Hopeful Time

Daily Devotionals for the prisoner's wife

© 2020 by Angela Pomeranz

Cover design and photos by Angela Pomeranz except bars, courtesy of William Warby (wwarby.com).

ISBN 978-0-578-65180-4

**Denotes selection from Angela's earlier work *To the Lady on the Outside: A 40-Day Devotional Guide for the Prison Wife* © 2014.

Scripture taken from the NEW AMERICAN STANDARD BIBLE, © 1960, 1962, 1963, 1968, 1971, 1972, 1973, 1975, 1977, by the Lockman Foundation. Used by permission.

A little about me

I'm an everyday widow. My husband isn't home to share the everyday moments with me. We are close, but cannot be close. We talk, but never as long as we want or need. We share, but always watched.

My husband is serving two life sentences. And without God's intervention, I'll be an everyday widow for life. I'm in a marriage without the everyday ability to share time and space with the love of my life, but I remain amazingly blessed every day.

This journey is all the more amazing when I consider what unsuccessfully tries to pull my husband and me apart. But God is in the space between it all, and He holds us together. And that makes it rich and beautiful. Sacrificial, yes, but astoundingly beautiful.

Prison is a tremendous journey of faith. It's painful, discouraging, and lonely at times, but it teaches more about love — and God — within the days. I keep learning the beautiful things of both.

I wrote many of these devotionals from my own need to be encouraged in the truth of God's word. God ministered to me, and I transferred His support into words that will hopefully minister to you. The Bible remains the centerpiece of my journey. I cannot stress enough how important it is to stay in God's word daily. My hope is that these devotionals will supplement your Bible study, not be a substitute for it.

Blessings,

January 1 — Keep Breathing

Psalm 145:18

The Lord is near to all who call upon Him, to all who call upon Him in truth.

There may be many times on this prison journey when you feel the wind knocked out of you. Unexpected and troubling events arrest your breathing and you feel as though collapsing is your only option. Grief and powerlessness rule in your body and mind at such times.

I think this is a natural reaction. It takes time to absorb the negative before you can process another perspective. All the things we read in Scripture, the truth we know, doesn't always immediately flow in confidence when hit with a painful or scary situation. With the initial deliverance of something bad, we have to get past the shock first. And that's okay.

I used to imagine how wonderful it would be to have such faith that at the word of anything tragic or scary, my immediate response would be a confident quote of Scripture with the true assurance in my heart behind it. I have never attained that. I always need time to be with the Lord, let Him speak to my heart, and then all the things I know to be true take a deeper footing in the situation I'm walking through at that moment.

Maybe it's a weakness in faith for me, but I have learned that God is never less real to me in those moments. My foundational faith keeps me breathing when I'm initially hit with hurt or fear that takes my breath away. That faith carries me until the chaos subsides to a meditative level. Then that's where God does His greatest work in me.

The awesome power of Scripture, the personal nature of God, and His loving assurance are acutely experienced when my breathing is steady and I'm seeking Him in solitude. I cannot seem to get to that place when I'm collapsed on the floor from that initial weight—literally or figuratively in my heart.

If you're recuperating from such an event or when one arrives, know that God is present at all points in your breathing. The point is to keep breathing. Let your faith sustain you, and God will be faithful to take care of the rest of your needs when your heart is best able to absorb it.

January 2 — Amazing Grace

II Kings 21:16

Moreover, Manasseh shed very much innocent blood until he had filled Jerusalem from one end to another; besides his sin with which he made Judah sin, in doing evil in the sight of the Lord.

    Manasseh was the most evil king in Judah's history. He was all about destroying the things of God and promoting idol worship. He promoted human sacrifices. He killed his own sons by throwing them into an altar of fire as part of his idolatry. He advocated sexual immorality in the worship of Asherah, an idol representing a female fertility god. He engaged in star worship. He practiced witchcraft and seduced the people to do evil. It's said that Isaiah the great prophet was sawed in half during Manasseh's reign. As stated in the verse above, he "shed very much innocent blood."

    Manasseh was a horrendous evil unleashed on Judah. Yet amazingly, God gave him opportunity after opportunity to repent and return to Him. God sent prophets to warn that his actions were a great sin against Him and the people. But Manasseh ignored the warnings, and, finally, God sent the Assyrian army to Jerusalem as judgment. Manasseh was captured and hauled away to Babylon as a prisoner.

    When finally distressed enough in his captivity, Manasseh cried out to God for help. II Chronicles 33:12 tells us he "humbled himself greatly before the God of his fathers." We also then read of God's amazing response. God forgave Manasseh and restored him to his kingdom. From that point forward, Manasseh, in stark contrast to his previous life, lived for God. He removed the idols, worshipped and served God only, and led the people righteously. His is an astounding story of redemption.

    When I consider those incarcerated for atrocious crimes, I need only remind myself of Manasseh to be encouraged that there remains hope for change even for the worst of criminals. Many crimes are quite sobering and nearly unbelievable, simply because they truly are heinous. But I also consider how deep God's mercy is. How much it must have grieved Him to look upon His great prophet Isaiah being murdered by Manasseh. Isaiah had an amazing call on his life, yet God's love was expressed in forgiveness to his murderer.

This is all amazing grace! We all need grace, because we all sin. Although deserving of God's wrath, great sinners were—and continue to be—redeemed. Take encouragement from this when considering even possibly your husband's crime or others in prison. Change is possible. The evil doesn't have to reign forever. But like Manasseh, a cry for help and for forgiveness must be heard. God is faithful to hear and restore a life to one reflecting tremendous good. And most amazingly, He extends salvation through Jesus to a humbled heart regardless of the heart's past.

January 3 Unhindered Courage

Joshua 2:14

So the men said to her, "Our life for yours if you do not tell this business of ours; and it shall come about when the Lord gives us the land that we will deal kindly and faithfully with you."

These were the words spoken by the spies to Rahab after they sought protection in her home during a reconnaissance mission in Jericho. Sent by Joshua to scout the city as part of his military tactics, the spies were part of the anointed mission to cross the Jordan and take the city. The Promised Land awaited. And because of her courage and agreement to help them, Rahab was kept safe.

Rahab was a prostitute, and her home is described in Scripture as a house of harlotry. Yet, her faith in God and courage to help the Israelites earned accolades as can be read in Hebrews 11:31 and James 2:25. She eventually became the great-great-grandmother of David.

It's also interesting to read as part of her request granted by the spies was not only to spare her life in the coming invasion, but also that of her family (verse 13). Can we assume that her parents, siblings, and in-laws were proud of her profession? Can we assume that there were strained relationships, arguments, and shame on the family's part for the reputation she earned? Scripture doesn't say.

But what we do know is that her faith brought her salvation, and it also enabled her to reach out to family members who had possibly rejected her because of her lifestyle. She was not bitter toward them. The crisis approaching Jericho may have been what spurred her on to reconcile herself to her family.

In the end, love trumped all of it: God's love for her and her love for her family. Despite her tainted and immoral past, God chose to use her in a mighty way. He required nothing of her but to have faith. This faith was used to impact not only her family, but also an entire nation.

Your husband may be like Rahab. His past may have severed relationships. His behavior may have earned a shameful reputation. In fact, all of us have a Rahab in us, because we are all sinners. But wrongdoings and regrets do not determine our future if we seek God and believe. God extends mercy to those who believe in Him. And His grace sustains us during crisis. It may have taken prison to bring it. But God doesn't define our potential based on our past. He uses our past to bring us to Himself, and to share with others the mercy we have received. Do not underestimate the power of a faithful life.

 January 4 New Devotion

Leviticus 23:24

"Speak to the sons of Israel, saying, 'In the seventh month on the first of the month, you shall have a rest, a reminder by blowing of trumpets, a holy convocation.'"

The Feast of Trumpets inaugurated by God during the time of Moses marks New Year's Day on the Hebrew calendar for today. God outlined various ceremonies for the Israelites in the Old Testament period. They were times of repentance, thankfulness, celebration, and often remembrance. The Feast of Trumpets was a time of focused rest to request God's continued favor. A burnt offering was the centerpiece of this festival. The all-consuming fire represented repentance of sin and all-consuming new devotion to God.

Prison may remain part of your calendar this year, but a renewed devotion to God can bring you renewed hope, joy, and purpose. God can use this year to grow you and your husband closer to each other and, most importantly, to Himself. You can close out this year in celebration of God's provision, encouragement, love, and mercy.

You may be thinking: "But my husband wants no part of God!" You might feel as though you're on this journey alone. If this describes you, then your burnt offering may need to be focused prayer for your husband.

Commit to pray daily for him. Commit to following God's will. Aspire to be like Jesus, and watch how God will move in your life. God's movement in your committed life will impact your husband.

This coming year may also involve severe challenges. Prison is challenging enough, but with additional life difficulties, days can seem eternal, life can be overwhelming, and energy to keep going can wane. Satan will use such times to seep into your marriage and focus on furthering the damage prison has already accomplished.

Do not give in to defeat. Let this year represent the line in the sand that Satan isn't allowed to cross. God will remain on your side and fight for you, but your devotion is required.

Let this year be the beginning of your all-consuming devotion to God. Prison may not leave the calendar this year, or the next, or the one after that. But God can bring you successfully through each day within each one if you seek Him. He's already seeking you. A new devotion to Him will be the most life-changing resolution you'll ever make, and in your future times of remembrance, you'll celebrate His faithfulness and goodness when life was at its greatest challenge.

January 5 — God's Loving Cover

Genesis 3:21

And the Lord God made garments of skin for Adam and his wife, and clothed them.

Sometimes we think our sins are too bad for God to forgive. Or we are too ashamed to even ask. I struggle to accept God's mercy when I commit the same sin—repeatedly. It's not my intent to engage in the same sin over and over, but in my humanness, I fail. I inherited this human tendency from our original parents, Adam and Eve. And when I consider the magnitude of their sin, I gain amazement for how big God's mercy really is.

The story of creation is popularly known. On the sixth day, God created Adam. He then created Eve to be Adam's partner. They were perfect; His creation was perfect. But sin entered the perfect world when Adam listened to his wife's words instead of God's. Eve had already fallen for Satan's temptation to eat from the tree of the knowledge of good and evil. She then offered Adam the fruit, and he ate, despite God telling him that the tree was off limits. Once Adam took a bite, Scripture tells us that both their eyes were opened, and they became aware of their nakedness. From that point forward, death became a reality for mankind and the earth.

Adam's sin brought eternal death to all his descendants, including you and me. Talk about regret! Adam must have felt below zero when the realization of that consequence entered his heart. How does anyone recover from such a sin? The answer Adam received came in the form of God's loving cover.

In their shame, Adam and Eve attempted to cover their nakedness, but their efforts were inadequate. God intervened and lovingly made clothing for them from animal skin. Despite the magnitude of sin, God was merciful and provided. He covered their sin out of His love. The consequences remained, but God didn't quit loving them. He met them at their need and provided.

More regret had to enter Adam's heart when the realization came to him that the first bloodshed happened as a result of his sin. An animal died, and soon to follow, his son committed the first murder. Sin brought death.

And it still does today. But God's mercy sent Jesus to us. Jesus came as a sacrifice to cover our sins. His blood shed on the cross mirrors the sacrifice of that one animal killed to provide a covering for Adam and Eve. Jesus brought perfection back to mankind. Regardless of the sin, Jesus's sacrifice was enough.

So when you consider your worst sin, consider what God did for Adam whose sin brought eternal death to all of us. Your husband may be struggling to believe his sin can be forgiven. If God's love was enough to cover Adam and Eve, His love is certainly enough to cover us. We only need to accept it. And the covering comes through Jesus.

January 6 — Justice & Mercy

Matthew 7:1-2

"Do not judge lest you be judged. For in the way you judge, you will be judged; and by your standard of measure, it will be measured to you."

I love rules. Since a child, I have been procedurally wired. I like details; I see ideals. This has helped me academically and on the job. But in my Christian walk, it can prostrate me on the foundation of legalism, aiming judgment at anyone who behaves contrary to Scripture. Ironically, I can recall engaging in the same or worse behavior when I was immature in my faith and blind to my own sin. God has His ways of reminding me of the old me.

One day, driving the interstate after visiting my husband—and of course driving the speed limit—I repeatedly encountered drivers who did the opposite. After a couple of erratic, speeding cars causing me to swerve and brake to avoid a collision, I felt a righteous anger when considering their selfishness, stupidity, and risk taking. And with another car passing at an excessive speed, my finger pointed firmly at the back of the car and my mouth sharply stated to God, "Those are the people I want judgment on!"

As I drove, my eyes took quick notice of any flashing lights along the shoulder as the miles progressed, savoring the hope of seeing one of my earlier nemeses getting what they deserved. But that retaliatory vision was never satisfied.

The following week, I traveled a city street heading toward my next destination. To my startle, I saw flashing lights behind me. I surveyed the scene and there was plenty of opportunity to pass me. I slowed and waited. But there he remained, behind me. Reasoning quickly arrived to the answer that there must be something wrong with my car of which he wanted to alert me. So, I pulled over and waited for my previous bewilderment to be confirmed.

But the officer didn't cordially inform me of a problem with my car. He gave me the opportunity to answer his rhetorical question: "Did you not see the flashing light at the school zone back there?"

My heart sank from the weight of the Lord's conviction and in the fall from the legalistic pedestal I stood upon the previous week. I was oblivious to my own guilt when that officer pulled me over. I loudly heard the intermittent siren the officer had to use to convince me that, yes, I was the target of his pursuit, and I loudly heard the voice of the Lord. Sighing as I sat waiting for the officer to return with written judgment, I humbly said to God, "I get it, Lord, I'm sorry."

Extending mercy to others—including my husband—doesn't come naturally to me. I need God's frequent reminders that I'm to love without hypocrisy. I got a ticket for going 38mph in a school zone. I was just as guilty of speeding as those who passed me the earlier week going 80. I sometimes forget what it's like to not be the "new" me, loving God and wanting to do right in His eyes. Thankfully, God didn't give me what I deserved those years ago when I was speeding along in sin, ignoring His authority.

God knows each person intimately and how best to bring conviction. We seldom know what may be going on in a person's life resulting in what we see. But God knows the clear details of that person zooming past me at 80, and I must surrender my upset to God's perfect ability to invoke change in that person from within, not from my pointing finger. If you're struggling with the same, pray for God's continued pursuit of whoever sets off your spiritual radar and rest in His ability to change those violating the rules of what you know is right. One of whom may be your husband.

January 7 — When All Seems Lost

I Samuel 30:6

Moreover David was greatly distressed because the people spoke of stoning him, for all the people were embittered, each one because of his sons and his daughters. But David strengthened himself in the Lord his God.

David had deserted to the Philistines to obtain some respite from Saul's continual pursuit. Six hundred men remained loyal to him and accompanied David in his fleeing from Saul's efforts to kill him. Now camped with the enemy, David finds himself facing off with his homeland Israel—and Saul. But despite David's apparent allegiance to the Philistines, the leaders didn't trust him. So he was commanded to return to Ziklag, a city within Philistia where David, his men, and all their families were living.

When they arrived, they found the city burned and deserted. The Amalekites had raided the city and taken captive all their families. With this discovery, David's men turned on him and spoke of killing him.

What a position to be in! David couldn't return to Israel, he couldn't go with the Philistines, his own family had been taken captive, and his closest comrades were making threats to kill him. He finds himself essentially alone, facing hostility on all fronts.

Who does David turn to in such a hopeless situation? God! The verse for today tells us that David strengthened himself in the Lord. This statement speaks volumes to David's reliance on God. And it captures the steady significance that God had in his life.

Prison can make you feel as if all seems lost. Everything may seem fighting against you. It's so easy to become discouraged when battling the forces of prison. You may be alone with no support. But God is always ready to help.

David sought the Lord and, in doing so, received the encouragement he needed to keep fighting. With God's assurance and grace, David was then able to spur on those men with him to keep fighting too. In the end, they pursued the Amalekites, won the battle, and retrieved all that was taken from them.

Like David, seek the Lord. He will faithfully show up when no one else seems to be on your side.

January 8 — Perfect Faithfulness

Isaiah 25:1

O Lord, Thou art my God; I will exalt Thee, I will give thanks to Thy name; for Thou hast worked wonders, plans formed long ago, with perfect faithfulness.

Isaiah is writing about the last days when evil is defeated once and for all, and all God's children will be with Him in perfection. This redemption of the world is certain. It has been a determined reality that every believer can count on. God is perfectly faithful in all things and His word. This includes not only the larger vision of Christ's second coming, but also your daily experiences until that day.

You can take great comfort in knowing that the mighty God who created and controls the universe and who remains sovereign over every moment within it also knows your situation intimately. And better yet—He faithfully remains at your side through it.

Notice that Isaiah uses the words "my God." God is personal. Isaiah had experienced God on a personal level and had written praises in responses to this. He's your God too! He's faithful to you.

When faced with each day, it's easy to lose sight of the faithfulness of God. The bad can seem already the victor. You can retreat to the position of merely endurance within the fallout. But always remember that God never leaves your side.

When faced with financial worries, health concerns, family issues, or simply the drain of dealing with prison, take encouragement that God knows all about it, and He sees the days ahead of you. He knows how it all ends. So with that knowledge, you can trust Him to lead you on the best path to the best end. And His presence remains faithful to comfort you, even when the path seems to not make sense.

This relieves stress! You can breathe easy and confidently knowing God's got your back. Seek to remain close to Him within your days. He's perfectly faithful.

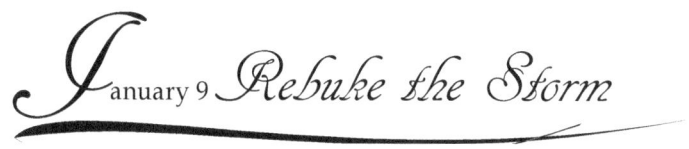

January 9 — Rebuke the Storm

Mark 4:35

And on that day, when evening had come, He said to them, "Let us go over to the other side."

    The disciples traveled with Jesus as He taught the people. He also regularly taught the disciples through preaching and experience. Jesus continuously addressed their faith. The verse above begins a passage where we can read of a teaching moment Jesus had with them.
    They had gotten into a boat to travel across the lake. Scripture tells us that Jesus took the opportunity to rest; He went to sleep. During their travel, a tremendous storm arose. Waves crashed into the boat and water began to fill it. The disciples panicked. They ran to Jesus, woke Him, and essentially began fussing at Him. "Teacher, do You not care that we are perishing" (verse 38)?
    The disciples had been obedient; they followed when Jesus said to go over to the other side. Maybe they assumed because Jesus said go that it would be smooth sailing. The disciples aren't unlike us. It's easy to believe and say our faith is solid when times are easy. But the testing of faith comes when the storms of life hit.
    Jesus had already told them they were going to the other side. Faith would have clung to this assurance that despite the storm, they would arrive safe. But the disciples' response was almost the extreme opposite. They became fatalistic, calling on Jesus in a manner as if to say, "You obviously don't care or else You wouldn't be ignoring all we're going through here!" Their sleeping refuge was not sleeping. The human part of Jesus was sleeping, but the deity of Him was fully in control.
    Prison is a storm. But Jesus is fully alert and in control. He will assure your destination is reached, through your pain, your fear, and even your unfaithfulness in belief. And in doing so, you'll receive lessons as the disciples did: be at peace; Jesus is here.

January 10 — Hidden Idols

Isaiah 46:1

Bel has bowed down, Nebo stoops over; their images are consigned to the beasts and the cattle. The things that you carry are burdensome, a load for the weary beast.

    Idols during the time of Isaiah were handcrafted items believed to possess supernatural power to bless those who worshipped them. It seems strange to us now to consider someone could actually believe such a thing. If a supernatural power depends on man for its creation, then it's obviously not powerful, and definitely not supernatural. So instead of worshipping the one true God, the Israelites succumbed to the idol worship of the time. But an idol can be anything that becomes more important than serving and worshipping God.

    I was challenged with this when even desiring and trying to do the things I knew that God was calling me to do. In my pursuit of my purpose, I became so burdened emotionally for its accomplishment that, in many ways, it became an idol rather than pursuing God.

    I failed to be content within the process of purpose. God encourages me toward an awesome future, but He also desires to be Lord of the days within the journey to get there. I wanted to skip the days in between and run full speed to the finish line. My intent was good, but I had inadvertently created a hidden idol. And that idol was dragging me down.

    I became restless in the present, weary within the days from the want not yet fulfilled. My attitude became frustrated when going through days that seemed wasteful. There was an urgency in me like being stopped in traffic when already late for an appointment. In my emotional exhaustion, the reality God showed me was that I was not late; I was exactly where He purposed in the timing He had orchestrated. My challenge was to relax and serve Him. I was to worship *Him* daily — not the goal.

    And this was clearly shown to me one day at a job that I was becoming increasing intolerant of, because I desired so much to be doing something "greater" and more directly related to my purpose. In the course of that day, I was able to minister to a young lady in a tough situation, share a little of my testimony (including the Gospel), and pray for her. I also encountered another lady I had not seen in some time, whom I had ministered to a few years prior after the death of her husband.

God's message got through that day: "I am your God, and I want to use you where you are—now." Peace also returned to my heart. It was a further lesson that idols can never satisfy, whether from good or bad intentions.

Consider what your hidden idols may be. It could even possibly be prison or your husband's legal case. Put God back where He belongs in your life. Seek to serve Him above all other things, and He will accomplish everything for your good, now and in the future.

January 11 *Victory in God*

Psalm 59:1-2

Deliver me from my enemies, O my God; set me securely on high away from those who rise up against me. Deliver me from those who do iniquity, and save me from men of bloodshed.

This is a Psalm of David. He spent a good deal of time dodging the pursuit and attacks of Saul. David faced this threat on his life repeatedly, but he always saw God as his defender, and with that understanding, his praise to God often accompanied his requests for help.

I have found that David's psalms reflect my heart for what my husband goes through, the danger he faces, and—at times—the defense he needs when threats on his life have been made. This is sadly the reality of prison. Prison wives also have to live with this reality. We wake daily, knowing in the recesses of our mind, there remains the possibility that harm could have come to our husbands in the hours while we slept. For me, there's a corresponding relief when the phone rings and I know he's safe, at least at that moment.

As long as there's prison, this reality remains. But we do not have to succumb to desperation. David humbly sought God's help, but he confidently concludes that God's power is more than enough to protect and deliver him. In fact, in this psalm, he rejoices in this truth. In verse 16, he says, "But as for me, I shall sing of thy strength."

When you're faced with this sense of danger or uneasiness about your husband's welfare, pray this psalm to God. Wherever you read "me" insert your husband's name. Intercede on your husband's behalf. The worry of your heart can be beautifully captured in David's words. Let the earnestness of your plea come through in the meditation of these words to God. Let the truth of God's power to deliver your husband and keep him safe calm your spirit. Allow God to minister to your fear. And when the phone rings, smile and thank God for His lovingkindness.

January 12 — Perfect Timing

Galatians 1:15-16

But when He who had set me apart, even from my mother's womb, and called me through His grace, was pleased to reveal His Son in me, that I might preach Him among the Gentiles, I did not immediately consult with flesh and blood.

Waiting on God to act in our lives regarding a particular concern is one of the hardest spiritual disciplines. Waiting on God while He works in someone else's life is equally difficult. In fact, His apparent inactivity in someone's life is ironically easier to experience for the person not aware of the process. They move along day to day, unchanged and seemingly unbothered, and we wonder why God is not doing anything.

We have a hard time understanding this. But the sovereignty of God will always be incompletely understood by us, because we do not possess God's attributes: all-powerful, all-knowing, and timeless. God's timing is always perfect, despite what appears to be indifference or a late arrival.

According to the verses above, Paul's life purpose was decided by God even before his birth. Yet, Paul was an adult before God revealed the plan to him. God allowed Paul to persecute the church and actively work against His will until the exact day arrived when He made Jesus known to him.

God's life purpose for each of us was decided before our creation as well. And learning from Scripture that God's timing is perfect, our patience in the waiting process should be encouraged. God has the exact day planned when the apparent inactivity preceding that day culminates to awareness.

If you're praying earnestly for the life change for your husband, do not give up. Years of living foul and opposed to God doesn't necessarily mean God has given up on him. Scripture does teach that God will only pursue each of us so long before giving us over to our own choice of rejecting Him, but only God knows the timing for this as well. Keep praying and keep believing in the sovereignty of God. We are all "works in progress," at different points in God's timetable. His grace pursues all of us and remains just as powerful regardless of what speed it seems to be traveling.

January 13 Good for Good

Proverbs 19:17

He who is gracious to a poor man lends to the Lord, and He will repay him for his good deed.

It's an interesting concept—lending to the Lord. He doesn't need anything, so why or how is this even possible? This verse is packed with all kinds of treasures from Scripture. We see God's grace and His sovereignty. We see how He uses believers and bestows eternal riches. We see the personal nature of God.

When the bank lends money, it's for a particular purpose the borrower has planned. None of us takes out a loan and accepts a monthly payment just because we can; we have something we want to do with the money. In God's economy, He has plans for our money, but just as valuable are our talents, personalities, experiences, and even our trials.

He takes these things and uses them in other people's lives for their good and for a particular purpose. It may be to bring a blessing, meet a need, draw that person to Himself, provide encouragement, teach that person, or any one of an abundance of reasons that's specific to that person. In return, He blesses us in the same way: individually and unique to our circumstance. Only a sovereign God could do this seamlessly, lovingly, and across all time. Besides being an interesting concept, it's an amazing one!

So being gracious to someone in need doesn't always involve money. Being gracious means being kind, compassionate, giving. The "poor" person may not be financially needy; she may need a hug, someone to listen, someone to help mow the grass, a ride to the doctor, or input regarding a big decision. For Christians, our desire to be gracious comes from a heart influenced by God's grace to us. And most powerfully, we show compassion out of the past pain and trials in our lives that God so graciously helped us through.

Allow God to use what you possess. Your skills, personality, and experiences, including possibly prison. He has invested or allowed these things in your life, and He can use even the bad to bless others. Allow God to use your life and watch how bountifully He repays you.

January 14 "With" Love

I Corinthians 13:1

If I speak with the tongues of men and of angels, but do not have love, I have become a noisy gong or a clanging cymbal.

As you grow more accustomed to being alone on this prison journey, it's easy to allow your responsibilities and routine to take the place of time you spend "with" your husband. Filling up your day with other things will become an easy pattern to fall into, simply because he isn't there to fill that time with you. Time with him mutates into the expected and routine of visits, calls, and possibly letters. All other time involves something else.

Paul teaches us in this chapter of I Corinthians that love is an action. It's about doing something, not feeling or saying something. It's about giving of one's self, considering others first. Beyond the routine events of a prison marriage, how can you show your husband that you love him?

Maybe it's doing something special for him that he wouldn't expect. If you aren't a letter writer, write a letter. Maybe you could learn about something he's interested in. Send him articles or a magazine subscription related to his interests. Follow his favorite teams so you can share in some conversation with him about it. Regularly send him pictures of things you're involved in or places you go. It may be making a priority of something he has asked you to do, even if insignificant.

It's hard to put your husband first when he isn't physically home. Work, home, and life demand our attention. Fight the tendency to become distracted by things or other people as you attempt to endure through the daily direct and indirect effects of prison. Entertainment technology, the internet, work, reality TV, going and doing become distracters. Establish a quality routine when you can spend time "with" your husband. Just going through the actions communicates love and that he's important to you.

January 15 — Not unlike Others

Romans 3:23

For all have sinned and fall short of the glory of God.

I was experiencing what I title A Hormonal Week. For me, this is when I'm easily tearful, mostly intolerant, and frustratingly forgetful. I do not know which I would enjoy more at those times: screaming or crying! Sadly, I'm also a poor reflection of Christ when my body is battling within the imbalance. Add prison to this and I can be curt in my words, unmotivated for excellence in my job, and somber in my mood.

The Wednesday of that week for me resulted in my being rather argumentative and rude to the optical shop employee when I was trying to resolve a contact lens issue for myself. A typical annoyance turned into one handled poorly. The employee conceded to my obvious attitude. Her abiding by the cliché The Customer is Always Right brought "victory" to me.

But even as the words were coming out of my mouth, I felt conviction. I knew I was being unkind and ungracious to a lady who was only trying to do her job—whether she was right or not. And long after the call ended, I struggled with the shame of my own behavior. I asked forgiveness from God, but didn't feel any better about myself. Or about my walk as a Christian.

In my thoughts, I hoped the workers at that shop would be gracious, knowing they likely had such regretful moments somewhere in a bad week for themselves. I had apologized to the lady before exiting the call and presented myself more gracious when I picked up my lenses later. But the overwhelming thought I couldn't escape was that the damage had been done; I would be a negative memory for them from that day forward. Feeling that way, I struggled to even rest in the forgiveness I knew God did extend to me.

Paul teaches us that all are sinners. All need Jesus to stand in righteousness before God. None are perfect. There are no perfect Christians. The fact that I'm a Christian is evidence that I realize I'm not perfect and need Jesus!

And while I continued to dwell on my less-than-godly week, the Lord provided me a vivid illustration the next day to remind me of what Paul says in the verse for today.

In a checkout lane at the grocery, I happened to be behind an associate pastor of the church. I knew he didn't know me since I was new to attendance there. I witnessed his mild disputing with the cashier about credits for advertised sale items. Did he handle it perfectly? Not really. But it sure gave me encouragement!

I smiled in the knowledge that God was reminding me that all fall short, even pastors. I need to make amends with those I harm by my words or actions to the greatest extent possible, rest in His forgiveness, and move on. I encourage you to do the same when the hormonal-type days, complicated by prison, happen in your life.

January 16 — Waiting on God

Jeremiah 42:7

Now it came about at the end of ten days that the word of the Lord came to Jeremiah.

Jeremiah went before the Lord on behalf of the Israelites in response to their fearful fleeing of Babylonian rule. A rebellious Ishmael had assassinated the Babylonian-appointed governor, and the people who had been encouraged to live in peace under the Babylonian rule were frightened to return. One of their own had murdered the governor. The people needed direction. Should they flee to Egypt or return to Judah and face the uncertain response of Nebuchadnezzar? Wow! If they ever needed to hear from God, it was then! But God waited ten days before responding.

Can you imagine the stress? Have you ever been in a crisis for direction to receive only silence from God? Why did God wait ten days in Jeremiah's case? Why does He wait before responding to our prayers at times?

It was a critical crossroad of faith for the Israelites, because the Lord's eventual reply was not what they really wanted to hear. He told them, "Do not be afraid of the king of Babylon, whom you now fear" (42:11). The Lord promised to deliver them from the oppression and restore them to their land if they would only return. But they simply couldn't believe that was the best answer, so they took matters into their own hands and proceeded to Egypt. This cost them dearly.

I have been in those moments where everything seemed to be falling apart with no clear answers as to what to do next. It's a test of faith to wait on God. And like the Israelites, I have not always liked the answer once it came. Being obedient to the answer becomes the second hurdle.

In even less urgent matters in my prayers for my husband, the answers do not always come quickly. From day one, I prayed every day, earnestly, for God to change my husband's heart, yet it was two more years before I even heard the words "I'm sorry" from him — for anything! The lack of results didn't mean that God had not answered. He always answers yes, no, under certain conditions, or not now. The "not now" answers are the hard places in life to be. I would have preferred a Damascus-road event to thrust our love to the point I so desired, but that was not how God chose to answer.

Your burden may be a delayed fulfillment as well. Do not give up on God; keep praying. In the case of my husband, allowing God time to work was best for us. I grew in my faith, I learned more about God, and my husband learned more about love. We would have never received these lessons if God had essentially knocked my husband on the head and said, "Straighten up!" There's richness in waiting if you'll only endure the process.

The great part is God doesn't leave you alone to endure by yourself. He sees the road and carries you through the rough spots. You can be faithful without fear, because God is faithful. It may seem scary, and it may not seem to always make sense, but trust God in His answers! **

January 17 — House of Wisdom

Proverbs 9:1

Wisdom has built her house, she has hewn out her seven pillars.

Scripture has much to say about wisdom. We are to pursue it, desire it, and allow it to permeate our lives. True wisdom comes only from God. He created us, thus our ability to learn and apply knowledge — wisely — comes from God. A person can be smart, but unwise. Prison houses many career criminals who are highly intelligent, but lack wisdom.

There's much to gain from godly wisdom. James tells us that applying godly wisdom to our lives — much like building a house on the pillars of wisdom — brings great benefit. He writes in 3:17, "But the wisdom from above is first pure, then peaceable, gentle, reasonable, full of mercy and good fruits, unwavering, without hypocrisy." If we focus on these benefits as the seven pillars in our decision making, then we will see the fruit of wisdom.

Early in our love, my husband frequently requested things of me that skirted on the edge of ungodliness. Wisdom would ask, "Is the decision pure?" My husband frustrates me at times. Should I respond in anger or rudeness? Wisdom would ask, "Would my response be gentle or peaceful?" When my husband was several hours from me, I wanted to see him both days of every weekend, which meant many miles to drive, much cost, and physical exhaustion over time. Wisdom would ask, "Is it reasonable?"

There may be times in your life when God asks you do to something that seems unreasonable—unwise. He sure has with me! You should always do what God tells you, because He has a special purpose for His specific instructions. But in general, aside from those times, Scripture teaches us how to make wise decisions. Read the book of Proverbs for a ton of practical, biblical instructions for becoming a wise person.

But be warned, godly wisdom will conflict with prison. Prison is very much as James describes in 3:15 as "earthly, unnatural, demonic." However, the truth doesn't change. God's wisdom is unwavering. Stand firm in what you know is right when walking this prison path with your husband. I know it's hard to swim against the current and cause friction with your husband possibly. But God will honor your actions.

January 18 Scented Love

Song of Solomon 1:13-14

"My beloved is to me a pouch of myrrh which lies all night between my breasts. My beloved is to me a cluster of henna blossoms in the vineyards of Engedi."

Perfume has been a part of culture for ages. Even Solomon used scent to describe his beloved. The sense of smell is a very strong attractor to a man. The perfume industry knows this! Living in prison provides few avenues for your femininity to be experienced by your husband, but perfume remains a doable avenue within the restrictions. Your femininity can flow and even stay with your husband within the separation.

I do not typically wear perfume, but it's a special thing I reserve for my husband's letters (when allowed by the prison) and visits. He loves it! I have worn different kinds over the years, but generally he knows the scents I like.

My scent reflects my personality in many ways and becomes another way of connecting.

He immediately inhales my scent when he opens a letter, placing the paper to his face and breathing it in almost with as much romanticism as Solomon describes of his beloved's scent. Accumulated letters kept in his locker bring the same aroma when he opens it. At visits, he gets the added pleasure of having my body attached to the scent. And this provides pleasant memories for the times in his cell when he enjoys the lingering aroma on a sheet of paper. The sense of smell is highly connected to memory!

Romance has to be intentionally fostered in your marriage. Perfume is a simple way to do this. There are so many fragrances out there now that it can be overwhelming to choose, but that's a good thing! Get creative, incorporate different scents for different wardrobes. Let your husband pick his favorite for you by scenting letters with sample fragrances. If the budget is tight, consider a body spray or lotion in the same line of a perfume that you like. The main goal is to communicate your attraction and love for your husband in the ways available to you.

January 19 *Emerods*

I Samuel 6:5

"So you shall make likenesses of your tumors and likenesses of your mice that ravage the land, and you shall give glory to the God of Israel; perhaps He will ease His hand from you, your gods, and your land."

What on earth are emerods! Having a difficult time reading and understanding Scripture? Emerods could be one example. In the King James Version, *tumors* as found in the verse above is another word for *emerods*. So why don't they just say tumors! If you're new to reading Scripture, do not let the translation be a barrier to seeking God through His word.

There are numerous translations and types of study Bibles. Some people say the KJV is the only translation to be used. I do not believe that. As long as it's a Christian Bible, God will speak to you through it. He isn't limited by word choice or confined to one translation. My former pastor highlighted this point by explaining the following.

The New Testament was originally written in Greek. Were the authors Greek? No. Jesus and the disciples spoke Aramaic. Then why did God choose for the New Testament books to be written in Greek? Answer: Because that was the language of the people He wanted to reach at that time. Rome was the center of that time period, and the people there didn't speak Aramaic. So if you think about it, God approved His word being translated into different languages and words to meet the need of the people.

The KJV is written using 16th century English. Do we talk like they did in 16th century Europe? No. That's why often the KJV is difficult to read. The structure and "emerods" become barriers to our study. God of course is still active in all versions, but do not be afraid of seeking out another version.

I tend to study using a variety of versions. This can help keep things fresh and encourage looking at Scripture from different perspectives. As your understanding of Scripture increases, you may find that you can return to other previously difficult versions and understand them more clearly.

Your husband may also need a different version. Most any correctional facility I have been in or prison correspondence studies my husband has participated in offer and use the KJV only. I think that's a misfortune. Not all inmates have the reading skills to make sense of that style and word usage. So if you or your husband are feeling discouraged in your efforts to study Scripture, try something different. God's grace and desire to reveal Himself to you through His word transcends grammar and sentence structure.

January 20 *Through People*

Mark 5:43

And He gave them strict orders that no one should know about this; and He said that something should be given her to eat.

Jairus had pleaded at Jesus's feet to come to his home and heal his daughter. His daughter was twelve years old and had fallen ill to the point of death. In fact, on the way to Jairus's house, others met them, informing Jairus that she had died. From their perspective, there was no further need for Jesus to come. She was dead; hope was gone.

But Jesus continued on to the home and performed a miracle, bringing her back to life. Not dwindling the awe of His power to raise someone from the dead, I'm struck by Jesus's words to her parents. He told them to prepare her something to eat.

It's fascinating to me to consider why Jesus raised her from the dead, but left her hungry or in need of food. He certainly could have supernaturally met this need as well. All He did was speak the words, and the little girl's life returned to her. It was definitely within His power to satiate her hunger, but He chose not to. He delegated that responsibility to her family.

This is a great example of how God desires to use people to meet our needs. Likewise, we are used by Him to meet the needs of others. Christians are the "hands and feet" of Jesus. And not necessarily physical ones.

When faced with prison, having other women in your life who understand your struggles is a great support. It can sometimes just be one person, but it brings tremendous blessings to you. She can encourage you, give advice, or just listen. And when needed, she's another person who would love to help when life surprises you with a car that won't start, a sick child, or any other interruption that creates a need. In turn, you can be that for her.

Oftentimes, prison can be a very lonely journey with a lot of valleys. Not everyone can understand what the correctional system requires of you logistically and emotionally. Not everyone understands the loss you experience in being separated from your husband. But another prison wife can relate.

God wants to use where you have been to help others on the same path. You may have come through many years of incarceration; do not keep it to yourself. Use what you know to help others. You may be new on this path; ask for help. There are others out here who would love to help. Then later, when able, you can help another.

January 21 Spiritual Lockdown

John 20:19

When therefore it was evening, on that day, the first day of the week, and when the doors were shut where the disciples were, for fear of the Jews, Jesus came and stood in their midst, and said to them, "Peace be with you."

My husband had called informing me that the prison was going on lockdown. There would be no further phone calls or visits for the weekend. Violence had increased the prior weeks and had come to a head with another incident the day he called. Lockdown eliminates movement on the compound; prisoners aren't allowed their usual routine if that involves leaving their cell or dorm. Prison officials use this strategy to diffuse the eruption in conflicts and bring more order and safety to what's already a controlled environment.

Spiritually, I can find myself in a version of lockdown. It's a paralysis of movement toward my calling or anxiety related to it. I may fear stepping out in the next step or worry that in doing so will be a misstep. In contrast to prison, my lockdown is usually of my own creation, not one imposed by God.

The disciples experienced their version of lockdown after Jesus was crucified. They feared the Jewish leaders would seek them out for harm as well. And with Jesus dead, they seemed to relinquish their hope with that reality. They still didn't anticipate the resurrection despite Jesus explaining this to them. Instead, they locked themselves away in response to the violence perpetrated on Jesus.

Their lockdown was indicative of their disheartenment. They were supporting each other by gathering in the time of crisis, but they seemed without direction. They were grieving. They were trying to regroup with the overshadowing fear of their circumstance.

Jesus entered their situation physically and spiritually to energize their hearts and direction. He put their anxiety at ease. His presence arrived when they needed hope restored. Jesus left them with a renewed motivation for the future.

If you're in a spiritual lockdown, God wants to get you moving forward—whether physically or emotionally. Prison can stagnate your motivation and hope. It can be tough to take the next step. But He brings peace with His presence and direction for your uncertainty. And most of all, hope within your circumstance, despite how dark it seems now. Release your spiritual restraints and experience joy as a result. Your next day is waiting, your next step is waiting. God says you'll be okay. Do not fear.

January 22 *Why Him?*

Genesis 50:26

So Joseph died at the age of one hundred and ten years; and he was embalmed and placed in a coffin in Egypt.

Joseph was the second to the youngest of Jacob's twelve sons. Genesis provides the account of how Joseph's brothers were jealous of him due to the favor Jacob cast upon him. The brothers originally planned to kill him, but instead sold him as a slave. They lied to Jacob about the whereabouts of

Joseph making it seem as if he was mauled by an animal, never to be seen again. Joseph never saw his brothers again until he was second in command of Egypt.

The story of Joseph is an amazing testimony to God's providence. And with any life history where so much difficulty is allowed, like Joseph's, we can become emptier of reasons when death takes a life that has so much potential.

Joseph was an astounding man of character. He persevered through frightening, dangerous, and lonely places, none of which he deserved. He resisted temptations of the flesh. He resisted bitter thoughts. God allowed Joseph to be mistreated by his brothers, sold into slavery, and imprisoned — despite his innocence. His brothers lied, created grief for their father, and did great harm. They were guilty. Yet at the end of Genesis, we read of Joseph dying before any of his brothers.

Joseph had proven himself a faithful servant, an intelligent man, a strong leader, and a forgiving family man. Could not have God continued to use him? For that day, he could have lived many more years. Yet God ordained Joseph's death for the day it came. Just as he had his experiences leading up to that day.

When considering prison, you likely have many questions of why? Why your husband? Why the life that led him there? Why the harm to him since being in prison? Life puzzles us when evil seems to prosper. Joseph experienced many steps in life that seemed as if evil won.

But if you read the story of Joseph, see God's providence within the pages. Let the observance of God's control encourage you to absorb and live within the days that are leading to places not yet known. Every day won't be like today. God miraculously brings perfection from pain to those who belong to Him. Even within events that seem to have no meaning, purpose for good, or the best good, God can be trusted.

And I believe that becomes the question to be answered when life — or prison — robs us of lives, futures, and blessedness: Can God be trusted? Even if your heart is weeping right now, please cling to the faithfulness of God to divinely pattern your steps — and that of your husband — from prison to the palace.

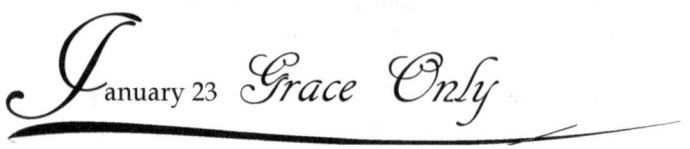

January 23 — Grace Only

Ephesians 2:8-9

For by grace you have been saved through faith; and that not of yourselves, it is the gift of God; not as a result of works, that no one should boast.

Paul was writing to the Gentile Christians in Ephesus. And he was encouraging them in their salvation despite not being of Jewish lineage. They were just as saved as the Jewish believers, who had a tendency to think Gentile believers still needed to do certain things to be fully followers of Jesus, like circumcision. Paul was always reminding through his preaching that the law didn't save; good works or keeping the commandments does not bring salvation or keep a person saved. God's grace saves us!

God doesn't hold a balance as a court of law and separate our good and bad actions, and then make a determination at our deaths if we presented enough mitigation to reduce or eliminate the consequences. Jesus's death paid the penalty of everything in our lifetimes we have done or will do that's sinful.

This is a hard thing to accept when our sin has been great in the eyes of man—or ourselves. My husband has a hard time not feeling as though he has to work his way back into God's favor because of all the bad he has done in his life. I empathize with this.

God's love is beyond comprehension. A prisoner's testimony is usually very powerful, because it's evidence to the mercy and grace of God. Despite the past, God forgives and prepares a place in heaven for the earthly criminal, just as joyfully as He does the man who has been a "good" Christian since childhood. How awesome is that!

It's not an excuse to delay a salvation decision, but it should encourage us to not give up on those we love who remain distant from God and the good. You may need to remind your husband of this truth, if he's still averting his eyes in shame when faced with the love of Jesus. Remind him that it's not about what he has done, but about who he believes has taken the penalty.

January 24 — Despite What's Seen

Genesis 8:15-16

Then God spoke to Noah, saying, "Go out of the ark, you and your wife and your sons and your sons' wives with you."

Noah and his family had spent a year inside the ark with Lord only knows how many smells, irritable moods, and trying logistics. Finally, there was dry land seen and waters on the descent. In verse 13 we read that "Noah removed the covering of the ark, and looked, and behold, the surface of the ground was dried up." Hallelujah! The family must have been overjoyed and eager to get out of that boat!

But we read that it was another two months before they exited. The surface of the ground was dry, but there was still mud below. They would have had a lot of stuck-in-the-mud livestock I suppose. Not to mention the even larger wildlife. So Noah and his family waited.

I'm struck by the obedience of Noah. Granted he had just seen God's power displayed and faithfulness to his family proved. But he was still human. His wife and sons and sons' wives were still human. There's no indication from Scripture that Noah or anyone in his family had to be rebuked for wanting to exit the ark before God told them to.

Noah was obviously a great spiritual leader of his home. No one seemed to question why they couldn't at least break open the door and step out onto the land, if not only a few feet. But Noah did nothing until He heard from God. Despite what he was seeing, he waited.

Life circumstances can seem, at times, like that dry surface. We can be tempted to move ahead when waiting has already been many days and the days before difficult. We just want where we are to be behind us! Especially if we see a better place ahead.

Learn from Noah. Rein in your emotions and remember God knows when it's safe to take that next step. It may be a job you cannot tolerate any longer, a large purchase that you think you cannot live without, or a move to another place. Stick your head out and breathe in anticipation of what you may see, but do not go until God says go. Things may look good on the surface, but there may just as surely be mud underneath.

More seriously, you may be experiencing prison as your ark. You have been in it for what seems an eternity, surrounded by daily difficulty. Maybe you want to exit your marriage, flee to better ground.

Oh, please wait on God! He's busy preparing the soil for a renewal! Trust Him to safely bring you and your husband through the flood.

January 25 Refusing to Panic

Psalm 27:1

The Lord is my light and my salvation; whom shall I fear? The Lord is the defense of my life; whom shall I dread?

Psalm 27 is an awesome passage of Scripture. It's one of my favorite chapters in the Bible. I have memorized it, because I want its encouragement and beautiful expression of faith on my lips when panic becomes my temptation. Faith is the refusal to panic. This psalm speaks of God's power and faith in His protection, whatever comes.

This truth helps ground me when I feel overwhelmed and losing heart for what's difficult. As a prison wife, I'm sure you have had moments when you wished for respite in life and its demands, particularly prison.

This truth helps me when I consider all the potential enemies surrounding my husband — officer or inmate. Any day could bring harm to him and he doesn't have to do anything to bring it; just being in prison brings a daily risk.

This psalm helps me when I feel alone within the struggles. Family, co-workers, friends, and acquaintances may not understand this prison life. But God does. And He will never forsake me! I can always go to Him for help and support even when no one else believes in me or my husband.

This psalm reminds me that God will always be there, guarding my life. I have eternal security for my future, whatever this life brings. Thankfully, my husband does too. This brings peace. I know that he will never be forsaken in his aloneness, surrounded by evil.

My heart takes courage when I read these verses. Let it encourage your heart too. God has already defeated Satan. Jesus's resurrection has claimed victory. You may think because of where your husband sits that evil has won. But this isn't true. There's no authority on this earth, including the DOC, outside the authority of the Almighty! Do not despair. You'll see the goodness of the Lord even in prison.

January 26 — Unbeknownst to Them

Matthew 9:12-13

But when He heard this, He said, "It is not those who are healthy who need a physician, but those who are sick. But go and learn what this means, 'I desire compassion, and not sacrifice,' for I did not come to call the righteous, but sinners."

It was a beautiful late afternoon to walk my dog. The air was mild, the sun warm after a chilly start to the day. We drove to the cemetery to get away from the traffic and noise that usually accompany our walks. It also provides a time of reflection and refocusing of meaning. How can one not consider the heavier issues of life when walking amongst the markers for those lives now gone? But that afternoon provided an opportunity for something more than I had planned.

While absorbing the peace on our stroll, my ears soon heard the sound of yelling and cursing. Severe cursing! Angry, foul words were being shouted by a woman walking along the road which ran alongside the cemetery. Her target was a man, possibly husband, possibly boyfriend, possibly something else. He walked many paces ahead of her, ignoring the verbal rampage. As she crossed in front of a house, the dog in the fenced yard began barking at her. That animal then received the most vulgar tongue-lashing! Her screams to both the man and the dog continued the entire length of the road. Pure ugly.

My first reaction was to be annoyed. I had intentionally came to walk in peace! I wanted to share the time with God, talk with Him, mediate on His goodness, and simply be still in my heart. But the interruption blaring in the not-so-peaceful walk of that woman couldn't be ignored.

I soon felt sadness for her. She must be miserable, I considered. My reflections became ones for her life, what her experiences have been, and why she has ended up with a heart and mouth so black. Is she drunk or high? What will her night be like if that man was in fact her mate? How miserable they must be as a couple if that was a typical fight between them.

So my talk with God became for her. I prayed for her to come to know Jesus and to find joy. I prayed for her heart. I prayed for the man. I prayed they both would grow into the purpose God had planned for them. Unbeknownst to them, someone was praying.

Soon I was leaving and heading to the gas station. I didn't go earlier in the day as was my routine. It seemed that day was not about my routine—or me.

Upon pulling in and waiting for a pump to be free, I heard screeching tires and, yet again, yelling and cursing. And, yet again, another weight on my heart in response to what my ears were hearing. Some near miss I suppose in maneuvering the parking lot. I knew that my being there at that time was no coincidence. There are no coincidences with God, only divine orchestration. I began praying for the persons involved.

As in the previous prayers for the couple at the cemetery, I may never know the outcome of each life, but I do know that God must be seeking them. My reason for sharing this story is to encourage you to see beyond yourself, prison, life's interruptions or changes in your routine. God may have a specific reason to take you a different direction. God will also use you if you make yourself available. You get to participate with God in lives that need Him—unbeknownst to them.

January 27 *Crisis of Hope*

Psalm 146:5

How blessed is he whose help is the God of Jacob, whose hope is in the Lord his God.

An attack on your hope is the most devastating kind. Hope is what moves us forward. It's what gets us out of bed. It keeps us in our marriages when there is no current evidence of why we should stay. An attack on your hope is dangerous, because it's what we need attached to all aspects of our lives to stay the course—especially when prison exists in our lives.

Most crises in my married life involved my husband's violence toward someone else. He has multiple stabbings in his prison record that document his hardened response to a perceived threat. In all cases, I had to absorb a lot of hope to process and move forward in my marriage. Each incident resulted in more years of confinement for him and nearly nonexistent opportunities for us to be together. But with God's help, my hope survived.

It was not until my husband was in a position to do the same for me that I realized my hope was more dangerously attacked when he failed to do so. His opposite response of anger sent me into bewilderment and a battle for a new level of hope. How could our marriage survive if I was the only one willing to do the hard stuff? If I could learn how to love him through the multiple crises that he brought into our marriage, why couldn't he do the same for me one time? I felt abandoned in my marriage to endure my crisis alone—and my hope was breaking apart.

But God provided the deeper level of hope I needed to stay the course of my marriage and endure my crisis. My husband was far behind me, entrenched in anger, but God continued to work on his heart while He gave me the strength I needed to deal with that as well. It was a truer feeling of being Jesus's bride which has always taught me more about how to love my own husband, even when my husband struggles to love me the same way. It's sacrificial. Jesus will faithfully and perfectly love me. And the more I mediate on this picture of marriage, I'm able to love my husband with hope.

My husband eventually climbed out of his anger and expressed more pleasant emotions. He learned a little more about love in the end and I was reminded what true love demands. If you're struggling to keep your hope, because of your husband's action or lack of loving behavior toward you, God can pick up the damaged pieces of what's left of your hope and meld it back to resemble your heart once again. You cannot walk this prison journey without hope. God can be your faithful resource to supply however much you need to keep moving forward in your marriage even if your husband seems to be lagging behind.

January 28 Train or Dumpster

Philippians 4:11

Not that I speak from want; for I have learned to be content in whatever circumstances I am.

Every wee morning of each Monday I used to be startled awake by what initially sounded like a machine monster set on gobbling up my house. What it actually imparted to my ears—in drowsy expectation—was the massive truck emptying the dumpster which sat on the other side of the fence. I got the joy of rising between 1:00 and 3:00 a.m. every Monday.

When I first moved into the house, this realization on what's already a somber start to the workweek had me whining and assuredly convinced the city was incompetent and indifferent to its citizens. I also knew that the driver of the truck somehow enjoyed his work, likely dropping and moving the bucket of metal repeatedly just to make more noise.

But on one morning, I decided to "get back" at my nemesis by actually rising early before he even arrived and spend time writing. Good versus evil, and my goal was for good to win. My thoughts were, "If you're set on waking me up, good is going to come from it." I thought through the circumstance and began to consider if God was using my location to stir me on in my writing.

Maybe so. But I also got a lesson on contentment. For while up, I also got to hear the regular passing of a train that made its way through the center of town. A noise that was just far enough away that it never awakened me, but once up, was clearly heard in the unobstructed night air. I then took regular notice of the homes that lined the tracks on my trips through that area. Humility followed.

Trains traveled through there seemingly every hour, blasting the alert at every crossing. Those poor people I would think. How could I ever complain about my once-a-week disturbance when they lived with their nemesis nightly, multiple times a night?

Paul teaches us in the verse in Philippians that contentment should be our goal in whatever circumstance. Because frankly—and usually—things could always be worse. It's when faced with the worse that we gain appreciation for our lesser circumstance.

Paul was in prison when he penned those words. He wrote several books of the New Testament while imprisoned. He maintained the faith that his message wouldn't be in vain. It would leave the prison even if he never did, being used by God to speak to the churches. His situation was harsh, yet he didn't let his surroundings and present condition to alter his hope or the call of God upon his life.

To learn to be content takes intentionality. It takes a disciplined attitude. It's also done best with the power of the Holy Spirit to energize our motivation. Surrendering circumstances to God brings calm to troubled or despairing thoughts.

Prison surrounds us with worries, barriers, fears, frustrations, and mostly negative experiences. It may rob you of sleep like the train or dumpster. When the negative presents itself, however, do not let what you experience trap you in a negative funk. Rise above in your thoughts, thank God for His mercies, and enjoy the inner calm that comes in knowing how blessed you truly are.

✝

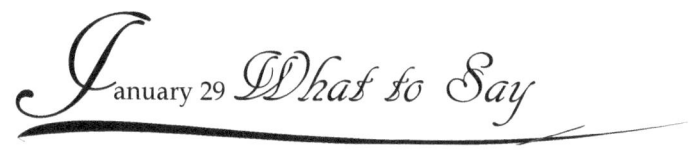

January 29 — What to Say

Proverbs 15:28

The heart of the righteous ponders how to answer, but the mouth of the wicked pours out evil things.

    I have often heard the comment: "I just don't see how you do it." I'm just as often not sure if this is a compliment or statement of pity. This of course is in response to my being in a prison marriage — and one for life. For me, not just being in one, but choosing one! Sometimes I may respond that it wasn't my idea, but God's. Other times I may take the opportunity to share about God's faithfulness in my marriage. Regardless, I'm addressing a common perspective by other people: they just don't get it. And with a similar sigh to the loss of the everyday with my husband, a sigh comes as those commenting persons walk away, because there's really no way for me to make them get it.

    As a prison wife, you likely live in a repeated state of explaining and attempting to justify why you're with whom you married. I have never known any couple more often asked to explain their marriage than those in a prison marriage. But it doesn't stop with that. What follows is the list of questions — some very intrusive — of love and intimacy, your husband's crime, or the one which is the most pleasure for me to field: when does he get out? Any answer to any question just creates a new set of questions. Instead of a conversation, you feel as if you're being interviewed!

    Such a conversation can circle in my mind in that spiraling downward loop to get my blood pressure rising and sighs replaced by huffs and puffs. I'm thinking, "How dare she ask me such questions! Does she ask every married person she meets such questions!" My mouth wants to pour out such thoughts in a less-than-godly reaction. But in my heart I know the wiser choice is merely to defer the topic or decline to discuss. And that's okay.

    I ponder how to answer based on God's word, His wisdom. If I feel I'm going to be the gossip shared over the dinner table, very little gets volunteered to another's frustration. My inherently quiet self has no problem doing that. If someone has a genuine interest in my well-being, I may be more open. If I can encourage someone by sharing some about my situation, I'll talk freely.

You'll need to decide how to answer others when marriage comes up. There will be variables that weigh toward different outcomes for the conversation. You're wise to ponder what you're going to say. The verse in Proverbs says that it's better to delay an answer to consider the best response than to impulsively engage from the wrong motivation.

January 30 — The Discipline to Wait

Exodus 32:1

Now when the people saw that Moses delayed to come down from the mountain, the people assembled about Aaron, and said to him, "Come, make us a god who will go before us; as for this Moses, the man who brought us up from the land of Egypt, we do not know what has become of him."

Moses was in charge of the Israelites and Joshua was his apprentice so to speak. When God told Moses to go up to Mt. Sinai where he would receive the Ten Commandments and laws for the people, Moses took Joshua with him. He instructed Aaron and the elders to wait for them until they returned.

Moses was on the mountain six days before God spoke. Why did He make him wait? Scripture doesn't say. But Moses waited faithfully. He had entered the cloud while Joshua waited beyond. It was forty days before Moses exited the cloud. But Joshua waited faithfully. Neither knew how long they were going to wait; God didn't tell them. Their desire to be obedient trumped the unknown.

The people on the other hand grew restless. They had waited long enough from their perspective. They pressured Aaron to make a golden calf for them to worship, since Moses had not returned with any instructions from God. Thousands of people died as a result.

The essence of prison is waiting. Waiting in line to be processed in, waiting in the canteen line, waiting on mail, and waiting—ultimately—for your husband's release.

Waiting may also involve the desire for change in your husband. It may seem like you have been praying for your husband for eternity, yet nothing has changed. And waiting is now growing wearisome.

Waiting can be draining emotionally in either case: time to progress or change to happen. It helps to focus on God, like Moses and Joshua did, instead of the wait, as the Israelites did. Time will progress at the same speed, but the drain will be less if you occupy yourself with the Lord.

I often use the time waiting in line to pray. The long drives to the prison also provide "quiet" for prayer or singing songs to the Lord. In the days without my husband I become purposeful by doing and enjoying the things of God. Prison moves forward with me, not away in the distance as I turn and go a different direction out of frustration. I wait, because I too know God is faithful. He changes people and circumstances in His timing.

Do not give up on God! Continue to seek Him through the many waits. He will richly bless your faith.

January 31 *Holy Help*

John 14:16

"And I will ask the Father, and He will give you another Helper, that He may be with you forever."

At a time when my husband went back to confinement for another stabbing, I was in desperate need for God. That grief, which radiates throughout my body at first knowledge of such events, flooded out of my eyes onto a soon saturated pillow. Hope for change buried itself with my face. I despised the thought of going through the fallout of his actions — again.

With the informing call that sent me to my knees, also came the weighty knowledge it would be many months before I could see or talk to him, and at least two years before I could touch him, because visits would be behind glass. The previous time gruelingly took four. I was an extreme mix of emotions, but I knew who would faithfully help me sort through them and comfort me in the process — and God faithfully showed up.

He reminded me as I sat in tears with my Bible that hope wasn't lost. The story of Onesimus, a useless man whom God redeemed for His glory and made "useful," met me as I opened God's word. The Holy Spirit latched onto that word, and when He prompted me to 2 Timothy, God stirred my spirit as I read many verses reassuring me that He would use the time to refine my husband, making him useful for His glory. He stressed that even though my contact with my husband was from that point restricted, He still had full access.

I was staying with a friend then. In response to the incident, we were discussing the different levels of custody within the prison and the levels of confinement. My husband, being "close custody" due to the nature of the crimes that sent him to prison, must always be within an armed perimeter. He was housed in "open population," but with the stabbing was transferred to "maximum management," which is the most restrictive housing level, even more so than death row. It was a conversation we shared without any anticipation that the upcoming Sunday I would read on a church sign along my route God Wants Full Custody.

God sent me a hug to reassure me again in the message He had spoken to me the previous days in my grief. In essence, "Take heart! I will use this time for his good. Hope isn't lost!" A soothing confidence came over me, because I was reminded my husband was in perfect hands. I actually became excited about all God was going to do with the time that seemed so bleak when first delivered.

The Holy Spirit allows me to experience such hugs from God. He's the one who enables me to understand Scripture and have it come alive when I read. I cannot imagine walking this prison journey, or life in general, without this divine help.

This holy help is available to you as well when you come to believe in Jesus. It's a beautiful relationship! God, Jesus, and the Holy Spirit. Three persons in one. Jesus is your way to God and the Holy Spirit resides in you with your belief in Jesus, so God is with you all the time. You have supernatural help available to you! God loves you and desires to be your help on your own prison journey.

February 1 Stepping Out in Faith

Zechariah 1:3

"Therefore say to them, 'Thus says the Lord of hosts, "Return to Me," declares the Lord of hosts, "that I may return to you," says the Lord of hosts.'"

The Israelites was experiencing a lull in their motivation to rebuild the temple. Their captivity under Babylon was over, and they were allowed to return home by the new Persian ruler. What joy! The initial response was marked by high energy and will to complete it. The foundation was laid with praise. But opposition soon followed.

Work ceased for several years, because the people allowed fear of the opposition to dominate them. The Lord sent Zechariah to encourage the people. The Lord promised to be with them, but they had to move forward. They needed to position their hearts as it was in the beginning. God promised to be with them, but they had to continue building. In the end, the temple was completed through God's provision and protection.

Scripture tells us that God comes close to us as we draw close to Him. He always takes the first step, but then He allows us to choose how close a relationship we desire. We will never experience God's best unless we choose to remain close to Him.

Prayer and reading Scripture are the keys to remaining close to God. The more you do both, the closer to Him you get, and the more you'll see His working in your life. A close relationship brings confidence in His provision and protection for your life and over your situation—including prison.

Do not walk this prison path without God being close. There are too many struggles to go it alone. He wants to help. Let Him.

February 2 *Even My Mood*

Colossians 1:18

He is also head of the body, the church; and He is the beginning, the first-born from the dead; so that He Himself might come to have first place in everything.

I have found this to be a very challenging verse when I consider my mood. In the heat of upset, does my response mirror what would be pleasing to Jesus? Do I surrender my mood to Jesus, allowing the Holy Spirit to reign in me rather than my flesh? Frequently, no.

I allow my heart, and soon words, to flow from an ugly attitude. I can be down on myself, mad at God, frustrated with "life," and have zero tolerance for people. I just want to scream and zap everything into something I can tolerate or beam myself and my imprisoned husband elsewhere for a vacation.

In those moments, I have surrendered to the flesh, and sometimes, in the worst of upsets, will inform God that I know I'm wrong, but "I don't care!" Thankfully, He does care, and He will wait until my tantrum is done, then lovingly remind me that I must rise above such moods and defeat them. If I do not, Satan will kick me when I'm down every time. And this does nothing to help me or my husband overcome prison.

And how is this done? Paul shares that he's able to keep going, even while imprisoned, because God's power mightily works in him. Paul knew he couldn't fulfill his purpose, keep the faith, and survive the earthly stress and temptations without God's help. He had ample reasons to complain to God and be mad. Yet, we read in Colossians that his mood reflects rejoicing while suffering. Wow!

I want my words and heart to be pleasing to God, but it will take His power to restrain my mood in such moments when I'm set on being defiant and mad at the world and life. The recognition is my opportunity to turn toward God and surrender to Him. He desires and deserves to be first in everything. The total me He wants, and that includes my mood.

As you go through this day, consider where God places in your life — even your mood. It will likely be the most challenging aspect of the day to surrender, especially when your flesh is enjoying the outlet.

February 3 — Just Like a Dog

Romans 7:23-24

But I see a different law in the members of my body, waging war against the law of my mind, and making me a prisoner of the law of sin which is in my members. Wretched man that I am! Who will set me free from the body of this death?

I usually always enjoy walking my dog. Rain and cold are the least favorite elements to endure on our walks, but I can usually find pleasure in it, simply because she does — regardless of weather. But the weather impacts my urgency to go and get back, yet she goes along at her usual pace, being distracted by most anything her nose senses along with way.

It's my dog's nature to want to sniff around when outdoors. If left to her own nature, we would never finish our walk. I have to sometimes drag her away from some spot on the ground that she has buried her nose to. What the goal is for her at those moments, I have no idea. It's simply what dogs do. But in my frustration, I'll usually remark to her, "Quit acting like a dog and let's go."

In the verses above, Paul is frustrated with his sin nature. He shares that the good he desires to do, he doesn't do, and the evil he doesn't want to do, he finds himself doing. He teaches us that our sin nature is always at war with our spirit. If you're a Christian, you have two natures living within you: the righteous and the unrighteous.

If left to our own efforts, our sin nature would win every time. We would be like a dog, doing something that comes naturally. It takes resistance and the Spirit of God in us to keep us on track and moving forward toward a positive outcome.

Paul further teaches us that disciplining our thoughts is the first step in defeating our sin nature. Setting our minds on the things of God, not of the flesh. Will we be perfect? No. Again, it will always be a battle between giving into sin and living for God.

But be also encouraged that you aren't left to fight alone. The Holy Spirit in you provides the power to overcome your sin nature. With the faith in what Jesus did for you on the cross, God's Holy Spirit now resides in your body too. Surrendering to His desires will bring victory.

Are you a believer and your husband not, or is he possibly losing more battles with his sin nature than you would like to see? Prison is a difficult place to live righteously, even for the believer.

If he doesn't have a relationship with Jesus, that becomes your utmost prayer. Because without Jesus, there's no war; sin resides fully in your husband's flesh. He will continue to act like what he is—a sinner without Christ. If he's a believer, but stumbling, pray for his strength to resist the evil around him. Your prayers become utmost for his strength and protection.

In either case, remember that God is on your side! He desires you and your husband to walk righteously and to have victory over sin.

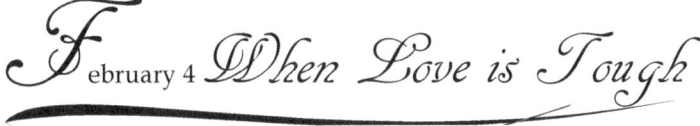

February 4 When Love is Tough

I John 4:11-12

Beloved, if God so loved us, we also ought to love one another. No one has beheld God at any time; if we love one another, God abides in us, and His love is perfected in us.

Saying "I do" may have come before or after prison. In either case, a covenant was made. Loving a prisoner is a tall order on many days. Besides the barriers and continual separation, our husbands' actions may not always be loveable. He may still gamble, owe money that you end up covering, drug and drink, lose his temper, or make trouble within where he lives. It's only through understanding God's love that we are able to fully love our husbands when they are difficult to love. It's supernatural love.

God so loved us that He sent Jesus to die. God loves us, but hates our sin. Remember it's your husband's sin you do not love, not him. The person you love is still there, he's just wrapped up in sin. He needs Jesus. And he can see Jesus in you by how you love him. It's a love beyond romance. It's seeing him as God sees him. And when you do that, loving him comes from a different motivation—a godly one.

God wants to love your husband through you. When fresh out of patience, kindness, or goodness, you can still love your husband by allowing God to be those things through you. Ask Him for help, discipline your focus, and watch the supernatural results. By focusing on how God loves, you can extend that love to your husband, even when he doesn't seem to deserve it.

And what also helps to remember is that you aren't easy to love all the time either! None of us are. I need God's faithfulness to love me when I'm difficult. I want my husband to show me the same loyalty.

It's a risk that our husbands get blamed for everything wrong in the relationship because of where they sit daily. But a prison marriage isn't unlike others in that we also must take ownership of how we make things difficult. If both parties pursue loving each other in this way, love is perfected, and this is most vividly seen when it's tough.

February 5 *Before & After*

Ephesians 2:1

And you were dead in your trespasses and sins.

Tattoos. Prisoners seem to have an abundance of them. They reflect a past, interests, possible gang affiliation, or a love. My husband has acquired many since being in prison. He has added to or revised those he wore at the time of his sentencing.

It strikes me now how they reflect his journey of faith. Many before were images of evil. Now, his body displays Scripture, the Lion of Judah (Jesus), and the overt evil images have been covered. True, getting work done is against the rules, but I cannot help but take joy in the motivation behind the new ink he now bears.

It's the power of God to change a heart. My husband isn't perfect. But he's thankfully not the same person which led to his incarceration. This is only true by the grace of God and His mercy to seek a prisoner's heart that cared nothing for good or godliness at the time.

Paul reminds the believers in Ephesus about their new life in Christ. He describes the sins of their previous lifestyle that equated to their spiritual death and contrasts their rebirth through God's saving grace. He stresses in the passages that they didn't earn their salvation; it was a gift.

His descriptions are harsh: sons of disobedience, children of wrath, indulging in the desires of the flesh. The Ephesian believers, if seen through today's lens, likely would be depicted with that array of tattoos representing their previous lifestyle. Yet we read that the worst of evils cannot surpass God's love.

The blood that once flowed as a result of a tattoo gun, somehow imparting a false sense of strength through an image only skin deep, was countered by Jesus's blood which flowed after being pierced fully through His body from the power of love.

Your husband's past is no match for Jesus's love. The heart behind the worst of tattoos can be covered.

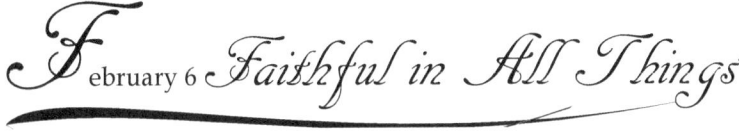

February 6 — Faithful in All Things

Genesis 24:14

"Now may it be that the girl to whom I say, 'Please let down your jar so that I may drink,' and who answers, 'Drink, and I will water your camels also'; —may she be the one whom Thou hast appointed for Thy servant Isaac; and by this I shall know that Thou hast shown lovingkindness to my master."

Abraham was in Canaan. Sarah had died. Isaac was still unwed, although God had promised Abraham that his descendants through Isaac would be like the sand of the seashore. It seems nothing happened quickly in Abraham's life. Isaac was forty years old and single.

Why the wait? Scripture doesn't say, but we read in Genesis 24 that Abraham sent his servant to request a wife for Isaac from Abraham's family. Charged with this assignment, his servant sought the Lord through prayer in finding God's choice for Isaac. We can learn a lot by studying this servant's heart for the Lord and his calling.

First, he was faithful at his job. Abraham had entrusted this man with all that he owned. He was an older man, likely having been with Abraham for some time. Being a servant was not glamorous, yet he was reliable, trustworthy, devoted, and obviously skilled at what he did. And he was rewarded through the increased responsibility given to him by Abraham.

Second, he loved the Lord. We read his prayer in verses 12-14. He prayed for God's blessing on his endeavor. He wanted it to be God's choice and he asked for confirmation. He prayed with belief and with details. He asked God to confirm His choice in a specific way. And God showed up. We read further in verse 26 that he was quick to give honor to God.

Third, he remained focused on his assignment. He had been charged with the task and resisted any delay in completing it. Rebekah's brother and mother wanted her to stay another ten days with them before leaving. Who can blame them! They had no way to emotionally prepare for her departure. But Abraham's servant declined. His business was urgent. In the end, Rebekah left and returned with him to be Isaac's wife.

If you're struggling with faith, take encouragement from this story. God takes care of those who are His. You're a prison wife and it's tough! Like the servant's role, it's not glamorous. But God will reward your faithfulness. Keep loving the Lord and thanking Him for His provisions in this journey of prison. God is always at work. Even as you pray, He's busy working things out for your best. And keep going. Stay focused on the good and to whatever assignment He has called you to while you actively wait for what lies ahead.

February 7 *Today*

Up at 3:00 and again nothing to say. Tears seem to be the only part of me that can speak. Futility is the only thing motivating. And that comes only through the shake of my head, wondering why I even try. But I suppose, even in this moment, words from frustration still move forward to form sentences—and this space—just as those from purpose. So the purpose for today's awakening might be to share the reminder that not all days are perfect, happy, or desirable.

I didn't want to get up today. I also do not want to go through the energy of searching for the energy to complete all that awaits me at my job— today. But I'm responsible and do understand that things usually get better; it just take more discipline some days to push my attitude in the same direction.

It's cold here. The furnace is churning, but fails to contently warm me. Another lull and whine of my mood I suppose. I feel nauseous. The consequence of sinus trouble—or too much coffee on an empty stomach. But even the progress of this page brings some upward momentum to my outlook.

Prison can often be this way too. Days that require more energy that you want to invest. Lack of motivation to continue. A desire for a little reprieve. Your husband, in his extraordinarily difficult behavior, may be adding to the weight you feel in your spirit—today.

But I can say that days that are imperfect, unhappy, or undesirable do not last forever; they do not define every day. I have been at this place many times before, and I know it does get better. God is interested in helping you also to move forward.

He's merciful, because He understands your weaknesses. He knows why you're sluggish in your mood. He knows you intimately. He knows how to meet your individual need—today.

So I do not think being sad is always a bad thing. Some may try to push you along through the pain and somber mood as if it's not okay to spend time in the dumps. You're a prison wife; you can expect some sad days! But I think sadness can be spiritual. It allows you time to reflect and be still. It's in these moments that God can minister most effectively to your spirit if you seek Him. When I have such days, I do not usually have the focus to "study" Scripture; I just need to hear from God. I need to be "hugged." So I allow Him to take me wherever He desires in His word. And I absorb the encouragement He faithfully provides.

Thus there's no Scripture reference for this devotion today. Read where God leads you, and be encouraged that tomorrow is in His care as well, whether you're still sad or feeling better.

February 8 — In God's Timing

John 9:1-3

And as He passed by, He saw a man blind from birth. And His disciples asked Him, saying, "Rabbi, who sinned, this man or his parents, that he should be born blind?" Jesus answered, "It was neither that this man sinned, nor his parents; but it was in order that the works of God might be displayed in him."

It's the age-old question even asked by the prophets and the psalmists: Why does God allow suffering? I have asked it in my confusion to events I see. I have asked it in my own life when it took an unexpected turn. It often remains a mystery not fully understood. But I do know that God remains good—all the time. And all things happen in God's timing.

Consider the blind man. Why did God allow him to remain without sight all those years before intervening? Jesus said that it was so others could see the works of God in him. The man endured difficulty many years, but in the end, God perfected it at a level we could see—but only in hindsight. Good did come from the bad. The man received his sight and became a tremendous witness for Jesus.

And why was the witness so powerful? Because everyone in town knew this man's past! They had passed him daily as he sat begging. They probably thought, as the disciples mistakenly did, that some sin brought the curse of blindness upon him. Jesus corrected them in this thinking. But He also presented to them a life changed, initially physically, then spiritually. Would the blind man say that the wait was worth it? Since the suffering brought his salvation—absolutely!

Prison may be part of your list of questions presented to God like mine. Why did God allow my husband to do what he did? Why did He allow him as a child to be abused and slowly pulled into crime and drugs? He was just a child!

Searching for those answers gets me nowhere. But when I focus on the possibilities and the ways God uses the path that led my husband to prison, I'm more convinced that God remains good. A great witness comes from a past redeemed by God! The greater depth brings the greater witness to the power of the resurrection and Jesus's ability to change a person.

Be encouraged in this! God isn't through with any of us. He was not through with the blind man who sat most of his life unchanged, begging, and in need of one thing—an encounter with Jesus.

Pray for that encounter for your husband. See prison as the catalyst to an astounding future that will never be without today's difficulty. Hang in there with God. His timing is always perfect. The good will come, and you might be surprised at how much you're praising God in the end. **

February 9 — Ambassadress

II Corinthians 5:20

Therefore, we are ambassadors for Christ, as though God were entreating through us; we beg you on behalf of Christ, be reconciled to God.

    I have never considered an "ambassadress." The word brings real femininity to my thoughts. As a Christian, I often have heard and continue to hear "ambassador" as used in the verse above. Ambassador tends to bring my thoughts to those of power, initiative, perseverance, and special assignment. As a Christian, all those descriptors should be true for me. I'm Christ's representative. But adding femininity to the word reminds me of the special role I have as a lady doing the work of the Lord.

    Femininity is a strength just as important as boldness or assertiveness that may reflect an ambassador. How we dress and behave reflect our commitment to Christ and our husbands. Do we talk respectively to and about our husbands? Or are we flirtatious toward other men in our dress and actions? What characteristic would come to mind if a coworker were to describe us? Peter reminds us that a gentle and quiet spirit is of great worth to the Lord (I Peter 3:4). A gentle and quiet spirit is a lady with a submissive heart.

    And with this consistent reflection, others will see you differently. They will know what you stand for. Your consistent strength of character will impart influence. They will see a lady who sticks with her marriage. They will see the power of forgiveness. They will see perseverance in the face of great challenges. They will see all these things done with grace and joy, because God is ultimately the source of your strength.

    You can be an ambassadress. You can be a feminine, yet ultimately powerful lady in the hands of God. You can influence your husband and those around you, and even those who watch your life from afar, like in a prison visitation room. They will see a lady embracing the special assignment she has been given in Christ through the circumstance of prison. Your quiet strength can be amazingly powerful.

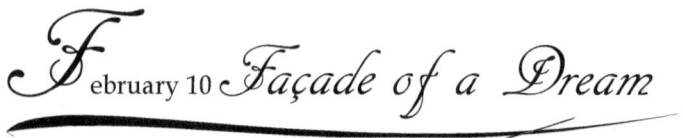

February 10 — Façade of a Dream

Proverbs 24:11

Deliver those who are being taken away to death, and those who are staggering to slaughter, O hold them back.

It was a disturbing dream. A blatant nightmare would have been less unsettling. The reality behind the images seen during my sleep represented the final fate for those not reached for Christ. Men on death row, being led away to execution, centered the activity of the thoughts. The image progressed through the individual face of each man awaiting his fate.

Death was coming. But the fear in my heart was not from his physical death, but his spiritual future once killed. I knew each man I saw didn't have a relationship with Jesus and hell awaited—eternally. There was a panic in my heart to stop the progression, to have more time to share what he needed, to pray that he would accept the offer of Jesus's salvation.

But strangely and more sadly, nothing came from my lips. I was walking amongst the progression, seeing other bystanders who appeared to be ministers, but I heard nothing. Everyone just watched.

Beyond the progression, celebration was seen. It seemed that a festival surrounded the event. But who were these people celebrating such a horrible outcome for someone else? I went among them and strangely words came. I pled and ridiculed them, angered by what I saw.

At awakening, there was an understanding that the faces I saw in the dream were never rescued. The dream didn't have a joyful ending. Those celebrating were Satan's servants.

That morning was sobering, because I knew, although it was a dream, everything it represented was actively real. Those marked for death in prison desperately need to know Jesus!

It could have been my husband at one time in his life. What if no one ever prayed or witnessed to him? The man I thankfully came to know and love was spared the execution chamber. But the greater sorrow comes when I consider that sentence being carried out and his never being in heaven. It's a horrible consideration.

Few of us know the date we will die. Every day is a gift for all of us. But a death warrant initiates a countdown to that knowledge. A precious window of time remains for the spiritual condition of that person to be determined, for eternity.

Please join me in praying for those men and women on death row who do not know Jesus. Time is precious. Prison locks that person into a progression possibly unable to be changed legally, but eternity holds a far greater punishment if that person dies without salvation.

The verse in Proverbs seems almost a plea; "O hold them back!" The words are desperate. But the author is at least speaking! I'm challenged by this. My actions in the dream were wasted on ridiculing the evil instead of investing my words in the lives needing to hear.

February 11 Spiritual Help

Psalm 51:10

Create in me a clean heart, O God, and renew a steadfast spirit within me.

David wrote Psalm 51. It's one of the most endearing, because it reflects the extremes of repentance and forgiveness. He had committed great sin when he orchestrated adultery and murder, yet his faith in God's love surpassed his guilt.

He desired to live a life pleasing to the Lord. But he also acknowledged his dependence and need for God to be successful. David admitted his sins and asked God's forgiveness, then asked God to help him going forward to be a testimony to what God had done for him.

Prison brings a need for spiritual help. The culture of prison is evil. Your husband lives amongst it daily. He may attempt to lure you within the culture through requests and participation in things that aren't godly. You may also become weary in your efforts to remain faithful to God and, in some circumstances, your husband. You may desire escape. An escape from the life you wake to daily.

A spiritual battle is really what we wake to daily. The origins of a weary heart may be like arrows surrounding you. And evil draws the bow. Satan will capitalize on the days and seasons when we are most often weary. He will kick us when we are down. But it's at these moments and on those days when the power of God can show itself to us if we surrender to the need and accept God's help.

It's an awesome thing to experience the power of God in circumstances when you know you had nothing to do with the outcome. Maybe you experience it when the Holy Spirit restrains your words when you feel ugly and want to unleash the feelings onto your husband. Maybe it's when you're faced with the attention of another man and the warning goes off in your heart to flee—and you do! Maybe it's when you're overwhelmed and have no energy to be kindhearted on the job, yet you find yourself ministering to someone "out of the blue."

In all circumstances as these, you can be wowed by the understanding that it was purely divine help that enabled you to be successful. God's power is seen greatly when you're at your weakest. Pursue His help. And when you see His power shine through the circumstance, you'll feel the warm hug in your spirit that whispers, "Well done, My daughter."

February 12 When Done Wrong

I Samuel 1:10

And she, greatly distressed, prayed to the Lord and wept bitterly.

Hannah was a lady often mentioned when depression is described of persons in Scripture. She was barren and tormented in her spirit by this truth. She longed for a child and wept to God regularly. To add to her distress, Peninnah provoked her. Both Hannah and Peninnah were married to Elkanah. Peninnah had several children. And despite what I may think about this arrangement, I'm drawn to consider Hannah's reaction to her situation.

Nowhere in the passage do we read that Hannah treated Peninnah or Elkanah poorly. In fact, we read that Elkanah loved Hannah, possibly indicating that he didn't feel love for Peninnah. And maybe this contributed to her disdain toward Hannah. Despite how many children she gave Elkanah, he continued to love Hannah and not her. What a household!

Do I think that Hannah handled the situation perfectly every day? No—she was not superhuman. But I think Scripture highlights for us the predominant attitude that she maintained. She was devoted to the Lord and sought the Lord's blessing in the face of years of unanswered prayer for a child. It even seems that Peninnah's antagonism escalated when the family traveled to the temple to worship—as if wanting to add salt to an open wound.

I admire Hannah. She represents so much of how Jesus handled His persecutors. She was gentle and quiet, yet steadfast. She knew the power over her circumstances remained with God. This drove her actions and ability not to retaliate when provoked. Hannah's faith in God to provide a child didn't falter, and this energized her reaction. She's shortchanged, I think, when only her sadness is highlighted. She was a powerful lady.

In the end, God blessed Hannah with a son. Samuel was a great prophet. He led Israel all the days of his life and remained the spokesperson for God. He anointed Saul as king and later David. Hannah's prayer seemed to take forever to be answered, but God answered in a huge way in perfect timing.

If you're facing a circumstance that's unfair, if you're being mistreated, if you're enduring antagonism, take encouragement from Hannah's testimony. Do not lose heart! Keep seeking God through prayer. God sees your circumstance and desires to bless your faithfulness. Resist the temptation to retaliate. When God unleashes His blessing, it will overflow and surpass your greatest desire.

February 13 — Fighting Fear

Matthew 10:28

And do not fear those who kill the body, but are unable to kill the soul; but rather fear Him who is able to destroy both soul and body in hell.

This is my challenge. Separation from my husband brings vulnerability within days of no contact. His environment isn't nice. Many who surround him are dangerous. My husband wakes to harm's way daily. It's a horrible feeling and often nauseating to consider his being physically hurt or, more frighteningly, killed.

If this horrible event happens to my husband, and his life is taken, I have the peace in knowing that his eternity is secure — and I'll be with him, eternally. With salvation comes life, not death. I'll grieve, but not as those who have no hope. This is the hope that I maintain for myself and my husband.

There was a time when I battled severe anxiety. This anxiety surrounded death and the kind that comes from unnatural events, such as accidents or crime. In my humanness, it seemed any unnatural cause of death I had better opportunity to control, thus preventing its occurrence. Sounds foolish I suppose, but my thinking was not perfect at that time.

I still have bouts of fear. I have to meditate on the hope that Jesus supplies when overwhelmed with worry that harm is headed my way or towards my husband.

God is sovereign. He has determined my days before I was even born. So it is also for my husband. And since we believe in Jesus as the Son of God, in His death and resurrection, in His forgiveness of our sins, there's nothing to fear—in the big picture.

When sin entered the world, so did death. We physically die. But spiritual death is what we should actually fear. And this death can only be nullified through Jesus. He's who we should reverence, because without Him, hell stands waiting.

If you battle anxiety for your husband's safety, pray. Pray for his safety, but more importantly, if he isn't a believer in Jesus, pray that he will come to know Jesus for salvation before he's ever taken from this earth. This is your number-one priority. And if he's a believer, rest in God's promise: He will never leave him or forsake him, especially not at death.

February 14 *Love & Desire*

Song of Solomon 7:10

"I am my beloved's, and his desire is for me."

Valentine's Day can bring a solemn acceptance of another special day not shared with your husband. Unless possibly it falls on a visitation day. But even with that, your desire to share is stifled by the setting and rules governing that time. You're together, but cannot share fully your level of desire. It's rather bittersweet.

What you must cling to is the part of your love that survives the challenges, making it a greater love to celebrate than most couples consider on this day. You show love every day when you support your husband during this time. There are challenges, but in the end, your love will be far richer than the surface exchanges of romantic cards on Valentine's Day.

For now, your flowers may be a blooming weed that survived the closely clipped yard at the visitation park. It's handed to you by your husband while you walk that repeated lap around the perimeter. Your chocolates may be a bag of candy purchased from the canteen on the same visit. For now, these may be your mementos for the day, but they also reflect the dedication to keep celebrating each other regardless of the situation.

Solomon in the verse for today is writing about the love between his new bride and himself. They are finally coming together intimately after a building courtship. Their love is new and exciting. They are all about each other.

This time of prison may be an extended courtship without most levels of physical intimacy, but if you nurture your desire for each other in spite of the situation, your love will grow deeper in other ways. Still send cards. Still get creative within the visitation park to celebrate. You may shed a few tears from unfulfilled desires, but always blend them with tears of joy for what you do share with him.

February 15 Chasing Perfection

Philippians 3:12

Not that I have already obtained it, or have already become perfect, but I press on in order that I may lay hold of that for which also I was laid hold of by Christ Jesus.

I'm from Kentucky. That means I was brought up watching basketball; specifically the University of Kentucky Wildcats. If you're a college basketball fan, you're likely familiar with the phrase "Chasing Perfection." UK's basketball team in 2015 was in pursuit of an unbeaten season, including all tournament games. March Madness took on a different goal than the usual Final Four bracket position and, ideally, the national title win.

Paul in his letter to the Philippians explained in the verse above that he was chasing perfection, but that which is of Christ. Perfection for those of us who follow Jesus is obtained when we enter heaven. The only perfect person on this planet was Jesus; the rest of us still have part of our sin nature in us. And because of that, while on this earth, we strive toward becoming like Christ by following His will.

Paul longed to be with Jesus. His goal was to reach heaven and see the Lord, who had saved him from a dead-end life—physically and spiritually. He recognized his failures in his humanness, but never stopped pressing on toward the goal.

With God's help, he tried to live a life pleasing to the Lord by being obedient to the calling God made on his life. Paul gave it his all. Like the Kentucky Wildcats, he chased perfection; he ran like an athlete. He competed in the spiritual battle to win the prize: eternal rewards with God.

This is the best we can do with our lives as well. We have a lifetime of mistakes behind us, and we will continue to sin as long as we are on this side of heaven. This is our nature. It's only through God's forgiveness and acceptance of Jesus as the Savior from sin that we are able to enter heaven despite a lifetime of failures.

If you're struggling with sin, take encouragement from this passage of Scripture. Perfection can be chased, but never obtained until your heavenly home is reached. There will be failures, you'll mess up. But this doesn't determine your destiny. Continue to ask for forgiveness for your sins and keep growing in your faith. Seek to be like Christ. There's no greater goal in life.

February 16 *Prison Neighbors*

Psalm 57:4

My soul is among lions; I must lie among those who breathe forth fire, even the sons of men, whose teeth are spears and arrows, and their tongue a sharp sword.

David could have just as well been describing my husband's cell rather than his time in the cave when fleeing Saul and his army. Evil and violence pursued David. He felt threatened daily. Saul threatened him verbally, and he attempted to murder David on several occasions. This sadly describes prison and the experience of many of the men there—both the victims and the pursuers.

The constant verbal garbage that smothers the good air in prison affects all the men there, regardless of participation in the exchanges. Cursing, lewd and vulgar talk, insults, threats—words are like the swords described by David. Lions surround the good and provoke and threaten for sometimes petty reasons.

My husband has often been on the receiving end of someone's rampage. He described once an inmate who had "shot" him up for literally hours. Then the next day asked to read my husband's newspaper. My husband declined for obvious reasons. Well this unleashed another round of insults and actual threats of physical harm simply for telling this guy no.

Are you for real! Just because my husband wouldn't let him borrow a newspaper? But this type of thinking and behavior is rampant in prison. Your husband may face the same. If not from other inmates, sadly from officers who misuse their position.

In David's case, he cried out to God to save him from the abuse and threats. In Psalm 57, he exalts God's faithfulness and lovingkindness and His truth. David praises God. He knew he was being wrongly treated by Saul, and he sought God for protection and deliverance.

This is a great psalm to pray if your husband has enemies in prison. Whenever the word "me" is used, insert your husband's name. The "sons of men" in verse 4 can be replaced with whoever is threatening or verbally assaulting your husband. Verse 7 can be your personal praise to God.

By speaking God's word back to Him, you tap into special aspects of prayer. David wrote the psalms under the inspiration of God. God knew you would be where you are today, facing prison and concern for your husband's safety. He knew you could relate to David's experience in the cave. That special connection can become the same heart-felt cry to God for the same deliverance. And God remains the same. The same God who rescued David is available to you and your husband.

February 17 A Wife's Belief

Judges 13:9

And God listened to the voice of Manoah; and the angel of God came again to the woman as she was sitting in the field, but Manoah her husband was not with her.

Manoah and his wife were the parents of Samson. Manoah's wife, who is unnamed in Scripture, was childless until Samson's birth. An angel of God visited her to announce her coming pregnancy and that her son was to be dedicated to the Lord as a Nazarite. God chose to primarily communicate with her, not Manoah.

She told Manoah about the angel's visit, and he seemed to believe the message, but one that came from possibly a prophet or other man. He desired the "man" to return so that he could question him further about how to raise the boy. To Manoah's credit, he desired to be a good father and to raise his son in a manner to be pleasing to God. He just didn't realize the extent of the special assignment that his wife and he were selected for.

In answer to Manoah's request, the angel returned, but again to his wife. She ran quickly to get Manoah, basically exclaiming, "He's back, come quick!" Manoah was able to ask the angel about how to raise his forthcoming son, but, humorously, the angel responded, "Let the woman pay attention to all that I said" (verse 13).

They had already been told how to raise their son; he was to be a Nazarite, a person who takes an oath of service to God. Manoah needed to hear it for himself I suppose. He really didn't understand it was an angel until miraculous things were done before his eyes. Even with that, he fell down believing they would die, because they had looked upon the angel of God. His wife presented more spiritual discernment by her corrective comments that God didn't plan to kill them, concluding that He would have never accepted their offering or shared with them all He had.

This unnamed lady of Scripture provides us an example of how God uniquely uses a woman in the life of her husband. Manoah's faith seemed less than his wife's. God began with her faith, then she was able to reach out to her husband. There's no indication that she doubted the angel; she ran eagerly to share with her husband each time. She repeatedly shared her faith in what God was doing. Manoah came to believe, in time, through his own experiences.

You may very well be the catalyst God wants to use in your husband's life. You may be God's go-to lady when He has something special in mind for your marriage. Embrace the assignment. Be open to what you hear from God and share this with your husband. You're a team for God, but for now, He may desire to use your greater faith to lead your husband.

February 18 *Emotional Mix*

Jeremiah 20:7

O Lord, Thou hast deceived me and I was deceived; Thou hast overcome me and prevailed. I have become a laughingstock all day long; everyone mocks me.

This verse begins a passage of Scripture where Jeremiah pours out his heart to God. His calling, which was to prophesy against Israel's sin and coming judgment by God, permeated his life and resulted in a colorful life of emotions. Part of this outcome involved the chief priest having him arrested, beaten, and put in stocks. Upon release, the verse above breaks forth his confusion with God and travels through his other emotions of anger, joy, depression, and the ironic passionate desire to continue preaching God's word to the rebellious people of Judah.

I love the example we have in Scripture of Jeremiah's life. His life was far from perfect, despite being obedient to God's call and remaining in God's will. Jeremiah voluntarily accepted a very difficult life out of his love for

God and desire to fulfill his calling. He's described as the "weeping prophet," because he didn't bottle his emotions; he was honest with God about how he was feeling.

I take courage from Jeremiah when I consider my marriage and the reality I face daily. My marriage to my husband while he was incarcerated has brought with it my own version of colorful emotions. And I regularly express them to God! But not from a hardened heart toward my life, but rather the active emotions of being immersed in God's will and the adventurous emotions I encounter as a result.

When I'm unjustly judged, I feel vulnerable and hurt. When prison corruption impacts my husband, I get angry. When I'm doing everything I can to be obedient to God, and yet difficulty comes, I question God. When I see the good coming from this life, I get impassioned for more. When I experience God's presence, I feel joy. When my husband taunts sin without conviction, I become discouraged.

Prison brings a spectrum of emotions. And that's okay! So long as you remain committed to God and your husband, your heart can express its feelings to God in sincerity. He knows how you're feeling already, so talking with Him allows you the opportunity to be nurtured through the difficulty.

But you must also participate with God in the management of your heart. You must allow Him to strengthen your faith, mold your character, and use the difficulty to mature your heart to better maneuver the experiences. In essence, you must grow spiritually to enable God to use your life more powerfully.

Emotions aren't a sign of weakness, but if not managed intentionally, they can stifle the journey of faith. Let's embrace the journey of prison and all the emotions that accompany it, handing them over to God to produce a beautiful outcome in and through us.

February 19 *Budget Minded*

Luke 5:11

And when they had brought their boats to land, they left everything and followed Him.

When Jesus called His first disciples, they didn't hesitate to drop everything and follow Him. I admire their faith. There's no indication in Scripture that they worried for their livelihood, bills, maintaining a household, or what their families would think. Of course, seen through today's eyes, we cannot imagine how any of us could make such a leap. We see today's culture as not allowing such freedom.

Such freedom is appealing. Not to say they had an easy road by choosing to follow Christ. Of course they didn't! But when seen through today's eyes, most of us aren't in a position to leap, because we are financially strapped. There are responsibilities and expenses we have acquired. And this requires an income.

Some expenses are unavoidable. We all have to eat, live somewhere, and have some type of transportation. It's the expenses that come through debt that usually interfere most with our financial freedom. Actively working toward decreasing your debt should be a goal, and this comes through budgeting.

I have found that my biggest barrier is discipline. I faithfully make a budget every month, but sticking to it is the hard part. There are always the unexpected and temptations I fall for that aren't necessities. My best strategy to stick to the budget is getting all money allocated toward debt out of my bank account as soon as possible! If it sits there, I tend to dip into it for other things. It hurts to release it, but it makes me accountable to the budget.

This also helps my husband stick to the budget. Once the money is gone, it's gone. His impulsive bartering has to have limits too. All too often his bartering blows the budget. He suddenly acquires something "on his face" and that sadly shifts to a priority payment that I hadn't planned. So it's not solely my responsibility to manage the money. My husband is just as responsible to spend with our budget in mind too.

This doesn't go perfectly every month. It has been most difficult when he has been in confinement, because very little of our communication is in real time. I may have just replaced a tire and then receive a letter informing me I need to send money for one of his unplanned purchases. Despite my telling him not to promise money we may not have, it does still happen at times.

But I keep the goal in mind: being debt free. I remain eager for the opportunities this will provide to bless others and to decrease the stress related to finances. While your husband is incarcerated, it's likely only your income supporting you and your family. This makes it even tougher. But even with only one income, managing the wealth you have is important, because if done well, you can bless others in Jesus's name too and better prepare for the future.

February 20 — Serious Words

Titus 1:12-14

One of themselves, a prophet of their own, said, "Cretans are always liars, evil beasts, lazy gluttons." This testimony is true. For this cause reprove them severely that they may be sound in the faith, not paying attention to Jewish myths and commandments of men who turn away from the truth.

One thing that can be said about Paul is that he didn't sugarcoat the truth. He was direct and bold. His way of evangelism mirrored his manner of persecution before he came to his encounter with Jesus on the road to Damascus.

In the verses above, he's instructing Titus on how to deal with Jewish opposition in Crete. Titus was left there by Paul to organize the church by appointing elders and teaching the congregation. Titus faced great challenges in this assignment. And like most of us, needed encouragement and advice.

I consider how much Paul's words must have meant to him. Titus was looked to as the leader; however, leadership can be lonely when things are going poorly. He needed a cheerleader. And Paul faithfully cheered him on through this letter, encouraged him to be bold and to lead the church with authority.

If your husband sounds like Titus, be his cheerleader! Living righteously is a hard assignment in prison, but all the more if he's attempting to teach others about Jesus and the truth. He's likely facing opposition, ridicule, and possibly threats. Let him know how proud you are of him. Tell and show him you're on his team.

Also entrust his personality to the Lord. Your husband may not sugarcoat things either, which can incite more opposition—and your fear. But God knows how to use the personality to be a positive force within the same walls. Pray for your husband's wisdom in how to handle himself without sacrificing the truth.

February 21 — Being an Intercessor

Exodus 4:24-26

Now it came about at the lodging place on the way that the Lord met him and sought to put him to death. Then Zipporah took a flint and cut off her son's foreskin and threw it at Moses' feet, and she said, "You are indeed a bridegroom of blood to me." So He let him alone. At that time she said, "You are a bridegroom of blood"—because of the circumcision.

Moses's wife intervened when he seemed unaware of the danger. Why did Moses neglect to circumcise his son as God had commanded the Israelites to do since the days of Abraham? Was he overwhelmed with the sudden assignment of returning to Egypt to free Israel from Pharaoh's reign? Scripture doesn't say, but we do read that God honored Zipporah's actions and spared Moses's life.

If like me, you pray near constantly for your husband. I seek God's protection, His will, and most everything in between on behalf of my husband. But when my husband has knowingly stepped outside of God's will, I pray for God's mercy.

Much as Zipporah took action to protect Moses from the consequences of his disobedience to God, I seek mercy for my husband. I trust God to handle the situation for my husband's ultimate good, and this may be allowing the consequences to come, but if there's a way to provide another opportunity for him to repent and make the right decision, I want him to have that opportunity.

God's wrath deserves reverence. My husband doesn't always see the threat. He rationalizes some choices and excuses the small sins as no big deal. Maybe Moses thought waiting extra days to circumcise his son would be no big deal. But neglecting God's command nearly cost him his life.

If you see your husband on a destructive path, be prepared to take action on his behalf through prayer. Pray for God's mercy, trust that God hears your prayers, and know that whatever the answer, God makes only perfect decisions for the best good. **

February 22 Furnace to Den

Daniel 3:25

He answered and said, "Look! I see four men loosed and walking about in the midst of the fire without harm, and the appearance of the fourth is like a son of the gods!"

We can take great encouragement from witnessing someone else's victory over impossible odds. Our faith can be bolstered. When we then encounter a faith crisis, we can know victory is possible. We hear testimonies of miracles, so we pray for our own. We hear of faith sustained in spite of not receiving a miracle. Good or bad outcomes can be faith builders when the circumstance overcame was severe. Daniel's three friends Shadrach, Meshach, and Abed-nego were miraculously spared certain death and this quite certainly impacted Daniel's faith when faced with his own later in the lion's den.

Nebuchadnezzar had ordered the three friends into the furnace following their refusal to worship an idol built by him. They knew it violated God's commandment. The officials reported this defiance to the king who became enraged. Oddly enough, the king had earlier promoted Daniel and recognized God as the "Lord of kings" and actually promoted Shadrach, Meshach, and Abed-nego upon Daniel's recommendation. Nebuchadnezzar displayed short-lived favor.

But Shadrach, Meshach, and Abed-nego remained true to their convictions and voiced such to the king. This enraged him further, and into the fire they were thrown. Where Daniel was during this event isn't mentioned. If he knew of the situation, he was likely pleading with God for their rescue. But what we do know is that God showed up, and they walked out from the flames without even their hair smelling of smoke.

Two kings later, Daniel would face his own faith crisis. A political ploy devised to get rid of him resulted in King Darius inadvertently sentencing Daniel to be thrown to the lions for his devotion to God. Daniel continued to pray to God despite the king's manipulated edict forbidding it. On his escort to the lion's den, he must have considered his three friends' miraculous rescue from the furnace. He knew it would be only through God's deliverance he would survive, but even if God chose not to, he could face death with heavenly assurance, as his three friends expressed prior to their fall into the flames.

And God showed up. Where Shadrach, Meshach, and Abed-nego were at the time of Daniel's faith crisis isn't mentioned. Daniel was an elderly man by then, so his three friends might have already died. The value of their testimony, however, lived on.

I wish Daniel had shared more about these things in his book. There must have been some comfort in knowing others before him had faced a similar circumstance. He knew of the Israelites' miraculous deliverance in the time of Moses, but Shadrach, Meshach, and Abed-nego were people he knew personally. He got to hear the firsthand account. And thankfully, he shared it with us through his writing.

Your prison experience—and the Lord's faithfulness to you—can be of great value to someone else on this same journey. The crisis may not be exactly the same, but you could lift someone else's faith by sharing your story. You have probably faced plenty of difficult circumstances and experienced God in the midst of your allegorical furnace or den. Consider sharing this with others. If you make yourself available for this, God will definitely connect you with the audience or lady who needs to hear.

February 23 *Prison To-Do List*

I John 3:16

We know love by this, that He laid down His life for us; and we ought to lay down our lives for the brethren.

Seems I never can get everything done on my to-do list. I have tried adjusting how I approach responsibilities, rearranging my efforts on the weekends, and trying new ways of doing things in hopes of generating more time in a day. There are non-negotiables such as time in the mornings with God and Scripture study. It's the negotiables that give me struggles, because my husband adds another list to my existing list most every week. If not careful, I lean toward making my own list priority and making excuses for his to be delayed.

It's a balance. But it's also a test of love. Love is sacrificial. It seeks another's good before its own. How much more than our spouses!

I often see my husband's list as just more work. Or I may simply not see it as important to "my life." He sends me topics for my reading, websites to check out, radio programs to listen to, things to type for him, sports news to print, tasks to do from exercising to spraying the house for bugs.

I have a tendency to lose heart when feeling overwhelmed. I just want to sit and do nothing, because the lists seem futile to ever stay ahead of. I can also get frustrated with my husband and somewhat bitter, because he simply doesn't grasp just how busy days are. He "forgets" about laundry, mowing the grass, grocery shopping, errands, paying bills, taking care of pets, and the unexpected needs that must be dealt with daily. To then get a letter with more things he expects of me can leave me with the urge to scream.

Having such an attitude, however, doesn't get things done and poses a threat to my marriage. Busyness and misdirected priorities are poisonous darts seeking to wound or destroy my marriage.

Love is sacrificial. This truth convicts me when I really stop to consider that my to-do list is often written from a selfish perspective. God allows enough time within each day to accomplish my purpose. And my primary purpose is to God and then my husband. If I'm faithful to these, my interests and needs will be taken care of through God's grace.

Our husbands desire to be respected. They want to lead, but being physically unavailable makes this difficult in the daily happenings at home. Within the separation, we can best do this by showing them their interests and requests are important to us. It becomes a way of showing love. It becomes our to-love list.

February 24 — Alien Beings

John 17:16

"They are not of the world, even as I am not of the world."

The television comedy *3rd Rock from the Sun* centered around four aliens who traveled to earth to research human beings. Humor was created from their odd behavior in trying to fit in. Despite looking like humans, they didn't know how to be human.

Christians are like aliens. This world isn't our home. We long for our heavenly home where sin doesn't exist, nor sorrow. God knew that we would need help and hope to live in a "foreign" world. He assures us in Scripture the ugliness and pain that accompany us in our lives here is only temporary.

Prison definitely adds to the sorrow of this life. It provides a concentrated dose of all that's wrong in this world. It can urge our longings for our heavenly home—for us and our husbands. Hope is more crucial when the environment is crueler.

Jesus is praying for His disciples when He speaks the verse for today. He was soon to be executed and was praying to God for the well-being of His disciples. They would soon be without Him. He didn't pray that God remove them from the world, but to "keep them from the evil one" (verse 15).

God leaves us here to share with others the hope that we have for heaven. Sharing this hope from prison or the outside can be met with evil opposition. Prison is a world of ungodliness and Christians do not fit in. Staying married to someone incarcerated doesn't fit in; the world would say leave him! But unlike the characters from *3rd Rock from the Sun*, we shouldn't try to fit in. Instead we should look to God to help us remain godly when surrounded by ungodliness and worldly beliefs.

Jesus warns us of the temptations we will face, but He also encourages us and prays on our behalf that we will successfully live as aliens in this world. Do not lose heart when everything around you seems foreign. It's a reminder that you're from a better place.

February 25 — A Well-Thought Day

Isaiah 26:3

"The steadfast of mind Thou wilt keep in perfect peace, because he trusts in Thee."

Prison has a way of depleting our emotional energy by keeping our minds fixed on the barriers and losses. Sighs accompany each morning on a path that has years before us. But God uses our trials to bring good. And with this knowledge comes the challenge of steadying our thoughts on this truth to keep our emotions from weighing us down within the present difficulties. It isn't just positive thinking. It's knowing that God is in control and is active, blending the good and bad to bring about the best.

I was reminded of this truth during a storm one early morning. Wind rattled everything beyond the walls within where I sat. Lightning, thunder, and heavy rain filled the sky, and an oil lamp lighted the space around me. Such times are blessings in the opportunities for stillness and contemplation.

And on that dark morning, the Lord used the events around me—specifically my pets—to speak His larger perspective to my heart.

My usually cheerful collie was frantic as she attempted to find some hidden place to squeeze herself into. Each clap of thunder intensified her panic. Trembling, she laid, drooling pools of saliva by her terrified panting. She never stayed in one place long, before she rose and paced again. I sat defeated in my efforts to console her.

I also looked upon the cat. He lazily stretched, repositioned himself, and returned to sleep, unbothered by the elements that warred against what seemed our meager shelter. He appeared more annoyed by the behavior of the dog at many points. Sitting there, I understood the message God spoke to my heart: I need to be more like the cat than the dog when the storms of life hit. This includes these days of prison.

Prison is a storm with few moments of relenting. It's a chain of days that inherently cover you with a black cloud. Maybe it isn't being able to see your husband for an extended time. Maybe it's the yard, growing by yards, but the mower is broke—and so are you, because there's now only one income. Maybe it's trying to cover your puffy eyes, because you spent the previous night in tears after an argument with your husband that a fifteen-minute phone call couldn't resolve. Each day can bring a different struggle.

Your challenge is to not surrender to the negative contemplations of your mind. Focus your thoughts on God's faithfulness and the truth of His word. Resist worrying. Draw on your experiences with God and what you read in Scripture to renew your thoughts with hopeful ones. God never makes mistakes. You can trust Him with your circumstances. And as you meditate on the evidences from His past provisions and His word, you gain peace within any current storm of prison or life and confidence for future ones.

February 26 Spiritual Happenings

Luke 10:19

"Behold, I have given you authority to tread upon serpents and scorpions, and over all the power of the enemy, and nothing shall injure you."

The Lord began revealing more to me of the spiritual realm as I got closer to Him. Overt things would happen within a day that I understood was from God. Just the same, the reality of evil became more overt. With my increasing intimacy with God, what I experienced in this realm was an extension of my conversations with God from His heavenly one.

One morning after my Bible study of the passage for today, I stepped out my back door to find a dead snake with its head smashed. It was just lying there right outside my door. I suppose it would startle most, but once I saw it, I instantly knew it was simply a hug from God. He wanted to encourage me in my purpose that He was revealing to me. He knew I would instantly recognize it as an encounter with Him, not a coincidence to figure out or a racing heartbeat to calm.

There was a later time when I was discouraged and feeling an eternity from reaching that purpose. I walked into my bathroom to see a scorpion on the wall. It was another reminder from God to reassure me of His plans for me. He had given me authority to tread on serpents and scorpions and over all the power of the enemy. Evil was trying to discourage me and that scorpion was God's reminder for me to recognize where my discouragement was coming from.

All my experiences such as those become a "hug" through the stirring of the Holy Spirit in me. God knows me intimately, what we talk about, what I have been studying, what patterns I'll recognize as His "voice." So a dead snake and a scorpion aren't freakish coincidences; they are spiritual happenings. They are part of the ongoing conversation I have with God. And the closer I get to Him, I "see" more of the spiritual realm active around me.

Do not ever let anyone tell you being a Christian is boring! It's an exciting journey. Even with years of my life having now involved prison, life is sweet. There are hard days. I struggle with depression. But my hope never fades, and God remains faithful to hug me when I need.

You choose how close to God you want to be. There will be no hugs without having the Holy Spirit in you. He comes to you with your belief and acceptance of Jesus as your Savior. And the extent to which you experience His presence depends on how close your relationship is to Him.

If you have not accepted Jesus, that becomes your first priority. The first four books of the New Testament provide details about the life of Christ. Read about Him. Consider the reality of your future—eternally. Consider your sin. Ask for forgiveness, and begin a journey with Jesus today. As you continue to walk with Him, your world will not be seen the same way again.

✝

February 27 — Undercover until Okay

Esther 2:20

Esther had not yet made known her kindred or her people, even as Mordecai had commanded her, for Esther did what Mordecai told her as she had done when under his care.

Esther was a young Jewish girl who was selected from a harem of other virgins to be queen. She was an orphan in the care of her uncle Mordecai. The Persian Empire was in place which placed the Jewish people in servitude. When selected as queen, Mordecai advised Esther to keep her heritage a secret for obvious reasons. That's until a plot to annihilate the Jews was orchestrated by a man within the king's palace. Mordecai challenged Esther to intervene on behalf of her people, questioning her famously if possibly she was brought into the royal family "for such a time as this" (verse 4:14).

The book of Esther is a great study. Well beyond just being a great story of courage, God's providence is the hallmark of the book. As a prison wife, it also provides me practical wisdom of how to approach relationships and how much to share about my husband's incarceration—if at all.

Early on, I simply avoided most conversation about my love life. The Lord had to develop in me boldness to talk about such a private part of my life—especially since it involved an inmate. My relationship was a good thing, and I treated it like a disease! I ran from the anticipated criticism and insane looks. So in the beginning, it was really more about me than my husband.

In time, I began to share more confidently with select persons. And with more time, a testimony was evident, and I knew that I couldn't continue to censor all that God wanted me to share with others. But I have gained wisdom from God to know that sometimes it's still okay to be like Esther.

I definitely do not feed the inappropriate, rude, and gossip interests of some people. I go into Esther mode, maintaining a silent strength in who I know I am. Some people can do harm with such information. They may use it against me or create problems for my husband on the inside. God gives me that sense or warning in my spirit when to be silent.

I'm probably more like Esther as I have settled into this life. My husband is a natural part of my life. If a conversation leads me to make a comment or tell a story about him that's okay. If someone has a question, that's okay too. I do not focus on the possibility of someone finding out or thinking critically in response. Conversations flow as would others when they talk about their spouses. I'm quiet by nature, but now I'm more so "quiet" in the normalcy of my marriage.

If God calls you to such a time to pronounce your connection to an inmate, do it confidently. If He imparts to you that a person isn't safe, remain quiet. It's okay either way. And remember, silence doesn't mean you're embarrassed of your husband. You're just being smart within a situation that demands a different perspective. And as you probably know all too well, not everyone will understand that. And that's okay too.

February 28 *Unnoticed Love*

I Corinthians 13:4-5

Love is patient, love is kind, and is not jealous; love does not brag and is not arrogant, does not act unbecomingly; it does not seek its own, is not provoked, does not take into account a wrong suffered.

I was on my way to visit when my car's engine just decided to shut off. Perfect! I was still an hour from the prison and flooded with worry. My mind scrambled through problem solving as I coasted, engineless, wondering what was wrong and how on earth I was going to take care of the situation. Thankfully, God's grace was at work when my car wasn't.

Aside from being in an actual town when the mishap occurred, I spotted a car parts store just ahead. My car had enough momentum to coast into the parking lot and into a spot right at the front of the store. Sigh...that was one hurdle overcome: getting off the highway safely.

The employees at the store were a blessing! They were able to determine that my battery was not holding a charge. They called a local repair shop and arranged for me to be seen. They charged the battery enough to get me there and didn't charge me a thing. So there I sat in a dirty waiting room with no air conditioning for two hours looking at an out-of-order snack machine knowing my husband would soon be worried as to why I hadn't arrived.

Once finally back on the road, my makeup was mixed with sweat, my hair frizzed from the humidity, and I felt filthy. And I was still an hour away. My thoughts slipped occasionally toward bitterness when I considered all the effort to make it to see him that day. There was no consideration of going back home, because that was my only opportunity to see him for several weeks. I tinkered with the complaints of his being oblivious to all I go through on this journey of prison. Even when I arrived late and explained everything, he made some comments about it, but quickly moved on to another topic.

In some sense that was not good enough for me. I wanted him to truly comprehend what a headache, worry, and financial impact that one day had on me. But it simply was not there. It seemed no big deal to him. I was then dealing with the true meaning of love: Love is being okay with the sacrifice without recognition of it.

I could have pushed the issue, continued to whine to him about the entire experience in an attempt to force his understanding or at least sympathy, but ultimately I knew that would be futile. Love accepts being unnoticed for such things.

My appreciation comes when I know that choosing to love without bitterness is fully noticed by God. His grace spared me from an even worse outcome. I could have been miles from a town with nothing but cows to witness my predicament. He orchestrated amazing help for me. And that's what I had to focus on. God knew the truth, the emotions I felt, and also the discipline over the same to not berate my husband into understanding.

Prison deals these circumstances to us as prison wives. I'm not the perfect wife at all times when hit with such days, but even within my failure, I acknowledge the truth of what love calls for. Take heart when you're faced with the same. God sees, knows, and blesses your efforts.

March 1 Ahead of God

I Samuel 13:8-10

Now he waited seven days, according to the appointed time set by Samuel, but Samuel did not come to Gilgal; and the people were scattering from him. So Saul said, "Bring to me the burnt offering and the peace offerings." And he offered the burnt offering. And it came about as soon as he finished offering the burnt offering, that behold, Samuel came; and Saul went out to meet him and to greet him.

Many things test our patience. But it's when we feel a sense of urgency or strong desire for something that patience can be severely tested. I recall my dad always telling me, "Never buy the first car you see." Regardless how appealing and "perfect" it may seem, it's wise to keep looking. He was really saying: do not let your emotions rule your decision making. When faced with a desperate situation, one that has us full of anxiety, it's even harder to wait for rescue or fulfillment.

Saul was the first king of Israel. Although reluctantly stepping into the role, once there, he repeatedly disobeyed the Lord. Samuel, the prophet and priest, had anointed him king by God's command in response to the people whining that they wanted a king just like all the other nations. God was their King, but they felt this wasn't good enough.

Saul's coronation as king was to be done at Gilgal. Samuel was to meet him there and offer sacrifices to God as part of the ceremony. But the Israelites find themselves pursued by the Philistines and cowered in caves, cellars, clefts, and pretty much anywhere one can hide. Samuel had told Saul to wait for him at Gilgal seven days, and he would arrive to offer the sacrifices and further instruct him as king. But due to the deteriorating situation and the people becoming restless, fearful, and scattering from him, Saul decided to move forward with the sacrifices and by his own way.

According to the law at the time, only a priest can perform the ceremony of sacrifices. Not a great warrior, not even the king. Saul ignored God's law. This ended up costing him the kingdom. God determined at that time to replace Saul with David, described as a man after God's own heart.

And we read from Scripture, Samuel didn't fail to arrive. He arrived right after the burnt offering was made, indicating that he did arrive just not at the time Saul preferred. This represents one of the hardest victories presented to Saul: faithfulness to God when it seems God is doing nothing to help.

If prison or life is pressuring you in ways that have you urgently wanting to move ahead in a particular decision, pause. Pray for clarification and confirmation especially for a major decision. If God has given you the answer, trust Him to be faithful to provide.

Buying that first-seen car may not be the perfect decision. God may have the perfect and better car waiting at another dealership on a different day. If that first-seen car is God's choice, you can take peace in knowing that it will still be there when you return, and you'll have demonstrated faith in God to provide, even when it seems imperfect to wait.

March 2 — A Heart's Intention

John 12:6-8

Now he said this, not because he was concerned about the poor, but because he was a thief, and as he had the money box, he used to pilfer what was put into it. Jesus therefore said, "Let her alone, in order that she may keep it for the day of My burial. For the poor you always have with you, but you do not always have Me."

    Jesus knew Judas's heart. He knew the underlying motivation for his reprimanding Mary for pouring a year's wages on Jesus's feet. It was not to benefit the poor, but himself. But Jesus didn't challenge Judas with the truth of his heart at that time. He focused on the actions of Mary and blessed her sacrifice. This takes great wisdom — the timing of when to challenge someone with the truth.

    I'm always with a searching heart for God's wisdom in dealing with my husband. I "see" so much for him, his potential, and his strength that God wants to use in powerful ways. It's difficult not to want to push him down that spiritual pathway. I know his heart isn't where it should be on some issues, but my words to him will not accomplish much — except possibly a response to stop preaching to him.

    God has taught me that my husband's heart must absorb the message before any step toward the good will be taken. Otherwise, his mind will understand my words, but his heart will not hear. His heart routinely doesn't hear in some cases, so I must pray for God's wisdom in how to handle the situation. I do not ignore it, but I pray for the right timing of when to bring it to his attention — if at all.

    Your silence may even be the best thing you can offer your husband. But just because you're silent, doesn't mean you're inactive. You're intentionally allowing God time to work in his heart so the truth will be convicting not by your words, but by the Holy Spirit. That's where real change happens. You'll battle your emotions in the process and be tempted to push things along quicker, but focus on Jesus, as Mary did with her perfume, and He will honor the intentions of your heart. With time, your husband will hear also. **

March 3 Lessons

Mark 8:2

"I feel compassion for the multitude because they have remained with Me now three days, and have nothing to eat."

    Jesus performed another miracle on that day. The people followed Him to a remote place. It had been three days and most available food amongst the people had been exhausted. Jesus fed four thousand plus people with the seven loaves of bread and some fish the disciples had with them.

    I'm struck by several things. One, the disciples had food with them, and I assume during those three days they ate. Two, it was Jesus who observed the condition of and expressed compassion for the people; the disciples didn't mention it. Three, the disciples seemed to forget the prior occasion when Jesus miraculously fed five thousand plus people from meager amounts of fish and bread by their words in verse 4: "Where will anyone be able to find enough to satisfy these men with bread here in a desolate place?" The circumstance provides rich lessons for us.

1. The disciples had Jesus with them who could meet every need of the people, both spiritually and physically. They just needed to share that good news.
2. Jesus intentionally went to a remote place for the lesson. Most times we learn greater lessons in life's "deserts," when resources are scarce and we have no answer except a miracle that only God can provide.
3. Jesus waited three days before bringing attention to the lesson. He would soon be dead three days, just as the people ran out of food in three days. But He rose on the third day and provided mankind eternal life, just as the bread and fish provided life.

    Even after the miracle on that day, the disciples soon forgot the lesson and had to be taught again of Jesus's sufficiency in all circumstances. This should be an encouragement to us when our faith diminishes only to be reminded later that God was always enough.

Whatever desert you may be in today, please know that Jesus has all your provisions. He may be waiting for you to recognize that He's the answer for the first time in your life or once again as in the disciples' case. And as you travel through prison with Jesus, well fed, be alert to others who are in need of nourishment and share your faith lessons.

March 4 — The Blame Game

Numbers 20:4

"Why then have you brought the Lord's assembly into this wilderness, for us and our beasts to die here?"

To hear my husband describe it, no inmate is guilty — at least in their own minds. They may have committed crimes, but there's always someone else to blame for why they had to do it. My husband sits in a cell 24/7 and listens to the rants of inmates, who often complain about whose fault it was they are now there. It's amazing they expect 100 percent of mitigating circumstances to account for their guilt.

This tends to be human nature. It's a connection closely fused to our pride. We are the center of everything, only good should happen to us, and if things go wrong, it's never our fault. Pride was the original sin and continues to keep us separated from God's best. We refuse to surrender and humble ourselves to God's authority.

The Israelites were infamously known for shifting blame. Moses had to deal repeatedly with their accusations that he was to blame for their discomfort. In reality, God had clearly told them why they were destined to wander in the desert for forty years. In Numbers 14:33, the Lord tells them, "And your sons shall be shepherds for forty years in the wilderness, and they shall suffer for your unfaithfulness, until your corpses lie in the wilderness."

Wow! Moses didn't sentence them to death in the desert; God did. And for what? They broke His laws. They repeatedly rebelled and acted unfaithfully toward God. But despite their obvious guilt and the Lord telling them this, they still deferred their role in their punishment onto someone else.

Sadly, God had promised them freedom. He freed them from Egyptian slavery and was using Moses to lead them to the Promised Land. But they forfeited this freedom. The promise would only be experienced by the next generation, Caleb, and Joshua.

Accepting blame and asking for forgiveness from God is where change, personal growth, and freedom lies. Walking humbly with God on the journey of prison results in life and a way out of the desert. A man may be imprisoned physically, but to continue in rebellion and shifting blame separates him from God's blessing while in prison. And, most likely, his continued freedom once home. Support your husband efforts to come "clean" of his guilt, challenge him as God leads when the blame game surfaces, and never stop praying for his freedom in all ways.

March 5 When Not Popular

Romans 8:31

What then shall we say to these things? If God is for us, who is against us?

I have a favorite picture of me and a friend that was taken many years ago. I noticed in the picture one day that my friend's hairstyle included bangs. I never gave it any thought, because bangs are popular these days. Then it struck me...that picture was not from "these days." She sported a style well before it was deemed stylish.

It can be the same for us as wives. Instead of a hairstyle, however, we sport an unpopular position to many. Being married to a criminal isn't fashionable — especially to those who work at the prison.

Many DOC employees look upon us as naïve, possibly being conned or desperate. For some reason, they feel we do not know our husbands' true selves. They see the good, bad, and ugly, and assume they know the "real" person whom we see in regimented segments. Maybe in some cases, this may be true, but like most all stereotypes, this perception gets spread across all of us.

Most of us know we aren't married to saints or they wouldn't be in prison. But unlike the officer who sees our husbands through a tainted lens, we actually know more of the good and the unique qualities which make our husbands popular with us. We are devoted through the difficulty. So we show up regularly at the gate to see an unpopular person and absorb the looks or comments about our unpopular love.

It's easy to feel embittered and downright resentful within such an environment. Being unjustly judged brings this natural reaction. But I only need remind myself that God is my biggest fan. I'm popular with Him. My marriage is popular with Him. Confidence in this makes walking through those gates commonplace. Like my friend who thought nothing of her hairstyle, not focusing on what others thought of her, she simply wore it daily and was content.

I do not look for acceptance by others when my marriage is considered. It's naïve of me to think I should expect acceptance. I focus on my husband and God's love of him and our marriage. This quickly diffuses the negative emotions which can smother my contentment and enjoyment of visiting my husband. My marriage isn't a badge of pride to be defended at every rude encounter with a DOC employee. It's about not really even thinking about what others think. The humility of being unpopular is seen in a strength that's unaffected by being a stereotype. Be reminded that God is for you and your marriage when faced with those who think differently.

March 6 *Equal Persistence*

Nehemiah 6:4

And they sent messages to me four times in this manner, and I answered them in the same way.

Nehemiah is one of my favorite books in the Bible. It's a story of his leadership in stirring the Israelites on in the rebuilding of the wall of Jerusalem. It's rich in practical application. It's inspiring. Nehemiah is an example to all Christians in how to face opposition. He loved the Lord, displayed great wisdom, courageously overcame trials, and genuinely cared about the people in his charge. Every leader should strive to replicate the characteristics of this great man of Scripture.

I'm struck by the tenacity of Nehemiah to not be deterred from his goal. He faithfully countered all attempts of the enemy to interrupt God's work. He anticipated the opposition and stood firm. The verse for today is just one example.

Nehemiah had received message after message from the enemy, trying to lure him into a trap. They wanted him to leave the work on the wall, remove him from a place of security, and plot his harm. Nehemiah didn't succumb to fright, worry, or alleged negotiations. He stood firm in his assignment. He didn't entertain even conversations with the enemy. He responded the same to each message.

Evil was persistent, but Nehemiah's persistence matched. They finished the wall with God encouraging them the whole way. We read in verse 16: "And it came about when all our enemies heard of it, and all the nations surrounding us saw it, they lost their confidence; for they recognized that this work had been accomplished with the help of our God."

Nehemiah's approach is something we can use in the challenges of prison. Stay grounded in the truth. Do not be swayed by things not of God. Flee the arena of the enemy by not entertaining their words (discouraging words of others can seem relentless). Stick close to God and seek His help.

God desires to lead you through this prison journey with victory. It's not an easy place in life to be. Persecution on any level can breed discouragement and bring doubt. Resist the impact on your heart and ultimately your actions. Evil will be persistent in its efforts. God will match this persistence if you allow His hand to remain on your life.

March 7 — Officers & Inmates

Acts 16:25-26

But about midnight Paul and Silas were praying and singing hymns of praise to God, and the prisoners were listening to them; and suddenly there came a great earthquake, so that the foundations of the prison house were shaken; and immediately all the doors were opened, and everyone's chains were unfastened.

Paul and Silas were imprisoned. The business of the local fortune tellers had been damaged when Paul rid their slave girl of the demon possessing her. This demon was the source of her divination abilities and their subsequent profit. These business men claimed the message Paul and Silas preached was contrary to Roman custom, deserving of punishment.

While in jail, we read in Acts that they were a testimony to the other prisoners. Their overflowing joy in the Lord couldn't be contained, and the other prisoners took notice. And before the night was out, God miraculously freed Paul and Silas's physical restraints and opened the prison doors.

What follows is their accompanying the jailer to his home, witnessing to him and his family. The jailer tended to their physical wounds while his family came to salvation and spiritual healing. They even celebrated over an evening meal. But what's striking to me is that Paul and Silas returned to the jailhouse afterwards!

The officials sent for Paul and Silas the next morning, and we read in Scripture that they were there, back in the prison, despite the freedom received the night before. Why?

Why did God so powerfully deliver only to have them return? He sent an earthquake all of things! The only conclusion I can draw is that the earthquake was not for them. It was for the officer in that jail and the prisoners.

I can sometimes be clouded by the familiarity of Scripture that I get wowed when something hits me like a brick that has been there the whole time. Paul was such an amazing man of God, and I easily attach such miracles and mighty acts of God to *him* — the great apostle, as if it was all about Paul being freed from prison.

But this story isn't about Paul. It's about the love of God for the prisoner and the officers in charge of them. God allowed Paul and Silas to be imprisoned for the sake of that jailer and the inmates who resided in the next cells. God desired for Paul and Silas — His servants — to take the life-changing message of Jesus to them.

So they knew the earthquake wasn't for their escape. It was a tool to get the attention of those cherished people within those dark walls. It provided a tremendous witness to their fellow prisoners. It also allowed a furlough to bring the Gospel to an entire household.

There are likely some or all of those men who were incarcerated with Paul in that Philippian jail in heaven today, because God loved them so much that He gave Jesus to die on the cross. But He also sent Paul inside the walls to tell them about it. We know for sure the jailer will be there. God desires none to die without knowing Christ — regardless of which side of the bars one lives.

March 8 Wicked Ways

Proverbs 4:14

Do not enter the path of the wicked, and do not proceed in the way of evil men.

Chapter four of Proverbs is instructions of a father to his son. It's his wisdom being handed down. When I read the verse above, I'm mostly struck with the self-direction that's implied. To enter anything indicates it's seen beforehand. He's telling his son: when you see the bad entrance ahead, stop. Go a different direction, away from it.

If my husband were to comment on this verse, he would say, "It's not that easy in prison, because there is nowhere to go!" He describes being surrounded daily by wickedness. It's hard to avoid the path when every direction you're confronted with it. Plus, he would argue, self-control is usually not a character trait mastered by most inmates, including himself.

What I would say to him would be that God always provides an escape from temptation. If a Christian, God promises a way. So when my husband comes upon the temptation to enter a wrong path whether it be gambling, consuming an illicit drug, looking at porn, or establishing connections with the wrong people, there will be the opportunity for him to go a different direction. He can choose to ignore the warning in his spirit, but it will be there.

Furthermore, to resist, he has to stop walking toward it! I pray for him to stop. When he sees the entrance, I pray for God to send conviction, warning bells, strength, an interruption, or a failure of a plan, anything to make the way of escape very obvious to him. I have also told my husband to ask himself: Can I ask God to bless what I'm about to do? I heard a pastor mention such a question and I have always considered it brilliant.

My husband already knows the right and wrong paths in the eyes of God. It's never a question of knowledge. But it's always a question of self-control. To see ahead and stop, or see ahead and keep walking. It's hard to watch him keep walking, because the consequences come to both of us. The wicked path harms him and harms us as a couple.

As a prison wife, you may find the paths surrounding your husband near impossible to block. It may seem futile for any victory. But God's word is truth. And if He promises the way of escape, it will be there every time. Your job is to pray that your husband chooses the better path.

March 9 Human Value

Luke 12:7

"Indeed, the very hairs of your head are all numbered. Do not fear; you are of more value than many sparrows."

    I love animals. And often times, I become more upset about animal mistreatment than a person's. In many ways, I see animals as more innocent, even when compared to the most righteous person. Even a child is seen with the understanding that innocence will not always be—the ugly in the heart will surface at some point. Animals will always remain pure in a sense. This makes reading of God's love for me more than animals hard to grasp.

    He loves me more than the innocent creature who has never lied or cursed? He loves me more than a beautiful bird that sings and brings delight? He loves me more than my beloved dog who unconditionally shows me affection and forgiveness when I take a bad day out on her? He loves me when I choose to stay home on a Sunday or become lackadaisical in my prayers? He loves me when I'm rebellious? According to Scripture, yes!

    The verse today is just one example of how great God's love is for us compared to animals. Luke explains that not one sparrow (valued at about two cents in that day) has ever been forgotten by God. He values even the smallest and insignificant sparrow, yet His love for us is greater.

    Of course, you cannot even get through Genesis chapter three without reading of how God killed the first animal to provide clothing for Adam and Eve—out of His love. He killed an innocent animal to extend love to Adam and Eve who just condemned mankind to an eternal, evil nature. In the end, He would offer Jesus, the only truly innocent and ultimate sacrifice to save us, because He loves us that much!

    This truth keeps me amazed. But it also proves that His love isn't dependent on our deeds. Whatever your husband did to find himself incarcerated isn't greater than God's love for him. It's another example of His amazing grace despite how badly a person messes up.

    So the next time you warmly smile at your beloved pet, watch any animal story which pulls at your heart strings or makes you weep, remember that your husband, regardless of past or present behavior, is valued and loved by God more than the most sweet, adorable, affectionate, and innocent animal. It's a humbling and astounding perspective.

March 10 Skills to Succeed

Deuteronomy 8:17-18

"Otherwise, you may say in your heart, 'My power and the strength of my hand made me this wealth.' But you shall remember the Lord your God, for it is He who is giving you power to make wealth, that He may confirm His covenant which He swore to your fathers, as it is this day."

The new generation of Israelites had made it through the desert and were about to cross the Jordan River to the Promised Land. God had been reminding them that it was only by His provision that they were successful thus far. And it would only be through their continued obedience to His commandments that their future success would be realized. He knew the tendency of man's pride to disregard God as success and ease enters.

This seems how we all behave when life is going good. Our need for God and our perceived dependency weakens. We get comfortable. It's only when luxuries are removed, whether emotional or material, and pain and discomfort return that we usually seek God more diligently. This is human nature; it's our sin nature. We think we do okay without God in a typical day.

I struggle with this just as much as anyone else. Usually it sneaks up on me. Life is stable, income is predictable, my husband is good, and I feel secure. It's really a foolish confidence from believing that I control the circumstances of my life. Anything I have accomplished is through God's blessing and power working on my behalf.

I certainly cannot take credit for my husband's spiritual growth. He isn't the same person that arrived in prison those many years ago. But I was merely the catalyst. God was responsible for the strength I needed in the process and the outcome it had on my husband. God taught me, and He gave me the skills to best serve my husband in very tough circumstances. In the end, we're both better people. But only by God's grace.

If you have a job now, thank God! He has blessed you with the skills to be successful at your job. If your kids are well-behaved or have grown into successful adults, thank God! If you have a successful marriage, thank God!

None of us can take another breath without God's help. We are fully dependent on God to take care of our lives whether we acknowledge this or not. Crisis can bring appreciation of this, but God desires each of us to stay close to Him on all days. Prison will bring a crisis or your life will eventually hit a rough spot. Do your best not to become complacent in your ease and wealth so when either arrives, you're armed with God's strength, not searching frantically for His presence.

March 11 Always Dating

Song of Solomon 7:1

"How beautiful are your feet in sandals, O prince's daughter! The curves of your hips are like jewels, the work of the hands of an artist."

Chapter seven of Song of Solomon is highly descriptive of a man's attraction to his bride. He compliments various parts of her body and praises her. She does the same for him in chapter five. It's a love story. I desire my husband to love seeing me in much the same way. My body isn't perfect, but it's perfect to him. I'm not the most attractive woman on the planet, but I'm to him. His praises makes me feel valuable. In return, I want to look good for him.

To me, going to visit is very much like going on a date. I get excited, plan my wardrobe, fix my makeup and hair to look their best, and head out the typical early hour with enthusiasm. I feel like a schoolgirl sometimes.

It's important to me to be attractive to my husband. Prison makes opportunities for all visual intimacy difficult. But even beyond my husband's sexual needs in this way, it's important to show him that I care about how I look to him—on all opportunities. "Letting myself go" has thankfully not been a comment I have heard from him.

Do I get dolled up every visit? No. He enjoys seeing me in different "looks," but the motivation behind maybe sweatpants and T-shirt is for him to experience that look, not from my apathy for getting ready. There's a big difference. There are some things I wear that are his favorites that I would never wear typically. I wear them, because it pleases him.

Is his love conditional on what I wear? Of course not. I just know that I want to be the bride in Song of Solomon for many years to come. I want my husband to feel important by the way I take time to get ready for him.

Visits can become very routine. To sit for hours on an uncomfortable seat or stand for hours with your ear smashed against a metal cutout just to be able to hear decently are the realities of this life. The drives can be long. The waits at every point in the process maddening. The exorbitant cost for glorified junk food in the canteen gets old. The best thing you have going for you at visits is the reason you're there—your husband!

Do not let the routine of visits or the length of time you have been on this journey dull your motivation for how you approach visits. Try to keep your look fresh and pleasing to your husband. Seeing you is the high point of his time. He looks forward to walking into the VP and seeing the love of his life. Be his bride every time.

March 12 — But the Snakes Remain

Numbers 21:8

Then the Lord said to Moses, "Make a fiery serpent, and set it on a standard; and it shall come about, that everyone who is bitten, when he looks at it, he shall live."

The Israelites were in the desert, grumbling against Moses because of the journey's hardships. God had rescued them from slavery, provided for them while in the desert, and had just delivered a victory to them against the Canaanites. But they complained anyway. The Lord's anger was roused, and He sent snakes through the camp. Watching people die was the reality check they needed to remind them how good the Lord had been to them and to confront them with their sin. They pleaded to Moses to intervene, asking God to forgive and relent. God responded, but probably not in the way they would have expected.

God didn't remove the snakes. He instructed Moses to make a snake out of bronze and only after the people looked at the snake would they survive the snakebites. God made them face their sin—individually—and would only save a person if he responded individually by looking at the bronze snake.

Even when God rescues and restores, He doesn't always take away the difficulty. He rather provides Himself within the problem. The snakes were a problem. God allowed the snakes to remain along with their deadly potential. But promised life in the midst of the threat.

God in similar ways does this for our husbands. There are deadly threats in prison. There's evil sleuthing, plotting, and striking within every prison. If our husbands live foul within prison, they are a snakebite away from a potentially deadly situation. They may seek God when faced with the reality of no other hope to survive what surrounds them daily. As wives, we are usually the ones holding the bronze snake pleading for them to look toward the good and receive life.

However your husband arrives to a repentant heart and desire for godly things, God will not abandon him to the snakes. He holds life now and eternal life in the future. Prison will always have snakes. But seeking God will provide your husband the antidote to survive what seems a hopeless predicament.

March 13 *Doing Joy*

I Thessalonians 5:16

Rejoice always.

I'll admit that being joyful isn't a quick, first response in my daily life. I'm very blessed. I have been spared known and most likely unknown hardships and happenings. I thank God as a natural flow in my day, but my joy gets smothered beneath my attitude on many days. And without a fresh and energized outlook, grumbling surfaces or the equivalent nonverbal sighing.

Paul often shares about his joy in his writings and tells us to do the same. In his letter to the Thessalonian Christians, he encouraged them to keep their joy, pray always, and give thanks until the Lord returns. This church was under much persecution. Paul had to leave the new Christians abruptly and he had grave concern for their well-being. He was later updated by Timothy that the Christians there were standing firm in their faith. He further rejoiced when he heard this report.

Paul's joy came from his relationship with Christ and his investment in other people. Essentially, things of eternal value. Paul took joy in his salvation. He took joy in watching others come to faith and grow spiritually.

Prison can contribute to my negative loop; it's a daily weight. It can smother my joy. My attitude is vulnerable to grumbling and sighing, because every day I want something better for my life and that of my husband's. I get tired of the restrictions, the worries, and the ugliness perpetrated within the system. I'm in my own little world of persecution at those times.

I can usually break that loop of grumbling if I can find a way to invest in someone else, using Paul as an example. My attitude lifts when I break away from my own troubles and spend time praying for someone else, reaching out to a friend to see what's going on in her life, writing my husband, or writing a devotional that I may share with someone. I meditate on my salvation and the hope I have in Jesus.

If you find yourself under the same weight, get into Scripture, sit quietly before the Lord. Consider your salvation and look for ways to share it with someone else. Invest in someone else's struggles by praying for them. Your joy is there, just waiting to be experienced anew again.

March 14 — It's in the Everyday

Proverbs 3:5-6

Trust in the Lord with all your heart, and do not lean on your own understanding. In all your ways acknowledge Him, and He will make your paths straight.

The problem with the future and the desires that overwhelm our focus is that the days only come one day at a time. Eagerness and time can be agonizingly incompatible. It's the nature of longings and yearnings. They can both paralyze our thoughts to what hasn't yet arrived, unhinging our hearts from the present.

I find myself in such a place when my heart lies within a future desire or vision the Lord has provided. I find it motivating in one way, because I know "now" will not be forever. But the light I see makes me want to sprint ahead — ahead of reason, practicality, and worse — God.

The challenge is finding peace within the days. I must focus an undisciplined mind on the present to keep my mood from sighing in the moments within the days that seem eternal. It's a level of surrender that isn't fun. It taunts my mind to think that there must be a way around the wait.

And I look! This is where Satan steps in the path and makes all sorts of options look appealing and doable. The sly maneuvering is the second-best path being dressed up to look like the right choice. I can push a door open if I belabor my efforts long enough. But I have consequently learned that it never ends up as that once desire or longing, because it was not arrived to by God's design, if arrived to at all.

God's journey has times of various speeds. Obeying the speed limit within the days is the mark of spiritual maturity and is the only successful way to travel with God. And like myself, you may be saying, "I hate this!" We want the life of the future, not these days when it seems nothing moves toward anything good—or moves at all.

Please do not waste the everyday in a lull of apathy because life isn't where you want it. No vision is reached if the everyday isn't purposeful. Dealing with restless emotions can be helped by making smaller goals within the journey. There's no way to reach the vision without taking steps. And steps have to have a direction. Spend some time with God, seeking direction and confirming He shares the longing of your heart. Then start moving. Actively work toward the smaller goals. Time will keep moving, and one day, you'll look back from a goal achieved—thanking God you went no other way but His.

March 15 *Seek a Better Day*

Joshua 24:15

"And if it is disagreeable in your sight to serve the Lord, choose for yourselves today whom you will serve: whether the gods which your fathers served which were beyond the River, or the gods of the Amorites in whose land you are living; but as for me and my house, we will serve the Lord."

Awaking to a typical workday, maneuvering my way to the kitchen light, I mentally roused to my routine. First was making coffee. Switching on the light, I surged into alertness, and the words followed, "What on earth!" The kitchen counter, the sink, and soon-to-be-discovered lower cabinet housed a literal colony of ants! Streaming back and forth in formation, marching atop the dish drainer, blanketing a saucer in the sink, and being unhindered by the toaster oven they maneuvered through, they traveled back down the cabinet to whatever entrance they used below. I spent the first minute simply overwhelmed by the sudden "project" and the consideration of how to even begin. My morning was thoroughly disrupted.

The temptation to fuss hovered over me as I faced the enormous, yet tedious cleanup. I didn't get coffee when I wanted, the dog didn't get taken out as she needed, and my attitude was teetering on the balance of the question Joshua presented: "Whom will I serve today?"

The built-up frustrations, tiredness, and life's unexpected difficulties have the ability to impact our attitude in a very sustaining way—they can rob our day of joy and the intended service God has for us that day. We choose our attitude.

Prison awakens us to days that are unexpected and full of frustrations. It can steer us toward a poor mood most any day. But do not let the setbacks and frustrations of prison rob your days of joy and usefulness to God. Interrupt the brewing. Rebuke Satan, telling him, "No! In the name of Jesus, I'm not giving you my day!" Break into a praise song, make a mental list of how you're blessed, do anything to pull your thoughts out of that rut that will only get deeper the more you spin there.

God entrusted Joshua with leading the Israelites following Moses's death. He was an astounding and faithful follower of God in his role. But falling away from the commands of God and worshipping idols tainted the Israelites' history. Joshua warned the people to consider their actions. They had the freedom to choose whom they would serve, just as we do.

Disciplining our reactions to events in life goes a long way toward making us available for God's service. Are we going to submit to our bad day and the fleshly desire to feel justified in our griping? Or do we deny the flesh and see the blessings in the day? Like the ants, only a few initially found food, but they returned with the colony. If you feed a negative thought, more will come. Prison will march in daily to disrupt your thoughts and keep you useless within the frustrations. Cut off the supply! Choose to serve God today. You'll find more joy—and peace—within this journey regardless of what type of day you wake to. **

March 16 Do Not Be Edom

Obadiah 1:12

"Do not gloat over your brother's day, the day of his misfortune. And do not rejoice over the sons of Judah in the day of their destruction; yes, do not boast in the day of their distress."

Prison wives need each other. We are the minority in the situation of our marriages. Most women we encounter aren't on this path, nor can they truly comprehend our experiences. It's disheartening to me to watch the competitive spirit and lack of courtesy or respect for one another at visit. Not every woman, not every visit, but with some regularity over the years, I have seen it. Maybe you have noticed this too. It may be cutting line through some selfish maneuvering, talking trash about another wife, getting mad when another couple unknowingly takes a "regular's" table, or even behaving to attract another wife's husband. The outcome is one wife doing something against another in a selfish, discourteous, or outright mean-spirited way.

Granted, a woman may behave that way regardless of circumstances; she may treat the mailman badly. The point is there's a unity of circumstances with prison and a wife should receive support and encouragement from another wife, not strife or rudeness. Visits are trying enough given all the negative that comes with the experience. Why add to that?

The Edomites were kin to Judah. However, they allied with the enemy to fight against their own family. So when Judah was down and defeated, Edom celebrated and took pleasure in this. Obadiah was a prophet who desired to encourage the Israelites and warn Edom that they wouldn't be laughing forever. God remained on Judah's side, and she would be delivered.

We do not have to be like Edom. We can make things right by seeing another wife's trials the same as our own—or possibly even worse. We all have stressors beyond our husbands' incarceration. Even though not everyone is joyful, patient, or even nice under the circumstances, we can be mindful of our behavior and attitude toward those struggling. We can consider another lady's experience and how our behavior or attitude impacts her.

If we feel comradery outside of prison, why not inside as well? It could be that a simple expression of kindness could be a huge encouragement to another lady. It may break through the bitterness or ugly attitude to relax her outlook, at least for a moment, to say, "We're family here."

March 17 *Innocent Casualties*

Joel 1:18

How the beasts groan! The herds of cattle wander aimlessly because there is no pasture for them; even the flocks of sheep suffer.

Joel was a prophet to Judah. As was commonplace among the Israelites, they forsook the Lord and did their own thing, bringing God's discipline upon them. Joel described the drought and plague of locusts which God sent that destroyed the land and life as a result. The verse for today describes how the drought impacted the animals as well. They were the innocent victims of the Israelites' sin.

For many men in prison, their children become the innocent victims. They must adjust to the changes and the confusion oftentimes about why their father isn't home. Even with the understanding they are in prison, the reason for the incarceration may be withheld depending on their ages.

As a wife, you're left often nursing the wounds your husband's crime has done to the family. You're faced with the children's questions. You're faced with the daily absence of a father that may be years before returning home. You may see your children slipping into wrong choices or onto a path which worries your heart for their future. Grief can follow for the losses your children experience now, and those possibly removed from their future.

But be reminded as Joel reminded the Israelites. God longed to redeem them and bring blessing to them. In the case of the Israelites, they needed to repent of their sins and turn back to God. If God longs to redeem the guilty, how much more the innocence of children!

God has always shown a special appreciation for children. Scripture frequently refers to children as blessings, possessing special qualities that we as adults should strive for. Be reminded that God has a special relationship with your children.

Your husband's crime can be redeemed for good. Not only his sin, but the consequences now brought upon the children. As Joel writes in 2:25: "Then I will make up to you for the years that the swarming locust has eaten…" God's word is true. There's a bright future and hope for your children. God still maintains an astounding purpose for every member of your family, despite how dry and damaged the surroundings may look now.

March 18 Trouble Follows

Acts 17:13

But when the Jews of Thessalonica found out that the word of God had been proclaimed by Paul in Berea also, they came there likewise, agitating and stirring up the crowds.

Paul was on his second missionary journey when the events in the verse today happened. While in Thessalonica, speaking in the synagogue over the course of days, many came to faith in Jesus. But the Jews were furious with the claims Paul was making. God had always told Paul that he would be rejected by the Jews and that his ministry would be primarily to the Gentiles. The events in Thessalonica supported this.

The Jews wouldn't stand by idle and listen to what they opposed. They went through the city stirring up the crowds and basically creating a riot. In verse five, they actually formed a mob to capture Paul, but not locating him, their anger spilled onto the man who provided hospitality to Paul during his stay.

With the unrest in the city and his life in danger, Paul headed out of town to Berea, which was about fifty miles away. However, we read in the verse today that the opposition of the Jews pursued him. They arrived in Berea and their ugly, mean-spirited efforts were repeated.

As a prison wife, you may feel like Paul at times. You try to do right by your marriage and husband, but receive ugly from others in return. This might even be by your own family members. In fact, you may leave one episode of turmoil to only end up in another one. It may seem as though opposition pursues you as well.

But consider how Paul responded. He didn't change his position. He just traveled on and spoke the same words with the boldness undiminished by the previous threats. He firmly knew the truth and didn't waver from this. He was wise and took heed about with whom to keep company and how long to stay in a hostile environment. Just because he left, didn't mean he was weak or loved Jesus any less.

In your journey, there will be people who will never be convinced that your marriage or husband has any value. They may openly ridicule you. They may withdraw and want nothing to do with you. But there are also those of us out here who are on your side. But more importantly God is! Human encouragement is powerful, but hearing from God—like Paul did—infuses you to keep walking this path with your husband. Seek God and those who will lift you up, not those who follow your efforts to only trouble you with their unbelief.

March 19 What's His Value?

Genesis 4:4

And Abel, on his part also brought of the firstlings of his flock and of their fat portions. And the Lord had regard for Abel and for his offering.

The idea of first place is a common thread throughout Scripture. It was proof of what's valued. From the beginning, honoring God was represented through the sacrifice of the first and best. Abel brought the first of his flock to God. Later, Israel showed their love to God by returning to Him the first and best of what He had blessed them with. The idea is that the person we love gets the best of what we have to offer, not the leftovers or damaged things.

God should always be first place in our lives. This is a given. But who is second? According to Scripture, your husband is second—in all things. And I believe the most difficult part of "all things" is time. Of all the things you have to accomplish in a day, where does your husband rank in regards to your time?

In the everyday, the challenge remains to keep him and your marriage in proper order. All marriages struggle in this it seems, but because our husbands aren't in real time with us, the challenge has to be even more intentional—or many days, it will not happen.

On weekends, after a hectic week, time with my husband gets replaced with chores, errands, and merely the desire to rest. He remains quiet in his lower priority—at least for a while. But the building frustration eventually explodes in a rant to me about things left undone that are important to him.

My first reaction is to be defensive. It's true he cannot comprehend all that I do in a day and the energy required to walk this path with him. However, I'm convicted when I do seem to find time for what's important to me. And with these things done, little time, if any, is left to invest in him whether through an affectionate love letter or doing things that he has asked of me.

So I must be more diligent to put him before other things. You'll be challenged in the same for your husband. If you're blessed to visit every week, your ways of putting him first may look different than a prison wife who has primarily letters to stay connected. I have been the latter for most of my marriage.

Try to do things for your husband that will speak to his value to you. If you write letters, write. Surprise him with something special. Take the time to do or follow-up on things that are important to him. It all may not get done, but the expression of his value to you will be evident. And the heart behind the sacrifice will make it all sufficient.

March 20 Doomed, but Not Dead

Psalm 102:20

To hear the groaning of the prisoner; to set free those who were doomed to death.

Death row doesn't have to equal death. What? That makes no sense. The truth is we are all eternal. The question at our physical death is: Where will we spend eternity? There are only two places: with God or in hell. The man on death row has just as much an opportunity to be with God in heaven at death as the greatest saint. This is because his deeds do not determine his eternity. It depends on God's mercy, and whether he's willing to accept this mercy which was given to all of us through Jesus.

In the verse for today, it states "those who were doomed to death." All of us are born into sin. If we grow up and never accept Jesus as our Savior, we will die in the same sin nature, damning ourselves to hell. That's right… we determine whether we go to hell or not. It's our choice. The State may execute a man, but he has the choice of whether the outcome will result in his eternal freedom or forever in hell.

God desires all to be saved. It's not His will that any perish. He hears the groaning of the prisoner who calls out to Him in repentance. He's willing to erase the bad, forgive the sin, and welcome him into eternity. Scripture speaks repeatedly of God's long-suffering and patience to allow as many who will come to Him to have the opportunity. But He will not wait forever.

There will come a day when all opportunities will be over. Either a man's heart will no longer see his own sin or Jesus will return, finalizing the eternities for everyone who chose not to believe. Every day is a gift, especially to those who aren't saved. It's only by God's grace that another day is offered.

If your husband is on death row, God's love for him is no less than for the grandest minister. He longs to be in relationship with him for eternity. How awesome is that! You love him, but God loves him more than you can even imagine. There's hope despite what his legal sentencing may be.

Keep praying for your husband's salvation. Know that God is on your side and desires the same. Share with your husband the hope for freedom and life, regardless of his current situation.

March 21 *It's Not Forever*

Habakkuk 1:6-7

"For behold, I am raising up the Chaldeans, that fierce and impetuous people who march throughout the earth to seize dwelling places which are not theirs. They are dreaded and feared. Their justice and authority originates with themselves."

One of my husband's greatest frustrations — and mine — is the corrupt activity of DOC officers. The guards who come on shift with the ugly goal of just being cruel. The ones who antagonize inmates just because they can. You likely deal with the same frustrations. It's in every prison system, every prison. It's the unethical rule of those who are supposed to be doing the right thing. I have experienced officers who are, quite frankly, worse than the inmates they supervise.

This was Habakkuk's frustration in his time regarding the rule of Babylon. He was a prophet who voiced this confusion to God when he saw God allow the more unrighteous to oppress the Israelites.

God answered Habakkuk by telling him evil will only be allowed to prosper so long. In essence, Babylon will get what's coming to it — in time. God had not forgotten the Israelites; He remained in control, and He reminded His prophet of this. Eventually, Persia conquered Babylon. It was with this change in power that the Israelites were allowed to return to their homeland and rebuild their lives.

God encouraged Habakkuk to not lose faith. He encouraged him to keep doing what's right despite the evil in charge, because He would deliver them. This is God's promise to all believers.

If your husband is a Christian, he already has the victory over the evil that seems to control the prison. His joy and assurance of his salvation will always outweigh any difficulty he must endure now. This life is a wink of the eye compared to eternity. And at the final judgment, evil will answer to God.

This should give us all hope! Not an enjoyment of seeing the evil damned, but more so the peace and anticipation of this world being made right again. As Habakkuk said in the close of his writing: "Though the fig tree should not blossom, and there be no fruit on the vines, though the yield of the olive should fail, and the fields produce no food, though the flock should be cut off from the fold, and there be no cattle in the stalls, yet I will exult in the Lord, I will rejoice in the God of my salvation" (verses 17-18). This is good news!

March 22 — Fully Qualified

Hebrews 2:17-18

Therefore, He had to be made like His brethren in all things, that He might become a merciful and faithful high priest in things pertaining to God, to make propitiation for the sins of the people. For since He Himself was tempted in that which He has suffered, He is able to come to the aid of those who are tempted.

    The book of Hebrews is all about Jesus being the all-sufficient person to make atonement for sins. It was written to the Jewish people who needed to know that the old system of going through the priest to seek forgiveness was no longer necessary. Jesus is all they needed. The author explains why Jesus is qualified. And part of this involved His willingness to become human, experience temptation, the struggles, and ultimately death, to help us trust Him with our lives. In essence, we know that He can relate to our lives, because He experienced the same—and worse.
    You're uniquely qualified as a prison wife to help other wives. You have gone through challenging times with your husband. You have experienced a unique pain and disappointment. I say this because most ladies you encounter likely do not have an incarcerated husband. At least that's what I find in my everyday world.
    And because of your experiences, you're the best and most qualified person to help another lady on this same journey. You'll be trusted to understand what she's feeling. Your advice or encouragement will be more readily accepted.
    When others try to encourage us or provide feedback without having a foundation from which to speak, the words are spoken with good intentions, but they often leave us feeling empty. They do not reach that part of our heart that's seeking understanding. Words from a "qualified" lady, however, can bring comfort not available from another source.
    Jesus ultimately is the best person to meet all our needs, but He also uses other people. He wants to use you. You're uniquely qualified to minister to

another prison wife. Regardless of how long you have been on this journey, there's another lady behind you just starting hers or one ahead needing a push to keep walking. There's a lady needing a welcomed and trusted support, and you can be that for her.

March 23 *Do Over*

Ephesians 1:7

In Him we have redemption through His blood, the forgiveness of our trespasses, according to the riches of His grace.

One of my favorite movies is *Star Trek: The Voyage Home*. Earth of their time faced annihilation at the hands of an alien probe which arrived seeking to know why communication had stopped with the creatures of the earth. The creatures were humpback whales—which by the time their "songs" reached the aliens had long since been extinct. Captain Kirk and crew traveled back in time to bring two humpback whales into the future. Man had, in essence, caused its own destruction by hunting the whales to extinction. But mankind was redeemed in the end, and was afforded a "do over." The whale species would be repopulated and the earth would be safe from harm.

This is a great analogy of man's sin being redeemed by Jesus. Sin has and will continue to destroy lives. But we receive a second chance for life when we acknowledge our sin and believe in Jesus.

It also provides a picture of how sin doesn't operate in a vacuum. We cannot sin and have it affect only ourselves. It impacts people around us, it can impact other people's futures, and it can impact through omission by removing the blessings from our own future by interfering with our purpose.

Your husband's sin impacted himself. It impacted the victim. It impacted the families of both. The ripple effect may have been profound, and in ways may never fully be realized in this life. But all his wrong choices can be redeemed.

But like the crew in the movie, action had to be taken. They responded to the probe by listening, seeking to understand, and answering. When the Holy Spirit stirs your husband toward repentance, he must respond. He must ask to be forgiven. Then he must trust that Jesus died because of his sins, but rose from the dead as Scripture says.

All of us are afforded a do over; your husband included. His life can be redeemed to one of hope. His future can be safe; his eternity secure. You may feel like the captain trying to command the rescue, but scared that it may be too late. But do not lose hope. In the movie, the people of the earth didn't know the great lengths Captain Kirk and crew were going through to save earth's future. There's plenty that God is doing in other places and times—all for you and your husband.

 March 24 Wickedly Lead

Job 1:12

Then the Lord said to Satan, "Behold, all that he has is in your power, only do not put forth your hand on him." So Satan departed from the presence of the Lord.

After this verse, we read that the Sabeans and Chaldeans attacked, in separate incidents, stealing Job's herds and killing the workers that were in charge of them. This is clear evidence that Satan uses his evil to influence people to commit evil acts. Satan was able to bring destruction and wrong to Job simply by using people. They were either possessed or influenced to fulfill Satan's plan to break Job's faith and have him curse God. But Job's faith prevailed.

The story of Job is a hard book for me to read. He didn't lose only his animals and hired help, but also his children in storms sent by Satan. Then he lost his health. His wife was still around and friends, but they were of the attitude that Job must have sinned in some way to have all that bad happen to him.

What we come to learn in Job is that Satan is the prince of this world—by God's allowable will. He doesn't sleep or tire in his pursuit to keep people from believing in or breaking their faith in God.

Your husband may have been influenced to do evil or he may have been the victim of it. Although we maintain our right to choose, when tempted strongly by Satan, we often fall. The thing we need to remember is Satan's power can only go so far.

God allowed Satan to pursue Job. This a very difficult concept for those of us who believe, because Job didn't deserve what happened to him. He was an upstanding and God-fearing man. But we can gain hope and confidence in knowing that God is always in control, even of the evil that attacks us. God doesn't allow it without purpose.

Whatever your husband is facing now, God is fully aware. A divine purpose is being played out. If your husband isn't a believer, you can pray that his current struggles bring him to faith in God. If he already believes, pray for his faith to be strengthened and for him to be victorious in the battle.

Evil activity is the reality of prison. Yet, it only has power the Lord allows. Let this encourage you and fuel your prayers also for those who succumb to being influenced by Satan to attack the men trying to live righteously in an unrighteous environment.

March 25 Fruit in the Waiting

Genesis 41:52

And he named the second Ephraim, "For," he said, "God has made me fruitful in the land of my affliction."

Is the land surrounding you today afflicting you? Prison is a fierce landscape. I once saw a dear friend who greeted me with puffy eyes and a worn look. A night of crying before the blessing of sleep—most of us have been there. Maybe you were there last night.

In her case, she and her husband faced two years of no visitation, because an officer made a false accusation against them. Appeals denied, the truth denied, and hope seemingly gone for any victory.

My heart wept for them, because it seemed another injustice within a system where evil rules the landscape. But they saw fruit from the affliction. Her husband was able to witness to men he would have never met otherwise; she was able to spend time with her grandchildren in memorable ways.

Joseph endured betrayal by his brothers, slavery, and imprisonment— many years of difficult circumstances. He was the victim of jealousy, greed, and unjust accusations. Yet though innocent, God didn't rescue him. God allowed the circumstances to continue. Joseph understood early that trusting God is for all times, not just when the days are easy.

God's purposes are never without meaning, even when our heart's question of why never gets answered. And if it does, hindsight is the only route it generally travels. Joseph arrived in Egypt as a slave, but advanced to royalty. He believed in God's providence, but tangible proof only surfaced when he finally walked free. God knew the big picture. He knew that

Joseph's trials would be the very thing that would lead him to running a kingdom.

Our experiences mold us for the next step in our purpose. Do not miss the fruit at the end of this journey of prison. God will use this time in abundant ways to fertilize the soil for your grander purpose. Cling to God from a wet pillow if you must, but always rise with the confidence that God is in control and the fruit will come. Ask God what lessons He desires for you to learn during this time. Seek Him. And watch Him deliver an overflowing bounty from what seems a barren landscape right now. **

March 26 Alive & Active

II Samuel 18:5

And the king charged Joab and Abishai and Ittai, saying, "Deal gently for my sake with the young man Absalom." And all the people heard when the king charged all the commanders concerning Absalom.

God uses Scripture to share His plan of salvation to unbelievers and to guide believers. The Bible was written by God. He used people to communicate the words, but the entire content is His words to us. The Holy Spirit works in tandem with the Bible. If you're a believer, you're guaranteed the Holy Spirit's involvement as you read. He will answer prayer, guide your life, or convict you of sinful ways.

The passage above is about King David and the troubles he experienced with his son Absalom who rebelled against him. When sending out troops to battle, he instructed them to basically spare his son during the conflict. Sadly, this didn't happen. His own troops rebelled against his order to "deal gently" with his son, killing him when opportunity provided.

On the surface, this is history being recorded for us. For me, personally, the Lord used this same verse at a time to provide guidance regarding a situation I faced.

My husband had once again used violence to escape a bad situation. He had stabbed his roommate multiple times, sending that man to the emergency room and himself to long-term confinement. It was a horrible experience to walk through especially since I was outside the gate waiting to visit when the ambulance arrived. I was suddenly faced with fear for my husband's condition and immediately snatched out of the group of waiting visitors to answer officers' questions. It brings a panic and dread to my body even in recollection.

In the aftermath of that surreal morning, I faced a burden in my emotions. I was fearful, angry, and horribly sad. I didn't know how to respond to my husband. I understood why things accumulated to the point he did what he did, but plenty of other emotions weighed down the balance on the other side. I was paralyzed.

I desperately needed to hear from God. Spending time in Scripture is where I knew He would answer. And He faithfully showed up. As soon as I read today's verse, the soothing comfort of the Holy Spirit moved in me.

I was not to fuss or preach at my husband, challenge his actions, or even shutdown emotionally from him. I was to deal gently with him. This put my unsettled and searching heart to rest. I knew I had been given God's will for me at that time. I hurt and cried on and off for what seemed like endless days. But even within the heartbreak, I gained strength in knowing God was in control and would guide me every step of what lay ahead for me and my husband. The first step was ensuring my husband that I loved him, despite the difficulty we then faced.

There have been other situations when God told me to respond differently, with more confrontation. I depend on the Holy Spirit to tell me what's best. So long as I'm in Scripture, God's sovereignty insures I'm reading exactly what He purposes. The Holy Spirit stirs within me and speaks to me through the words, providing the answer I seek. This is why the Bible is described as alive and active.

You can experience such peace in this prison journey regardless of the hard days. God's word can live with you within these days. He can comfort you in ways you cannot imagine. He can guide you in the simple steps or those that leave you vacant of direction. Open the Bible and read. You'll come to understand how God speaks to you. The words will come alive!

March 27 *Beauty Must Suffer*

I Peter 5:10

And after you have suffered for a little while, the God of all grace, who called you to His eternal glory in Christ, will Himself perfect, confirm, strengthen and establish you.

Rag curls were a common way to put style to hair before the days of hot curlers or curling irons. Strips of cloth mimicked the rod onto which sections of hair were wrapped. After a night of sleep with tossing and turning, the knotted removal could be painful. An elderly lady once shared the words spoken by her mother in response to her complaints of pain: Beauty must suffer.

Are you suffering right now? Not from fashion, but from the experiences of prison you now face? Scripture shares with us the value in suffering and how God uses it. He will use the painful experiences of your life to bring about a better tomorrow if you'll allow it. This is because the bad times are usually when we seek God more, and the closer we get to God, the better our life becomes.

Not better in the sense that we will be wealthy, healthy, and breeze through all days. But our character will mature to one of greater strength, usefulness, and testimony to God's love. Suffering has the tremendous ability to refine us and make us better people.

Peter speaks to this in the Scripture for today. Coming through the trials in life in victory can be inspiring to others. They will see your confidence and ability to overcome and wonder what inspires your strength. God's help and confirmation on your life to sustain you through the difficulty will hopefully encourage them to seek God also.

God uses suffering to grow us up spiritually. In His economy, waiting and perseverance cultivate faith. He rewards those who remain faithful despite their circumstances. The refining fire of suffering brings about precious qualities in you that would otherwise not be found.

The key to realizing the benefits of suffering isn't turning your back on God in anger or loss of hope. He's faithful to bring you through this time to a better future if you'll trust Him. You can experience tremendous peace and confidence that your life is safe, God is in control, and He's orchestrating all your circumstances for your good.

The knotted removal of your circumstance may take time and tedious effort that tempts you to want to scream to God, "Stop it! This hurts too much!" He wants to love you through the pain to reveal to you just how beautiful you can be when the suffering is over. Trust Him to perfect, confirm, strengthen, and establish you through this journey of prison.

✝

March 28 God's Word is Enough

Exodus 5:3

Then they said, "The God of the Hebrews has met with us. Please, let us go a three days' journey into the wilderness that we may sacrifice to the Lord our God, lest He fall upon us with pestilence or with the sword."

The Israelites were enslaved by the Egyptians. Moses had been called by God to lead them out. In this call, God didn't threaten Moses (or the Israelites) with disease or death if they failed in their efforts to leave. In fact, God assured him of His help to be successful. In fact, God spelled everything out for Moses, including what to say and what to expect from Pharaoh. Yet when before Pharaoh, he and Aaron embellished and added such words seemingly in hopes to better convince Pharaoh to grant their request.

Moses later, out of anger and frustration with the Israelites, struck a rock with his staff to miraculously bring water instead of speaking to the rock as God instructed. He again took back the battle and did things his own way, seemingly out of emotions. This cost him the opportunity to walk into the Promised Land with the people.

When being led by God, we do have to do our part. Moses had to go, he had to approach Pharaoh, and he had to take action as being the leader. When faced with no water and God's solution, he had to follow through on his part. Just as if we are unemployed and cannot pay our bills, we cannot sit and pray for money with no other effort; we have to do our part like apply for jobs.

Being available and faithful are our responsibility. But part of being faithful is believing God's word. In reality, God doesn't need our help with anything, but He chooses to use us to perform His will. In carrying out His will, He will always give us exactly what we need to be successful.

If you have heard from God regarding an issue, that settles it. You do not have to ponder the answer, make a backup plan, or get a second opinion. His word is enough. Your responsibility is to carry out what He has told you to do.

Prison can seem a formidable enemy, just as Pharaoh seemed to Moses. Leading over a million Israelites out of slavery was a huge assignment! But God's word was enough. Victory came as promised.

March 29 When Fear is Near

Judges 7:10-11

"But if you are afraid to go down, go with Purah your servant down to the camp, and you will hear what they say; and afterward your hands will be strengthened that you may go down against the camp." So he went with Purah his servant down to the outposts of the army that was in the camp.

Gideon is a person in Scripture that people can relate to. His assignment from God brought nervous apprehension. In fact, it says that he was afraid. He needed reassurance, not to maintain his faith, but rather to conquer his fear in spite of his faith.

The Lord had dwindled Gideon's army to 300 men. The enemy they faced was enormous; they filled the valley to capacity. How on earth was Gideon expected to engage this enemy without sure defeat? Gideon was obedient in reducing his men from 32,000 to the chosen 300, but his hope may have been quivering as thousands turned to return home. God saw his need for encouragement.

He sent Gideon and his servant down into the valley to assure him of the success awaiting. Even sending someone with him again showed God responding to Gideon's timidity. Gideon received clear affirmation when overhearing a conversation between two enemy soldiers. In fact, he even heard his name in the exchange! God wanted him to know confidently that he was hearing from Him.

Anxiety, worry, fretfulness, fear, uncertainty — these are emotions counterproductive to our calling and Christian walk, yet we are human and they creep in just like in Gideon's life. Prison can catapult us into any of them on any given day. But the beautiful thing about God is that He understands our fears and compassionately provides what we need to encourage us to keep moving forward. He communicates assurance personally to us, but also uses other people in our lives for support, like Gideon's servant Purah.

You may be walking toward the valley or right in the middle of one, wondering how on earth you can succeed. You may need to hear your name spoken of victoriously. Be assured that God knows your fear. He hasn't left you to battle alone. In fact, He has already planned the victory! Ask Him to provide you your signs of encouragement. Read the entire story of Gideon's life in Judges. He was an astounding man of God and someone I trust you can relate to.

March 30 — Home

II Corinthians 5:2

For indeed in this house we groan, longing to be clothed with our dwelling from heaven.

If you have experienced dementia, possibly with a parent or other elder, then you likely have addressed the issue of "home." As memory and feelings of security are lost, a person longs for home. "I want to go home," "take me home," or other versions of this request become a repeated plea.

The problem is home isn't usually a tangible place. Even if the person is physically taken to homes of the past, it still isn't "home." That's because the place is actually a feeling of security, a place where everything makes sense and seems "right." We tend to associate these feelings with home, because home is connected to our feelings like no other place. When the brain is broken as in dementia, the *sense* of home is fleeting in the confusion and never can be grasped.

The effects of prison can also disrupt our security and create longings for that place in life where all seems right. And it generally resides with our regrets for choices that could have possibly been done differently, removing the consequence of prison which now permeates our lives. But like dementia, finding a home of the past isn't available any longer. To move forward in peace, we need assurance now and hope for the future.

Paul compares this life, our bodies, as a tent or house. And while in this mortal body, if we have a relationship with Jesus, we long for our better home in heaven. For in heaven all the burdens of this life will be over. No more tears, sorrow, difficulties. We will finally be in a place of eternal peace and security. We are in some ways like that person with dementia, but with the realization that our eternal home will not be found in this life. We long for it, but understand that this world isn't our home.

Jesus has told us that He's preparing a place for us. This gives us hope! Be encouraged in this truth. Whatever this world or prison throws at you, it will never remove the security of your future if you know Jesus.

March 31 Case of TMI

II Kings 20:13

And Hezekiah listened to them, and showed them all his treasure house, the silver and the gold and the spices and the precious oil and the house of his armor and all that was found in his treasuries. There was nothing in his house, nor in all his dominion, that Hezekiah did not show them.

Humility doesn't always come with being a prison wife. At least not for me. And it's because of the struggles that pride can take root and front itself when with others. It's a version of woe is me that's fueled by pride, not a sincere need for understanding, support, or to encourage others. It took me several years to gain the confidence to even mention my romantic interest sat in prison. And now these years later, with sturdy confidence, I hover around the line of boasting to all I have endured or continue to endure. When brought down by God, a sickening disgust for my own behavior follows.

The reality is I can do nothing without God. Any success that I have had in my marriage has been dependent on His mercy or grace. So my heart's efforts at times to be a testimony must be reined in and refocused to exalt God, not myself.

Hezekiah reigned over Judah. During that time, God delivered Judah miraculously from Assyria. A destroying angel went through the Assyrian camp which was preparing to invade Jerusalem and killed them all. Later, God miraculously healed Hezekiah of a terminal illness and granted him fifteen more years of life. Then what we read soon after seems almost too unbelievable to be true. Hezekiah actually entertains the Israelites' future enemy and flaunts Judah's wealth as written in the verse above.

It seemed he was trying to impress the Babylonians by a show of wealth and to indicate the power wealth brings. It was a case of too much information without acknowledging the source of Judah's blessing—God. Isaiah, the great prophet of God, quickly delivered God's rebuttal to Hezekiah's behavior, humbling him with the knowledge of all that lay ahead. Babylon would invade and rule over the Israelites for those infamous seventy years.

God's blessings on our lives, our testimony, can be a valuable way to encourage someone else. But when it expands—puffed up by pride—the power it holds is deflated. This is because God steps out of the way, figuratively and literally, leaving us standing on our own merits, which will always be zero without God's sustaining power.

Sadly, we can be oblivious to the motivation which spawns the words we speak. That's the power of pride. So, the best way to combat this power is before you open your mouth, ask yourself this question: Am I trying to impress with the negative? If the motivation is to showcase all the bad you have endured to your own glory or to gain accolades for the same, then it would be best to not speak at all.

Humble yourself through silence. Too much information without the support of the Holy Spirit are worthless words. The enemy Satan will use your pride to keep glory from God and to drain your testimony of the mighty power it possesses.

April 1 Be Unashamed

Psalm 145:5-6

On the glorious splendor of Thy majesty, and on Thy wonderful works, I will meditate. And men shall speak of the power of Thine awesome acts; and I will tell of Thy greatness.

I chose to be a wife of an inmate, trusting God with the plan that He affirmed through my own fears and "This is insane!" moments. Every day of my life with my husband has involved prison. He's nearly twenty-five years into his sentence; I have been with him for the last seventeen at the time of this writing.

For a redemptive end, God brought together polar opposites, separated by geography, the prison barriers, and personalities. I'm the fairy to my husband's monster, the Lady to his Tramp, the velvet to his rawhide. These differences fuel even further God's amazing transformation of both me and my husband to solidify our union.

And having plans for this beautiful union, God will not allow me to retreat to silence. Early on, He spoke to me in His way: "Angela, there is a tremendous witness in all I'm doing, but there is no witness unless you start opening your mouth." I knew He was right. But oh, how hard this was for me at first.

In the beginning, opening my mouth was expectantly met with looks of disbelief, the awkward silence as others tried to search within the void of words for what would be an appropriate response to something smothered in their skepticism and their own "You're insane!" attitudes. It made me want to retreat to that place where quiet people spend their days, where it's safe.

Unexpectedly, I also became angry by what I viewed as the arrogance of some to think they knew better than God regarding what was right for me. They questioned my ability to understand how God leads me when I had heard clearly—repeatedly. I spend every waking moment with Him, in His presence. I'm in conversation throughout each day with Him. I study His word and pray. Persons whom I knew read a five-minute devotional on a good day and some not having even opened a Bible in months were actually convinced they knew best. Mature Christians even portrayed unbelief in their attitudes toward my decision and where I knew God had called me to be—the wife of a prisoner.

Yet through it all, I took courage from knowing that I was in the center of God's will. He encouraged me daily and loved me through the difficulties. I found that I loved God more than avoiding the criticism, the disbelief, and the hurtful words of others.

You may be experiencing similar trials. Even if you didn't choose to be a prisoner's wife, your challenges aren't beyond God's help. I want you to know that you aren't alone. God is with you! Others might discourage you, even if not intentionally. Their best words of concern can cause your discouragement. Your husband might even be your biggest challenge. But stand firm! God has a tremendous plan for your marriage. It will be as unique as you are. It will be unique to your marriage.

Prison doesn't extinguish or put your marriage on hold. It becomes another place where God's power can be seen. So do not retreat into shame or silence because of prison. Let people see the glorious work God is doing through it.

April 2 Be Mad at Prison

Colossians 3:14

And beyond all these things put on love, which is the perfect bond of unity.

The ring of the phone steadily became louder in my mind as I stirred awake. Oh, it's my Baby calling! I slumber to find the light and the receiver. I'm also greeted with my congested head and a nasally voice as I say,

"Hello." Once the computer-generated voice goes through its monologue, I'm soon hearing my husband's voice.

I'm listless from the minor illness which plagued me over the weekend, weak in my voice, and quick to be reprimanded by my husband's words, "You've got to speak up!" Followed by his list of all the bitter reasons from his surroundings for why I needed to, all deciphered through static and staccato words from a prison cordless phone nowhere near its receiver.

My reaction was initially anger and the words, "Let me wake up first!" It was an arrow shot back to remind him that I'm dealing with my own crap on the other end because of his situation. And for that moment it was being woke up out of a dead sleep when I'm already sick, anticipating also another wake-up at 1:00 a.m. by the garbage truck emptying the dumpster mere feet from my window, and the coming hours of another Monday at work.

Essentially, we were both aggravated with the situation, not so much each other. But in our human nature, we attacked what was available. The call ended with a sigh and regret that the precious fifteen minutes afforded us only biweekly was over and prison had once again made the simplest way to connect difficult.

I usually see clearly the forces at work after the fact, but while in the moment, I'm undisciplined in my spirit to respond differently. I think that's the case for many of us. Emotions get the best of us and our husbands receive the worst of who we are. And vice versa. The challenge becomes anticipating the difficulty and being prepared to respond differently. This takes intentional thinking and deliberate words that may fight against how we feel. Those words may not seem like they satisfy like those fired back in anger. But the healing impact recognizes our unions against the true enemy, instead of damaging each other by the verbal darts which only poison.

And sadly, while prison remains, you'll have plenty of times to practice staying united to your husband when faced with the frustrating situations of prison. Divert that angry energy into a weapon to fight prison by not succumbing to the temptation of battling your spouse. Be mad at the circumstance, not him.

April 3 Always Moving

Numbers 33:1

These are the journeys of the sons of Israel, by which they came out from the land of Egypt by their armies, under the leadership of Moses and Aaron.

This chapter of Numbers provides a journal of all the places the Israelites camped after leaving Egypt until arriving at the Jordan River. Moses had kept this list, not as an itinerary, because they didn't plan the route; God led them. Moses was rather obedient to documenting the journey as God instructed him.

If you read this chapter, you may be astounded, as I am, to just how often the Israelites pitched camp on their journey of forty years. Forty-one times they moved. Some camps only lasted a few days; others a year or more. I can just envision the exhaustion from the logistics, especially considering the size of the Israelite nation and the energy of pitching tents, repeatedly.

You may be exhausted with your journey involving many transfers for your husband. DOC typically moves inmates regularly. It comes with this life it seems. You get somewhat comfortable and adjusted, then bam, he's somewhere else and you have to regroup and begin again in a new place.

But God is in control of every move, every time. The frequent transfers may be a consequence of living in DOC, but they also can be a tool used by God for the good. It may be for protection, lessons to be learned, or faith to be developed—both in you and your husband. This prison frustration isn't beyond God's sovereignty. Keeping this in mind helps mitigate the deflated feelings that come with the sigh, "Here we go again."

So once again, take heart! Another move doesn't move you away from God's presence. He's there ahead of you, purposing your experiences, maneuvering you through a path for a divine reason. Like the Israelites, it may seem like desert wanderings, but when orchestrated by God, the meaningless detours are leading to a tremendous blessing. Rest in this peace.

April 4 — From Self to God

Genesis 29:35

And she conceived again and bore a son and said, "This time I will praise the Lord." Therefore she named him Judah. Then she stopped bearing.

The happenings between Leah and Rachel overflow with human tendency. Jacob loved Rachel and worked seven years for her father to earn her hand in marriage. But her father tricked Jacob on the wedding night, shielding his eldest daughter Leah's face, sending her to him instead. She became pregnant from this deceptive embrace. He then had to work another seven years in exchange for Rachel whom he loved and desired from the beginning.

So Jacob now has two wives. Leah realizes she's the unloved, the unwanted. Her response is to try to earn Jacob's affection through giving him many children. In this effort, she does give him ultimately six sons and one daughter. She even sent her maid to him and he had two sons by her which in those times became an extension of the wife.

This giving of children, however, never did change Jacob's heart toward her as she desired. He fondly loved Rachel to the end. What's interesting to note is how the naming of Leah's children changed from self to God.

Her first three sons' names reflected her focus on her struggles and her desire to be desired by her husband: "Because the Lord has seen my affliction." "Because the Lord has heard that I am unloved." "Now this time my husband will become attached to me." It isn't until her fourth son that this attitude shifts to focusing on God alone. "This time I will praise the Lord." And this son is named Judah, the eventual tribe through which Jesus is born.

Leah is so much like us when going through difficulty. Our tendency is to become self-focused. Our hearts overflow with the attitude of "Woe is me." We do not know how God may have been dealing with Leah over those years, but something changed at the time of Judah's birth. And rightly so. The heritage of Christ doesn't seem fitting unless solely attached to praising God.

But even when she seemed barren, her maid brought further sons to Jacob and their names reflected a happy heart, not a bitter one. There's no indication that Leah's situation changed. But her attitude and heart seemed to. Sure, she was not perfect in her attitude 100 percent of the time; we read later of her slip into resentment. But, overall, we read of a shift from self to God.

Prison is unloving and undesired. But focusing on God continues to be the antidote for bitterness and self-defeat. A happy heart can live within a difficult circumstance. When you take a step toward God in your attitude, He responds in His grace to make a difficult time doable, and surprisingly, joy can be found. You may not be perfect in this effort, but He understands this as well. He remains faithful and perfectly attached to you, because He loves you.

April 5 Tune Out

Ecclesiastes 1:18

Because in much wisdom there is much grief, and increasing knowledge results in increasing pain.

    The book of Ecclesiastes isn't the most cheerful book. Solomon is thought to have written it, but there's no certainty at this point. It's the author's solemn reflection on life with and without God. He determined that without God, all life is meaningless. He shares with us in the verse above that as he came to understand this, his grief increased.

    Ignorance can be bliss, because we are shielded from often painful realities. But with the reality of this world's depravity and glorification of sorrow through the headlines, we wake daily to news of death, corruption, heinous crimes, and generally any emotional caption which results in our sighing. For a Christian, headlines of the sins of this world can be even heavier to our hearts when absorbed.

    News is important. Jesus tells us we are to be active in this world, not retreat from it. But there are times when we need to take a break from the bad. We need to tune out the news, which overwhelmingly remains negative.

    Dealing daily with prison brings its own sighs. Adding to this, often throughout each day, the sad, negative, or sinful displays of this world's depravity can bury us in a defeated spirit. It can drain us of motivation and sightings of the good.

    Access to smartphones, technology, and instant information has its place, but it also seeps into a compulsive need to always stay connected, streamed at a touch or click into our minds. This level of access to the world's events, family issues on social media, politics, Hollywood gossip, or even the retelling of a rescued animal from mistreatment must have limits.

    Consider a media fast or—at the least—intentionally limit your screen time. Use the time to recharge, spend time in true life, and connect with God, not your computer. Face prison from a balanced perspective that there's bad, but you choose to control its place and impact on your life.

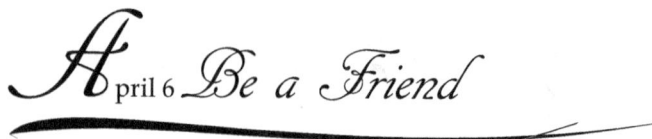
April 6 — Be a Friend

Genesis 38:12

Now after a considerable time Shua's daughter, the wife of Judah, died; and when the time of mourning was ended, Judah went up to his sheepshearers at Timnah, he and his friend Hirah the Adullamite.

    Relationships in Scripture are fascinating to consider. Family, friends, enemies, leaders—the lives of people doing life are recorded for us. Some such stories are mere glimpses, such as the relationship between Judah and his friend Hirah. We do not have any details about Hirah's personality, his feelings about some of Judah's actions, or how they became friends. But what we can know is that he was a long-term friend whom Judah obviously trusted and spent time with.

    Judah was not a saint. He had the idea of selling his brother Joseph into slavery. He married a Canaanite woman which was forbidden by God. He pursued a prostitute who turned out to be his daughter-n-law. She deceived him, because he didn't keep his word to give her his son as a husband. She became pregnant as a result of the immoral act. But despite the tainted past of Judah, we know that the Lord Jesus was a descendant from him.

    Hirah likely had no knowledge of his friend's role in the coming Savior. We do read that he remained a friend to Judah through some very trying times: the death of Judah's two sons, the death of Judah's wife, and the shameful act with his daughter-n-law.

    True friends are there through the good, bad, and ugly. Close friendships can endure times of conflict and the parts of personality that can be hard to bear. A true friend is willing to accept your personality annoyances, frustrations, and things about you that make being a friend to you difficult at times. It's kind of like family: we love our family even though they try our patience or anger us on some occasions.

    You may never know what influence you may have on a friend for the good. As a prison wife, having a good friend is special. Your husband's incarceration may be a point of conflict or it may be further evidence that a friend loves at all times. Appreciate your friendships. Invest in them as Hirah did with Judah. They will likely be one of your greatest blessings when you need them most.

April 7 Spiritual Rest

Exodus 20:8-10

"Remember the sabbath day, to keep it holy. Six days you shall labor and do all your work, but the seventh day is a sabbath of the Lord your God; in it you shall not do any work, you or your son or your daughter, your male or your female servant or your cattle or your sojourner who stays with you."

Life is hard enough without prison. There seems to never be enough time or true rest. Even come Sunday, resting can be just another stressor if not approached with the right perspective.

How can that be? Well, you can physically stop doing stuff, sit on the sofa, and tell yourself it's alright to do nothing. But all the while, it might drive you crazy, because there's still laundry building, chores left unfinished, and errands waiting. The mental effects of these burdens can remain despite your body not moving.

God built into us a rhythm for life. Part of the rhythm involves resting. But "resting," more than anything, is to be spiritual. It's more about your heart's condition, than your body. It's a time to focus on God, renew your mind, and recharge your spiritual energy. This is best done without the distractions of work and life's demands. But it doesn't mean God doesn't understand when we fumble toward this goal or events trump our desire. Sundays (or whatever day of the week is your "Sunday") shouldn't be legalistic.

Legalism can take root and make you think that if you lift one finger of activity on a Sabbath that you're sinning. Please do not be so hard on yourself! God understands what we have going on in life. He understands what season of life we are in. He knew how all our days would be before we were even born. He's more interested in your heart's condition, than the sacrifice of your body.

To the greatest extent, physically rest at least one day a week. But when you're in a season of life or an overwhelming weekend, still try to focus on God. Turn your work or chores into worship. Listen to praise songs as you clean. Use the time in the car running errands to pray. Between chores, spend time on your knees in prayer. Ask God to help organize your schedule to allow more physical rest. You can still pursue and obtain spiritual rest with the benefit of feeling renewed in your heart for God if done with the right perspective. God will meet you wherever you happen to be, and He will continue to help move you toward the ideal holy day.

April 8 Falling into Place

II Corinthians 9:8

And God is able to make all grace abound to you, that always having all sufficiency in everything, you may have an abundance for every good deed.

It was an extremely hectic week at my job. I felt overwhelmed and unsure of how all responsibilities were going to be accomplished. It was pushing my hopeful and optimistic outlook downward, much as the worried and stressed appearance I'm sure I carried with me. In my acceptance that the outlook looked bleak, I asked God on my drive into work to please orchestrate the day for my productive benefit. Because without His divine help, I knew victory wouldn't be the reality.

And amazingly, I was blown away by the grace of God! Necessary tasks were blended into the unexpected to allow both to be accomplished. This was even without the fervor of stress that I often battle when hit with mounting responsibilities and deadlines. Everything fell into place only by God's orchestration.

Paul is writing about the nature of God's economy: sacrifice with the right attitude brings blessings. My attitude changed when leaving for work that day, and God responded with His blessing. This way of working in our lives can be seen in many areas. Just as Scripture reminds us that if we seek first God's kingdom and His righteousness, He will take care of our needs. This economy works in all settings: home, family, work, and even prison.

It's very freeing to see the activity of God in our lives. It reminds us of His interest and involvement even in the details of the everyday. Nothing is missed; we are never alone in our trying and difficult days. He goes before us clearing the path to guide us through or around the troubles heading our way. We just have to trust His sovereignty and ask in faith for His help. He will show up. He loves us that much!

Your life may be speeding along on a hectic highway. Your responsibilities may be paired with little time. Surrender your schedule and life's demands to God. The stress of prison, work, family, and home can be perfectly managed by God. His grace will show up to bless your efforts when done with a submitted heart.

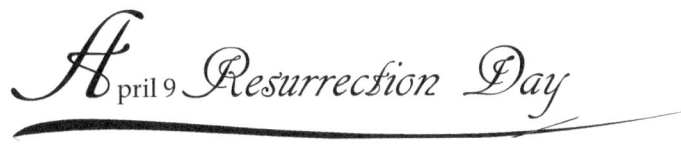

April 9 Resurrection Day

Matthew 28:6

"He is not here, for He has risen, just as He said. Come, see the place where He was lying."

April brings Easter into full bloom. Easter Sunday is the most important day to a Christian. It varies by calendar date year to year, but consistently remains evidence to why there's hope. Jesus came back to life three days following His execution. He died to remove the eternal death sin brings to mankind. If a Christian, your worst day is never your worst day, because of resurrection day.

Without the resurrection there would be no hope. Unless Jesus died on your behalf, hell would be your future. If not a Christian, the critical decision you must make is whether you believe your sinful nature demands a Savior and that Jesus is that Savior through His death and resurrection.

If you have made that decision, you travel through your days looking through a lens of hope. Hope for the days to come. Hope for eternal life. Regardless of the struggles in this life, a better day awaits. Nothing can separate you from this hope.

This is critical when facing prison every day. The fears, violence, and corruption are met with hope. Your worst day involving prison is an indistinguishable wisp of air in the blink of this life. Your entire season of prison is just another part of the blink. You need this perspective to soldier through the tough days and years ahead.

Jesus warns us that we will have trouble in this world. But because of His resurrection, He has overcome this world, including prison. Sometimes you need to step back from the daily trials and consider the big picture. It's a glorious picture where there's no more pain, tears, or heartache. There's freedom. This describes your eternal home if you have faith in Jesus and His resurrection.

Hopefully, your husband has an end of sentence within this blink of time. Prison will hopefully only be a season. Regardless, your spirit will be lighter and despair will not be able to settle on your heart when Jesus has secured your future. This will make all the difference in the world—through the good and bad of it all.

April 10 God's Word First

Luke 23:56

And they returned and prepared spices and perfumes. And on the Sabbath they rested according to the commandment.

Following Jesus's death, Mary Magdalene, Mary the mother of James, Joanna, and other women followed Joseph who took Jesus's body from the cross and laid it in the tomb. Their desire was to return to the tomb to anoint His body with large quantities of spices and perfume.

Jesus was killed on a Friday. Scripture tells us that He died at 3:00p.m. The Sabbath would begin at sundown and continue until sundown of Saturday. According to Jewish religious law, no work or business is done on the Sabbath. So after learning of where the tomb was located, the ladies did as much as they could to prepare for the anointing before sundown arrived. But then they rested as God commanded.

I admire these ladies greatly. What discipline they had to show over their emotions! They had just witnessed their Savior crucified. They were grieving. Yet despite this, they clung to God's word. They didn't let their emotions rule their reaction.

I wonder if within the group there was varying levels of faith. Maybe there was a lady who full of emotion wanted to disregard the commandment and provide Jesus a proper burial—without delay! Maybe of the group, one had to intervene and remind her of what God's word says. I would have probably been the one justifying not doing the Sabbath "as usual" because of the events just experienced. I have definitely rationalized not doing my Sabbaths (going to church) for far lesser reasons.

But If Mary and the other ladies could be obedient to God's word when faced with the execution and burial of Jesus, I should be able to in less significant circumstances. Do I have to be rude when frustrated? Do I have to overspend when happy? Do I have to slam a door when angry?

I continue to struggle in this area, and typically find that I cycle through obedience because of my feelings. Sad, discouraged, angry—how I feel impacts my motivation for obedience. But I always come to realize, again, that Scripture is always right regardless of how I feel in the moment. I can never go wrong being obedient to God's word.

Whatever you're facing in your journey of prison that has your emotions low, meditate on Scripture. Feeling hopeless, facing criticism, bearing anger — read a Psalm or one of the Gospels. Are you struggling with feeling worthless? Read about Jesus's crucifixion and meditate on the truth that He willingly placed Himself on that cross because of how much He loves and values you. Put God's word first, like the ladies who spent time with Jesus. Put it ahead of your emotions, your impulsive feelings, because it is the absolute truth for every choice.

April 11 Per-Mission

Daniel 1:8

But Daniel made up his mind that he would not defile himself with the king's choice food or with the wine which he drank; so he sought permission from the commander of the officials that he might not defile himself.

Daniel and his three friends were prisoners of war taken to Babylon for intellectual training and physical preparation to serve the king. The king's goal was to bring the best and beautiful into his service. The steps in this mission called for these young Hebrew men to eat and drink from the king's rations. The food and wine offered were considered unclean to the Hebrews, because part had been sacrificed to idols. God was clear that the Jews should keep themselves separate from idol worship of any kind. Daniel had to make a choice within his captivity: would he be on God's mission or the pagan king Nebuchadnezzar's?

Daniel didn't seem to hesitate in his choice. He kept himself focused on God's mission and serving the only true God. To this end he asked permission of the king's help to allow them a different diet for ten days as assurance that the king would still be pleased with their appearance. Sticking to God's mission brought Daniel and his friends favor with God and the king.

It takes boldness to remain faithful to God when in the enemy's camp. Standing up for God's will and values, knowing persecution is a strong possibility, takes courage. What we learn from Daniel, however, is that God provides favor when we seek to serve Him.

Dealing with prison, for yourself and your husband, provides daily faith choices that require evaluating your mission. Your battlefield is paved with concrete and dreary paint, corrupt authority, lonely awakenings, and crumbling hope when the enemy has you surrounded. But do not allow the enemy's mission to deceive you into believing you have no choice within your captivity.

Prison cannot rule your choice to follow God. Courage it takes, yes! But God never forsakes you in the battle. His favor is on those who seek to follow Him. Choices come daily. Keep your mission before you and trust that God has you surrounded as you step out into His will.

April 12 — Do Lord, Oh, Do Lord

Luke 23:42-43

And he was saying, "Jesus, remember me when You come in Your kingdom!" And He said to him, "Truly I say to you, today you shall be with Me in Paradise."

Oh, do remember me! The familiar tune "Do Lord" has been recorded by various artists and sung by children for decades. The repeating phrase "way beyond the blue" indicates the heavenly home for those who accept Jesus as their Savior.

The thief hanging on his own cross beside Jesus believed in who Jesus was and pleaded with Him to not forget him in the afterlife in heaven. It was his version of singing "Do Lord, oh, do Lord. Oh, do remember me. Way beyond the blue." Jesus responds by assuring him that, yes, he would enter heaven.

This Scripture is also great assurance that salvation is based on grace, not works. This unnamed thief admitted his guilt from the cross. He committed a crime which earned him the death penalty. But his legal punishment didn't eliminate his salvation. God's grace saved him, eternally.

Scripture doesn't say at what point in this thief's life he confessed salvation. A common interpretation is that he came to salvation at the time of his execution. If true, this is further evidence of grace!

It's never too late in this life to be saved. A lifetime of wrong choices and sin can be erased with belief in Jesus. A deathbed salvation is just as secure as a childhood faith. It isn't dependent on what we have done, but on what Jesus did for us. He died on His cross in our place. The thief received an earthly consequence for his sin, but Jesus took on his eternal one.

Every prisoner has the same offer as the thief. Accept Jesus and enter into Paradise. It makes no difference the crime, but only the heart condition. Jesus remembers and knows those who are His. And He allows nothing to separate His own from Himself.

Let this encourage your heart! Let it encourage your husband! He doesn't have to balance the scales to set his eternity right with God. Jesus has already done that for him. He need only rest in God's promise that heaven awaits for those who believe.

April 13 A Couple's Prayer

Mark 10:8

"And the two shall become one flesh; consequently they are no longer two, but one flesh."

Praying with your husband is a highly effective way to build and strengthen your marriage. The first time my husband spoke the words to me, "I want us to pray," we were sitting in a crowded visitation park. He took my hands in his, and we bowed together as close as we could physically be in that moment. It was as if all the years of prayer I had done for him, alone and hurting, were evidenced in the fruit of his now praying over us. It was absolutely beautiful! His words to God were beautiful. I suddenly experienced all that I knew God had been telling me about my husband's future: he will be a mighty man of God! I felt safe, I felt peace, and I felt God's Spirit pouring over us as one.

Was my part of the prayer well scripted and fluent? No. Praying aloud in front of others is a difficult thing for me. It's another challenge for my shy and quiet personality. Plus at that moment, the butterflies in my heart were exploding as I considered the great step we were taking. This caused a further impairment in my mouth. But that was okay! The important thing was that I was praying for and with the man whom God had given me as a life partner. It wasn't about the words, but the power of the One hearing them.

We have prayed together nearly every visit since that time, and on the rare occasions that circumstances prevent us, there's grief within me. My soul yearns to connect with him in that way. We need it. It's a way for my husband to spiritually lead our relationship in real time. He needs that!

It's a special connection that you can have with your husband too. It's the most important way you can strengthen your marriage. But if you — or your husband — aren't there yet, continue to pray and ask God to bring your relationship to that deeper level. There's a comfort that comes with frequency. So, if you're uncomfortable praying aloud now, that's okay too. Keep praying, and it will get easier.

Remember, it doesn't have to be scripted and fancy. The persons who sought after Jesus came to him with a specific need, simply stated: I want to walk, save my son's life, heal me of this bleeding, restore my vision. He already knew their deepest need; He knows yours too. But He still desires you to ask. And joining with your husband in asking brings special delight to God.

April 14 — Yielding to Love

II Timothy 2:24-26

And the Lord's bond-servant must not be quarrelsome, but be kind to all, able to teach, patient when wronged, with gentleness correcting those who are in opposition, if perhaps God may grant them repentance leading to the knowledge of the truth, and they may come to their senses and escape from the snare of the devil, having been held captive by him to do his will.

It was the disturbing news that I repeatedly dreaded: My husband had once again turned to violence to escape an oppressive prison situation. Within my initial mix of emotions was definitely anger. My heart was raging toward my husband, and as usual, he was nowhere around to hear my pain. He was sitting in a confinement cell, and I was pacing the outskirts of that cell in my thoughts and hurt, shaking my fist at him, screaming, "I am not going through this again!"

But seeking God for comfort, reading the Scripture above, I received the salve to ease the wounds to my heart and allowed the nature of love to have victory over bitterness. God's standard of love resonated like a warm breeze over me.

God's first command to me when He brought me my husband was simply "Love him." That hadn't changed with the incident. God reminded me that my only real responsibility was to love my husband; He would change him. I knew my husband had been tempted toward violence by Satan, and he yielded to it. It has always been one of his greatest weaknesses. I also knew that my husband sat in remorse for the situation he brought into our marriage, feeling insecure in his thoughts that he might certainly hear the words that raged in my mind. Satan certainly desired for me to say those words, to remain bitter, and ultimately to give up on my husband and our marriage. But the power remained with God and His word.

In that first letter following the incident, I focused on assuring my husband of my love, and most importantly, that I forgave him. I could rest in God's control over the situation, and I was free to communicate that peace through peaceful words to my husband, not angry ones, because it truly was the nature of my heart by the time pen reached paper.

Did I share with him my pain? Yes. But I didn't share it with a retaliatory attitude as the one raging in my flesh when I first heard the news. Yielding to God's Spirit and His guidance that I had read in II Timothy gave me the strength to respond to my husband in a way that would have been impossible otherwise. And our marriage benefited.

Applying what you read in Scripture will always bring a reward. Going through prison with a closed Bible denies you the encouragement, wisdom, and help you need to deal with the ugly days and Satan's efforts to destroy your marriage. Your motivation to apply Scripture can only come by staying in Scripture. As you commit to remaining close to God through His word, He remains ready with exactly what you need to read to deal successfully with the situation you face—the usual bad of prison or the unexpected worse.

April 15 *Unlikely One*

Ruth 4:13

So Boaz took Ruth, and she became his wife, and he went in to her. And the Lord enabled her to conceive, and she gave birth to a son.

Growing up in Moab, Ruth wouldn't have been destined for any astounding future. The Moabites were enemies of Israel. They were people included in God's list of those forbidden for Israel to intermarry and imitate. They worshipped false gods. They actively battled against Israel. Moabites were the descendants of Lot's son Moab. A son born from Lot's sexual act with his own daughter.

Ruth didn't come from a very noble background, but while in Moab, she was introduced to an Israelite whose family had traveled to Moab because of a famine in Judah. They married, but Ruth remained childless for the duration of their marriage. This man died, leaving Ruth in a blended heritage.

Ruth had grown close to her mother-n-law Naomi. Out of her love for Naomi, Ruth relocated to Judah when Naomi decided to return home. Naomi had lost everything at that point, both her sons and her husband, which prompted her decision to return.

Once there, through God's providence, Ruth met Boaz, a close relative of Naomi's. They married and Ruth had her first son. This unlikely coming together of a foreign woman from an enemy land and an upstanding, godly man birthed a son who would be one in the continuing line of sons to whom Jesus would be born. Wow!

God used the unlikely, the wayward, and the sinful to show His mercy and redemptive power. He orchestrated the heritage of Jesus to be linked with immoral and pagan ancestors. His heart for reaching the lost is amazingly evident.

Your husband may be lost. He may have an immoral and severely wayward past. Most people may see him as an unlikely person to achieve anything of value—especially for God.

But thankfully, God doesn't operate based on our righteousness. He operates out of His nature of grace and redemption. Your husband is a prime candidate for an astounding purpose in God's story. He can be further evidence of an unlikely one being used to bring others to Christ and glory to God.

April 16 Talents for God

Exodus 35:10

'And let every skillful man among you come, and make all that the Lord has commanded.'

What are you good at? There are innate abilities given to us by God that often have been developed through practice and experiences of our lives. Oftentimes our personalities are uniquely fitted to what we enjoy and what we are good at. It's important to discover and develop our talents, because a platform for serving God is available there. As prison wives, our talents can also be a rewarding way we can invest our time, which so often presents itself as our enemy.

In the verse today, building the tabernacle was in progress. God had provided Moses the details of how it should look and the materials to be used. A natural and practical expression of how this was accomplished is read. Assignments were given based on skill. Men and women talented in working with cloth, metals, and wood contributed to the work in ways they were good at.

God made you with great foresight. Even before you were born, He planned your skills, personality, and how both should be used for His glory. Of course, He also gave you free will. You do not have to use these attributes for good. There are plenty of examples in this world of people who use their talents for unrighteous things or things of no eternal value. Even the Israelites are later noted in Scripture to use such skills of woodworking and blacksmithing for making idols, in direct opposition to God.

God purposes your talents to be used for Him. Life takes on a depth of joy not available otherwise when you use your talents for how God designed. God gave Moses the design and skilled men and women went to work. What joy they must have felt knowing they personally contributed value to such a holy structure as the tabernacle.

Using your talents with the same perspective can bring you such joy. And prison cannot squelch it, because the daily reality of prison difficulty is balanced by purposeful living within the wait. There's satisfaction of contributing something of eternal value, not just finite pleasure. I challenge you to consider what you're good at and look for ways to use your talent in godly ways.

April 17 Eventual Victory

Judges 20:18

Now the sons of Israel arose, went up to Bethel, and inquired of God, and said, "Who shall go up first for us to battle against the sons of Benjamin?" Then the Lord said, "Judah shall go up first."

Israel consisted of twelve tribes. Judges chapters nineteen and twenty tells of the war between the tribe of Benjamin and the eleven other tribes. This war was the result of the rape and murder of a Levite's concubine by men of Benjamin. In preparation for going into battle, the eleven tribes sought God's input. In the verse above, God instructs them to send the tribe of Judah to battle first.

Reading further into the chapter, you'll read this initial battle was unsuccessful. Israel lost 22,000 men. In fact, the next attempt was not successful either, despite their once again seeking the Lord's face before marching out. The second day they lost another 18,000 men. It was not until the third battle that they gained victory.

This is part of the nature and ways of God that can be difficult to comprehend—if at all. You would think that with God's green light to go, victory would be certain the first time. But He allowed the Israelites to be defeated before bringing victory. Why?

It could be they asked the wrong question. Instead of "who" should go up first, maybe the question should have been: Should we go up against our brother Benjamin? In their emotional response to the murder, they may have skipped this important question. Maybe they were still too angry to think clearly.

They had a righteous anger toward men who committed a heinous crime against their own, and they desired to be vindicated. It seemed they assumed God would agree and bless their efforts. But God delayed the victory. Maybe it was His way of teaching Israel this important lesson. It's the part of Scripture that we can never know for certain.

The important lesson we can learn from this passage is how faithfully the Israelites continued to seek God despite the bewildering outcomes. In the face of defeat, they returned to God each time, asking Him for guidance. They prayed, they fasted, and they wept—desperate to hear from the Lord. In their human emotions, they may have erred in the steps, but God was gracious in His perfect way.

Within the missteps of your best intentions, take encouragement that God doesn't abandon you in the battle. The prison path comes with stumbling, both for you and your husband. It's a difficult battlefield in which to learn. But God will wisely teach you within it, and this, in itself, may be to your victory in the war regardless if the initial battle brings consequences.

April 18 Waiting by the Brook

I Kings 17:3

"Go away from here and turn eastward, and hide yourself by the brook Cherith, which is east of the Jordan."

Drought was coming to the region and Elijah was God's spokesman to Ahab about this determined event. No rain or even dew would be seen for years. Once this message was delivered, God instructed Elijah to head for the brook Cherith. Despite the negative consequences on the land, the Lord would provide for His servant during the hardship. While at the brook, God provided food and water to Elijah.

Aside from his physical needs, I wonder what Elijah did while at the brook? He was alone, secluded. He knew the drought was going to last years. Did he take supplies with him? Aside from being God's prophet, did he have a hobby that he could possibly continue during the wait? It's interesting to consider the details not told to us in Scripture, but what I'm sure he did was actively listen for God's next directive.

This can be the most difficult part of following God: the time between the steps. It takes discipline to cling to the truth that God's timing is perfect. Getting restless within the wait is our natural reaction, because it seems God is inactive. But that's never the truth.

God is continuously managing the seen and unseen aspects of our lives. He just asks us to trust Him while we are waiting. Elijah trusted God and remained alert for His voice. We can do the same if we keep the truth in our hearts that God will speak. He will not let us miss the step if we are actively listening and desiring to be obedient to what the next step reveals.

Scripture doesn't say how long Elijah stayed at Cherith. At some point, he left at God's command and traveled to Zarephath. While the drought was still in progress, God remained faithful to Elijah and miraculously provided during that next step through a widow.

While you wait, try to relax between the steps, seek to serve God within the wait. Continue to listen for the next step in your assignment. All the while, be assured that God will provide as you trust His leading.

April 19 *A Jesus Encounter*

Mark 5:20

And he went away and began to proclaim in Decapolis what great things Jesus had done for him; and everyone marveled.

The Gospel writers tell of a man so evil and violent that the community kept him in chains and iron shackles in attempts to control him. But he was much too strong. Repeatedly breaking their efforts, he ran loose and naked.

He lived in the tombs, away from his family, crying out and cutting himself with rocks. He was greatly feared and overtly mentally ill due to demon possession. There wasn't one demon; Scripture tells us there were many. This man presented little hope for change—that's until he met Jesus.

In stark submission of the many to the person of Jesus, the demons pleaded with Jesus not to send them into the Abyss, the place John writes about in Revelation where Satan is imprisoned during the millennial reign of Christ. These dark angels possessing this man were terrified of Jesus, because they recognized Him, believed in Him, and revered His power. With one command, "Go!" Jesus sent them into a herd of two thousand pigs. The pigs ran down into the sea and drowned.

Jesus valued that one man more than two thousand animals, and He loved him despite the depth of the evil controlling his life. He personally intervened and saved him. And this man was different as a result. The community was shocked with the transformation that occurred in him. He clothed himself, acted civil, and spoke in his right mind. He begged to go with Jesus, but Jesus told him, "Go home to your people and report to them what great things the Lord has done for you, and how He had mercy on you" (verse 19).

There are men in prison today whom society has said there's no hope for. They are believed to be evil with no hope for rehabilitation. They are segregated, feared, and believed unable to live in society because of a history of violence or lengthy offenses. And they may have clearly earned their sentence. There's an unseen world where evil spirits operate, and they seek to destroy lives. But Scripture is clear about Jesus's love and willingness to redeem the worst of those influenced for evil. I cannot read about Jesus's healing of one similar and not believe there's always hope. Meeting Jesus changes everything.

April 20 — Patient Endurance

Hebrews 12:1

Therefore, since we have so great a cloud of witnesses surrounding us, let us also lay aside every encumbrance, and the sin which so easily entangles us, and let us run with endurance the race that is set before us.

To endure something indicates it isn't moving quickly. It almost indicates a grueling effort. So how is it that the writer of Hebrews can tell us to run with steadfast endurance? How does one run patiently, especially in a race? Running a race conjures the image of moving as fast as one can.

The idea put forth seems a contradiction, but when we consider it in a spiritual sense, our race demands determined, vibrant activity. The race is becoming more like Christ through holy living. We actively run toward Christ and away from sin.

But sin is a powerful competitor. Satan pursues us, enticing us to sin. He gnashes at our heels the whole way. He steadily keeps up with our pace; he patiently waits for us to tire or stumble. To run this life in a holy way requires endurance.

In this prison journey, worry is the sin which quickly entangles me. I have to battle this nearly daily. There are plenty of worries that come with prison, but I must consciously run toward what I know to be the truth of God's' word: Be anxious for nothing! I wake up daily, patiently enduring against this competitor.

Your race may be littered with other obstacles to trip you up and discourage you. The great thing is you have God on your side. He's your cheerleader and strength to keep winning the daily race. You have the men and women of Scripture to encourage you. You can read how their imperfections and sin didn't determine the outcome of the race. They stayed in the race with God's help and won the prize. Moses, David, Gideon, and the heroes of the faith as listed in Hebrews, chapter eleven, can be your mentors.

But most importantly, you have Jesus! When you're weary from the race of prison which seems to move agonizingly slow, remember what Jesus endured on your behalf. Ask Him for help, and He will lead you in triumphant victory.

April 21 Prison Christians

John 15:18-19

"If the world hates you, you know that it has hated Me before it hated you. If you were of the world, the world would love its own; but because you are not of the world, but I chose you out of the world, therefore the world hates you."

My husband frequently mentions how hard it is to live godly in prison. There's continuous encounters with temptation, oppression, and evil. Christian values aren't valued in prison. Choosing righteousness can cause problems. It becomes a form of persecution that's hard to escape, because there's nowhere to escape to.

Jesus has forewarned all believers that we will be in conflict with the world's values. Sin is human nature and this will never go away until Jesus returns. The world awards sin, glamorizes it, and accommodates it. It seems the more degraded the world becomes, prison follows the same course, because the officers and inmates enter the gates bringing their worldly values with them.

Prison persecution that my husband may face concerns my heart more than any I might ever receive on the outside. It's just another opportunity for harm to come to him. A simple exchange can escalate to violence. Prison etiquette demands certain things, and when not followed, relationships can be stressed, even the best of ones. There are expectations in prison, unwritten rules. Christianity conflicts with the prison culture, just as it does in the outside world.

Jesus encourages His disciples to look forward to the hope of eternal life when all things will be made right. Evil's time is finite. God doesn't rescue believers from the world, but He provides the Holy Spirit to help us live godly when the surrounding world doesn't. This promise doesn't change with prison. Your husband can take heart that the Holy Spirit hasn't left him to battle his surroundings alone. This truth along with your prayers are a powerful combination to help him overcome the world in which he lives.

April 22 Safe Steps

Psalm 119:105

Thy word is a lamp to my feet, and a light to my path.

I was walking my dog one early hour, my favorite part of the day. Everything was still and incredibly peaceful, except the tweeting of birds occasionally and the rustle among bushes as we passed. I particularly cherish the time, because I can focus on God's magnificent creation above while talking to Him. I usually make a comment on the moon if seen: "Oh, look, Lord, there's your moon," as if I were informing Him of something He might have missed.

On that early morning, there was no moon to be seen; a clouded sky obscured its view. Walking with flashlight in hand, yet not used, we made our way with the aid of intermittent light poles. Before I realized it, the ground beneath my feet changed and my footing slipped. Without the light, I had slowly veered from the straight path I thought I was walking and stepped off onto the grass. My sense of direction had been lost, because my sense of sight diminished.

This is how it is with God's word. Psalm 119 is about God's word—the Bible. The psalmist describes it as a lamp and a light. Spending time in God's word will guide you clearly through this journey called life. If prison seems to have sent you off into the grass, God wants to help you find your sure footing. His word is alive and never outdated. It's His word to you for encouragement, decision making, relationships, and anything you'll ever face in life, including prison.

But like my flashlight, I must use it to have it make a difference in my steps. I encourage you to read your Bible daily. The more you read, the more God will reveal Himself to you. Do not walk this prison path without God's help and direction. Chances are you'll likely end up off course and in a worst position than when you started.

God's plan for your life is perfect. He knows the steps that are safe—the right decisions to be made, how best to handle your husband, your finances, that difficult boss, but most importantly, how to fulfill your unique purpose in life. God hasn't left you because the darkness of prison has entered your life. Turn on the light of His word and see just how much peace comes from knowing where you're walking. **

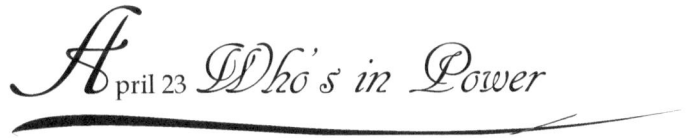

April 23 Who's in Power

Jeremiah 2:8

"The priests did not say, 'Where is the Lord?' And those who handle the law did not know Me; the rulers also transgressed against Me, and the prophets prophesied by Baal and walked after things that did not profit."

God was confronting the leaders of Judah who were responsible for leading the people. The priests, the prophets, and the rulers were no longer doing their part. They were to be the example and accountable to keeping God's law, and in doing so, keep the people faithful to the covenant originally delivered through Moses. But as was the history for the Israelites, they fell away from God and became corrupted by the people around them who didn't follow God.

I cannot help but think of many of the officers in the prison system who have been corrupted while supposedly serving in a position of power. By forsaking their oath, they have fallen for the things that do not ultimately profit. They perpetuate evil and exert unethical power. They are no longer trustworthy representatives of the uniform.

It's a frustrating aspect of prison. Officers make a lucrative profit on contraband, they take pleasure in demoralizing the men serving their time, and their promise to uphold the laws of the position is forsaken. All of this contributes to the bad that's already so prevalent.

But just as Jeremiah warned the Israelites that judgment would eventually come, the evils perpetuated by ungodly persons will one day be called into account. God remains ultimately in power, regardless of the powers He currently allows to remain in place on this earth, including in prisons.

Prison can seem a huge foe that seems impossible to impact for good, because those in charge actively seek ways to circumvent it. But this is only temporary. God's law, His values, and His kingdom will come. And this eternal outcome will victoriously place all persons under the authority of the righteous leadership of Christ.

April 24 True Knowing

Hebrews 12:3

For consider Him who has endured such hostility by sinners against Himself, so that you may not grow weary and lose heart.

Today marks the anniversary for a past arrest for myself. I spent a few days in jail before posting bond; yet, I faced prison ultimately. It was the most difficult experience I have ever been through. I experienced injustice and wrong impressions cast upon me. I was labeled and negatively viewed. One wrong decision seemed to erase all the good I had ever done in my life. And most frustrating to me, no one seemed even interested in hearing about the good. I was surrounded by hostile persons and attitudes.

My heart for the prisoner enlarged in a way I never expected. I experienced a small glimpse of what my husband and others experience daily—and it made me weak with sorrow for them. It was the epitome of not knowing how someone truly feels until you have walked in their shoes.

Weariness was great during that time. I was mentally and emotionally exhausted, yet the legal blows and injustices continued to come. My life was in shambles, and my energy was running on fumes.

I drew much comfort from Scripture such as today's verse. Jesus endured the worst of injustice and died as a result. He was openly criticized, hated, and targeted by devious men. He was mocked publically.

I took comfort knowing that Jesus knew exactly how I felt, because He had walked in my shoes. He endured far worse than what I ever had or will. So during that time when the Holy Spirit spoke to me from Scripture or through my circumstances, it came from someone I knew truly knew what I was experiencing. That's a special thing.

When you're going through your valleys, especially when opposition unfairly targets you, there's no greater comfort emotionally and mentally than a spiritual embrace by God to energize your mood to keep walking this journey. You can rest in knowing that the power that raised Jesus from the dead will confidently lead you out of the valley, because He loved you so much to go through His own. He endured when the hostility by sinners unjustly arrested, tortured, tried, and executed Him. He endured injustice for you. Please hang in there with Him now. He's faithful.

April 25 — Beyond the Shame

John 4:28-29

So the woman left her waterpot, and went into the city, and said to the men, "Come, see a man who told me all the things that I have done; this is not the Christ, is it?"

Prison can be a shameful reality. Not so much the place, but the crime which led to its reality. I experienced great shame with the arrest mentioned in yesterday's devotional for an action I didn't know came with such a severe consequence. Sadly, once arrested, my shame was broadcast in the newspaper, my employer was notified, and social media was lit up with the news. The shame I felt was numbing.

I didn't want to walk my dog, believing any passing car brought recognition of me. I averted my eyes from people I passed coming and going from stores. I tried to do all my errands at times when there would be few people, and hopefully, fewer opportunities to enter the path of someone who knew me. It was a prison without the physical restrictions, and I felt devalued.

I allowed shame to travel with me everywhere, despite God's forgiveness the moment I confessed. I had never experienced such a negative weight traveling through my days. But God in His intimate care of me wouldn't allow the situation to keep me in such a worthless state. In my Bible study, He compassionately reminded me through the story of the Samaritan woman that shame doesn't have the victory. Jesus redeems the shame and reaches out to others through it.

The Samaritan woman had many failed marriages, she was living with a man in sin, and her reality resulted in her altering her days to avoid public encounters. She was at the well to draw water at the hottest time of the day when most anyone else wouldn't go. Scripture leads us to believe it was only Jesus in the area after His disciples went ahead into town for food.

Jesus shared with her how she could have "living water," indicating salvation. She came to believe through the encounter that Jesus was in fact Christ whom was prophesied to come. And with her belief, she excitedly returned to town to tell others.

It struck me in my reading that this woman ignored the shame that had followed her to the well. She had met Jesus and she wanted everyone else to know they could meet Him too. Her desire to share Jesus trumped any negative past feelings about herself and what she knew others knew about her. She willingly sought out an audience for her testimony.

My perspective of the negative has now changed to one of redemption. I can confidently carry on with my life in the forgiveness I received through Jesus. I can use the situation to better someone else's life—hopefully yours—by sharing how God has loved me through the bad.

Jesus waits at the well for you too. He came to the well just for you. He desires to show you how your shame and current situation can be restored. And once you experience His living water, either for the first time in salvation or from a thirsty reminder as I needed, you'll feel valued and loved. And this will cover you, not your shame.

April 26 — Doing Life Together

Ecclesiastes 4:10

For if either of them falls, the one will lift up his companion. But woe to the one who falls when there is not another to lift him up.

I have always struggled with Christian community. Being an introvert, social situations have always been less attractive to me than spending time alone. In many ways, I realize that my marriage to a man serving a life sentence fits better with my personality than if I were needier for companionship. More amazing evidence of God's sovereignty.

But I also realize that God designed us to be in community—introvert or not. We need other people. And if a Christian, other believers are the people who should be standing ready to assist when we have a need.

God has routinely and symbolically slapped my hand for avoiding community and not fostering relationships with persons within the church. A church "home" as an adult has often eluded me. Sadly, God got my attention in a severe way through my arrest and legal issues.

I was thrown into a crisis. I experienced the trauma of the arrest and jail time. I bonded out to discover I had lost my job as a result. I lost my housing, because with no income I couldn't afford rent. My life was spilled out in pieces under the foreboding reality that I also faced prison. I do not recall being more frightened in all my life. But what I also experienced for the first time was the importance of community.

In my case, my (former) coworkers poured over me love and support in ways never expected. Each new day brought another encounter of this. I was truly taken aback by how they rallied around me during that time. Financially, logistically, prayerfully—people that I never knew cared so much came out of the woodwork and were there for me.

I got the message. I got to experience what true community is all about. Those coworkers were Christians, and I couldn't help but realize they were the church in my case. Oh, yes, I attended church, but was not connected relationally. God gave me an example of why getting involved and developing relationship in a church is so important. My loner tendencies will not serve me well in a crisis. Just as so, I may need to be that person helping another when crisis hits.

A prison marriage can be an isolating experience. It may take boldness to seek out support. God, however, desires you to be involved in Christian fellowship. You may need to start out in small ways if you struggle with this area as I do. These relationships take time and must be nurtured. My coworkers' responses would never have been the same if they didn't know me personally from having spent time with me and sharing experiences. Find a church and begin.

†

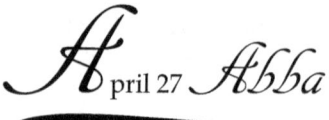
April 27 Abba

Romans 8:15

For you have not received a spirit of slavery leading to fear again, but you have received a spirit of adoption as sons by which we cry out, "Abba! Father!"

When I learned that I was facing prison, I was desperate for rescue. I cried out to God from my fear, reminding Him that I was His daughter. I needed Him to be my protective Daddy. I wanted to run to Him and have Him take care of everything. The next evening after my cries, I had a dream that my father (who died in 2000) had been resurrected. In the dream, I ran to him, and he hugged me close. I asked him, "Did God tell you that you were going to be resurrected?" He responded, "A Lion told me."

It struck me in the following days that God spoke to me through that dream. Jesus, my resurrected Savior, was also my Daddy. I could run to Him just as I could my earthly father.

"Abba" is the equivalent to "Daddy." It reflects the intimate, secure, and almost childlike relationship to a father. Complete dependence. Paul in today's Scripture is reminding the Christians in Rome of this relationship. As believers in Jesus, they had been adopted as sons of God. With this adoption, they could boldly call upon God as their Daddy. If you're a believer in Jesus, you have this right to.

Take comfort in this. Whatever you're facing, whatever prison difficulty, whatever frightening situation, your Abba stands waiting with His arms open. He will hug security into your spirit to remind you that you're His daughter. He's your protector. He will take care of you through this difficult time.

After that dream and understanding of God's message to me, I still fought fear. But I only needed to meditate on the truth to calm the anxiety creeping into my heart. Like the Romans, I needed a reminder. I needed to focus my thoughts on the truth, to remind myself that my Daddy was actively taking care of the situation for my good.

It's okay to cry out as often as you need. That's what your heavenly Father—your Abba—desires of you. He so loves you and wants to show Himself strong on your behalf. Run to Him.

April 28 — Silent Hours

Psalm 39:12

"Hear my prayer, O Lord, and give ear to my cry; do not be silent at my tears; for I am a stranger with Thee, a sojourner like all my fathers."

My smart phone has a feature that allows me to set "silent hours." These are scheduled times that the phone will not ring or ding or make any alert according to a set of rules that I set. I love the feature! I love knowing that I'll not be interrupted or awakened during those hours. I also love that it allows exception to this. I can specify certain numbers which will ring or text through. This ensures that I'll not miss important calls from important people.

Have you ever felt like God must have His silent hours set and you aren't on the list to break through when you try to reach Him? These are those maddening times of silence when you desperately want to hear from God, to have your prayers answered, yet there's no indication that your prayers are getting through. You may wonder if He's even aware that you're calling out to Him.

David wrote many heart-felt psalms when he desperately sought God's presence. There were times when he feared God was far from him. When convicted of sin or pursued by enemies, David was a man who cried out to God for rescue and help. There are many other writings of David expressing that he often had to wait on God's deliverance or answer. This led to the many psalms of praise in the end.

The silent hours before God are hard places to be. It's a crucible of faith. David learned that God is faithful through the wait and silence. He acknowledges God's power to know his situation intimately and His ability to help. Why God chooses to be silent must fall under the same mysteries that demand that we trust He's in control and is working behind the scenes in His perfect way.

Scripture encourages us to keep seeking God, keep praying, and keep trusting. God knows exactly what you're facing. He hears your cries for help. He's working in the situation. If you're a Christian, you can undoubtedly know that you're on His VIP list, entitling you access to Him at all times. He will lovingly break through at the most perfect time.

April 29 When It Seems Unfair

Jonah 4:4

And the Lord said, "Do you have good reason to be angry?"

Luke 15:27-28

"And he said to him, 'Your brother has come, and your father has killed the fattened calf, because he has received him back safe and sound.' But he became angry, and was not willing to go in; and his father came out and began entreating him."

Where does envy rank in your life? Do you have trouble being happy for other women who seem to have the life that has been taken from you because of prison? Are you bitter about your situation or toward your husband? Do you think that you deserve better or others do not deserve what they have?

Jonah couldn't be happy for God's forgiveness toward Nineveh. He believed they didn't deserve it. The prodigal son's brother couldn't be happy for his brother's return and the father's blessing on him. He felt that he was entitled to better treatment and his brother didn't deserve such favor. Both he and Jonah would have likely taken joy and had a sense of peace if disaster and ill will resulted, somehow satisfying what they felt was justice.

Being a prisoner's wife is fertile ground for envy, jealousy, and pride to take root. You have to be content with the life that you now have. You have to believe in the value of your life despite prison. You have to believe that your life has been perfectly orchestrated by God and it's special because it's meant just for you, not anyone else.

Someone else's life and apparent blessings and favor you see doesn't mean that your life is void of the same future—in time. God orchestrates all our lives with an eternal view. Trusting Him with where you are now goes a long way toward being content and reining envy's efforts to keep you bitter.

Pride and the feeling of entitlement will blind you to your own blessings. It diminishes your reverence for God and His right to be sovereign over everything—the good and the bad. It's impossible to love as God commands with envy, jealousy, or pride in your heart.

The genuine emotions for another can be judged by the amount of peace in your heart. Are you at peace when you see a wife embrace her husband at the gate at his release when you're waiting in line to visit yours? Are you oddly satisfied when you learn of a lady's "free-world" marriage—which you have always envied—having problems? How you feel in either scenario reflects the amount of love in your heart.

None of this is easy! You aren't a terrible person if you struggle with this. It's human nature to a great extent. But you'll stifle your own joy and diminish the life that God has blessed you with if you focus on what you're lacking or what you see in others that you do not currently have. You're walking a unique path. No one can walk it for you, but no one can experience the treasure of blessings God has reserved just for you along the way.

April 30 In God's Eyes

Matthew 19:6

"Consequently they are no longer two, but one flesh. What therefore God has joined together, let no man separate."

I used to feel it was the only thing about me that people saw: She's the lady who married a convict. There was a time when I felt as though every interaction was clouded by that known headline that I was sure was running across my forehead. Walking away, I usually still felt as though eyes were on me. There must have been something written there too I was sure. Every conversation had to be negotiated to steer it away from the discussion of love or to prepare for a response to the questioning that could be seen—or believed to be—coming toward me.

There are times when I'm the focus of others' considerations of my situation through the eventual questioning I encounter if I tarry in a conversation. Learning I have been the subject of gossip sadly confirms my vulnerability is further justified at times. But I still expect the condemning responses of others too diligently.

I know there's an ambulance chaser in most of us, and I expect my relationship is some version of this in the curiosity it creates. The looks, the gossip, and even the research into my husband's crimes looking for that information that puts fuel in the ambulance—it all accompanies me on this journey. The impact can have me feeling as if I were the one judged guilty.

Not talking at all about my husband often becomes my solution to this fear. But it leaves me in solitude and unable to share the joy and blessing that my husband is to me.

I do know that my marriage and husband aren't beyond hope or value. Yours isn't either. Both have extreme value in the eyes of God—and His are the only ones that ultimately matter.

Not everyone is interested in seeing your marriage from this perspective. Chasing the ambulance is more interesting, and it remains easier to condemn a mug shot than someone you know more personally.

God's eyes see a relationship that represents His love for the church. He sees a covenant that no man should separate. He sees two people remaining faithful to their vows regardless of circumstance. God's perspective helps you walk confidently away from the murmuring or knowing looks, or to sit in the air of jokes about inmates or prison without it uprooting you from the solid foundation in knowing God is all for you and your marriage.

May 1 Restoration

Joel 2:25

"Then I will make up to you for the years that the swarming locust has eaten, the creeping locust, the stripping locust, and the gnawing locust, my great army which I sent among you."

I walked to the mailbox with the dog, accomplishing two tasks with one trip. The dog took her usual direction in a portion of the yard in front of the house. I leisurely allowed her to explore the familiar area, while I mindlessly looked about the sky, across the road, and eventually to the ground. I startled to see plants covered in huge grasshoppers. It could be described as a swarm. I made our exit hurriedly, yet gingerly, through the crop of disgusting critters, careful not to disturb their activity. A few hours later, I looked at one specific plant, and it was eaten down to stubs. A plant nearly a foot high was no more—and so was the grasshoppers. They had moved on to new growth.

Joel describes the destruction of the land by locusts. God rendered judgment because of Israel's sin and unfaithfulness. Their land would be unfruitful due to the locusts and drought. It would be total destruction as indicated by the waves of locusts in four intervals. The plague would devastate life and land.

Yet the mercy of God remained. He promised restoration of all that was lost. His blessings would once again rain down on Israel both physically and spiritually. Life and land would be restored. He promised this, because Israel was His chosen people.

When I saw the locust swarm in my yard, aside from the immediate disgust, I also couldn't help but be encouraged. Sounds crazy I suppose. It was what I needed to "hear" that day so badly. I was at a place in life wondering if I would ever recuperate from damage that God allowed to happen. It was His reminder to me, His daughter, that He would piece my life back together. In fact, He would make it even better than before.

You may see a swarm of locusts over your life right now. They have eaten away at everything good. There may be parts of your life that remain only in jagged stubs. This may be from relentless consequences of a bad choice or circumstances merely allowed by God. Either way, if you're a child of God's, He can make up for the years that the locusts have eaten.

And it may be years. I'm glad God's mercy isn't time limited, because I need a lot of years restored! And my hope rests in this. God reminded me that day in the yard, and continues to do so as I need. Consider this devotional your reminder.

May 2 Peaceful Living

Romans 12:18

If possible, so far as it depends on you, be at peace with all men.

I remember when I told my great aunt about my marriage to a man incarcerated. All seemed okay once she got over the shock. She stumbled over her words as most people do, mustering those surface comments you say in such situations: "If you're happy, I'm happy for you." But a little while later, I got a call from my mother, asking me to please call my great aunt and try to reassure her of things. Apparently, she called crying to my mother over the situation. I knew her reaction was one of concern for the difficulty that awaited me. She was not going to disown me or avoid me at the holidays.

I believe relationships with family members that have been typically good will weather the storm of prison. However, if your family is your biggest critic, Paul's instruction above is a huge challenge. It's hard enough to deal with criticism from others, but these pains can run deeper within families. Arguments spawn from bitterness. Resentment can distance you further. Being at peace may seem an impossibility.

You want your family's support and acceptance, but if they are entrenched in their position, let it be. Seek peace. Do not fuel the arguments. Proverbs further teaches us in 17:14: "The beginning of strife is like letting out water." So abandon the quarrel before it breaks out. Confidently continue in your marriage, include the subject of your husband as you feel comfortable. In the end, let your marriage be its own testimony.

But this doesn't mean you have to put yourself in hurtful situations, repeatedly. To keep the peace, you may need to avoid some individuals until the immediate hurt lessens. There may be relatives that you maintain a distance from if they are the ones stirring unrest. We can express more liberty with our words with family, and if charged with anger or hurt, the conversations likely will not go well. Take some time apart and see how it goes later.

Jesus taught a lot about relationships. He taught about not repaying evil for evil, considering others before yourself, loving and praying for those who persecute you. This verse in Romans blends with the others. It isn't an easy assignment, but thankfully, you're only responsible for your part in keeping peace.

May 3 The End Is Better

Ecclesiastes 7:8

The end of a matter is better than its beginning; patience of spirit is better than haughtiness of spirit.

I love this verse. It attaches itself to hope and keeps me assured that despite how hard things may be, the future will be better. Life and Scripture reflect this truth for us.

The race of the steadfast isn't in vain. A farmer harvests at a later time than he plants. The ant works hard and stores its food so there will be plenty later. The caterpillar strains against the cocoon to exit as a butterfly. There's an anticipation of hardship and toil to receive the good in the end.

This is particularly encouraging when there seems no earthly reward to exchange for the current difficulty. There's no guarantee for a comfortable life, but there can be joy and hope, because we know what awaits in the end.

If we see no good outcome, we still understand that this world isn't our home. This allows us to keep walking forward through the difficult days.

I kept this in mind when my uncle was approaching his execution night. For the bad he experienced in life, sitting in the electric chair seemed not a better end to anything. But he had his salvation. So his years of negative experiences, his years on death row, didn't remove the hope secured for him after this life was over. The end remained better.

This is an assurance that all Christians have, whether it's seen in this life or later in heaven. There's no difficulty that hope doesn't trump.

Prison must be seen from this perspective. The nature of a prison sentence is the anticipated difficulty before there's any freedom. The end will be better than the beginning. Let this encourage you when your hope slips away from you. Hope always brings you faithfully to the end—and the end will be good.

May 4 No Worry Too Great

I Peter 1:13

Therefore, gird your minds for action, keep sober in spirit, fix your hope completely on the grace to be brought to you at the revelation of Jesus Christ.

Peter spends the first part of his writing encouraging the Christians of his day to keep their salvation in mind, especially considering the persecution in the area. If they focused on this hope, even the threat of death could be faced with confidence. This encouragement can be applied to anything that we face in life, from the daily struggles to the more serious life-threatening events. The verse above I have used to combat my sin of worry.

I'm a worrier by nature. I contemplate. I consider scenarios from all aspects of possibilities, and I try to anticipate results from the hypothetical. These tendencies in themselves can be positive when making decisions, but when used to merely mull over concerns, they lead to the unproductive state of worry. Worry then leads to anxiety. Anxiety then leads to physical effects such as fever blisters, headaches, and acne.

According to Peter, my mind is the key. I need to control my thoughts. When worry creeps in, I need to direct my thoughts to my salvation. If this is the key when facing such things as persecution and death as was the

Christians then, and still do today in parts of the world, this should surely be applicable for the day-to-day worries that I face.

And it does work. I accept that whatever is imposing worry upon me can never be so great or detrimental to remove my salvation. I have the hope of a future when all these yucky, difficult days are behind me. This brings peace.

Consider trying this yourself. Write this verse on an index card, post it where you can see it daily. Memorize it. When you find your mind going into overdrive with concern, rein it in. Do not allow your thoughts to race undisciplined through every possible negative end that could occur. There's no worry too great for God's grace.

May 5 Be Not Ignorant

II Corinthians 2:11

In order that no advantage be taken of us by Satan; for we are not ignorant of his schemes.

My husband has been in prison nearly twenty-five years at the time of this writing. He has never touched a computer. He only saw a "live" cell phone for the first time within the last few years. In the days of dial-up internet, I would complain to him about the slow speed, but the next week, receive a list of things he wanted me to download, print, and send to him. He never conveyed an understanding that his request would take hours, because he really didn't understand. I had to take a deep breath and again explain why it would be awhile to do. This frustrated him, which then frustrated me.

My husband has lived life through mostly secondhand avenues. He still does pretty well at keeping up with current issues, but often he has no practical application. He tries to give me advice or help me make decisions, but he truly has no basis from which to judge in many cases. Satan will use such situations in his ammunition to cause a rift between us.

Satan is constantly looking for avenues to destroy marriages and godly relationships. Little arguments can multiply. Discontentment can grow as a result. In the verse today, Paul is encouraging the church to be wise to Satan's schemes. In this case, a member had sinned and had expressed repentance, but apparently, the church was unwilling to accept him back. Paul saw the danger of Satan capitalizing on this response. He associates the division within the church as part of Satan's schemes to destroy it.

We read popularly in Scripture that Satan prowls around like a roaring lion, seeking someone to destroy (I Peter 5:8). We are told to put on the full armor of God to withstand the schemes of the devil (Ephesians 6:11). We are told to resist the devil and he will flee from us (James 4:7).

We cannot be ignorant of our enemy. My husband's ignorance on certain matters cannot tempt me to fall for Satan's schemes to use such little nuisances to dig that wider rift. Satan spoon feeds us his schemes generally to catch us ignorant of what's happening until the damage is done.

Be wise. Be alert. Do not let Satan sneak into your relationship. Do not allow him to take the difficulties of maintaining your marriage and use them to separate you more than the bars and razor wire already do.

May 6 Remaining Close

Genesis 2:24

For this cause a man shall leave his father and his mother, and shall cleave to his wife; and they shall become one flesh.

As the lady on the outside, you may find the hurt from repeated fights and the exacerbated problems created by prison subside as you substitute your energies from the prison system to a typical lifestyle, going back to things you did as a single person. It may seem harmless at first, but take caution. The small exceptions from the wrong heart are enough for poison to seep through any weakened framework in your marriage. Any newly defined limits or heart condition can cultivate seeds of a variety of temptations that will poison your marriage with Satan's goal being to ultimately destroy it.

For many marriages, routine happens with time. Passion then often leaves. Emotional distance becomes the next step away. When there's distance, a risk of that void being filled by things or persons other than your husband arises. New enjoyment is found in things other than your marriage.

Prison already promotes this distance. Prison has an abundance of routines that create familiarity. Our marriages seem to begin at a deficit in both these areas, so Satan is closer to the goal from the beginning. It becomes a greater challenge for us to keep that void small by not walking in the opposite direction of our husbands — emotionally or physically. Letting other things or people distract our attention cultivates this wrong path.

I'm not saying that you should never go out with friends or you should never have fun with others. The danger comes, when in doing so, your marriage—by default—receives the leftovers of your time and energy. This may be a sign your heart is drifting from your marriage. It becomes easier and easier to make that shift away from the close connection with your husband the more it's allowed to happen.

I'm sure this definitely sounds like work. But any marriage demands work to keep the passion alive and the relationship fresh. A prison marriage is uniquely challenged in this. However, there's a richer level to love when connection and enjoyment remain visit to visit, phone call to phone call, or letter to letter. Your marriage can achieve this when it remains all about you and your husband, helped by God.

May 7 Betrayal

Luke 22:21

"But behold, the hand of the one betraying Me is with Me on the table."

When lying down that night to sleep, my heart was hurting. I had received several letters earlier that day from my husband, most of which were not the supportive, empathetic expressions of a man trying to show his wife love and care. They were rather full of anger and ugly words. I felt betrayed. The one person I longed to hear from, to share my struggles—which were enormous at that time—was nowhere in the words I read. I was numb in disbelief that he was so cold toward everything I was going through and treated me so unlovingly.

My habit when I lie down to sleep is to read a passage of Scripture. I have no pattern. I just pick up my small New Testament and read. The goal isn't to study, but merely to spend a few moments with God before sleeping. That night, however, God met me in the most intimate way.

My Bible opened to the passage in Luke when Judas betrays Jesus. There was no mistaking the warm message to my hurting heart: Jesus understood my pain, and He was reaching out to basically hold me and love me when I was hurting so badly.

Judas was one of Jesus's disciples. He was chosen. Jesus loved him. Yet despite being in Jesus's inner circle and sitting under His teaching, this man betrayed Him. Judas's actions led to Jesus's arrest and execution. Jesus knew Judas's heart. He knew that Judas would go through with his plans. Yet He still experienced the raw emotions of a friend's betrayal.

That's why the message to me was so comforting. I knew Jesus knew what I was feeling. God's loving nature faithfully showed up to give me what I needed in that moment. It made the disappointment and hurt more tolerable, because I knew God was right there going through it with me—and He understood perfectly.

You may feel betrayed on this prison journey. Your husband may do things that make you feel abandoned on your side of the fence. His environment may breed harsh reactions that are unloving. Always remember that Jesus endured rejection and betrayal. He knows your pain intimately, because He's your Creator. But He also experienced the same while on this earth. He longs to carry you through the hard places you may be right now.

May 8 When It Hurts

Hosea 1:2

When the Lord first spoke through Hosea, the Lord said to Hosea, "Go, take to yourself a wife of harlotry, and have children of harlotry; for the land commits flagrant harlotry, forsaking the Lord."

Hosea had a very grievous assignment: He was to marry an unfaithful woman—intentionally. He was God's prophet to Israel, and Israel was unfaithful. God used Hosea's life as an illustration of His relationship to Israel. Israel was unfaithful, but God continued to have compassion on them and desire their whole-hearted return. There were to be consequences for their "harlotry," but God never gave up on them or quit loving them.

Hosea married Gomer, and as anticipated, she remained unfaithful. She had children by another man (or different men). She left Hosea to pursue different lovers. Yet, Hosea continued to love her, sought her out, and brought her back home.

Gomer didn't stray after marrying Hosea; she merely continued in her lifestyle *despite* their marriage. Her character was immoral to begin with. But she was not beyond redemption, nor was their marriage. This is what God was communicating to Israel. He loved them and longed to restore their relationship. He wanted Israel to quit worshipping idols and return to Him, the one true God.

You may have found yourself in a marriage to some version of a Gomer. You may have faithfully stayed with your husband prior to and now within prison, yet he still strays. He may still be unfaithful in his words to you, his promises, and his actions. Your pain is great.

If this describes you, please seek God's guidance. God may have special plans in how He wants to use you in your husband's life. You might be the exact tool God will use to bring your husband to repentance. There may a grand blessing at the end of all this.

There's no way I can say how your situation will end. I do know that God can work mightily through a faithful wife even in the presence of an unfaithful husband, whether he be unfaithful emotionally, spiritually, or physically. God can provide you the answer to His will in your situation. Seek Him through Scripture and prayer. Healing of your hurt will involve His love for both you and your husband. Be faithful to God, and He will work out the rest according to His perfect will.

May 9 Vow to Be Kind

Proverbs 3:3

Do not let kindness and truth leave you; bind them around your neck, write them on the tablet of your heart.

A wedding ceremony includes the exchanging of rings. They represent the lifelong commitment to each other. It's a bright and hope-filled day. And as with most weddings, the love on that day is bubbling with emotions and the couple sees through their figurative glasses, roses covering everything, including their spouse. It should be joyful and carefree. But when I read the above verse, I think this verse would make great advice to the new couple.

Kindness is a simple etiquette that oftentimes becomes less practiced as our marriages move forward. We relax. We become comfortable with each other, showing our good and bad sides without much censorship.

This proverb is telling us that it's wise to be kind. Such a small gesture can infuse positive energy into your marriage. Its removal can stir up arguments in an instant or slowly poison your relationship. Using it encourages respect and shows love. The book of Proverbs is full of wisdom about how to use words and how to behave. Kindness is powerful.

I usually reflect on this after I have failed at it! It becomes so easy to let words fly out or an attitude act out. It truly is a discipline for me when I anticipate conflict churning between me and my husband. I say to myself, "Be kind, be kind," as I usually take a deep breath in that moment.

The writer speaks to keeping kindness close, let it become a part of who you are. Like a wedding band, let it be a reminder and representation of your love for each other. You likely will not have a literal kindness necklace, but if written in your heart, it will be seen just the same.

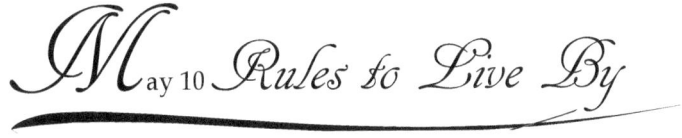

May 10 Rules to Live By

Leviticus 25:18

'You shall thus observe My statutes, and keep My judgments, so as to carry them out, that you may live securely on the land.'

There's difficulty in living by all the nuisance rules established by the DOC. They are tedious and wearing on both our husbands and ourselves. They usually do not encourage connection or contentment on this journey. They usually exasperate us in their presence. But God calls us to live under the authorities in our lives—willingly.

This is a challenge outside of prison, to keep every rule we encounter in life. How many of us drive a few miles over the speed limit at times or in certain situations? The smaller the offense, the more we minimize our thinking to "it's no big deal."

In Old Testament times as reflected in today's verse, God was all about the little things too. He provided Israel with all kinds of rules to live by. In this case, He was giving them instructions on land use. In exchange for their obedience, He would bless them.

But God was always more interested in their heart's obedience, than their actions. That's why a repeating refrain throughout Scripture is God calling His people to love Him with all their heart, soul, and body. God tests our hearts by our obedience to His commandments.

I have been tested by God in this area and have failed. I have justified actions, gave into my husband's ungodly requests, and have grieved God's heart. I have suffered consequences for living outside of God's will. They have been hard lessons, but God only calls me to obedience for my good, and He disciplines me for my good.

So thankfully, I'm forgiven and once again trying to live by rules placed on me by the authorities of this world—and honoring God by my actions. My heart desires obedience, and I'm more content within the myriad of rules now than in the past. Living by the rules brings freedom and security to my heart, because I know it pleases God.

May 11 Eye for an Eye

Deuteronomy 19:21

"Thus you shall not show pity: life for life, eye for eye, tooth for tooth, hand for hand, foot for foot."

Supporters of harsh, equal retribution often reference this verse from the Old Testament. They use it in response often to death penalty cases. They want a life for a life. They want the criminal to "get what he deserves." In context, however, this verse actually refers to a person who has provided false testimony. During Old Testament times that person would receive whatever punishment the accused would have received if found guilty. This law was to deter a person from making false accusations against someone else.

People who quote this verse in ignorance usually show no further familiarity of what Jesus taught in the New Testament. I say this to encourage those of you who have to endure such comments because of your husband's crime. People make comments from their hurt and from a heart that doesn't know Jesus.

There are hundreds of laws from the Old Testament that would seem ridiculous to us and extreme. A woman caught in adultery could be stoned to death. A rebellious son could be stoned to death. Why take one law, like the one above, and discard the rest? Is it right to use a verse out of context and argue that someone should follow it?

Words hurt. People say things without considering the impact on someone else or even the truth of what they are saying. When others say things that harm your heart, try to filter it through what Jesus would say. Jesus revolutionized the thinking of His day. He taught grace and truth. Jesus challenged the executioners who had no sin to cast the first stone at the adulterous woman. He compared the angry hearts of men to those who physically kill.

It becomes clear that caution must be used when listening to or speaking from Scripture. Know the truth and do not absorb the hurtful words of others who do not know it.

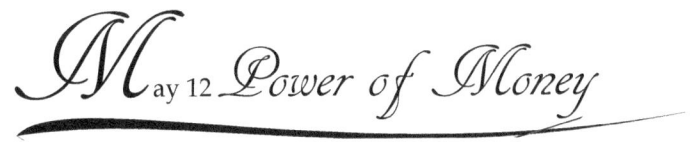
May 12 Power of Money

Judges 16:5

And the lords of the Philistines came up to her, and said to her, "Entice him, and see where his great strength lies and how we may overpower him that we may bind him to afflict him. Then we will each give you eleven hundred pieces of silver."

Samson had great physical strength, but Delilah's love of money was stronger. She agreed to betray Samson for a large sum of money. And she was persistent. Time after time she manipulated and badgered him with her words. He finally gave in. This cost him dearly.

It seems Samson's lust and backslidden lifestyle blinded his heart to just how low he had fallen. He immersed himself in a foreign, pagan culture. He sought after pagan women against God's law for an Israelite. The union with Delilah drew him further away from the Lord. In the end, the sin of her heart overpowered his heart for godly things. The Philistine lords provided her an offer she couldn't refuse. And with no mitigating values of God, she accepted without any apparent reservation.

The outcome of Delilah's payment was Samson's hair being cut which went against the Nazirite vow he was under, his eyes being gouged out, his imprisonment, and his untimely death. Delilah was likely killed in the collapse of the stadium (verse 30) with no amount of money being able to save her.

Money remains a driving force for unethical and illegal behavior today. Prison is full of this foundational motivation which led to incarceration. It's the primary tool to participate in a sinful lifestyle like drug use. Despite a cashless economy within most prisons, money remains a key to bartering. Your husband may be a Samson. He may be participating fully in the lifestyle of prison, blind to the continuing slide to what will be his eventual bottom. Money may be enticing him to do evil like Delilah. It may seem like an undefeatable power. But it isn't.

Keeping close to God is the key to your husband resisting the harmful influences of money and those who love it more than righteousness. Pray for his strength to resist the temptations. Pray that God would send him a Christian friend to help combat the negative influences. Pray for his conviction when he strays. And always pray for God's mercy.

Even when Samson reached his bottom, God was merciful when he repented. God restored Samson's strength. He can do the same for your husband.

May 13 Watchful Faith

I Kings 18:43-44

And he said to his servant, "Go up now, look toward the sea." So he went up and looked and said, "There is nothing." And he said, "Go back" seven times. And it came about at the seventh time, that he said, "Behold, a cloud as small as a man's hand is coming up from the sea." And he said, "Go up, say to Ahab, 'Prepare your chariot and go down, so that the heavy shower does not stop you.'"

The Lord had told Elijah that He was sending rain. The drought was finally coming to an end. The people and land had been under judgment for three years due to idolatry perpetrated by King Ahab. Baal worship hallmarked Ahab's reign over Israel. Elijah prophesied the drought, and now God was sending him back to Ahab to inform him rain was on its way.

After Elijah bowed and prayed for the rain to come, he sent his servant to look out toward the sea to confirm the coming storm. But there was nothing. There's no indication he doubted or showed panic that possibly the Lord was not going to fulfill His promise in this case. Elijah's confidence in God remained rock solid. He continued to pray and he sent his servant back to check on the outcome. His servant had to go seven times before the smallest cloud was finally spotted.

Elijah was one of God's great prophets, yet he didn't receive an immediate outcome to his prayer. He knew God was faithful, and he continued to pray faithfully. He continued in his expectation that God would show up. And God did—as promised.

It takes courage to have faith when so much is on the line. Especially, when many eyes are upon you. To speak faith over an outcome that remains in the future invites criticism and embarrassment if it fails to arrive. It takes courage to stand confident when no evidence of an answer to your prayer is seen. But if God has given you a promise, you can trust that it will arrive.

You may be watching in faith for God to work in your husband's life. You're waiting for possibly his heart to change. But you may still be returning from each visit with no rain in sight. Nothing seems to be changing; his heart is still possibly dry and barren.

Keep praying and watching! God is faithful. You'll not always understand why God chooses to delay, but you can trust Him with your outcome. The rain will arrive. And it will be at the perfect time and in the perfect way.

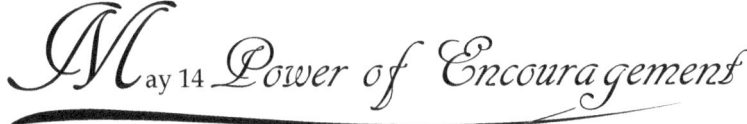 May 14 Power of Encouragement

Ezra 10:4

"Arise! For this matter is your responsibility, but we will be with you; be courageous and act."

This verse quotes the words of Shecaniah to Ezra when Ezra was deep in grief over the sins of Israel. God had orchestrated their return to Jerusalem and freedom from Babylon exile; however, Israel had forsaken the command of God to not intermarry with the pagan people around them. Ezra discovered that this had happened. In response, he wept before the Lord and remained distressed.

It seems Ezra was so overwhelmed emotionally that he was paralyzed in his grief. He was so ashamed and burdened by the guilt of the people's actions. He understood the grace and mercy extended to Israel by God with their freedom from Babylon, so the knowledge of their rebellion in light of God's love profoundly grieved him.

Shecaniah recognized that Ezra needed to move from his grief to hope in God's lovingkindness to forgive and restore. He acknowledged Israel's great sin as well, but was assured that God had not forsaken them. He believed in God's forgiveness and prompted Ezra to grab hold of that and rise up.

The people looked to Ezra as their priest and leader. He had led the first group of Israelites home from Babylon. Shecaniah knew the people needed to hear from Ezra. He still needed to lead and put the people back on track. With God's mercy, Shecaniah knew this was possible. He just needed to encourage Ezra in this.

Ezra did what Shecaniah encouraged. He rose up, called the leaders to action, and reconciled their relationship with God. Just as so, you may need to be a Shecaniah to someone. There may be another lady you know who is new in her grief related to prison. She needs hope. She needs encouragement to rise up and believe in God's mercy.

You may be that lady needing hope. Let me be your Shecaniah. There remains hope! God is loving, compassionate, and merciful. Your grief is okay, but do not let it paralyze you. God welcomes your repentance and tears either for yourself or your husband. God knows your heart and is willing to meet you in your grief and restore what prison or sin has taken.

May 15 For the One

Matthew 11:4-5

And Jesus answered and said to them, "Go and report to John what you hear and see: the blind receive sight and the lame walk, the lepers are cleansed and the deaf hear, and the dead are raised up, and the poor have the gospel preached to them."

    I think we can sometimes get immune to things we know about Jesus and read in Scripture, not always absorbing the awesomeness of what we're reading. Jesus did some astounding things for individuals when He walked the region where He was living. The verses above are His response to John the Baptist's question to confirm the Jesus he was hearing about was the Jesus whom he prophesied.

    Reading the affirmation of miracles Jesus reported back to John, I cannot help but consider the individual blessing on each person. Imagine being blind, then seeing perfectly again. Imagine having a permanent, life-altering disability, then being healed of it. Imagine having your face disfigured from leprosy, then healed. Imagine being deaf, then hearing the voices of loved ones, nature, and music. Imagine being raised from the dead and getting another opportunity to right relationships and witness to loved ones.

    Jesus was all about the individuals—the one. Even within a crowd, miracles were bestowed individually. He saves each person, individually. This is one of His awesome characteristics. He looks intently on the person, knows each heart personally. The power of God was bestowed on the person deaf, disabled, blind, poor, or dead.

    Each person who encountered Jesus's healing during His ministry obtained a fabulous testimony. But I'm sure they could never quite capture in words the joy they felt when their body was renewed. The amazing things God does in our lives settle into a part of who we are that cannot be easily explained to another. Nothing seems adequate.

    That's the special intimacy we get to enjoy with God. And His attributes have not changed. Jesus is your personal Savior. He intervenes personally in your life, because He loves you. God sent Jesus personally to you so you could be with Him forever. And He still does miracles! Meditate on these verses and consider the awesomeness of Jesus.

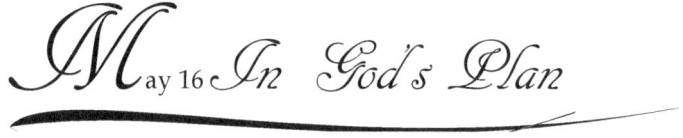

May 16 In God's Plan

Esther 5:1

Now it came about on the third day that Esther put on her royal robes and stood in the inner court of the king's palace in front of the king's rooms, and the king was sitting on his royal throne in the throne room, opposite the entrance to the palace.

Queen Esther had been informed by her cousin that the Jews were planned for annihilation by a devious ploy of Haman of the king's court. Esther was a Jew and she grieved for the fate of her people. She planned to go before the king, risking her own life, to request favor for her people. The verse above describes her approach to the king. He accepted her approach and questioned what she wanted. In preparing her request, she planned a series of feasts for the king, inviting Haman too. She would divulge the ploy to the king in Haman's presence.

What's recounted in the prior chapter is while in the midst of her preparations for the feasts, she and her maidens fasted. For three days, they went without food and drink. So when Esther approached the king "on the third day" as written in the verse above, she had not eaten or drunk the prior three days.

Fasting is part of petitioning God. The deprivation of food or drink disciplines a person's thoughts on God. Prayer is taken deeper within the sacrifice. Esther and her people's earnest appeal to God matched the severity of their need.

The irony of Esther's plan is that while preparing a feast, abounding in wine and delicacies, she refrained from both. Fasting is a discipline. How much more when surrounded with preparing a banquet!

I admire the strength of Esther. I admire her faithfulness to her people. I admire her wisdom. I admire her courage to trust God with the outcome. In the end, Haman was executed for his plot and the Jewish people were vindicated.

God's sovereignty is seen throughout the book of Esther. Esther's situation was very frightening. An enemy was directly attacking her life and persons she loved. But God had arranged all the details before the crisis hit to bring about the divine result.

God's sovereignty hasn't changed. He's in control over everything that touches your life and your husband's. Nothing takes Him by surprise, and He already has the plan of escape. If you're in a prison crisis, be assured that it has been filtered through the hands of God. He already has your rescue planned. He desires for you to seek Him during this time. He responds to the cries of His people and never abandons them to the enemy's plot.

May 17 What God Says Goes

Psalm 85:10

Lovingkindness and truth have met together; righteousness and peace have kissed each other.

My soon-to-be-husband and I were looking forward to our first contact visit. Years of letters and non-contact visitation had culminated to one final review when he would receive contact visitation privileges. I was beyond excited! But when his classification team reviewed his case, their recommendation was no.

When my husband sent that recommendation home, my heart was sorely disappointed—and angry that he had been arbitrarily denied without any consideration it seemed of all the good he had done up to that point. Ironically, during my Bible study and prayer after learning of the recommendation, the Lord gave me the verse above.

I was rhetorically talking to God, "But, Lord, are you not aware of the recommendation? Are you not aware that what they recommend goes?" You see, the verse spoke to my spirit that my husband and I would finally get that first kiss, but all evidence was to the contrary.

When my husband went to his hearing to formally process the recommendation, he was prepared for the outcome. An officer from the state office attended such proceedings to also give input to what the determination should be. Amazingly and out of character for the DOC, the state officer didn't agree with the prison's recommendation and my husband was positively reviewed. And part of that determination granted him contact visitation privileges. Absolutely amazing!

When I learned of the turn of events, I was overwhelmed with praises to God. I cried. I danced. I fell to my knees and thanked God. I also learned about God's faithfulness. He told me I would get to kiss my husband, and the following week I did!

Despite the evidence you may see around you, believe God for His promises. He's always working behind the scenes in ways and through people we aren't aware of. If He has spoken to you about an issue, you can be guaranteed He will be faithful to His word. What God says always goes.

May 18 Find Grace

Hebrews 4:16

Let us therefore draw near with confidence to the throne of grace, that we may receive mercy and may find grace to help in time of need.

I experienced death with regularity when I worked at a nursing home. It was rare to go any month without having one or more residents die. On one morning, however, the deaths were of two ladies, both named Grace. This couldn't have been anticipated and, with its rarity, confusion happened when the funeral home arrived to pick up "Grace." As you might already be thinking, the wrong Grace went to the wrong funeral home. Well, thankfully "grace" was found amongst all involved, forgiving the unintentional error.

The writer of Hebrews is encouraging us that Jesus is also forgiving of our human imperfections and our mess-ups. One of the reasons Jesus accepted the experience of becoming human was to show us that He can be trusted to understand our failures. He understands what it's like to experience temptation. He also never forgets that we are born weak and with a sinful nature, making mistakes most days.

Sin comes with being human. We are born into sin. There's no solution to this condition except asking God for forgiveness and believing in Jesus, His birth, death, and resurrection. Once we have done this, we are assured forgiveness for past, present, and future sins. God will be merciful to us. And we will always find grace going forward.

Be confident therefore! The guilty burden you may be carrying is likely only there because you have believed a lie. You may believe that you're not worthy to be forgiven. But this is precisely why Jesus died for you. He's merciful.

He also understands how hard being human can be. He understands how ugly and mean-spirited people can be. He understands how it feels to be unfairly treated. The wrongs of life done to you can be buffered by grace. He can orchestrate your experiences for your good. This includes prison. Through His grace, you'll discover just the right help at just the right time.

He longs to show you love through grace. So if you're a believer, cling to this assurance. Be confident in your salvation from sin and come boldly to the throne of grace when you mess up. If you aren't quite sure you believe in Jesus, ask God to reveal Himself to you. He will show up in His mercy, and you'll find grace too.

May 19 Creation's Calm

Genesis 1:12

And the earth brought forth vegetation, plants yielding seed after their kind, and trees bearing fruit, with seed in them, after their kind; and God saw that it was good.

One of the best ways to relax and refocus is to spend time in nature. Get outside. If the wilderness isn't around, do the closest thing. Even just sitting on the porch is helpful. Live in an apartment? Find a park or take a ride out of town. Get in God's creation.

Take in the birds, listen to all the different songs. Watch insects scurrying to some goal, with seemingly no concern in the world. Look at the variety of grass or trees, even the tiniest flower on a weed. Soak up some sunshine.

Creation is a work of God's genius and power, yet imparts simplicity into our mood. There's something calming about meditating on the awesomeness of what God has created. It seems oblivious to the stress of the world. The birds do not worry about their finances. The flowers do not worry about politics. The butterflies are consumed by their simple flight from bloom to bloom, not terrorism.

Creation also represents something of this world that to some extent remains pure—whether the animals or the outdoor world where they live. A tree may be growing in the heart of a city, but the city cannot change what a tree is—it's still a tree. A squirrel can live in town in the same tree, but it still spends its days doing what squirrels do.

You're busy like everyone else, but you have the added stress of prison and its impact. When feeling overwhelmed, you might be surprised how therapeutic the outdoors can be. God created nature for our use, enjoyment, and management. Take advantage of it when you can.

May 20 Resting Securely

Genesis 32:1-2

Now as Jacob went on his way, the angels of God met him. And Jacob said when he saw them, "This is God's camp." So he named that place Mahanaim.

God promised in Genesis 31:3 to be with Jacob as he traveled home. There had been strained relations between him and his brother Esau, so Jacob remained uneasy about a reunion following so much strife. He notified Esau of his planned arrival. But his anxiety only intensified when messengers returned to tell him that Esau—along with four hundred men—were approaching. In fear, Jacob divided his people and possessions to limit any harmful intentions of Esau. After this protective decision, Jacob went to God in prayer, pleading for deliverance from his brother.

Sound familiar to our response when faced with trouble? God promised to be with Jacob. He even sent angels to assure Jacob of His protection. But when things looked threatening in Jacob's eyes, what happened to his faith? He seemed to forget about the angels. He seemed to forget God's promise. Even before seeking reassurance from God in prayer, he took things into his own hands by dividing his traveling company. This sounds a lot like us!

When life gets complicated and the unwelcome experiences approach, we lose our confidence. We panic and think we need to do something to address the problem instead of being still, remembering who God is and what He has promised.

One time, another prisoner threatened to find and hurt our family. It was extremely unsettling to know I was a target to be found and harmed. It angered me, it scared me, and it made me sick with worry for my husband. I became acutely aware of just how many opportunities my routine and life allowed for harm to come. I quit walking the dog, I did my best to get home before dark, and I remained vigilant of my surroundings. Fear imprisoned me.

Faithfully, God reassured me of His presence and protection. I sought God and took what I saw were reasonable precautions. But the unreasonable reminded me when I had forgotten to rest in God's protection and peace.

Prison may be presenting you the same kind of fears. Let you and I both learn from Jacob. God's power to deliver us is greater than any foe that seeks our harm. Seek God first, cling to His assurances, and remember that He has the powers of heaven and earth at His disposal to carry us safely through any frightening situation. **

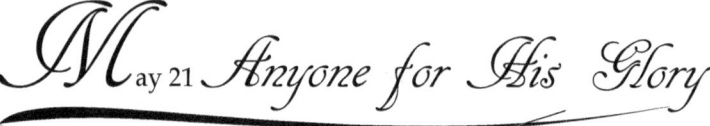

May 21 Anyone for His Glory

Ezra 1:2

"Thus says Cyrus king of Persia, 'The Lord, the God of heaven, has given me all the kingdoms of the earth, and He has appointed me to build Him a house in Jerusalem, which is in Judah.'"

Persia had come into power over the Babylonians, fulfilling the prophecy that the Israelites would be under Babylonian captivity seventy years. King Cyrus was more open to the gods of other nations, unlike the ruthless Babylonians, and with that, God stirred this pagan king's heart to allow the Israelites to return to Jerusalem. They were allowed to return to rebuild the temple which had been destroyed by Nebuchadnezzar when Babylon took the city.

If you ever find yourself wondering how God can positively impact your husband when he's up against corrupt officers, unethical and ungodly prison leadership, or an ungodly judge, consider that God can use the enemy for your husband's good. God can stir the hearts of anyone He chooses, even the ungodly, to bring about His will.

God can orchestrate circumstances, change hearts, and use the negative. King Cyrus was basically bragging that another god specially appointed him to do another great work. Cyrus really didn't care about the Israelites; they were still in bondage. He was only doing what he thought benefitted him as king. God used the negative of this man's personality and arrogance to bring about the good.

You can pray for God to do the same in your husband's case. From the warden to attorneys, pray for God to stir hearts and use any negative power to bring about favor for your husband. There's no limit to what God can do or through whom He chooses when it comes to His glory and the betterment of His children.

May 22 — The Hard Truth

I Kings 22:8

And the king of Israel said to Jehoshaphat, "There is yet one man by whom we may inquire of the Lord, but I hate him, because he does not prophesy good concerning me, but evil. He is Micaiah son of Imlah." But Jehoshaphat said, "Let not the king say so."

Captain Ahab in *Moby Dick* was stubbornly defiant and wouldn't listen to his shipmates. His desire to hunt and kill the whale which disabled him drove his decisions, not wisdom. Ahab was warned by others of the dangers and unavoidable defeat, but he refused to listen. In the end, it cost him his life and all but one member of his crew.

King Ahab of Israel had similar qualities. He desired to make war with the king of Aram and recapture land taken from Israel. King Jehoshaphat of Judah was visiting, and he wisely suggested that the Lord be asked first. Ahab thus called on the false prophets, because they always told him what he wanted to hear. Jehoshaphat saw through this and suggested a true prophet of God be sought out. This was Micaiah.

Ahab had previous dealings with Micaiah, and because he always spoke the hard truth, Ahab avoided his input. Scripture says that Ahab hated him. And as anticipated, Micaiah told Ahab that the plan to engage the Arameans wouldn't be successful. And true to form, Ahab ignored the warning, because it was mostly in his heart to do what he wanted—regardless.

Just like Captain Ahab's outcome, King Ahab didn't survive the battle with the Arameans. His selfish goal ended in prophesied defeat.

Sometimes as a prison wife delivering the hard truth to your husband is needed. You may not be a prophetess, but as a woman, you have God-given intuition. You can be the warning bell to your husband when he's headed in the wrong direction or not seeing the dangers around him. He may need encouragement to seek God's input, just as Jehoshaphat intervened with Ahab.

If you have heard from God on an issue, it's your responsibility to tell your husband. God has likely imparted the truth to you for that reason. You can ask God to affirm and help you in delivering the message if you're uncertain. Your husband may be stubborn and plow ahead regardless, but you'll be assured that you made the most loving choice in telling him the words that were not easy to hear.

May 23 In Humble Need

II Chronicles 20:12

"O our God, wilt Thou not judge them? For we are powerless before this great multitude who are coming against us; nor do we know what to do, but our eyes are on Thee."

Jehoshaphat was king of Judah. His reign was marked by an overall love of God and desire to please Him, but still with messy mistakes along the way. I love that lives such as his are included for us in detail in Scripture. They reflect the humanness and humble need that we all experience as we move through our lives.

In the verse above, Jehoshaphat is in desperate need for God's help. Judah was being invaded. They were the absolute underdog with no chance of victory. Jehoshaphat was not above expressing his fear and crying out to God for deliverance. Chapter twenty records his beautiful prayer, which reflects his trust in and need of God. He knew the only way out of the circumstance was God's intervention. And God responded with the miracle needed.

Jehoshaphat was the leader of the people and the entire community came to him for the answer to the terrible circumstance that faced them. But he didn't have an answer. He knew there was nothing he could do in his own power to bring victory. He didn't try to placate the people or give them false hope. He encouraged them not to stand before him as king for deliverance, but to stand before God.

Prison is likely your invading enemy that presents nothing but defeat when you look out across the multitude of years you face. You feel powerless. This is the perfect time to lower your human efforts and let God take over. It doesn't mean that you do nothing, but it's through your humble surrender to God that appeals for His mercy.

He knows your heart. He knows how and when you have failed. Yet, He also honors your humility. As God responded to Judah (verse 17), "Do not fear or be dismayed; tomorrow go out to face them, for the Lord is with you."

May 24 Spiritual Virus Protection

Ephesians 6:16

In addition to all, taking up the shield of faith with which you will be able to extinguish all the flaming missiles of the evil one.

You cannot safely operate a computer and access the internet without good virus protection software. If not, it's only a matter of time before you'll be defeated by a computer virus when you aren't even aware you're being attacked. With protection software, you're usually alerted of risks or notified when an attack has been stopped. It provides peace of mind.

Just like a computer, we need spiritual protection to identify and stop Satan's attacks on us. Ephesians chapter six contains the strategy "software" for not being defeated in such attacks. Satan will attack, but we can limit the damage he causes by following Paul's teaching in Ephesians.

Specifically, the shield of faith is a powerful weapon of protection for the prison wife. Satan comes at us to propagate fear, doubt, and hopelessness. When that flaming missile comes to you in the form of a disappointment, negative event, or hurt, you need to immediately remember that with God all things are possible. He's your protector. He's your life and circumstance changer.

Satan is the father of lies. Scripture says that when he speaks, he's a liar, because that's his native tongue. He speaks to deceive you. That blow to your emotions can be mitigated if you do not listen to the negative words that accompany the attack.

And it seems Satan's timing is when you're emotionally vulnerable, stressed, or physically drained. Be wise to that. See the attack for what it is and get behind your shield of faith. You'll be amazed at the power you possess to protect yourself from spiritual attacks with godly armor.

May 25 Memorials

Joshua 4:21-22

And he said to the sons of Israel, "When your children ask their fathers in time to come, saying, 'What are these stones?' then you shall inform your children, saying, 'Israel crossed this Jordan on dry ground.'"

It was important to God for Israel to remember His faithfulness and how He had delivered them from great perils. Teaching the succeeding generations about their heritage and God's actions on their behalf, including His laws, was essential for the Israelites. After crossing the Jordan, God instructed Joshua to set up twelve stones (one from each tribe) on the riverbed. This was to memorialize the location of the victory God granted them. Joshua also set up another memorial of twelve stones at the lodging place after crossing. Both were to be reminders to them and the children to come.

On this journey of prison, it's important to remember God's faithfulness. It's easy to succumb to doubts and fears when considering the mammoth corruption and difficulty your husband faces daily or in your challenging life outside the fencing. You can begin to believe that prison is bigger than God. But once you read how powerfully God acted on the Israelites behalf, you can confidently know that the power remains with God.

Keeping a journal could serve as your twelve stones. I'll admit, I'm horrible about journaling! I appreciate the benefits, but find it a cumbersome duplication for my routine. I tend to document God's workings in my life within my Bible. You'll have to find what works best for you. The point is to capture in writing for later reflection the circumstances of life, your feelings possibly, and more importantly, how God intervened.

I find great encouragement from reviewing all those notes and dates sprinkled throughout my Bible. They take me back to a time in life and spawn the memories attached to it. I'm usually wowed, grateful, or simply assured by considering where I'm now these many days later and how God sustained me through the situations that at the time were so difficult. Start to record your journey with God. It's a priceless path and one worth remembering.

May 26 A Crucial Connection

Colossians 4:2

Devote yourselves to prayer, keeping alert in it with an attitude of thanksgiving.

    Prayer is a mighty resource for the Christian. Prayer is a mighty resource for the prison wife. I often say that my husband is the product of prayer. Because he is! Urgent, daily, and earnest prayer was spoken to God from this prison wife who needed help when loving my husband was difficult, when I wept from pure desire for him, and when I longed to see changes in him for the good. Prayer continues to be what holds us together, because we are dependent on who we are praying to. My marriage depends on God, and I only stay connected with God when I pray.

    If not a Christian, it's an unfamiliar resource. This is where I would again encourage you to seek God if not in a relationship with Him. He will show up! You need the power of the Holy Spirit in you for prayer, and He comes when you enter into a relationship with Jesus. But for those of us who do believe, why is it so hard to maintain a daily prayer life?

    Often we are too busy. Our schedules spill over with little reprieve. Prayer gets substituted by busyness, or not even scheduled at all. Even our relaxation is filled with activity. Many times, I close out a weekend, but do not feel any more rested than when it started. The pace of life demands attention even when not working. Spiritually, busyness robs us of the simple, quiet time we need with God.

    Our busyness also communicates a drift easily — yet naively — into self-sufficiency. It generally takes a sudden depletion of a comfort, relationship, or resource to have us hit the floor in dependency. God desires us to run to Him in a crisis, but He also doesn't want that to be the only time He hears from us. We become preoccupied with our lives and ourselves, leaving God in the distance until help is needed.

    Paul instructs the Christians at Colossae to devote themselves to prayer. They were being led away from the truth by false teachings, and he was reminding them of holiness and godly living according to Christ. Prayer would help keep them from drifting.

    Paul consistently stressed the importance of prayer. He often let his readers know that he was praying for them daily. He knew the power of prayer to affect change in a person's life. He knew it was crucial to staying connected to God.

The importance of prayer is discussed throughout the Bible. It's a discipline. Devotion to prayer implies commitment. It means consistent follow through. Busyness is likely going to remain your biggest rival when it comes to praying.

Do your best to make prayer a priority. Mornings tend to be more fruitful, because less of your day has encroached on your time. Regardless, start where you can to establish a routine. See the life you want for your husband and your marriage and begin to pray. You'll never regret the time invested when you begin to see God move in response to your devotion.

May 27 Glorified Release

Psalm 142:7

"Bring my soul out of prison, so that I may give thanks to Thy name; the righteous will surround me, for Thou wilt deal bountifully with me."

David spent time on the run. Saul jealously and relentlessly pursued him, desiring to kill him. David's own son Absalom also became a pursuing enemy. In his efforts to avoid capture, he traveled from place to place, living in caves for protection. Psalm 142 was written by David, referring to one of his times in a cave. David survived being hunted like an animal in both cases and later returned to his rightful and anointed place as king. God remained with him.

Besides being a shepherd, soldier, and eventual king, David was a musician and poet. He played the harp and penned many of the psalms. His artistic talents expressed his emotions—whether despair or joy. He was a man after God's own heart, and he vulnerably writes about his heart condition.

In today's psalm, David was appealing for God's rescue, to deliver his life from his pursuers. He equates it to a prison. And part of his anguish was in knowing that he had no hope except God's deliverance. He was eager to write a psalm of thanks and praise in response.

If your husband is facing a long-term sentence, possibly life, you may feel like you're in the cave wanting to be rescued from the fate of the enemy. There may be no legal avenue at this time for release. You're in a dark cave with the only light at the entrance having multiple layers of razor wire, clanging metal doors, and guards. You may be struggling to maintain hope.

In prayers for deliverance, recognize foremost that God does all things and uses all things to bring glory to Himself. David recognized this. I struggle with this in considering my desire for my husband to one day be released. Of course, I'll praise God! But is my heart's desire to have him home more so for me or for God's purposes? This is quite convicting most days.

But in my cries to God, I know that He knows my heart and my longings. I pray this psalm for both reasons. I want to share life with my husband in freedom, but I also want that realization to further glorify all that God can do. I believe He knows that we will be faithful with the blessing.

I pray that every released prisoner considers God's hand in their survival during prison and the opportunity to walk out the mouth of that figurative cave with the enemy defeated, rescued by God. If you get to enjoy your husband's release date, please do not leave God out of your praise and consider how He wants to use the experience for His glory going forward.

May 28 Spectators

II Corinthians 3:12

Having therefore such a hope, we use great boldness in our speech.

There are plants in Florida that are quite popular with homeowners. Landscape efforts reflect the appreciation of these varieties. I look at them, however, and cannot understand what people seem in them. I feel guilty to describe them as ugly, but they are a far cry from beautiful to me. Some have a few seasonal weeks of redeeming qualities when some colorful blooms make their way out, but this seems not worth their presence the rest of the time. While driving past another reminder of my bewilderment of someone's taste in plants, I consider how many of us are on the receiving end of such opinions about our marriages.

To love and be married to a criminal brings with it opinionated spectators. Some people cannot understand what we see in our husbands. They harbor opinions as if we whole-heartedly agreed with the choices that resulted in our husbands' incarceration. The first response or impression is usually not directed toward a lady who takes her wedding vows seriously or about the strength of character being a prison wife demands. The positive is usually not seen first—or at all.

But spectators aren't interested in knowing the why behind the affection we hold for our husbands despite the circumstances. Like my plant opinion, it doesn't mean that much to me to seek and determine what attracts people to plants I find distasteful. I just see it, and say to myself, "Yuck. Who on earth would want that in their yard." And I go on. Even if I told the homeowner my thoughts, I highly doubt if anyone would choose to uproot the plant and get rid of it on account of my opinion. Spectators and passersby do not have that much power.

And just the same, do not allow the spectators of your marriage to hold more power than they should. They see your marriage from afar and do not know the history and heart for why you choose to remain with your husband. Spectators aren't around for the long haul so why give them a say into your life by dwelling on their opinions? You may not know them anyway. Your confidence remains in the Lord and His love of you and your marriage.

Paul describes in the verse today that his confidence and boldness in sharing the Gospel came from the Lord and the hope of salvation. His adequacy as a minister was not based on his own skill and strengths, but through that which God supplied. He could boldly share in the face of slander and criticism, because he knew the truth.

This is how you can stand firm when others condemn through their opinions or words. You know the truth of God's love and support of your marriage. You know God values your husband despite what he looks like from the "curb." And you can always trust that God's opinion is always a correct assessment of what beauty really looks like.

May 29 Once Chosen

Jeremiah 24:7

'And I will give them a heart to know Me, for I am the Lord; and they will be My people, and I will be their God, for they will return to Me with their whole heart.'

Jeremiah received the word from God that exile was coming. Israel would be in captivity to Babylon due to their continual rebellion against Him. But for those who willingly submit to this, the promise of restoration will be theirs. They would be allowed to return to Jerusalem. To rebel against Babylon would result in defeat.

God chose Israel from the beginning. And through the tribe of Judah, Christ was born, allowing the rest of us to be chosen as well. Part of being chosen evidenced itself throughout Israel's history of defiance and God's forgiveness and deliverance. In Christ, we cycle through the same. We sin, and God forgives us, repeatedly. He never stops loving us as His chosen children. He never stopped loving Israel.

In all of history, God always makes the first move out of His love. He chose Israel. As God says, "I will give them a heart to know me." Israel would have never chosen God without His choosing them first. None of us would come to God without His Spirit drawing us to Himself. He created us and put it in our hearts to know Him.

Just as so, God seeks after us like He sought the Israelites. He's ready to forgive and restore our relationship to Him. He didn't send the Israelites off to captivity without multiple warnings, nor did He leave them without guidance once they were there. He continued to lovingly provide for them.

In His restorative plan, He never initiates separation from His chosen people, but He does allow each person to choose to leave. He gave the Israelites that choice. We can choose to go our own way as well. But living outside of God's will and protection is never successful.

Take encouragement from this aspect of God's character. God is slow to anger and full of mercy. He's long-suffering. If your husband is a Christian and his spiritual journey has many U-turns or detours, God's nature is to seek after him. He may not escape the consequences of the wrong path, but God never stops loving him. Oftentimes, God uses the consequences as a means to draw him back—hopefully with his whole heart.

May 30 Steps to Better

Zechariah 4:10

"For who has despised the day of small things? But these seven will be glad when they see the plumb line in the hand of Zerubbabel—these are the eyes of the Lord which range to and fro throughout the earth."

Prison sets life on a rebuilding path. It interrupts relationships, finances, and plans. It damages each, and in some cases, destroys completely. Repairing or completely starting over can seem an impossible task. It can seem that all that was lost can never return to its previous state—and it's unreasonable to think that even if achieved, it could ever surpass and actually become better.

But the Lord is in the business of renewing and replacing with the best. What was destroyed with a bad decision can be put on the path of rebuilding and a grander outcome. Even when the steps to get there seem insignificant and far from all that was lost. It may look different, but the quality will always be better if God is the architect.

Zechariah was one of God's prophets. He was called upon to encourage the rebuilding of the temple in Jerusalem following the Israelites' return home; they had been in exile under Babylon for seventy years. The foundation had been laid, but work had ceased.

There were many who had seen the prior temple before it was destroyed. They seemed to have a nostalgic grief when looking upon the new efforts — like it would never compare to the first. They failed to consider that when the Lord is building, it's for His glory, and this is never second best or diminished by His earlier work. In regards to the temple, the Lord told Haggai, "The latter glory of this house will be greater than the former" (Haggai 2:9).

The first temple was built under better circumstances; peaceful ones. The second out of hardship and opposition. The greater work structurally of the first was replaced with work within the hearts of the people in the second. They learned lessons in God's faithfulness and grace. We see a tremendous picture of God's forgiveness and love for His people. God built each temple, and His will was perfect, regardless of how He chose to complete it. Each temple led ultimately to the glory of God coming to us in Jesus Christ.

The days of small things when surrendered to God will bear fruit of greater proportion. God is a redeemer. He brings life from death, beauty from ashes, and hope from despair. See the blessing in each small step of prison. Be assured that it's leading you to something grander. Stick to the steps, and God will see to it that your next "temple" is completed. And most importantly, the hearts of those involved will be renewed for the better.

May 31 Because of One

Ezekiel 22:30

"And I searched for a man among them who should build up the wall and stand in the gap before Me for the land, that I should not destroy it; but I found no one."

Ezekiel had the sad duty of living in exile, knowing his homeland was destined for destruction with an unchanging outcome. It was too late. God orchestrated the removal of whom He wanted, and Nebuchadnezzar attacked, removing further Israelites to Babylon.

Ezekiel was part of the second round of Israelites who were exiled to Babylon. He was primarily a prophet to the Israelites who were in captivity with him there. Within this role, he prophesied the coming destruction of Jerusalem's temple and wall due to Israel's idolatry and rebellion against God. But he also prophesied its restoration.

In Old Testament times, God used prophets to communicate with the people. Noah, Abraham, and Moses were some of those early prophets. In the verse for today, God expressed the reality of how far Israel had fallen. He said there was no true prophet in Jerusalem; false prophets only.

This is a very sad verse to me. God is so willing to provide second chances—third, fourth, and more. He warned and He sought, but the people ignored Him. He could find no one to intercede for the people.

God spared Noah and his family from destruction. The people watched him build that ark for years, yet no one turned back to God during that time. Abraham pled for the city of Sodom, bargaining that if fifty righteous people could be found God would spare it; this number had to be repeatedly whittled to only ten, which accounted only for Abraham's nephew and family. Moses repeatedly went before the Lord asking for mercy on the people in the face of their coming destruction, and God responded due to Moses's faithfulness.

The brighter side of these stories is knowing God cares about individuals. He looked for even one person to justify relenting punishment. He responded to individuals who remained faithful. One person can be mightily used of God to impact many. We have seen this throughout Christian history.

You may see prison and its corruption as that pit of rebellion and sin against God. But you can make a difference. Your prayers can make a difference. A man on the inside trying to live righteously can make a difference. One person can make a difference, because God is always seeking that one.

June 1 Not Doing Harm

I Corinthians 8:1

Now concerning things sacrificed to idols, we know that we all have knowledge. Knowledge makes arrogant, but love edifies.

My husband is a Christian. He knows truth. Just as I know the truth. So he hates when I "preach" to him. He knows when he's messing up, and he doesn't need me to quote Scripture. Yes, he needs accountability, but I have learned that most often, he needs love. Sometimes, the best way I can love him is to be silent. It may be praying, or it may be expressing support in ways I can. I seek God in knowing how best to respond.

Paul is addressing an issue for the believers in Corinth. Mature Christians knew that their obedience and relationship to God wouldn't be adversely affected if they ate meat which came from an animal that had been originally sacrificed as part of idol worship. Paul states the knowledge that there are no other gods, only the one true God, so the sacrifice to any other believed god has no power.

But a new Christian who sees them eat such meat, may struggle with guilt if they try to do likewise. Their knowledge is less regarding the grace of God, and their confidence is weak.

Paul says that the mature Christian should focus on loving the new believer by refraining from eating the meat, rather than pushing knowledge on them that their heart cannot adequately absorb. Paul knew that more words wouldn't take away the guilty feelings the new believer may experience.

My husband can be similar to the new believer in Corinth. He has knowledge, but his heart hasn't always fully absorbed the truth. And there's no amount of preaching that will speed that process along. He usually has to walk with God for more time and let God impart that truth through experiences, not my condemning words.

Preaching in such a way only puffs me up, expresses pharisaical arrogance, and puts roadblocks in the way. But loving my husband means accepting where he is in his walk with the Lord, praying for him, and restraining my impulse to correct and badger him with how he should be thinking or behaving.

If this describes your journey with your husband, you'll be faced with scenarios which demand wisdom. There are times when preaching is needed. There are usually more times when it isn't. Seek God's direction to know which way of loving your husband is best.

 June 2 Trust God's Ways

Jonah 1:3

But Jonah rose up to flee to Tarshish from the presence of the Lord. So he went down to Joppa, found a ship which was going to Tarshish, paid the fare, and went down into it to go with them to Tarshish from the presence of the Lord.

God chooses different times to intervene in regards to our straying and sin. This is part of His personal nature. He knows when best to rescue, when best to allow consequences, and at what point it's best to do either. Part of God's nature is that He's just, but merciful. Both can be seen in how He deals with individuals.

Jonah was given the charge by God to go to Nineveh and preach. Nineveh was lost in sin. Although the book of Jonah doesn't specifically comment on what sins the people of Nineveh were involved, God had determined the rebellion demanded judgment. But as is the way of God, He wanted to provide the city an opportunity to repent.

Jonah was not in favor of this plan. He didn't want God to show mercy. Nineveh was a pagan city and Jonah seemed to desire the people to get what they deserved. So in his effort to escape God's call on his life, he pursued sailing the opposite direction from Nineveh. And God allowed him to. This is when the timing of God's intervention and how He chooses to intervene is seen.

Jonah made travel plans. He looked for a ship headed to that opposite destination. He made the necessary arrangements. He boarded the ship, then took a nap, as if to rest in relief that he was free from the previous burden of God's plans.

God could have intervened at any point. He could have removed the availability of a ship. He could have caused Jonah to lose his money for the fare. He could have influenced Jonah to take a nap prior to boarding the ship and causing him to miss the sendoff. He could have created a sailing problem with the ship, stranding it to dock for needed repairs. There were countless ways God could have intervened to prevent the outcome of what Jonah ultimately experienced: being thrown overboard, consumed by a fish, and existing in the bile of the fish's stomach until puked onto the shore.

This is where the question of why often arrives to us, especially when considering prison. Why did God allow this or that? Why didn't God prevent this or that? Why didn't God act when lies were being told, information was not allowed, or the good was being suppressed? We ask why God spares some and not others.

These are the tough questions of faith. God's omniscience and sovereignty must be trusted. Consequences came to Jonah. He was three days in his own type of prison, but the experience set him back on God's path, and ultimately, more than 120,000 people of Nineveh were saved. God allowed Jonah to go so far in his rebellion to spur on the most effective repentance in his life and the life of others.

Everything that touches you or your husband's life has been filtered through God's loving hands. Some things will pass through to have a negative impact, some things will be withheld in mercy. Either outcome becomes okay when you know God is trustworthy.

June 3 Accusations

Exodus 5:23

"Ever since I came to Pharaoh to speak in Thy name, he has done harm to this people; and Thou hast not delivered Thy people at all."

Moses had responded to God's call, approaching Pharaoh and speaking the command from the Lord to let His people go. The Israelites were in slavery to the Egyptians. The slave work at the time of this passage was making bricks. The Israelites were forced to produce a quota of bricks daily.

After Pharaoh heard Moses's request, he became very angry. He instructed the foremen and slave masters to expect the same number of bricks daily, but to no longer provide the straw; the Israelites were told to gather their own straw. And with this new and unrealistic order, success was futile. In response to their diligent, yet unsuccessful efforts to keep up with the work, the Israelites were beaten and taunted, being called lazy.

The Israelites' response was also anger toward Moses and Aaron. They blamed them for the abuse they now suffered. Moses, in turn, accuses God of not keeping His promise. We read his reaction in the verse above. He became despondent, crying to God in disbelief and confusion.

I empathize with Moses. How many times I have pled to God from a place of accusation. Where are you God? Why have you allowed this to happen to me! Speaking from an unfaithful heart in response to what seems like abandonment from God, I would surrender to fussing at God for not honoring my faithfulness to Him. Maybe some days it's from an overflow of emotions, because most often, once calm in my spirit, the right perspective will follow: trusting God when not understanding. Oh, how often I have been through this cycle on this journey of prison! I'm so grateful that God considers my humanness and knows I'm flesh and weak.

My ultimate hope is to gain a stronger faith for God's providence and faithfulness. I believe in it, but I desire to let that belief reign over my reaction when hit with what seems the opposite and impossible. Like His dealings with Israel, He had not forsaken them. He was planning an even greater deliverance through a circumstance that seemed to only be getting worse.

Do not lose faith in God's ability to bring a victory over your circumstances. Resist complaining to God. Cling to Him. Ask for assurance from a faithful heart, not a despondent one. Even if everyone around you has withdrawn their support, shown spite, or even called you a fool, believe what you have heard from the Lord. He's faithful. He will show up. God delivered the Israelites in a mighty way, His way. He's working on your deliverance as well.

June 4 The Good Shepherd

John 10:2-3

"But he who enters by the door is a shepherd of the sheep. To him the doorkeeper opens, and the sheep hear his voice, and he calls his own sheep by name, and leads them out."

I was walking my dog along the road which was a combination of dirt and sand. It was packed hard at points and shifting at others where ruts turned up heaps of sand. I was enjoying the early morning to take in nature and spend time with God. The moon could still be seen in the sky along with the dawning light.

My life at that time was quite a mess, so it was nice to absorb the simplicity that walk provided. I talked with God about all the unknowns and my fears. I shared my hopes and need for His mercy and restoration.

My dog was oblivious that I was walking more for me than her. We walked a fair piece, then turned around to head home. What I noticed immediately was the footprints in the sand by my earlier steps. More interestingly, the tread design had an intermittent oval with a cross in its center. Granted the shoe designer likely didn't intentionally mean for that to be a Christian cross, but a cross it was. And it spoke volumes to my needy heart.

It was a reminder that God was walking with me through the mess. In fact, He was leading me out of the mess. All I needed to do was to keep listening for His voice and follow where He was leading.

At that moment, my dog pulled and desired to go all kinds of directions with her nose leading her, ignoring my leading. A yank finally got her attention. I further considered how I had already experienced God's "yank" on my life to get my attention. I was experiencing an extremely hard lesson from a sinful choice. I knew going forward that I wanted to be nowhere except near the Shepherd, not off in the weeds, chasing a dead-end goal.

John shares with us Jesus's parable about the sheep and shepherd. Jesus describes Himself as the Good Shepherd who lays down His life for the sheep. Satan only desires to destroy the sheep. He schemes and sneaks in another way to gain access to the sheep. He tries to deceive the sheep into going another direction.

But Jesus knows His own and they know Him. Nothing can snatch His sheep from Him. Staying close to Jesus protects the sheep from being led astray.

During that stressful time, I could rest in knowing God was close, and He was leading me to better mornings and better days. God wants to do the same for your mess. He hasn't left you. He's walking right along with you. He desires you to stay close, listen for His voice, and follow His steps. He will lead you through the debris of your wrong choices or that of your husband's and to safe pastures.

June 5 The Good Shepherd 2

Isaiah 54:17

"No weapon that is formed against you shall prosper; and every tongue that accuses you in judgment you will condemn. This is the heritage of the servants of the Lord, and their vindication is from Me," declares the Lord.

I was walking my dog again along the same route the next morning. Same pleasant weather, same quietness, and same mess of my life on my mind as I talked with God. I looked for the moon in the morning light. I also looked down to find my footprints from the previous morning. Amazingly, many still remained, despite the traffic which had passed over the road throughout the day and evening. The oval encompassing the cross still distinguished itself in the sand. My little footprints had survived multiple tire treads. The verse for today came to my mind.

My mess found me surrounded by enemies in the form of bills, joblessness, health concerns, legal problems, and prison. There was not enough of some and too much of others. Every direction I turned was a major barrier. It seemed I was surrounded with no escape, like the tire treads I saw around my footprints.

But the Lord provided His assurance that He had not left me. He was working within the mess to lead me out. Sure He just reminded me of that the previous day, but repetition in Scripture signifies importance. God was confirming that truth with the repeated message to my still needy heart.

In the verse today, Isaiah was writing about God's message to the Israelites. God had sent enemies against Israel due to their rebellion and idolatry, but He had not forgotten them. They would be restored, and He wouldn't allow them to be destroyed.

In my case, I knew God lifted His hand of protection due to my personal sin. I was suffering a severe consequence like the Israelites. Unfortunately, life's typical demands didn't go away either. But in the end, God would be my Divine Defender. His lovingkindness and compassion for me wouldn't be removed.

You can be assured of the same. God is faithful to His own. He will lead you—His lamb—and protect you from your enemies. He may allow consequences at times, but this doesn't remove His favor from you. He's working behind the scenes to clear a secure path for you on which to walk.

June 6 *Confidently Upheld*

Micah 7:8

Do not rejoice over me, O my enemy. Though I fall I will rise; though I dwell in darkness, the Lord is a light for me.

Micah prophesied the coming punishment for Israel, but like God's message through other prophets, there always remained hope for restoration. God's discipline would be followed by renewal. God always left a remnant when dealing with Israel. He remained faithful to His covenant. Micah wrote beautifully of this.

The enemy of prison may knock you or your husband down—repeatedly. This may be from your own choices. Maybe like Israel, you have strayed from God, putting Him further down on the list of importance. But there always remains hope if you're a child of God.

Stay focused on God, not the circling enemies. Acknowledge why some of the enemies are there—any ungodly choices—but then let your worry for the future get turned into positive prayers of confidence in God's deliverance. The verse today is a great verse to speak out loud to Satan. He might bring more ammunition in his discouraging attacks, but he doesn't have the power to extinguish God's presence or light.

You'll rise with God's help. But to get up, you must look up. Sometimes this means denying how you feel and trusting God's nature. Guilt may be weighing you down. Your confident beginning may be the act of looking up. It may be surrendering the next, unseen step to God. Despite the fear and whatever emotions accompany it, get up in faith. The enemy wants you to remain in fear, powerlessness, and defeat. Rising up clears the cloud he's trying to smother you with.

From days of old, God's love has been unchanging. He's love. He has always been love. You can trust Him to respond when you call. You may call from wherever you have fallen. It doesn't matter how low. It doesn't matter how dark your life has become.

June 7 *First Contact*

I John 4:19

We love, because He first loved us.

In the movie *Contact*, the character Ellie played by Jodie Foster obtained a love interest early on. This man Palmer, played by Mathew McConaughey, pursued her faithfully throughout the movie. Ellie openly rejected him, turned away from him, and intentionally avoided him. Yet, he kept pursuing. He was a man of faith; she was skeptical of faith. Although the movie was about alien communication that Ellie discovered through her work as an astronomer, the film illustrates how God pursues us to teach us about faith and true love when we are lost and faithless.

Palmer challenged Ellie to consider faith and the existence of God like she searched for alien life. He encouraged her to search for the truth, which was parallel to what she was doing in her professional life. In the end, through Palmer's steadfast devotion and her experiences, she began to show the sprouts of faith.

If Ellie seems like your husband, please know that God powerfully pursues through supernatural orchestration. He may be using you to teach your husband about Himself and love. You may be a Palmer. In which case, you're the conduit for God's power. God's Holy Spirit will ultimately draw your husband to faith, but you can be a vital part of that process.

God always initiates first contact. His loving us teaches us how to love. We all love to the extent we understand love. Knowing this helps us dissolve frustration and hurt that we may experience at the hands of our husbands. I remind myself that my husband is loving me as best as he knows how to love. I rest in the assurance that as he gets to know God, his ability to love will increase. That's true for me too. It's true for you and your husband.

It will also help to remember that it isn't your job to bring your husband to faith; it's God's. Your responsibility is to love him as Christ has loved you. You're to be devoted and let him see love in action by how you behave toward him and how you live your life. In doing so, you may plant a seed of faith, you may water what's already there, or you may harvest someone else's spiritual investment in him. Regardless, in every part of the journey of his faith, God's love never falters, even when your husband seems to be running the other direction.

June 8 *Common Love*

John 13:34-35

"A new commandment I give to you, that you love one another, even as I have loved you, that you also love one another. By this all men will know that you are My disciples, if you have love for one another."

Do you find it difficult to be in groups because of your husband's incarceration? I think this is most evident for me, sadly, when connecting in a church. We are encouraged to share, be vulnerable, seek support from others, and "do life" together with other believers. This sounds great, but I think even within these scenarios there's a "typical" set of struggles. When involved in a church, I have never met any other person dealing with an incarcerated spouse.

This is likely impacted by the size and location of the church. In small, rural churches I have never even met anyone dealing with prison on any level. Larger churches, in larger cities I have found some, but for most of the group events, it seemed I was again the solo prison wife.

My cautious skepticism remains when I begin attending a new church. I have those familiar pangs of "Is it safe to share?" "Will I be the outcast here?" If I can persevere through the repeated and awkward encounters in the get-to-know-you phase, I do okay. Usually people remain cordial, but that polite acceptance always has me wondering what they are really thinking. So trust is a huge hurdle.

We all want to be loved and accepted. And this is especially wanted when we are part of a church. We think that of all places we should be, but this isn't always the case. Jesus tells us that Christians should especially love other Christians. In doing so, people outside the church will get to know the love of Jesus. They will see unity and that unity comes when believers treat other believers lovingly. In essence, we should be following Christ within the church and outside of it.

In following this teaching, I must also be willing to love those I'm in fellowship with at church. And I use "fellowship" loosely, because my personality tends to retreat when in social gatherings. If not in word, in my heart. So my challenge to be involved in the lives of others and theirs in mine is two-fold: my own fear of rejection and my introverted tendencies.

But it cannot always be about me. I need to take the focus off my own fear of acceptance and get involved in the lives of others. I cannot be vigilant with every interaction that a person may ask me about something personal, like my husband. Oh, what a challenge!

Even though you and I are prison wives, we have something we can contribute to God's people, His church. We will never be used to the extent He desires if we stay in our comfort zone of silence or avoidance. As people get to know us, they will be better able to love us as Christ teaches in this passage of John.

You may always be the only person impacted by prison in your church. Expect that. Also be careful that you do not hold it against its members by distancing yourself from the lives of those there.

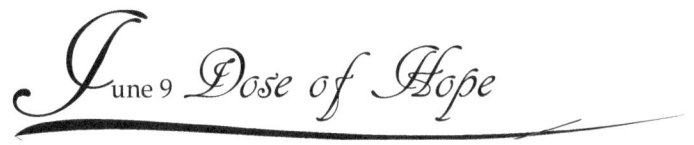

June 9 — Dose of Hope

Romans 15:13

Now may the God of hope fill you with all joy and peace in believing, that you may abound in hope by the power of the Holy Spirit.

    As the years of prison progress, my husband has shown an increasing need for hope. He has shown more weariness in this journey. His tolerance has shown decline. The energy for the daily endurance has become harder for him to find. I do what I can to encourage and support him, but what I have come to realize is that I cannot be his hope. The power he needs must come from his relationship with God. Within the daily battle, there has to be something far greater in his heart than his love for me. He needs to love God more than me.

    In loving God, his relationship with God gets closer. Through this process, he will see God actively move in his life to be an encourager greater than any presence I can provide. God is there in places I have no access to. He's there when the unexpected happens. He's there to speak to my husband in precisely the moment that he needs. The supernatural power of God transcends the physical and logistical barriers that I face in supporting him.

    My husband will find his purpose in God when he remains close to Him. Knowing what God has uniquely called him to do will energize him. Living within prison with purpose is huge! Time has more meaning and hope remains between the meaningful moments of visits, phone calls, or mail.

    I think men with a long-term sentence are in more desperate need for hope. Most definitely for those facing life or capital punishment. There isn't a release date to keep the heart hopeful. The light is dim if not seen at all. The power of knowing God through Jesus is the only answer to infuse such a path with anticipation for a better day and to live within the present one with optimism and unique enthusiasm.

    You may worry for your husband's state of mind and emotions. You love him dearly, but your worry comes from knowing that it doesn't seem to be enough. It's a vulnerable and defeating feeling.

    But do not give up in the battle! Do what you can, and trust God to be there to do what only He can do. Pray for your husband always. Pray that he comes to know God and grow in his love for God. In loving God, joy and contentment will find a home in his heart and hopelessness will get pushed out.

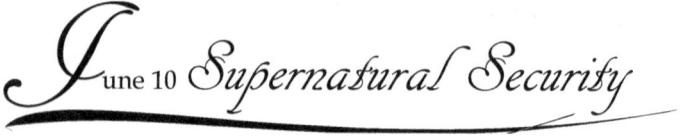

June 10 Supernatural Security

Nahum 1:7

The Lord is good, a stronghold in the day of trouble, and He knows those who take refuge in Him.

There are very few positive verses in Nahum. He was a prophet foretelling the destruction of Nineveh, an Assyrian city. His words are directed to Nineveh and the Israelites. One for their warning; the other for their encouragement. Jonah had previously preached to Nineveh and they repented, but this didn't last. They once again were oppressing God's people and judgment was coming. Although the Israelites repeatedly strayed resulting in such oppression, God always showed mercy and delivered them.

Nahum reminds the Israelites that the Lord is good. He's just, but sovereign, faithful, and good to His children. Those who seek Him are promised refuge in the time of trouble. He disciplined them for their good, but always promised restoration. This promise holds true for us today through Jesus.

A stronghold is a military term. It's a place of protection against an enemy. It's strategic for defense. It's built to withstand attacks. Taking refuge in a stronghold provides security.

God is a stronghold. He welcomes His soldiers into His care and protection in times of trouble. But unlike a physical place, His protection travels continually with those who know Jesus. His protection has no limits and is always more powerful than any foe.

Your husband needs a place of protection within prison. He needs a refuge of protection from the enemy attacking him. He's in a daily battle with harm on every side. Jesus has all the power of heaven available to protect him. Let this encourage you! But also let it encourage you to pray for your husband's deliverance and protection. Consider a prayer like this.

Father God,
I know you are the protector of your children. Let your Holy Spirit reign in my husband's dorm this day and throughout that prison. Restrain Satan's activity to do harm and violence. Let my husband have peace today. Surround him with your

angels. *Do not let anyone who wills to do harm against him enter the space you are protecting. I know my husband struggles in his obedience and continues to make ungodly choices, but protect him as your anointed soldier while he grows into understanding and living fully into his calling. I know you love him. I know you love the ones who are counted as foes. Intervene in the lives of those in that dorm, both officer and prisoner, for the good. I love you and praise you for your goodness. I ask all this in the precious name of Jesus, Amen.*

June 11 The Samaritan Challenge

Luke 10:33

"But a certain Samaritan, who was on a journey, came upon him; and when he saw him, he felt compassion."

    The parable of the Good Samaritan spoken by Jesus was recorded by Luke. It was an illustration of what loving our neighbor should look like. The victim of robbers lay wounded beside the road. Two religious leaders had previously passed by the man, intentionally avoiding him. A man from Samaria took notice of the man's need, went out of his way, and did what was within his means to help. He provided first aid on the scene, took the man to an inn and provided further care. He paid for the man's stay and assured the inn keeper that he would return on his way back through town and cover any additional expenses the man may have incurred.

    A particular point of the parable is the man loving and serving the stranger was a social outcast. The Jews hated Samaritans and considered them unclean to the point they wouldn't even step foot on their land. They would go out of their way just to avoid traveling through their territory.

    Jesus doesn't say if the wounded man was a Jew, but that's one of the lessons I think He is teaching. The Samaritan showed compassion for a man who possibly was someone who on any other day would avoid any encounter, let alone let a Samaritan touch him! In contrast, the religious leaders didn't stop to help one of their own. They were content to let the man lay there and die.

    Prison portrays severe divisions: officer and inmate, black and white, this gang and that gang. Strong emotions are affiliated in the mix. There's open hostility between the opposing groups.

    Jesus would say your husband's neighbor is the officer working the booth, the racist roommate, or the untrustworthy gang member. His neighbors are those persons he encounters daily. Jesus says your husband's love for these individuals should match the love he has for himself. This is a severe challenge in prison when most neighbors aren't neighborly. How do you show compassion for someone who despises, antagonizes, or threatens you?

It really comes down to a heart issue. Your husband has to begin to see people differently — as a person Jesus died for. God loves every officer and every prisoner. To show compassion and love for another person, a possible enemy, can only be channeled through a heart surrendered to Jesus.

Your husband can begin by praying for those men around him. Maybe he cannot tolerate engaging them at this point, but he can always pray. Maybe he has to begin praying for his own heart to see people differently. Prison desensitizes people to their own humanity and that of others.

Your husband may not be anywhere near ready in his heart to be a "Good Samaritan." It does take a spiritual intention. It takes a desire to mature spiritually. But this doesn't mean he will never be there. And hopefully, if ever in a wounded situation like the Samaritan, someone will see him and extend compassion regardless of his background or affiliation too.

June 12 Speckled Vision

Luke 6:42

"Or how can you say to your brother, 'Brother, let me take out the speck that is in your eye,' when you yourself do not see the log that is in your own eye? You hypocrite, first take the log out of your own eye, and then you will see clearly to take out the speck that is in your brother's eye."

There's a picture of me and my siblings when we were quite young, sitting on a fireplace hearth, all smiles. When we came upon the photo, my sister claims she isn't in the picture. She adamantly believes the one girl isn't her. The rest of us have no question about it. It looks exactly like her! But for whatever reason, she cannot see her own resemblance in the picture. Despite plenty of evidence in that photo — my sister's features, my mother affirming it, unanimous agreement from others — she refused to accept it. She wouldn't entertain the idea at all.

This is how sin is a lot of times in our lives. It's easy to see it in someone else, but be blind to our own. And pointing it out to someone usually doesn't enlighten if the person isn't willing to consider it.

I have to be cautious in this area when managing my husband's accountability and my tendency to be rigid and legalistic. My heart's intention is my concern for him, but it isn't always accepted that way. He can feel badgered and judged, like he can never measure up. He also has a quick-witted way of calling me out on my own spiritual shortcomings.

And he's right. I have enough of my own issues and sin to deal with that focusing on his is what Jesus is teaching about in the verse today. Let me get right with God before I try to police anyone else's walk with the Lord, especially my husband's. Jesus hates hypocrisy.

It doesn't mean there will not be times when I must challenge my husband about his actions. There's accountability. But there's a prayerful way to approach that. And I must be pure in my own heart at that time.

I also have to remember that the Holy Spirit convicts of sin, my words never will. My husband's sin cannot be badgered out of him. He must sense the conviction by the Holy Spirit and repent. Like my sister's photo. She will have to "see" it for herself before she will believe and have a change of heart.

Focus on your walk with the Lord, deal with your own sin. Then you'll be in a better position to help your husband with his. Seek God's heart on issues of sin that are weighty that you think you need to address with your husband. It may not go well. He may deny and refuse to change. At which time, you continue to pray for the Holy Spirit to do the work only He can do.

June 13 *Expectant Faith*

Mark 11:21-22

And being reminded, Peter said to Him, "Rabbi, behold, the fig tree which You cursed has withered." And Jesus answered saying to them, "Have faith in God."

Peter addresses Jesus in this passage as if he was shocked to see the tree withered. The previous day, Jesus cursed the fig tree for not having figs on it. During their walk past the tree the following morning, Peter exclaimed to Jesus to look at the tree, because it was then withered. Jesus responded by telling the disciples to have faith.

I take the interaction with Peter as Jesus saying, "Peter, you should have expected to find the tree withered." If they had faith when witnessing Him curse the tree, the withered tree would have been expected. It was a done deal when Jesus spoke the words.

Jesus proceeds to describe faith as it relates to prayer. The popular writing about faith moving mountains is found in this passage. Confidence in Jesus's power will energize your prayers, but will it really be so powerful to move mountains if you asked God to? Will your prayers get your husband released early? Will your earnest prayers keep your husband safe while in prison?

This is a difficult passage, because I know there are plenty of prayer warriors who still didn't receive what they prayed for—despite their faith in God's ability to deliver. I have prayed earnestly for God to intervene before my husband hurt someone, to only arrive at the prison the following morning to an ambulance departing with the outcome of my husband's actions on a stretcher.

Faith must also rest in God's perfect and allowable will. You pray to God, because you have faith in Him. Faith in His goodness and sovereignty accepts His will despite not experiencing results you want. If you confidently pray for something that you know is in His will, it will granted. If He allows a negative outcome within His allowable will, you still have faith that He decided correctly.

Because God is omniscience and omnipresent, He makes decisions based on information that you do not have. If you had all the information, you might likely not being praying as earnestly for that one thing that God ultimately withholds. Faith is trusting in God's answers.

So you should pray with expectant faith. And yes, faith in God's power believes He can move mountains if needed to accomplish His will in your life. If He doesn't move your mountain, you still can have expectant faith that He has something more perfectly planned.

June 14 Like Lot

II Peter 2:7-9

And if He rescued righteous Lot, oppressed by the sensual conduct of unprincipled men (for by what he saw and heard that righteous man, while living among them, felt his righteous soul tormented day after day with their lawless deeds), then the Lord knows how to rescue the godly from temptation, and to keep the unrighteous under punishment for the day of judgment.

I have more recently related to Lot in how he handled himself in regards to Sodom. Granted he gets a bad rap most of the time, but amazingly Peter records for us that he was righteous within his time in Sodom. But Lot did endure the impact on his spirit from living within such a sin-filled city.

I experienced a similar "torment" when being in the presence of my husband's sinful choices that were persisting. Like Lot, I was initially living on the outskirts of the sin. But in time, became more accommodating of my husband's choices. I was still trying to be righteous and be that rebuking voice, but the constant knowledge of God's displeasure of the situation remained ever present in my spirit. It made me weary at points in trying to balance my husband's choices and what I knew to be right. My prayer was forever that my husband's heart would be convicted, and we could walk out of the situation together.

What I have learned the hard way is that sometimes I may have to walk away on my own. I cannot camp too close to the sin as did Lot. I cannot get pulled into ungodly situations with my husband, merely out of the hope that God knows my heart's intention. In trying to be the light and witness for God's will, I accepted things not of His will—and this made me miserable in my spirit.

Lot was miserable too. He initially settled in the area of Sodom because of the quality land. Why he moved closer to Sodom and eventually lived in the city isn't known. Even after Abraham rescued him from being a prisoner of war after Sodom was attacked, he returned to living there. Maybe he was trying to be a righteous witness for the people there. His heart may have been good, but staying close to God and sin were incompatible.

You'll have to make the same decision in regards to your husband's actions. Hopefully, he's already a righteous man. Not perfect, but trying to live righteously. This will make your Christian walk and marriage much smoother in dealing with prison.

If he isn't, your spirit will remain unsettled as you watch his participation in things that are ungodly. The best choice you can make is to not camp too close. You can have a clean heart before God even though your husband persists in doing things that you know are displeasing to Him. Not participating in the unholy will likely be the best thing you can do for your husband.

June 15 — All In

Mark 10:50

And casting aside his cloak, he jumped up, and came to Jesus.

    Bartimaeus was blind. He sat begging beside the road; this was his life. But he desired more. When he heard that Jesus was passing by, he cried to Him for mercy. Jesus called him over, and with that summons, Bartimaeus threw his coat aside and eagerly went to Him. Jesus healed him, and Bartimaeus didn't look back. He joined the others who were following Jesus on the road.

    Bartimaeus was all in once he heard the call from Jesus. He possessed very little. He was a beggar. Yet he threw aside likely his only possession of value—his cloak—to come to Jesus. It was diminished greatly in comparison. The thing of upmost value to him awaited his arrival.

    There was no hesitation by Bartimaeus. He leaped up and got to Jesus as quickly as he could. He was also not discouraged by those around him who tried to stifle his cries in the first place (verse 48). He wanted to hear from Jesus, not the naysayers. And Jesus rewarded his perseverance and faith.

    This is how we should strive to live for God—all in. Ignoring the discouraging remarks of others, enthusiastically following after Jesus, and loosening the grip on things which hold us back from complete devotion.

    What a challenge! This seems to be harder when we have more possessions, better health, and a smooth-going life. It could also be that prison has taken most of that away, and you feel like Bartimaeus more now than ever before. Life has mostly become about survival. Maybe your security has been diminished to only a few things of value. Your challenge may be the fear of losing the few things you have.

    The men who brought Bartimaeus to Jesus told him, "Take courage, arise! He is calling for you" (verse 49). When Jesus calls, you can trust that whatever you leave behind fades quickly in comparison to what you receive. Bartimaeus regained his sight. Just imagine what opportunities this provided in his life!

    Jesus desires you to be all in. He has amazing blessings and plans for your life. Take courage! Come to Him and "see" for yourself.

June 16 · The Will to Know

Colossians 4:12

Epaphras, who is one of your number, a bondslave of Jesus Christ, sends you his greetings, always laboring earnestly for you in his prayers, that you may stand perfect and fully assured in all the will of God.

    I pray regularly that I stand perfect and fully assured in God's will. There's peace knowing that God will answer this prayer. I can be assured of that. Decision making can be impacted by so many false perspectives and less-than-perfect options. I frankly do not trust my ability to always discern the difference. Feelings get blended into the mix, and these are even less reliable.
    I must labor earnestly to stay in God's will. It seems this becomes even more imperative as I grow closer to God. Spiritual haughtiness can seep in with maturity, dampening my sensitivity to my own sin. This will always steer me away from the best path. Temptations then operate with even more stealth.
    But I also have a more yearning desire to be in God's will. This can sometimes paralyze my decision making. I'm so afraid of making a mistake that I vacillate to the point of exhaustion. I have what I refer to as "spiritual stress." God never intends for me to be stressed in this way.
    God will not withhold His will from you. He wants you to be in His will, so He isn't going to intentionally make it such a mystery to be figured out or deliver it through some cryptic message. He wants you to stand perfect and fully assured in it.
    When you find yourself vacillating, step back and meditate on this verse from Colossians. Always be mindful of your blind spots as you mature in your faith. This is also a great verse you can pray for your husband. You can be like Epaphras, praying earnestly for your husband to stand perfect and fully assured in God's will too.

☩

June 17 Amply Supplied

Exodus 15:27

Then they came to Elim where there were twelve springs of water and seventy date palms, and they camped there beside the waters.

    The Israelites had just been delivered through the Red Sea. It was an amazing show of God's power. It seemed the previous miracles, along with the pillars of fire and cloud, were not enough to have them believe the supernatural accompaniment of God's provision, so Moses was once again faced with a rebellious group. Yet God again miraculously rescued when they saw no hope for survival. The sea parted and they crossed, escaping the pursuit of the Egyptians.

    They left that experience and found themselves three days without water. And the grumbling returned when the hopeful treasure of water they finally came upon was too bitter to drink. God, however, had plans for their rescue again, and turned the water into sweet refreshment. A sad ending of His test of their devotion.

    Now with a mountain of miracles behind them and God's mercy, they headed out from there and came to Elim. It was paradise in the desert — twelve springs of water and seventy date palms. An abundance of provision. They camped there and enjoyed the blessing. It was as if the Lord had forgotten all their recent mistakes and went overboard in grace.

    This is the beauty of God's love for us. He longs to be gracious and bless us — despite our mistakes. We mess up. He forgives and blesses. In the midst of the desert, He provided the Israelites a resort. Fresh water, food, and nice shade. A welcome rest from their travel. It was as if the Lord was saying, "Trust Me and watch Me deliver!"

    Whatever difficulty you're facing today, the desert of prison being one of them, the Lord takes pleasure in blessing you. You may have guilt for previous failures of devotion, but God's nature hasn't changed. He will welcome you back, and it will be as if nothing before happened. It's not about your deserving the twelve springs of water and seventy date palms. It's about His grace.

June 18 The Best of Yourself

Proverbs 16:32

He who is slow to anger is better than the mighty, and he who rules his spirit, than he who captures a city.

    I face multiple moments when my spirit isn't ruled very well. I say unworthy words, and as they are exiting my mouth, I know they aren't going to be helpful. Yet, in that moment, I don't care. I want the satisfaction of speaking my mind. My body language is just as guilty even when my mouth is silent.

    It takes a much stronger person to control negative emotional reactions than whatever force is displayed when they are unleashed. Once unleashed, the person impacted is then forced into the same scenario. And like myself, doesn't always rule his or her spirit well either. It deteriorates from there.

    I then sigh with disappointment that I, once again, didn't handle the situation better. My pride may have been spared, but my character and pursuit of holiness took a step in reverse. Then comes the guilt and the new battle within my spirit that I must manage.

    When I do have successful moments of controlling those negative reactions, I find that in the end, it was really okay to drop my verbal or nonverbal weapon. The situation passed and the earth didn't stop on its axis because of my emotional silence. Also, I got a boost of confidence knowing that my response was pleasing to God and was a step to a stronger character in myself.

    The more you practice this the better you get at it. Thankfully! It feels horribly awkward on first attempts and may never quite go away, but learning to rule your spirit has great value for your relationships.

    You may find that writing this verse on a card and reviewing regularly a great benefit. If you and your husband tend to argue on the phone, having it handy at those times might be a great resource. And always remember the Holy Spirit is always with you to help. Say a quick prayer when you're tempted to respond in impulsive anger. With success, you'll be in unique company of those mightier than rulers and stronger than the physical strength of those they command.

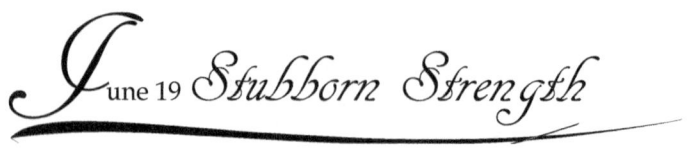

June 19 Stubborn Strength

Ezekiel 3:8-9

"Behold, I have made your face as hard as their faces, and your forehead as hard as their foreheads. Like emery harder than flint I have made your forehead. Do not be afraid of them or be dismayed before them, though they are a rebellious house."

    The Old Testament prophets didn't have a glamorous job. It was a high calling to be the mouthpiece for God. But as they often were sent to warn Israel, God often warned the prophets of the difficulty that awaited them. In Ezekiel's case, God repeatedly remarked to him that his calling was determined whether Israel listened or not. He would face an obstinate, rebellious people. However, we read in the verses above that God didn't send His prophet out unequipped. He provided the strength he needed to match the opposition that awaited.

    The popular principle "God will provide where He leads" comes to mind when I read about many of the prophets. A calling by God can be a nervous consideration. It usually challenges us, calls us from our comfort zones. There's a deepening faith when our lives are stirred up by the Almighty. Our foundational faith is added to the new strength God provides to accomplish His will.

    God knew Ezekiel would need strength to match the opposition and to endure the calling. God was going to ask him to do the unusual, the unpopular, the physically demanding, the emotionally demanding, and the overall sacrificial. These would be the demands to accompany a difficult message to an unaccepting audience.

    Being a wife to your husband is part of your calling. It isn't glamorous at this point. It's sacrificial in ways that are unique to a prison marriage. Remaining with your husband may not be popular and often you may face a rebellious husband and definitely an ungodly system. You may face situations outside your comfort zone.

    But the stubborn strength of what you face will be matched by God's power. He desires to outfit you with what you need to take on the calling that you now have. He's faithful to do just that. Do not be afraid or dismayed. Move forward in the strength you have and trust that God will take care of the rest.

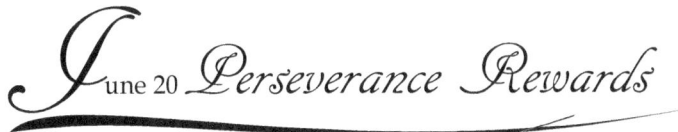
June 20 Perseverance Rewards

Revelation 2:3

'And you have perseverance and have endured for My name's sake, and have not grown weary.'

    I was leaving one afternoon to run a few errands. Hearing my keys jingle, my dog with a surge of excitement runs for the door wanting to go along. In disappointment, she watched me exit without her. To my amazement when I turned to lock the door, I see her head and both front paws sticking out the tiny doggie door available to the smaller terriers of the house. She was strenuously trying to make it out, determined not to be left behind. In greater amazement, I learned a few days later that, indeed, my 35-pound collie eventually managed to work her way through that six-by-nine inch door.

    Throughout the Bible, perseverance is stressed. Persevering in our love for God and His word, our work ethic, our morals, our character—everything related to Christ calls for excellence and perseverance. However, with this positive determination also includes persevering through persecution and enduring hardship. Following Jesus has never been easy, but it has always been worth it. God rewards our perseverance in living a godly life.

    The church of Ephesus as described in Revelation was being praised by Jesus for their perseverance. They stuck with God and remained vigilant against sin and false teaching. They weren't a perfect church—there never has been. But they tried to keep Jesus as King of their lives, not growing weary when faced with opposition.

    You'll find God's grace on this path of prison if you do not give up on the life that He calls you to live. A righteous life can be led within the hardships of separation and struggles you face. In sticking to what you know is right in the eyes of God, you may experience friction with others, your husband, and even persecution on some level, but your faithful decision will never be in vain. God sees and rewards.

    And expect to be imperfect. The Ephesus church became immune to their sin. They lost their sense of dependency on God. I read the passage of Revelation as if they were running on cruise control and not realizing they were actually going in reverse, allowing other things to replace their desire for God.

Jesus says the answer to this heart condition is to get back to the things of God. Do the things you did at first. The goal is to stay alert to where you have been and what God has done for you. Stay energized in the race. God's presence will go with you. He will not leave you behind in your struggles. He will reward your faith and determination to follow Him.

June 21 I'm No Job

Job 1:22

Through all this Job did not sin nor did he blame God.

Wow! This is astounding to me. Mostly when I consider how I would fare under the same circumstances. Job lost everything except his faith. He lost his livelihood when all his herds were stolen and his employees killed. He lost all of his children in a storm. He then lost his health. And through it all, his wife remained, but she was of no support.

To read about Job's life and his reverence for God to the extent that he never blamed or cursed God when not even understanding why the bad kept happening leaves me awed. I'm ashamed to consider how I have responded in my past when even a slight annoyance happens. I never lost faith, but my reverence was lacking.

When overcome by emotions, my emotions fail me. I often consider if Job was by personality wired with a calm and positive attitude. Or did his love for God overshadow his natural tendencies? I do recognize in my own life that the closer I remain to God, the more discipline I have over my spirit. The annoyances have less power. But I'm still no Job. But I do not think that's why we have his story.

See his story as encouragement that your struggles aren't an indication of some sin you have committed or from God's lack of love for you. Sin certainly has consequences, but as we learn from Job, bad circumstances also happen to good people who live righteously and love God.

See Job as a remarkable man to learn from, not as a reason to feel defeated thinking you could never be like him. Consider the positive habits of his life which kept him close to God and learn ways you can practice similar ways in your own life. Satan will not like it, but his attacks may just be from his anger and attempts to discourage your faith, not your failure of faith.

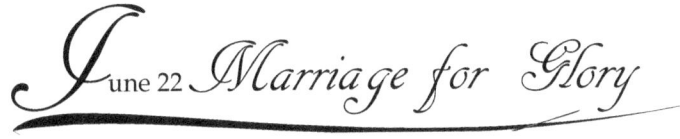

June 22 Marriage for Glory

Ephesians 5:27

That He might present to Himself the church in all her glory, having no spot or wrinkle or any such thing; but that she should be holy and blameless.

After I met my husband, God had to increase my boldness to even share about our relationship. I was my usual quiet and private self within my days. It was a blending of my personality and the anticipation of negativity and questions from others that had me shying away from the topic of love, especially of one incarcerated. When I mentioned that I was even writing my husband, the joking remarks followed: "Now, you're not going to be one of those women who falls in love with a convict, are you?" Little did they know, I already had.

And I consider my husband my greatest blessing. Unlike all my relationships before, God brought me this one. Not a drink, not loneliness, not for status or acceptance, or from anything originating in me—God brought me this one for His glory.

Paul teaches us in Ephesians that marriage is a reflection of Jesus's relationship with the believers. The husband (Jesus), should love his wife (believers) like Jesus loves His church. The wife should respect and follow her husband.

Marriage is primarily for God's glory. Ideally, two believers are brought together in marriage to fulfill the great commission. Individually, each of us has that assignment; as a couple, it still remains. Sharing Christ and bringing God glory—this is our marriage assignment.

But we are often far from this as couples. My husband and I aren't there yet. Yet I remain hopeful of all that God is doing in both our lives, individually, that I know we will resemble more of that one day.

Try to look at your marriage in the same way. It will lessen some of the emotional losses when you consider the grander reason for why you're together. God desires to work within your marriage to teach you more about Himself. In following His design for marriage, you'll discover a deeper love for your husband. And in that depth, separation and the unique challenges of your marriage can be overcome—to the glory of God.

June 23 — He's Bigger

Psalm 61:3-4

For Thou hast been a refuge for me, a tower of strength against the enemy. Let me dwell in Thy tent forever; let me take refuge in the shelter of Thy wings. Selah.

Since being on this path of prison with my husband, I have grieved the loss of countless memories not shared with him. And most are the experiences of the everyday. Prison brings an acute awareness that the beauty of love is found in the simple things of each day, not so much the vacations or holiday events. These more notable times hold special meaning, and I miss having him home to share them, but the sharing of the simple is where my yearning settles.

As a prisoner's wife, the loneliness and desire for the everyday are there to create a residual ache for me as I live on the outside. I long for the things most seem to take for granted in their abundance of it. I have a daily reminder as I continue in the same surroundings that are the stage for such moments to be created — or observed in the worlds of others — whether it's around the house, in the yard, at the grocery, or in the car with a list of errands to be completed. Oh, how I miss doing the uninteresting with the one I love.

But as a prisoner's wife, I get accustomed to doing the typical days of life alone in many ways, especially given the lengthy sentence as my husband is serving. He's involved to the extent he can be, but many of the daily decisions, the logistics of doing most all decisions, and the simple experiences of life become a solo endeavor. To sit and share with each new day isn't available. There's no morning talk over coffee or conversation over dinner. The luxury of conversation is a fifteen-minute phone call on a regimented schedule and visits that are even less frequent. We are only able to experience the everyday to the extent we are able to place it on paper, squeeze its events into that fifteen minutes, or unload it at one time on a visit.

This absence of the simple and the presence of the routines of prison might be your struggle today. Your struggling thoughts see the prison barriers and more days ahead of the same. The anticipated energy to overcome the barriers can exhaust you before the days even arrive as the contemplations in your mind begins to spiral downward. If not careful, your sighs can accumulate to the point you lose heart within the discouragement of the regimented and restricted life you face in your marriage. You then risk giving up that space in your heart where joy and contentment usually reside. If you succumb to those discouraging feelings, a season of sorrow enters your days. Oh, how long the journey seems in such moments.

This is why God wants to be the most cherished partner in your marriage. He wants to be your spiritual energy to comfort and encourage you in the everyday. He interrupts those battles in your mind through encouragement and assurance. When you're emotionally exhausted, He provides what I call "hugs" to refresh your perspective and give you the lift you need to keep walking this path—whether it's the bigger path of prison or those disappointing walks from an empty mailbox on days when you really need to hear from your husband. Without God's presence, the grey of the prison can become a constant cloud, casting a shadow over your outlook. If you face the everyday under that persistent cloud, the journey you see ahead looks overwhelming. But God's Holy Spirit reins you back into today with that fresh perspective and reminds you that God remains bigger than prison.

June 24 Written to Remember

I Chronicles 16:12

Remember His wonderful deeds which He has done, His marvels and the judgments from His mouth.

My Bible is very much my journal. It's my treasure I depend on when the rumblings of difficulty encroach. Any Bible I own has dates, study notes, insights from God, and underlined verses sprinkled throughout the pages. A review of God's faithfulness recorded in the margins may be an answer to prayer, an encouragement, or the more difficult voice of conviction. When all seems out of my control, I can absorb comfort through reading God's word and the reminders I find along the way. I can rest in my faith in who is greater than the storm, because He has proven Himself faithful every time before.

David wrote about God's faithfulness and the verse today is part of a song he wrote in praise to God's strength, goodness, and love. In chapter 16, they are celebrating the return of the ark to Jerusalem. The Philistines had captured it in an earlier conflict, and once sent back to the Israelites, it remained in different cities until this final stop.

David says that the purpose in remembering God's deeds was to keep close to Him and remain faithful to His will. David recognized that the more God's word is part of your daily life, the better both of these are accomplished.

By writing down moments God has moved in your life, answered prayer, blessed you with a miracle, spared you, encouraged you, and even disciplined you, you can preserve precious evidence and memories that might possibly get lost as life moves forward. These can be crucial reflections when really needing to hear from God at a later point.

And in one of those later moments, you'll gain amazement for what God has done. You'll hopefully look back even on prison and all the journal notes of God's faithfulness during this current time and have a deep awe in how He carried you through. You'll peruse times when you didn't see how you were going to make it, yet there you'll be sitting and reading of it from the other side of the pain and difficulty.

Find a way that works best for you to capture your walk with the Lord. Use the margins of your Bible, a separate journal, or basic loose-leaf paper. There's no best way; just what promotes the routine best for you.

June 25 Words Done Differently

Proverbs 15:1

A gentle answer turns away wrath, but a harsh word stirs up anger.

One thing I have learned that helps when my husband and I are having issues is to tell him that I love him before I even enter a conversation that I know has the potential to go badly. This puts a positive word and value on our relationship before the conflict has the opportunity to smother out the good. I might say, "I love you. I adore you and you're my greatest blessing." I then share or respond to the issue that's causing difficulty.

Just the process of intentionally approaching the conversation with worthy words *first*, the conflict holds less power. Furthermore, the limited time we have to even discuss the issue is more productive and less likely to end prematurely with our being mad and frustrated when the prison restriction says, "time's up." It's a horrible feeling to hear dead air or end a visit without the opportunity to say "I love you."

The wisdom found in Proverbs affirm this approach. And most of us can attest that it works. We are more apt to respond aggressively when someone aggresses toward us. We stay calmer in our words when someone speaks to us respectfully. The discipline we can show over our words can diffuse an argument or make it less severe.

However, this is very difficult to do in the moment of upset. I often say a quick prayer when answering my husband's phone call when I know I'm mad about something. It's my acknowledgment to God that I'll need help to manage my words calmly. I do the same at visits when I know we are having issues. I know too well that once my husband's anger is sparked, he's all in verbally. This does the conflict no good at that point.

It really is hard to swallow my own anger for the betterment of resolving an issue. It feels unnatural in many ways. It feels close to losing in a competition of some sort. But I have to cling to the greater victory which happens for our marriage when I surrender my words to a godly response.

All marriages are faced with this issue. But for those involving prison, communication is a greater challenge, because you simply do not have the time and setting to encourage sharing on the level issues demand. You start at a deficit before you even open your mouth. It's a wise strategy to put this proverb to use. You may bite hard on your tongue to accomplish it, but try it. You have nothing to lose, but possibly a less severe tongue-lashing from your husband in response.

June 26 Your Mind's Defense

James 4:7

Submit therefore to God. Resist the devil and he will flee from you.

Satan is very good at taking advantage and orchestrating damage to your marriage through what he speaks into your head. He has a brilliant way of lurking in the shadows until you're hit with pain, depressed, or simply drained by life, then he whispers discouraging and despairing thoughts to you. He might be yelling for all we know, since it's another realm where he and his demons operate.

But he has been doing it for a long time, and the fierce landscape of prison isn't where he limits his efforts to destroy. If he can keep you frustrated in your days, irritable in response to little things that needle you, and doubting your future, he can methodically rob you of your joy, and this will impact your marriage.

The key to stopping Satan in his devious tracks is to replace those negative, defeating thoughts with godly ones. Tough assignment! Anyone who has tried knows how hard it is to discipline a mind that's easily swayed by what it sees, hears, or imagines. But the negative chain begins with one thought, and that's where you begin your efforts—that first thought. The beauty of the promise to anyone who has a relationship with Jesus is that once you resist, the devil flees.

Negative thoughts come in all versions: immoral, unkind, impatient, prideful, discouraging, lying, worrisome, jealous. Any thought not godly is negative. If you consider changing how you think based on such a list, it does appear a daunting task. Just as the journey you face in the time of your husband's sentencing, it looks overwhelming and bleak for any success if you consider all the days ahead collectively. So it is with your thoughts. You cannot possibly win the battle if you already see yourself as defeated in the war.

So do not dwell on the difficulty you face. Do not dwell on your failed attempts from the past. Satan will be right there to discourage you before you even begin. Think of each negative thought as a battle. Focus on winning that one battle.

Often, just stopping and taking a deep breath are the keys to defusing an upsurge of mental frustration. It lowers your blood pressure and lets your mind have victory over your body's innate response when stressed. Use the exhalation to say a quick prayer to God for help: "Lord, refocus my spirit on the good."

Sometimes a song is a great distracter. You can immediately start to sing a hymn. Do something positive. Get in God's word. Speak Scripture aloud when needed. You may need to speak to Satan directly and tell him, "You can stop right now in the name of Jesus!" in response to his needling your emotions. The devil loves to speak lies when you're at your weakest. Expect it, respect it, but your challenge remains not to embrace it.

It may take you time to recognize the subtle building of negative thoughts. You do not realize how often you say negative things or think negative thoughts, until you're consciously trying to stop the ground they have in your mind. Remaining steadfast in your perspective and focusing on God's sovereignty allow you to move forward each day, following and focusing on the good, not running from the bad which wants to demand all your attention. Your husband and marriage need the good to reign. With God's help, the power of your thoughts become an ally on this journey of prison, not the enemy.

✝

June 27 — Hugs from Above

Psalm 23:4

Even though I walk through the valley of the shadow of death, I fear no evil; for Thou art with me; Thy rod and Thy staff, they comfort me.

One day, with a heavy heart and a heavy sky above me, I was making my way home. Traveling along the road, weary from the day, I saw before me a brilliant rainbow seemingly with its end resting over my house that remained unseen in the distance. My heart lifted toward that realm of peace when such a reminder of God's power and control over this world — and my circumstances — came before my eyes.

It was a soothing comfort that appeared frequently the days prior in various and unique places to form a familiar pattern. A person's shirt, the cover of a catalog, the words in a song — regularly experienced with the stirring of the Holy Spirit in each moment and my responding, "Oh, look Lord, another rainbow," in innocent communion as if I was informing Him of something that He might have missed. So when I saw the patterned rainbow resting over my house, I knew it was a hug from God simply to say, "I see what you're going through, and I'm here. Do not fear."

Remarkably, that comfort appeared again in the sky the following day, a rainbow resting with its end in the homely distance toward which I was traveling. God's goodness and intimacy poured over me as my face again lifted in a smile. Repetition in Scripture indicates importance. I knew the significance of the repeated rainbow. He was stressing His words of comfort through a giant hug from the sky as I continued to battle the same stress and emotions that were trying to smother me in their relentless presence.

The next morning, I was unable to keep my scanning eyes from the clouds to see if there would again be a rainbow. But the sky was clear — and that was okay. I had absorbed the message. But for me, God's presence is a longing in any avenue through which He chooses to reveal Himself. I live in expectation of His presence and communication to me, and that was my state on that drive to work that following morning, talking and communing with God.

It was a conversation that I carried to my desk to begin another day of responsibility within the world that so overwhelmed me previously. I checked my E-mail. But unlike previous mornings, one stood out in brilliant font, because the Holy Spirit soared within me. It was titled "A Hug Certificate for You." After I clicked the message, my heart was further consumed with the intimacy of God. I read, with building tears: "If I could catch a rainbow, I would do it just for you."

The Lord has rainbow hugs for you too. There's no better way to walk through life—or prison—than with God Almighty. When you have the infinite power of God at your side on this journey, you'll experience indescribable assurance. There's no one on this planet who can support you like God can. He knows you so intimately; He's your constant companion. There's no one who can love you like He does. Invite Him into your life and begin to experience the astounding presence of the Holy Spirit going along with you now and into eternity.

June 28 Be Holy

I Peter 1:15-16

But like the Holy One who called you, be holy yourselves also in all your behavior; because it is written, "You shall be holy, for I am holy."

In all my behavior? I consistently fail at this. However, with renewed desire to draw closer to God, I'm taking steps in a better direction. It has been consistently hard because of prison. My husband's struggles with holiness impact my efforts of the same. It's a version of the proverb which states that bad company corrupts good character. My husband's influences and prison culture make it hard for both of us to be righteous. I can be in a moral war most any day.

Peter was quoting from the book of Leviticus where God had instructed the Israelites in holiness. In the Old Testament, holiness was equated to keeping God's law, thus not sinning against Him. Like the Israelites, holiness comes down to our turning from sin and toward God. And it's usually in the small things that trip me up in my pursuit of holiness.

What I have to focus on is loving God more than my sin, regardless how small it may be. The small sins put Jesus on the cross just as effectively as the large ones. If I can discipline my responses from that perspective, my decisions, thoughts, and actions naturally progress toward being holy.

Does my husband always agree with my convictions and change in behavior? No. It does create conflict and this becomes another example of how prison marriages are hard. He's saturated in a culture that isn't holy.

Prison is pagan. And just as my husband's behavior can influence me negatively, he's influenced by the people around him. His good efforts are corrupted by bad company.

You likely face many of the same battles in your efforts to be holy. Let Christ be your example and always remember that you're His witness. He has given you the Holy Spirit to help you resist temptations that hope to trip you up. Your love for God can motivate you to not participate in the sins of your husband. God can use your desire and consistent, godly choices to draw your husband toward holiness, and with that, there become fewer battles within the holy war between the two of you.

June 29 Intentional Work

Proverbs 16:26

A worker's appetite works for him, for his hunger urges him on.

Prison marriages take intentionality, energy, and time — in more ways than the obvious. Our multitasking in the kitchen while catching up on the day's happenings with our husbands isn't available. Time with our husbands must be carved into our routines. We must set aside additional time through writing, talking on the phone, or visiting to share our days. Often, our husbands are housed a great distance from us. Visiting them for six hours can easily take twelve, and for many, an overnight motel stay.

Spending time with our husbands means the yard doesn't get mowed, the house doesn't get cleaned, the laundry doesn't get done, and the grocery shopping is delayed. All that doesn't get done, because of the regimented demands of prison, must find another place in an already busy schedule. This takes work.

The proverb for today basically says that we work for what's important to us. Our time is spent on what's important to us. Our money is spent on what's important to us. Priorities become challenged when a spouse is incarcerated. Time management is essential to get everything done. And if something doesn't get done — if you have prioritized right — it will be okay anyway.

You should be commended for the investment you continuously make in your marriage. Keeping the important things in focus will keep you making the right decisions for your marriage. Your hunger is to make it through prison and support your husband. You feed your daily appetite to this end through your daily choices.

If you sense your urgency for supporting your husband waning, take a look at what you have been "eating." Where are you spending your time? Is your heart motivated for things as they used to be? Has your priorities changed?

It's natural to have lulls in motivation, especially when doing a prison marriage. But refresh yourself! Renew your appetite for the things that matter. Make some intentional decisions that puts your marriage first. There may not always be money to visit or to talk on the phone, but there still remains ways to invest your time and energy in your husband. Keep the goal in mind and keep working intentionally!

June 30 *Truth or Feeling?*

Hebrews 10:22-23

Let us draw near with a sincere heart in full assurance of faith, having our hearts sprinkled clean from an evil conscience and our bodies washed with pure water. Let us hold fast the confession of our hope without wavering, for He who promised is faithful.

A few years ago, I was brought under conviction by the Holy Spirit for an issue. I immediately repented, but going forward, I really struggled to pray. And it broke my heart. I felt estranged from the source and enjoyment of my days. I loved and revered God so much that the unworthiness I felt about myself in comparison made me shy away. I almost felt as though someone more worthy than me should talk to God on my behalf. It was a horrible feeling.

But that's all it was—a feeling that Satan beat into my mind; it wasn't the truth. Someone more worthy than me had already intervened with God on my behalf; that was Jesus. I could come boldly to God in prayer, fully restored and forgiven. What followed from one of those depressed evenings was a morning hug from God to remind me of this truth.

Walking up the hallway on my morning shuffle to the coffee maker with the distant light from the bedroom behind me, I felt the unusual below my feet. "What am I walking on?" I said to myself within the cloudiness of my morning mind. Switching on a closer light, I saw the source. A curtain that hung, separating the hallway from the living room, had been torn down. I knew the message to my heart immediately. God said, "Come." Tears flowed, and God's love swallowed me up in such a sweet moment.

Some would say there's a logical explanation for it: the dog probably tore it down. My rambunctious dog during the night could have. But once you walk with God, you learn how He communicates with you through the inanimate, situations encountered in your day, and yes, your dog sometimes. You learn to hear His voice.

And the joy of forgiveness was like none other. God had forgiven me the moment I repented, but it took some time before I let that absorb into my spirit. I let my feelings interfere with my closeness to God. Scripture tells us that we cannot trust our feelings. Our hearts can deceive us.

There may be times when you have to simply believe God's word when you feel otherwise. You may feel unworthy, but God's word says you're loved. You may feel useless and without purpose, but God's word says you were uniquely planned for a very special purpose. You may feel as if you have done too much bad to be forgiven, but God's word says, "Come."

July 1 — He Knows His Name

Luke 19:5

And when Jesus came to the place, He looked up and said to him, "Zaccheus, hurry and come down, for today I must stay at your house."

Your husband lost much of his identity when he went to prison. An inmate number got attached to him which becomes more important almost than his name. Most mail cannot be delivered to him without it. Likely every piece of paper connected with his prison file includes the identifier. If not referred to by this number, he's addressed by housing and bunk information or simply the generic "Inmate."

Places like prison go to great lengths to remove the personal face from the criminal. No one seems to care about his story or his value as a person. He's a number to manage and control in the name of security.

Jesus, however, knows your husband by name, even before he was named or born. Your husband is loved deeply by God. Jesus is personal and died personally for your husband—and for you. This level of intimacy is remarkable. We find in Scripture that the amazing way Jesus ministered while on earth was individually. He spoke to crowds, but healed with a personal touch or word.

When traveling through Jericho, there was a tax collector named Zaccheus who was eager to see Jesus, but because of the crowds and his small height, he couldn't see him. So he climbed a tree for a better view. Jesus walked near and called Zaccheus by name. Jesus didn't say, "You there, in the tree," or ask someone near, "Who is that man above in the tree?" Jesus knew Zaccheus, knew what he did for a living, and most importantly, knew he needed a Savior.

Reading further in Luke 19, Jesus states why He came to earth: to seek and save the lost. That mission was the same the day your husband was born. He came to seek your husband by name and to save him.

The crowd ridiculed Jesus for accompanying Zaccheus to his home, considering association with such a sinner disgraceful. It was Jesus's grace that saw the sinner and yet felt compassion. Jesus desired to be a guest in the house of a sinner. He went to Zaccheus's home. He can also come to a prison cell.

July 2 A 3-Legged Dog

Jude 1:4

For certain persons have crept in unnoticed, those who were long beforehand marked out for this condemnation, ungodly persons who turn the grace of our God into licentiousness and deny our only Master and Lord, Jesus Christ.

Many years ago, I was visiting churches in the area to find one to attend regularly. On a Wednesday evening, a lady stood up in the congregation and handed out a Bible study. I took one. During the upcoming days of study, I was skeptical of the author and the content. There was nothing overt, but I had a very unsettled feeling when I tried to read it. But more eerily, the analogies the writer used in the study began playing out in my life. The final one involved a small dog statue in the front yard.

The study had used the illustration of a 3-legged dog. On my trip to the mailbox later that morning, my eyes were drawn to the small dog statue left behind by my in-laws when they moved on to another house. It was toppled over. I retrieved my mail and went to stand it upright only to discover that one of its legs was missing. It was nowhere to be found. And the Holy Spirit stirred and confirmed what I was feeling: the study was false teaching. Further investigation into the publisher found an organization without a mention of Jesus in their mission statement.

I was experiencing the Holy Spirit's warnings during those days, but also the evil presence that was heavy in my home. I recall sensing evil when I laid down at night. So much so, I prayed for protection and for Satan to be cast out. After I destroyed that study, the sense of evil was gone.

Did the lady at that church realize what she was distributing or was she a victim of the false teaching? She seemed well-intentioned, but Jude warns us that false teachers operate covertly. They sneak into congregations and seek to deny the truth of Scripture. They hope to lead people astray. Ultimately, they deny the true Jesus.

If you're a new believer, please be cautious about what you read and what you hear preached. Always do your own study of God's word to make sure you're receiving the truth. Take your Bible to church. Do not rely on the jumbo screen to reflect Scripture accurately. If you're a mature Christian, keep fresh in the word and call out error when you encounter it.

As prison wives, we can be vulnerable emotionally and some religious groups can be welcoming and sympathetic to our situations. It may be easy to get pulled into a false religion that subtly presents itself as Christian, yet blends error into it. Pray for discernment and for the Holy Spirit's warning to keep you safe from their ungodly attempts.

July 3 *An Assumed Offense*

Joshua 22:16

"Thus says the whole congregation of the Lord, 'What is this unfaithful act which you have committed against the God of Israel, turning away from following the Lord this day, by building yourselves an altar, to rebel against the Lord this day?'"

In the settlement of Canaan by the Israelites, there were three tribes which didn't make their home on that side of the Jordan. They preferred to remain on the opposite in the land of Gilead, because the land suited their livestock and tribe. Moses allowed them this request, and Joshua fulfilled it with his leadership once Canaan was possessed.

The tribes of Reuben, Gad, and the half-tribe of Manasseh considered the geography, the fact that the rest of the Israelites were separated from them by the river, and decided to build an altar there representing their devotion to God. They were concerned that in forthcoming generations, their affiliation with Israel might be discounted or believed unworthy, because of the geographical separation. An altar would be a memorial and symbol of their continued membership with Israel.

The tribes in Canaan learned that the altar was being built, but didn't know the reasoning behind it. They became angry in response to what they perceived as their brothers' rebellion and disregard for the Lord's commandments. An altar in their minds could only mean idolatry was happening. They immediately went to Gilead to confront the tribes.

What's interesting to read is how they went about dealing with the assumed offense. They didn't storm into the area and pull down the altar. They didn't become aggressive and battle their brothers in their anger. They didn't expel the tribes from the rest of the community and leave them to their assumed idolatry. Instead of any of these options, they asked questions.

Their concern for the behavior demanded a response, but by asking questions first, they avoided further damage and civil war. Granted, their questions contained assumptions, but reading further in the chapter, they also extended grace to their brothers by encouraging them to return to the rest of the Israelites if they were tempted to follow other gods in their physical separation from the rest of the tribes.

The three tribes responded to the concern, and with the explanation, the leaders accepted the reasoning, and everyone returned to their homes pleased with the outcome.

When you may be presented a situation with your husband that seems concerning on the surface, remember to ask questions first. It may not be as it seems. Even if the information comes from official sources, officials do not always have your husband's best interest at heart, and sadly, cannot always be trusted. Confront when necessary with a heart to discover the truth, not confirm an assumption.

July 4 Freedom in Christ

John 8:36

"If therefore the Son shall make you free, you shall be free indeed."

I have never heard of any prisoner ask to remain incarcerated after completing his sentence. Not that he would have any choice in that regards either. Many might return, but none can stay a prisoner once set free.

I often think of the *Shawshank Redemption* character Brooks who was finally released, obtaining what all inmates yearn for. But once "home" he couldn't adjust. He had no support really. He lived alone in a changed world that he couldn't relate to. He committed suicide when he could no longer live under the burden of being out of sync with everything around him. If allowed, he would have probably returned to prison.

Thankfully when Christ returned to heaven after His resurrection, He didn't leave us alone to continue living in an alien world in our new spiritual freedom. We have the Holy Spirit in us to be that support, comfort, and guide to help us remain free—free from sin.

But spiritual freedom does come with a choice, both to receive and to maintain. If you have believed in Jesus's death and resurrection, recognized and asked for forgiveness for committing the sins which placed Him on that cross, He has granted you freedom. You're no more under the penalty of damnation. Heaven awaits you after you physically die. This is good news!

But many Christians, including myself, struggle to remain free. Not that we can lose our salvation, but we take back the chains and shackles, return to our cell, and never take hold of the power that comes with having the Holy Spirit living in us. We let sin imprison us, and there we remain.

We trip over the same issues. We become discouraged. We stay lethargic for life, aggravated by our circumstances, and struggle to remain content. This isn't how God purposed us to live. This isn't why Jesus died!

We can have victory over the sin that keeps us down. We can live a life of divine purpose. We can wake up and have a truly good day. But we must desire contact with who holds the power to make all this happen. Our freedom comes with this choice.

Push through the tendency to give up because life has gotten stale and difficult. Come out on the other side of a difficult day, mood, or circumstance with a renewed hope. Allow the Holy Spirit to intervene and sustain your freedom.

✝

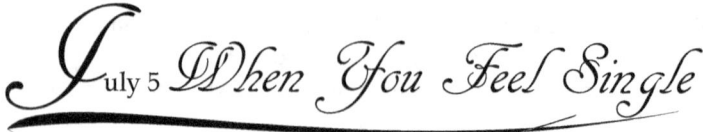

July 5 — When You Feel Single

I Corinthians 7:7

Yet I wish that all men were even as I myself am. However, each man has his own gift from God, one in this manner, and another in that.

The little things that so affectionately inject energy into the typical marriage flow within the everyday. Flirting comments at the kitchen sink, fighting for space on the sofa as a movie plays, calling for a towel from a steamy shower because of forgetfulness, and simply enjoying each other's company — the real-time flow of the little expressions of love balance the drain of those hard days of marriage.

But as a prisoner's wife, in the singleness of your days, there are few avenues for the natural exchanges and encouragement of the everyday to infuse your marriage. You do not have the everyday with your husband to recharge your emotional batteries. Your emotions drain daily in the contemplations of its absence.

I have found that God is the only answer to this type of singleness. My contentment in the Lord makes the singleness of my days doable. He keeps me company, makes me laugh, encourages me, comforts me, and leads me in my purpose — daily.

God regularly shows up in my life through intimate patterns to remind me of His presence or prepare my heart to hear from Him. This can be in Scripture or in my surroundings. The Holy Spirit stirs in both cases to let me know God is near. Once I have recognized the pattern, God uses it as an avenue in my everyday walk, along with my daily Bible reading and time in prayer, to communicate with me. It all blends in a pattern of intimacy to confirm, guide, encourage, or correct my walk — with my husband or in the days without him.

Paul was a single man. He expresses his wish that everyone could be that way. Why? His singleness allowed him to focus solely on the Lord. He had no distractions. He saw it actually as a gift from God. He came to learn that there's no greater contentment and fulfillment than his relationship with the Lord. He couldn't get enough of it. He wasn't opposed to marriage, but he longed for others to experience the closeness he enjoyed with the Lord through his singleness.

I believe a prison wife can enjoy some of the fruit Paul was referring to simply because of the separation we experience. This is especially true for those of us without children or other family commitments in the household. There's nothing of course wrong with those things, but it just makes cultivating the fruit more challenging. I experienced my own version of this when I was working sixty hours a week with no day off; it greatly impacted my ability to invest in my relationship with God. So I understand if you aren't in a place in life that Paul wishes for us. Life is hard!

But wherever you are in life, God wants to be personal with you. He wants to show you His love and to be your contentment, every day. He's already with you and waiting to be the fulfillment you have been longing for. He can make the singleness of your days doable.

July 6 Fruitfulness for All

Galatians 5:22-23

But the fruit of the Spirit is love, joy, peace, patience, kindness, goodness, faithfulness, gentleness, self-control; against such things there is no law.

When I read the list of the fruit of the Spirit, I consider how opposite those attributes are to the culture of prison. I do not see an abundance of love, joy, peace, patience, kindness, goodness, faithfulness, gentleness, and self-control in prison. There's an abundance of the opposite. Beginning in verse nineteen, Paul lists the opposites which are the deeds of the flesh. Both lists represent the heart within the person—for the good or bad.

We are all prone to sin from our fleshly desires without the restraint of the Holy Spirit. He can teach and guard our hearts to grow and preserve the good fruit. But without His presence, fleshly fruit of all the negatives are produced. Prison is just congregate housing for people producing bad fruit, because the Holy Spirit isn't active in their lives.

This is why prayer for a prison can be a plea for all those who comprise what makes the fruit of that place so evil. You can start with the prison as a whole, then pray more specifically for a dorm, then a wing, and then down to that neighbor or roommate who is making your husband's life so difficult. Because it all comes down to the individual hearts of those there.

It seems overwhelming, but God hasn't given up on the men there. Just as so, there are men on the inside trying to bear fruit of the Spirit with God's help. They could use additional help through your prayers.

Jesus is needed to bring salvation and a new heart to those bent on evil. The Christian men living in that environment need help to deny the fleshly desires that bombard them daily. God's Holy Spirit needs to reign within the walls to make the culture there a better place for the good of all.

July 7 Time Starved

I Peter 1:3

Blessed be the God and Father of our Lord Jesus Christ, who according to His great mercy has caused us to be born again to a living hope through the resurrection of Jesus Christ from the dead.

My husband has spent the majority of his years of prison in confinement. One day when considering this, I figured that less than two years out of the previous twelve, at that time, were spent in general population. Our ability to share the same space at visit or talk on the phone had mostly been restricted. It had varied from no contact to only a biweekly visits and phone calls. And while in confinement, visits were on a weekday which further complicated seeing each other because of my work schedule. When we did see or talk, in all its inadequate volume, I came away with an overwhelming knowledge of just how time starved I was for him.

To go year after year in that scenario can drain the hope from the best of us. And I cannot imagine living this life without a hope for something beyond prison, especially considering the life sentence my husband is living. But there's hope! And my hope comes with the accompanying knowledge that this life isn't my husband's or my home, and my purpose that I find in Christ brings satisfaction to my days while we are separated.

Peter praises this aspect of what he knew to be the truth for believers in the first chapter of his epistle. He reminds us that we have a living hope in Jesus. Living hope! Jesus actively intercedes and is present with us. He preserves our future in heaven and helps us during our days now. And Peter reminds us too that we can rejoice in this even during trials and feelings of distress, because these difficult days are temporary. I know that a life sentence for my husband is a blink of an eye when compared to eternity.

Meditate on this truth for yourself. Let it sink into your motivation each day to keep walking this path with peace and perseverance. There's no other peace that satisfies that longing you now have for time with your husband. Time will pass with more satisfaction, because the desire for your husband will be blended into purposeful days in Christ to maintain the energy you need to keep walking while prison remains a part of your life.

July 8 Night Messages

Deuteronomy 31:6

"Be strong and courageous, do not be afraid or tremble at them, for the Lord your God is the one who goes with you. He will not fail you or forsake you."

My car was once again missing — in my dream that is. I have noticed a pattern of this theme when I'm stressed in my waking world. Either I cannot find my car when in a parking lot or my car was stolen, because I knew exactly where I left it. I have a helpless feeling and I'm always alone in my efforts of trying to find the car or solve the problem. It's a horrible feeling of abandonment without any resources. I usually watch myself walking and searching through various scenes, never finding the car.

I learned that my patterned dream is a common theme for other people. It's supposedly an outgrowth of anxiety and uncertainty about life's direction. It could also represent a desire to go, but unable to make any steps forward. It was somewhat a relief to discover the commonality, because I could draw some confidence by the pattern for others in why I was having the same nighttime problem.

I know I'm not to worry. The level of my stress becomes more obvious when the dream occurs. I do not realize how much anxiety I have allowed to enter my thoughts until the familiar search at night is revealed the following morning. It sneaks up on me.

In response, I have to focus on God's word to remind myself that He will guide my life. I'll never be lost if I stick close to Him and seek His will. And thankfully, the reality is that I always have Jesus with me. I'm never alone, even when facing a struggle that seems mine alone to deal with. There's comfort knowing that all my feelings are known by God: my fear, worry, helplessness. He never leaves me or forsakes me — even if the problem was my fault to begin with. He's faithful.

I'm not one to believe that every dream has a practical application for waking hours, but there are evenings when they accurately send a message. I also believe that God will still use dreams to speak.

Consider how stress and anxiety creep into your thoughts. A dream may be a warning that you aren't managing your emotions as well as you thought. Meditate on the truth of Scripture. You aren't alone in your trials. God is right there with you. You have no better protector. Rest in this truth.

July 9 A Servant's Heart

Acts 28:3

But when Paul had gathered a bundle of sticks and laid them on the fire, a viper came out because of the heat, and fastened on his hand.

If you read the events leading up to Paul's snakebite, you would read of an astounding survival of him and others through a northeaster. Before that, he was arrested and attempts were plotted to kill him. He was in the custody of guards and being sent to Rome to be tried before Caesar. On the way, the boat was wrecked and they had to risk swimming to shore. They made it. Despite the ordeal Paul had been through, not to mention he was still under arrest and awaiting trial, we read of his gathering wood to help keep a fire going.

Was he made to gather wood? Scripture doesn't say, but given Paul's personality and character leading up to that moment, I think he probably jumped right in offering to help. The fire would help his captors, his fellow inmates, and the ship's crew. It was still raining and it was cold. They were exhausted, likely hungry, and wanting nothing more than to lie down and recuperate from the previous days.

Maybe others did. But not Paul. He immediately served others, and he continued to serve and use the detour for sharing the Gospel. Paul saw every encounter and experience as God's divine orchestration to some purpose. He didn't always know the details, but he remained faithful through the experience to not whine or diminish into self-pity.

What an encouragement Paul's life is! Prison dumps difficulties on us all the time, but we can be encouraged by reading of Paul's outlook. He encouraged others while the storm pounded them, and he continued to be a servant once safely on shore. God was right there encouraging him so he could encourage others.

Do not let the difficulties of prison stop you from being productive and serving others. In fact, investing in the good of someone else can help take the negative focus off yourself and redeem the time or bad experiences.

Time will keep moving regardless of how you choose to use it. See the opportunities within a day, not just the clouds. Allow God to bring this journey of prison to a good outcome for you and those He brings into your path on the way.

July 10  Doing Love Differently

Song of Solomon 8:7

"Many waters cannot quench love, nor will rivers overflow it; if a man were to give all the riches of his house for love, it would be utterly despised."

Separation—it's the very nature of a prison marriage. Your husband is separated from society; you're separated from each other. It's tough to do any marriage when separation is frequent. But unlike the traveling businessman or musician whose absence is usually intermittent, even if for months at a time, our husbands are away continuously, oftentimes for years. When added to the other frustrations that come along with prison, it can easily and more quickly separate your relationship in all ways. It will take subtle steps toward the destination of destroying your marriage. Staying connected with your husband becomes an essential challenge on this path of prison.

For a typical marriage, connectedness remains a difficulty over time, so how much more for ours. We face a deficit in connection the moment the gate closes behind us each visit. Within the prison rules that discourage connection, we must find ways of doing love differently to win this battle. We must encourage growth in our marriage, because relationships aren't meant to be stagnant—prison or free. Life changes; we change. Prison stifles growth through its redundancy, and the routine stales a relationship if allowed.

For a change, you might try writing even if you have calls and visits regularly. There's something special about the opportunity to stop from the hustle and share time with your husband through writing.

Take pictures of places you routinely go or the little things that happen at home. Such visuals help your husband feel a part of the life that's separated from him. Remember that most color has been taken from his world. He sees brown and blue all day, every day.

Take selfies to share "you" as the days play out. Your 5:00 a.m. look, your just-having-mowed-the-grass look, your Saturday look, and your Sunday look—all your looks.

Read the same books. Talk about the characters, the story, and your favorite parts. Read his favorite books in an effort to share what he enjoys.

Use the same Bible. It allows you to study from the same version and to know exactly the footnotes and cross references the other is reading. Read and share devotionals.

Get the same newspaper subscription, magazines, or listen to the same radio programs—anything that creates times of oneness. Using the internet, you can usually listen to the radio station that he does. You can read the local news where he's at, the weather for the day, and virtually any aspect of the area where he's experiencing his day. Your husband can receive the local newspaper where you live. He's able to read about what's happening in your area.

It may seem silly and a lot of effort, but the mundane becomes the significant when you're striving to stay connected. You want to share your life with him, so the small experiences are important. The absence of such small things risks creating the common loneliness and distance. If your husband were home, you would be spending time together, so now the focus must be on not disregarding this time, but finding new ways to share it. Your priorities will definitely be challenged! Get creative and make it a goal that your love will not be quenched by the waters of the world or prison.

July 11 A Purified Life

Malachi 3:3

"And He will sit as a smelter and purifier of silver, and He will purify the sons of Levi and refine them like gold and silver, so that they may present to the Lord offerings in righteousness."

The tribe of Levi was appointed by the Lord to be responsible for the temple. This duty was serious business. All items used in worship, the material used to construct the temple, everything associated with God's temple was to remain pure and holy. The priests were Levites, and they were responsible for teaching the people and holding the people accountable to God's commandments. During the time of Malachi, the Levites had become lax in their duties. And God reprimanded them.

God's discipline can be considered as being refined. When metals are purified, the impurities are separated from the metal by fire. The process doesn't destroy the metal, but it brings out its best.

We can look at God's discipline in the same way. He can allow distress and hurt to enter our lives to draw us out of our sin toward a more purified life. He disciplines us out of His love. He knows a pure life is the best life.

Our slide into impure, unrighteous behavior usually happens a little at a time. One small decision to the next. We allow sin to blossom and look appealing, because when it was just a small sprout, we made accommodations and excuses for it.

This world is so saturated with unholy things that a purified life has to be very intentional. The small sprouts have to be uprooted quickly. This is a challenge when prison presents its unholy self in full bloom daily. It's hard to separate from the impurities. We can only take comfort in the truth that God knows our hearts. We do need His chastening when we voluntarily slide away from righteousness, but we also receive His grace when we have no choice but enter a sinful arena and do our best to stay clean before Him.

July 12 Even the Prodigal

Luke 15:24

For this son of mine was dead, and has come to life again; he was lost, and has been found. And they began to be merry.

God loves the prodigal equally as the one who never strays. Luke chapter fifteen popularly testifies to this love. One son demands his half of the inheritance, while the other son stays home. The prodigal leaves and lives a life of pleasure and irresponsibility, exhausting all his money. He finds himself at his bottom, eating with the pigs. For a Jew, this was the lowest. He made a decision to return to his father, who according to Scripture was already waiting and watching. His father extended mercy and celebrated his return.

That's the beauty of God's vision for the prodigal. He watches without becoming weary. Scripture tells us He never sleeps or slumbers. He's the Shepherd always on the lookout for His child, desiring to draw him near where it's safe. But He also gives him the opportunity to roam free, if he chooses. But with that choice, God doesn't stop loving him. He's constantly working behind the scenes, seeking that one that strays.

God's vision isn't limited to the past of wrong choices, sinful actions, and outright defiance. He has a divine purpose for every person and desires to guide each person—even the hardest criminal—back from the darkness into the awesome future reserved for him.

While working on this writing, I was thinking on my husband, all the hope I have for him, all God has done in him, and all the hugs God uses to encourage me in our future. I went to church the following morning to be welcomed with a hug through a version of the sweetest hymn from my youth that spoke volumes to my heart regarding God's heart for the criminal. I looked at the screen and read.

O perfect redemption, the purchase of blood,
To every believer the promise of God;
The vilest offender who truly believes,
That moment from Jesus a pardon receives.

Those are words from the hymn "To God Be the Glory."[1] The chorus tells us to praise the Lord, praise the Lord, let the people rejoice! I was praising God from a heart that truly believes that God loves each and every incarcerated man, regardless of what put him behind the rolls of razor wire.

God desires to bring your husband home spiritually through salvation, and He will never let him stray without seeking him. I also pray he returns to you physically, but with a heart that will be praising God for the great things He has done.

July 13 Always Personal

II Samuel 22:29

"For Thou art my lamp, O Lord; and the Lord illumines my darkness."

David's heart just sings in this chapter! He's praising God for rescue, blessings, and protection. David's life was full of stressful times; he faced danger regularly it seemed. He became king, but not without sacrifice. He sacrificed easy living to follow God's plan. The path of his life presented trouble; some he was responsible for, most came in response to God's call on his life. But regardless of what led to the difficulty and darkness of the path

---

[1] Crosby, Fanny J., "To God Be the Glory," Convention Press, *Baptist Hymnal* (Nashville: Convention Press, 1975).

at the time, David knew that God knew his situation perfectly and personally.

God isn't a faraway god not interested in the happenings of your life. He isn't too busy to care about your struggles. When the path of life becomes dark, God knows intimately what you face.

God is personal. Your struggles with prison are known to Him. He's gentle and loving and longs to show you both on this journey. When you're weeping, His heart longs to help. When you're angry about injustices, His righteousness agrees. When you do not know what to do, He knows the way. All the things of your life, He knows.

This is beyond the human mind to comprehend. God's omniscience and omnipresence mean that He knows everything and He's everywhere all the time. And the great thing even beyond this is that He loves you and wants to be a part of your life, to show you grace and the light of His way through your darkness.

He also never tires of listening and helping. You're His greatest creation, and He stands available to you all the time. In the middle of the night, in the middle of a tough conversation with your husband, in the middle of traffic on a stressful day. You can call on Him anytime, anywhere.

Just like David, you have the same opportunity and access to God. His character hasn't changed. He remains personally interested in each person—you, your husband, the guards, the warden, the vendor employee who stocks the canteen. He's personal. Let this comfort you when you feel as though no one understands. God understands, and also possesses everything you need to brighten your path.

July 14 *Grace Abounds*

I Timothy 1:13-14

Even though I was formerly a blasphemer and a persecutor and a violent aggressor. And yet I was shown mercy, because I acted ignorantly in unbelief; and the grace of our Lord was more than abundant, with the faith and love which are found in Christ Jesus.

The screech followed the direction of the neighbor's cat as she skirted quickly across the yard. She had accomplished a mission and was carrying away her trophy—a little bunny. Into the brush, the cat retreated with her prize while I frantically called after her, "Gracie, drop it!"

My mission was to rescue the poor little creature that remained panicked within the grasp of the ironically named "Gracie." But each time I approached, she darted off and the screech followed. It was a horrible feeling to consider the fear and pain the innocent bunny was going through for the simple nature of the cat. Because once dead, her interest would travel from the bunny to the next lively bug or creature in the yard. I never rescued the bunny, and walked into the house, speaking out loud my disgust and anger at that cat.

Ironically, the neighbor had arranged with me the day prior to feed and care for the cat while they were away in the upcoming days. I gladly agreed. But after the yard incident, on that walk into the house, I found myself saying, "Stupid cat! I can't believe I now have to take care of you after what you've done to that little bunny!" I had no grace for Gracie.

I can understand why people have a difficult time extending grace to criminals. They do not deserve it. Possibly like Gracie, they indiscriminately harmed others. They may have had multiple opportunities to do the right thing, like I encouraged of that cat, to only run the other direction, deeper into crime.

God reminded me through that incident that His desire to extend grace to the prisoner remains unwavering. Despite the harm perpetrated on others, the inmate hasn't fallen outside the desire of God to care for him. Unlike me, God doesn't have to muster up the love and concern when the sin nature of one of His creatures wreaks harm. It remains constant.

So I resolved to care for the neighbor's cat with the overshadowing thankfulness to God that He doesn't harbor resentment for my sinful nature or those whom society has deemed even more unworthy because of past actions.

July 15 *Negatively Protected*

Jonah 1:17

And the Lord appointed a great fish to swallow Jonah, and Jonah was in the stomach of the fish three days and three nights.

We often think of Jonah's consequence for disobeying God as his being swallowed by a fish. But the reality is God sent the fish for Jonah's protection. He had been thrown overboard and was sinking into the weeds and debris of the water. He was becoming disoriented and close to death.

And in this distress, Jonah cried out to God for rescue. Thus a fish was sent as Jonah's rescue boat.

Once safe in the fish, three days and nights passed. I'm sure some initial time was spent recuperating from his near-death experience, then the reality and possible fear that accompanied his surroundings. Scripture seems to indicate that after the third night, Jonah had surrendered. His prayer follows in chapter two.

So for many of us, our initial cry for help comes easy, but it may take a few days to consider our circumstances and decide that God's way is best. It's true that as we draw close to God, He draws close to us. He responds to our cries, but He also wants our devotion to remain beyond the initial rescue.

Prison can serve as God's rescue boat. It's a negative event, but can be protective for some. It may be the fish sent to keep a man from certain death if left to continue in a lifestyle which led to incarceration. It can be a place, like the fish, where a man can consider his life, the path he has been on, and with time, consider God's will for his life. And hopefully, like Jonah, surrender to God's will.

We would like to rescue our husbands in other ways usually. It takes faith to trust God in how He rescues. There's such great pain to many as a result of prison, but always remember that it was our husbands' sin or that of others that resulted in prison. It was sin that set Jonah on the path which led him to being thrown overboard and left to die in the sea. It was also God's mercy for why the fish entered the picture for Jonah, and possibly for your husband's incarceration too.

July 16 Strength to Love

Luke 22:43

Now an angel from heaven appeared to Him, strengthening Him.

This is an amazing verse to me. In Jesus's humanity, He needed strength from God to carry out the plan of redeeming us from sin. Jesus was in tremendous distress while in the garden prior to His arrest and crucifixion. He prayed to God to remove the plan if that were His will. God didn't remove the plan, but strengthened Jesus to endure it. Out of His love for us, God strengthened Jesus so He could finish the most loving act for us—die in our place.

Jesus's act of love—His loving us—took Him to His human limits. His sweat was like drops of blood; He was in agony. He persevered in His love for us, and God helped.

I find a deep treasure in meditating on this when my husband may be hard to love or when prison has worn me down and pushed my emotions to my limits. I can consider what Jesus endured in His love for me and be refreshed in my encouragement. I'm also reminded that God can give me the strength to love.

The best way I have found to receive that strength is by staying in His word. He gives me reminders and tangible words to read when I need them most. It gives me opportunity to meditate on the truth. It encourages me. It calms my emotions and gives me hope.

In compassion, God strengthened Jesus. In compassion, I know that He will strengthen you to love through this journey of prison. Love can be a tall order on some days, and human effort alone will fall short. To love in the most perfect and unconditional way when your strength is gone, you need God's help. Be assured that He will faithfully provide what you need.

July 17 — In Times of Trouble

Psalm 34:4

I sought the Lord, and He answered me, and delivered me from all my fears.

Several years ago, my husband was having difficulty with a cellmate. I had been in prayer about it, but one morning, the prompting to pray hit me like a brick. It was urgent. It was so much so that in my Bible-study time, the Lord called me to fast too. I had never fasted at that point in my life, and wasn't even quite sure how to approach it, but the need was undeniable. My concern for my husband was excruciating, because I knew the response God was calling of me had to equate to the need on his end.

The next two days were spent in earnest prayer and fasting. On the second day, the feeling of peace was just as overwhelming as that initial urgency. The anxiety and concern were all gone. I couldn't even make myself worry about the situation. It was surreal. My fast ended and life resumed as normal.

My husband was able to call the next day and the first words out of his mouth were "I got a new roommate!" Come to find out when God called me to pray, my husband had planned to stab this other man to force a move out of the cell. It had gotten that bad. Thankfully, God intervened and orchestrated a positive move that my husband was oblivious to until I could explain on that phone call. There's power in prayer!

Why does God call us to pray? He certainly doesn't need our prayers to do His will. He's omnipotent, which means He's all-powerful. But it's clear that He desires us to pray. It's also clear that He responds to prayer.

The clearest determination I have made is that it's about being in relationship with Him. He desires to be in relationship with us, and He does this through prayer, engaging our lives through the Holy Spirit. It's a way of doing life with Him as we look to Him for guidance, strength, and comfort through prayer, while He responds through His word, our circumstances, or others to impart changes.

So we see prayers answered. We see a direct connection between prayers and outcomes. We see lives changed, because someone prays. We will never completely figure out the ways of God, but we can trust that He uses prayer to work in our lives for our ultimate good—and those whom we pray for.

July 18 Your Inner Minister

John 14:26-27

"But the Helper, the Holy Spirit, whom the Father will send in My name, He will teach you all things, and bring to your remembrance all that I said to you. Peace I leave with you; My peace I give to you; not as the world gives, do I give to you. Let not your heart be troubled, nor let it be fearful."

I'm a prisoner's wife who needs a cheerleader, someone daily to encourage me, to understand how hard this life is, and to walk faithfully with me through all moments. I need guidance in how to deal with a rebellious husband. I need someone to be there from those days when I suddenly have no contact with my husband to the better ones when I get to enjoy being with him more regularly. Because within all of the days, I need to keep walking this path with contentment and joy—for my marriage.

God's Holy Spirit is that person, my cheerleader. He isn't a silent observer. He actively participates in my days to express love, encouragement, and guidance. His presence keeps my heart at peace and enables me to look forward to another day, knowing God is in control and He has a special purpose for all I'm going through. I can keep walking with joy when the larger picture of love and the reason for the path are considered. Excitement returns to the journey knowing God is doing something awesome in my husband and my marriage for His glory. I can focus on my purpose with my husband and not prison. The journey remains doable.

And isn't that what we all desire when faced with prison—a doable journey? More good days than bad, fewer tears and more smiles, assurance not worry. We want a way to come through somehow better, not broken. We desire to meet our husbands at the gate one day, more intimately blended in our union than ever before, because we survived and flourished through a circumstance that did nothing but attempt to defeat us. Oh, how we want this!

But the journey lying out before us is constructed to neither encourage this kind of reunion at the end, nor a union at all. It's an inherently unkind and lonely journey, wrought with pitfalls, both outside the walls where you remain and within a prison fence where your husband experiences each day. Ugliness, tears, worry, and separation are the primary construction materials to pave the path that you now so concededly walk.

It may not have been by choice to become the spouse of an inmate, as was God's will for me, but you do not have to forfeit your daily joy and awesome future as you negotiate this new life with your husband. You can experience fulfillment and joy while you wait, and your marriage can survive this journey.

But I assure you it will be an incredibly long journey if you envision the only joyous and fulfilling day as the day your husband is at the front gate. You must have a deeper running contentment that will nourish your spirit and bring you fulfillment in lieu of that day. What about those of us who may never have that gate reunion? How can the journey be doable if we are living for a day that from all legal circumstances will never come?

That fulfillment and comfort are only found in God's daily presence through His Holy Spirit. Your emotions cannot sustain you on the hard days, especially when the hard days come in years. Emotions are volatile, drain easy, and fail us. God is steady, all-powerful, and faithful. The Holy Spirit communicates with your spirit to minister to your every need. As you remain in a personal relationship and seek His direction for your life, regardless of how long the fencing remains a part of your days, you can keep walking.

✝

July 19 Willing to Forgive

Matthew 18:21-22

Then Peter came and said to Him, "Lord, how often shall my brother sin against me and I forgive him? Up to seven times?" Jesus said to him, "I do not say to you, up to seven times, but up to seventy times seven."

    My husband has been a prodigal; he has victimized others. He has been that straying sheep that God goes looking for out of His love. And at no point did God ever not value him or stop loving him. I clung to such comfort when things got immensely difficult between us. If God hadn't given up on him, could I? I believed in God's ability to change him, and I knew God purposed our love for His glory.

    But change is slow. The husband who was hard to love showed up regularly early in our relationship, and shockingly, at times further into our love, which in some way made the hurt even harder to bear. There were days when I sat and absorbed his words about his latest heroin deal that provided him the "best" high for only fifty dollars. He shared as if he expected me to rejoice with him, but I only stared through eyes becoming moist from the hurt stirring in that depth where his words plummeted.

    It's no wonder we battle the acceptance of our loving men who seem unloving and unworthy. Evil holds fast to them and even once in prison, it surrounds them. My husband continued to be violent throughout our relationship despite the steps toward the good, and it was always difficult facing another explanation of why we couldn't visit on weekends or why I hadn't seen him for months when he was in confinement. I always gravitated toward silence, because I knew the hope and grace I extended him would end in the space between my words and the person before me. And usually I didn't want to muster the energy to endure the condemning looks or those of pity.

    Peter is discussing forgiveness with Jesus in the verse for today. How often should we forgive when done wrong? Jesus teaches that forgiveness should be limitless; that's what seventy times seven indicates. God forgives us every time we ask, and for innumerable sins. Because He forgives us, He instructs us to forgive others when they sin against us. He doesn't say for some sins and not others. It includes all.

Regularly forgiving your husband will include those times when he doesn't ask or deserve it. He may often deny doing anything wrong. This can be infuriating, and you may want to do everything but forgive him. But try to think of how God forgives you when you do not deserve it. Out of that appreciation, it will help you extend forgiveness to your husband.

Forgiveness is about staying close to God even if there still remains an unresolved issue between you and your husband. Forgiving your husband in your heart, speaks volumes of your love for God. It says you're trusting God to work in your husband's life, while you faithfully love him when he's hardest to love.

July 20 *Time Shared*

Hebrews 12:14-15

Pursue peace with all men, and the sanctification without which no one will see the Lord. See to it that no one comes short of the grace of God; that no root of bitterness springing up causes trouble, and by it many be defiled.

Having a supportive family is a wonderful thing, but it may also be the most difficult thing to balance in sharing time with your husband. There's only one visitation time. How that time gets shared can be touchy.

My husband and I have experienced this difficulty. His family desires to see him as well, but as a couple, we have so few opportunities to simply share the same space together, to sit and look into each other's eyes, to laugh, to talk about the serious and not-so-serious stuff. Our world is finally brought together for a few precious hours—and we need it. We long for it.

Bitterness can seep in when this treasured part of our lives is asked to be given over to someone else. In such a moment, I may rant to God, "Why don't we lock their husbands away for years and see how willing they are to give up time with him!"

Oh, how the Lord will grow you in this situation of prison! Through the difficulties and the sacrifice, God will always be more concerned with our character than our comfort. Thus, my rants get turned into conviction, and my embittered attitude gets corrected. I have to return to my motto "I love God more" and take the high road when He calls me to climb.

The writer of Hebrews talks about the damage bitterness does to others. It isn't holy behavior. It causes trouble. It damages the embittered person and those around. It does nothing for keeping the peace. Bitterness and a peaceful heart do not mix. One has to go.

I remain far from perfect in keeping bitterness from sprouting in regards to visits. Even when unable to see my husband, the reality that others are sitting with him in that moment, taunt my emotions toward that root.

Fortunately, my husband's family accepts our expressed need for alone time. Do they consider our situation perfectly every time visitation plans are made? No. But for the most part, both our imperfections get sorted out, and things move forward okay. When I'm unable to see him, they are empathetic to the impact on me when they visit freely.

Pursuing peace goes against our human tendency at times, especially when emotional issues are at hand. But stuffing bitter emotions generally erupts later at a high price. It hurts to sacrifice time with your husband, but oftentimes there's greater, long-term damage done to relationships when this conflict isn't resolved. God knows your heart behind the sacrifice and will bless your efforts.

July 21 Keep Walking

Numbers 21:4-5

Then they set out from Mount Hor by the way of the Red Sea, to go around the land of Edom; and the people became impatient because of the journey. And the people spoke against God and Moses, "Why have you brought us up out of Egypt to die in the wilderness? For there is no food and no water, and we loathe this miserable food."

Are you becoming impatient with this journey of prison? Is your journey getting longer and more miserable? Are you missing the life you used to have to the point you're considering returning to it—but without your husband? My words to you are "Please, hang in there!"

Routine and looking back caused the Israelites to give up on God and Moses. They tired of the routine, the same food every day, the same scenery of desert before them. They got tired of doing things God's way, because God's way was taking too long and seemed to be getting them nowhere.

Prison may look this way to you now. The routine of visits that never changes, the same food in the canteen that never changes, the same restrictions, the same life of routines where you see no end. You may be tempted to look back, desiring your old life. But who is your guide?

God guided the Israelites, and He provided for their every need. He tested their devotion. Prison is a severe test of devotion! But God will supply everything you need to make this journey successful. He can also bring you peace within your desires so those inner longings turn into something that will bond you closer to your husband rather than pull you away from him.

Get into the Bible, pray, and seek God's direction for how to sustain your marriage. He may lead you in a direction that you do not understand, and it may seem grueling at times, but you can trust that He knows where He's taking you. Special blessings for your marriage may be in the detours. There may be changes in you and your husband that can only be done while in the desert.

This world provides plenty of opportunities and justifications to quit on a marriage involving prison. But you'll possibly miss one of the greatest blessings of your lifetime if you quit on God now. You may be the precise tool God wants to use to bring your husband to salvation or to spur him on in his calling. A supportive, praying wife is a powerful tool in the hands of God! He can use you to make amazing changes in your husband. Whether his sentence just began or your walk on this path has years behind you, God is the way to keep walking with a renewed hope that the other side of the desert will be reached—together. **

July 22 God's Deliberate Delays

Isaiah 55:8-9

"For My thoughts are not your thoughts, neither are your ways My ways," declares the Lord. "For as the heavens are higher than the earth, so are My ways higher than your ways, and My thoughts than your thoughts."

Walking with God imparts the understanding that He orchestrates this world from an entirely different perspective—an eternal one. We operate in the present, and such are our desires. We like God to fulfill our desires quickly, because as we see it, it would be for our best.

Trusting God's timing and His plans are easy when things are moving along as we desire. It's when we are delayed or stopped altogether when the test of wills begins.

I often think of a pastor's story of plans to purchase a specific property on which to construct their first church building. The congregation had been meeting in a restaurant. It had been their earnest prayer and search for the ideal spot. At last, the location, price, and opportunity seemed perfect. There was great excitement, and plans were moving forward. Then at the last minute, another bid took away the dream of what seemed to be an answered prayer.

The pastor described anger with God. He recounted the story of his sitting at his kitchen table with his Bible, slamming it shut, stating to God, "You're wrong on this one!"

With time, however, another opportunity arrived. It was a better location and provided plenty of property for expansion. The landlocked location of the previous dream had grown to be highly congested at a major intersection with no growth opportunity. God answered that faithful congregation's prayer, but from an eternal perspective.

The desires which accompany you on this path of prison likely yearn deep from within you. They fill your mind daily and likely ache your heart at the same time. You may be questioning God about why He hasn't intervened, why He has withheld your desire, or worse yet, moved your desires even further from you. But you can trust what God is doing even when it seems He's doing nothing at all. He's always up to something good.

July 23 A Prayer Example

Mark 1:35

And in the early morning, while it was still dark, He arose and went out and departed to a lonely place, and was praying there.

When my husband was nearly three and a half hours from me, I would get up at 2:00 a.m. to make the drive to be there by visitation time. Having worked the days before, getting up at that time, driving seven hours for the day, and sitting on a plastic chair for the four hours in between exhausted me. I could barely get myself home to collapse on my bed, yet not before completing all the other logistics of life that do not go away just because I'm tired.

On those days, I used the time in the car for my more intimate prayer time. The drives complimented the times on my knees the days prior. Not a substitute for the time, but God knew my heart. He brought me this marriage, and I know He understands the efforts to maintain it. This includes those long drives.

But on a typical day, focused prayer is what I know is needed. It's what you'll need to sustain this path with your husband. Even Jesus took time away regularly during His ministry for prayer. Away from others, away from the distractions, away from even the good of all that He was doing—He did this to maintain His connection with God and to be an example to us.

In praying for my husband and our marriage, I pray regularly for certain things: his protection, his walk with God, his health and nutrition, his temptations, the passion and purity of our marriage. I pray for the officers and other inmates on his wing. I pray for the chaplain.

The specifics of this list change in focus depending on the day and on what my husband and I are going through, but these things regularly make it into a petition to God. You may find it helpful to pray through each of these areas or come up with a list of your own. A visual list can be helpful to your focus.

But prayer isn't to be approached as a formula that if you pray every day on your knees you'll be blessed. Blessings come from it, but it's about who you're talking with that's important. It's all about the relationship, not the sacrifices. Prayer is a discipline, but it isn't about the routine, but the relationship that's deepened because of it. Reverent prayer is blended with all other aspects of your life with God as part of being in a relationship with Him.

And because it's about a relationship, not a formula, during times when being a prisoner's wife plays out more difficult and demanding, God remains a loving Father who extends grace. He wants to be in relationship with you. So this may be behind the wheel of your car on some days. And that's okay.

July 24 A Crown of Support

Proverbs 12:4

An excellent wife is the crown of her husband, but she who shames him is as rottenness in his bones.

One of the greatest ways you can support your husband is through how you speak about him to others. We aren't married to perfect men. Most have done a terrible wrong to place them in prison. However, his value to you must see beyond the crime and to the man you love. And loving him best requires selective speech when not doing so could bring him shame or a further negative image.

The proverb above equates shaming your husband to rotting his bones. Such action eats away from the inside. It occurs in the unseen place of the heart really. It's a slow process—it decays over time. Most of us know how others' words can affect us. A compliment goes a long way; an insult usually further. Over time, others' words build into us for the good or strip away the same. Your husband needs to be built up.

Yes, he may have clearly earned his place in prison. He may continue to do things that are wrong, but as his wife, you shouldn't be part of the camp which ridicules and shames. You should believe in him and his ability to change—with God's help. This will impact how you speak about him. He's in an environment that ridicules and devalues him already. Be different than what surrounds him. Encourage him in his strengths and the positive parts of who he is—or who you hope he becomes in the future.

This may mean possessing a silent tongue at times when others are complaining about him. You may share the same feelings in the moment, but loving and respecting your husband means supporting him. If there are no counter comments to share him in a positive light, then silence is the best option. An accumulation of careless, negative words is difficult to recover from, especially if he sits within the same conversation.

An excellent wife is the crown of her husband. When someone wears a crown, he stands taller and prouder. It shows accomplishment and often victory over incredible struggles. A crown is evidence of favor and honor. When a crown is figuratively placed on your husband's head through positive changes others see in him, it should be clearly evident that your support is what helped put it there.

July 25 — As One of Us

Philippians 2:8

And being found in appearance as a man, He humbled Himself by becoming obedient to the point of death, even death on a cross.

The movie *Galaxy Quest* has a female alien character who falls in love with one of the men who returns to her ship to assist them defeat an enemy destined to destroy her alien race. Throughout the movie, she and her "people" take on human form to aid them in communicating and interacting with their human assistants. At the end, when the human crew was planned to return to earth, the female alien chose to leave her world and go to earth to be with her new love. She gave up everything—even her natural appearance—out of love.

This reminds me of what Jesus chose to do for us. He chose to be born into this world through a human female, giving up His heavenly home, out of love. He became human for our benefit. God became flesh and blood so we could relate to Him. We can trust that He knows our struggles, because He walked in human shoes.

The female alien came from a more advanced world. Their technology was incomparable to anything on earth. The best earth had at that time was science fiction entertainment which was misinterpreted by the aliens as reality. In humility, the female sacrificed great advances.

Christ humbled Himself to come live among us, sinful man. He was innocent and sinless, yet loved the world so much that He accepted a human life and eventual death so that we could have a way into heaven to be with Him forever. He came to defeat death.

Most of us would decline such a circumstance if given a choice. The sacrifice would be too great. Thankfully, Jesus willingly accepted God's plan for our salvation from sin. He sacrificed Himself for you and me. And thankfully, He rose from the dead to prove to us that He has the power to resurrect us as well. Death has no power over us when we believe in Jesus.

Believing in His death and resurrection is the most important decision you'll ever make in your life. Life is difficult enough, but death without Jesus will be eternal hell. Prison will end one day, but eternal separation from God will never end. And thankfully, an eternity with Him will not either. Choose for yourself and share with others the better place to be.

July 26 *Learning to Pray*

Luke 11:1

And it came about that while He was praying in a certain place, after He had finished, one of His disciples said to Him, "Lord, teach us to pray just as John also taught his disciples."

Following my relocation to be near my husband, I found a church to attend and planned to go on Wednesday evenings for what was called "House of Prayer." It was their Wednesday night prayer meeting. I had been praying for my husband for years, and I knew the power of prayer, so I eagerly wanted to be there. But not having been part of a small church in decades, I was rather naïve about what to expect from a prayer meeting.

All was fine—initially. Singing praise songs, worshipping through music, and petitioning God collectively—I thought all was well. But at the close of the service, the pastor instructed us to break into groups of two or three and to pray for the needs of each person in the group. My face must have resembled the panic-stricken features of someone in shock. A fear came over me that could have pulled me through the floor if it weren't for the chair I was sitting in with a sudden deadweight. The worst part was there was no escape as those around started to turn towards me.

After brief greetings and expressed concerns, we joined hands and prayer began. Everyone in the group prayed, and then that dreaded silence lingered as all waited for my prayer to begin. But there remained only silence. I was frozen inside, and I simply couldn't do it. I was so distracted by my own anxiety that I couldn't have formulated a prayer except maybe for myself anyway. A simple prayer it would have been: "Help me, Lord!"

I was never so grateful to exit a building in all my life! I left with building tears to God, embarrassment, irritation for something I hated about me, and guilt for feeling the way I did. I resented what everyone else seemed to do with ease. Weeks went by, and the difficulty remained. It remained guilt-laden and a dreaded part of the service to me.

So I understand how uncomfortable it can be to pray in front of someone, even if it's your own husband. However, with time—and practice—it gets easier. Practice? Yes! Prayer is something that we learn and must practice. The disciples asked Jesus to teach them to pray.

Many people use the ACTS acronym as a guide to prayer: adoration, confession, thanksgiving, and supplication. Basically, start with praising God for who He is, then confess your sins, then thank Him for your blessings, and finally, present your requests to Him.

If you can commit to practicing prayer (even aloud in your private prayer time), you'll find a precious jewel within you, ready and available, to support others in a time of difficulty. I know, because I have been prayed over in such a way. Practicing also enabled me to become more comfortable praying aloud over my husband. And that's been even a grander blessing.

July 27 More Than a Wife

Jeremiah 29:11

'For I know the plans that I have for you,' declares the Lord, 'plans for welfare and not for calamity to give you a future and a hope.'

Prison consumes much of our lives in the intentionality it demands. And we get accustomed to its presence, because it's the reality that must be dealt with daily. But with this, we can sometimes let prison define who we are and not what God has fully purposed us to be. Prison must be accommodated, but there's more God wants to do through us while here. He desires us to be foremost a helper to our husbands. But He also reserves for each of us a special assignment that will shine brighter than any level of darkness the prison tries to smother us with.

Our vision must be bigger than what we view through the rows of fencing. Our purpose must be more than the lengthy waits in every type of weather outside the gate and the ridiculous hours that we invest just to be in that line first thing in the morning. Our purpose must be more than the energy to get through the days between visits, until we can do it all again the next weekend. It's only in living out God's purposes for our lives that the life of prison becomes more than the routine of regimented time, separation, and the sighs as we face another day of both.

The verse above was God's words to the Israelites. They were in exile in Babylon and He was assuring them that He had not forsaken them. After the seventy years in captivity, He would restore them to their homeland. He had their future planned and it was something to be hopeful about. We can apply this principle to our lives.

God's purposes bond us to hope, and hope keeps us moving forward. It motivates us to persevere through the difficult days, to see beyond how things are right now, and to experience a further meaning to our lives despite it being altered by prison.

You have an assignment that God desires for you alone to accomplish. Knowing that God can—and will—use you for an extraordinary purpose while in this situation of prison brings hope and a solid direction you can trust to follow even as your husband remains away from you.

Your purpose found in God has a higher calling that will circumvent the heartache of the daily longings and the flow of tears that may follow as a result. His presence will sustain you, because while walking the smaller steps of your purpose and the everyday of prison, God is just as much there providing guidance, laughter, joy, and most importantly — fulfillment in the absence of your husband.

You have been uniquely gifted by God to fulfill a special purpose. It can be an exciting journey. Pray and see how God desires to use you, then start walking into your calling.

July 28 Funding Prison & Home

I Peter 3:1

In the same way, you wives, be submissive to your own husbands so that even if any of them are disobedient to the word, they may be won without a word by the behavior of their wives.

Finances may be the most difficult area to balance between your responsibility and your husband's leading. You logistically handle the finances: pay the bills, buy the groceries, keep the car running, and handle all other life's demands. Without your husband home, it's difficult for him to be involved quickly or to follow the flow of expenses that life becomes, thus easily adding to frustrations and difficulties when his expectations differ on how money should be spent.

It's the *planning* financially that's difficult for my husband to see. My blessed dog, which he insisted that I have, is one example. He tends to forget that there are often ongoing expenses with such decisions.

In this case, dogs equal fleas. And when we were looking at a very tight budget and summer flea season upon us, I knew the monthly budget had to absorb another fifty dollars for flea control. I was then suddenly hit with his need for me to send money. So the budget took the punishment through absorption of an expense that there was no money to cover except through less groceries or the sacrifice of a dog — and house — full of fleas.

What does help is my sending him our budget every month. He can see where every penny goes, and I think it helps him better understand what I face trying to make everything work. He can see the reality of life that becomes the anticipated, but not monthly expenses, such as the summer fleas or the car registration and oil changes. He "forgets" these realities enter life all the time, so putting the anticipated on paper reminds him. This decreases the frustration for me and financial conflicts between us.

It's not a perfect conversation every month and we still fight over finances at times, but having the conversation honestly is key. He has to be upfront on how he's spending money and I have to be honest with him from my end. I have to let him have an input to our finances to the greatest extent possible. I simply pray about the rest and trust that God will convict us both according to His wisdom on how we are ultimately using His money.

July 29 — Preparation for Battle

I Samuel 17:37

And David said, "The Lord who delivered me from the paw of the lion and from the paw of the bear, He will deliver me from the hand of this Philistine." And Saul said to David, "Go, and may the Lord be with you."

At a time of intense difficulty, I think it's our nature to question what led to it, why it arrived, and what the outcome will be. When we see no meaning to why we suffer, the ache seems more severe. It's through hindsight that our understanding gets some relief from its searching. And with this understanding comes the ironic praise for how the past days of difficulty prepared us for today's triumph.

The story of David and Goliath is rich with principles we can apply to our lives. Within the verse, we read that the very battles in David's past unknowingly prepared him for the infamous victory over the Israelites' enemy representative Goliath.

Goliath was nine feet tall! David was still a youth. Goliath was decked out in weaponry and armor. David declined the same for the familiarity of a slingshot and rocks. Goliath had been a warrior for years. But David also brought his experience of personal battles which could be arguably more frightening than facing the giant.

To pursue a battle with an attacking lion and bear, especially when food is involved, is astounding to me. David tells of how he did such to rescue a lamb which had already been well pinned within the jaws of the powerful creature. It would seem a death sentence for both the lamb and David. But the Lord mightily provided David the courage to enter the battle and to win.

Did David know there was a future battle awaiting him with a violent human enemy? Not that we are told in Scripture. But the boldness with which he assumes the challenge, he portrays seemingly less fear and unwavering confidence that the Lord would bring him victory.

In contemplation, I envision an unexpected fight with a wild animal more dangerous than a premeditated one with a man. The fear, the aloneness, the innate strength of an animal, and the odds seem less than squaring off with a human foe in a planned and voluntary encounter.

David seemed to agree. He recalled these prior experiences, and they provided him the courage to take on Goliath. He may not have known at the time how those negative and frightening experiences would prepare him for Goliath. But if he had any doubt for why he had to go through them, he certainly understood in that moment.

As a Christian, you understand that without answers, God can still be trusted. You can trust that whatever the physical pain, heartache, fear, or even prison, it doesn't arrive to you without purpose. It may be the very experience God uses to bring an amazing victory in your future.

July 30 Spiritual Wealth

Psalm 49:10

For he sees that even wise men die; the stupid and the senseless alike perish, and leave their wealth to others.

Prisoners are usually not wealthy. Their families aren't either, or else the ability to purchase the best attorney would be seen more often. Statistics are clear: the poor and disadvantaged fill our prisons. There's the likelihood that as the wife, you struggle financially to keep the household above water. Although money is a necessary part of our lives, and prison contributes to its lack for some, spiritual wealth will always be of greater value.

Psalm 49 reminds us that putting our faith in money and material wealth is foolish. It comes with no guarantee or ability to impact our eternity. You can't take it with you, as the cliché says. And you cannot purchase salvation for your children or those left behind from whatever money you leave them.

It's a far greater pursuit to invest in things that endure time—beyond prison or death. Your husband's life has astounding value and potential to impact the world for good, and money has no control over his ability to carry out his purpose. He can be wealthy in a way that richly blesses others. How?

It costs no money to pray for others. It costs no money to share his testimony. It costs no money to love you or his children. These actions carry the potential to change the lives of others through the anointing of God. His actions could lead another to faith in Jesus. What greater legacy!

Your husband can find value in spiritual wealth. His incarceration can be redeemed without money. It's really the only thing that has lasting value. Applaud the non-financial ways he contributes. Remind him of the power he possesses that has nothing to do with money. He can provide himself with God's help to richly share with others. You can too.

July 31 Anger's Motivation

John 2:15

And He made a scourge of cords, and drove them all out of the temple, with the sheep and the oxen; and He poured out the coins of the moneychangers, and overturned their tables.

I heard a financial advisor make a comment that getting mad about one's debt is usually the best motivator to getting out of it. Such anger is close to righteous indignation. It's the good kind of anger. It motivates positive action. This can be true for many things.

Jesus gave us an example of positive anger. The disrespecting of the temple stirred Him to severe action. The outer courts had been turned into a marketplace. He physically drove out the people misusing His Father's house and the animals they possessed. Scripture provides us this example and teaches that anger in itself isn't sin. Jesus didn't sin by His actions.

Most of us have plenty examples of unleashing our anger in negative ways, even when our cause is righteous. We say ugly words, harbor resentment, behave unlovingly toward someone else, or devalue our own worth for the mistakes we have made.

In moments of reflection on my life, I can get angry at my circumstances, the barriers, and the things I wished were different. It could be my own debt, a decision that I wish I could do over, or possibly a mishandled conversation with my husband leading to an unnecessary argument. The negative outcome motivates me to desire the better. And I move forward with intentional plans toward that goal. But I struggle regularly for how I express my anger.

The key is to recognize good anger and use it as a tool for the good. It can be a motivator for positive change. Just as so, contemplate how to do things differently next time when it's unleashed in a sinful way. Sometimes just taking the first step is all that's needed to move things along with a refreshing perspective and toward that positive outcome.

So repent of the sinful anger. Ask God to keep you energized for all you're working toward to manage your expression of what angers you. You may find a deeper study on anger as helpful to identify what triggers your anger.

Remember that anger is a God-given emotion. In its purity, it's not sinful. It's only sinful when unleashed in a sinful manner. The power of anger can be transforming in your life. Discipline its use and take it out on the right targets.

August 1 Translate & Interpret

John 16:13

"But when He, the Spirit of truth, comes, He will guide you into all the truth; for He will not speak on His own initiative, but whatever He hears, He will speak; and He will disclose to you what is to come."

Prison has its own language. I still get stumped sometimes when my husband throws a phrase at me. Going psyche, what's the lick read, rip, pipe, mule. Inmates in confinement often know basic sign language to enable them to communicate from a distance or through a window. Whether written, spoken, or gestured, if you do not know the language, the message fails to be understood. For an unknown language, the form of the communication dictates whether you need a translator or interpreter.

"Translate" and "interpret" are frequently used interchangeably; however, they are quite different. Translate involves the written word; interpret the spoken or signed word. When it comes to understanding God's word, the Holy Spirit serves both. He helps us understand Scripture whether it's written, spoken, or signed. He goes even further to communicate through circumstances, things we encounter in our day, or our emotions. He alone can speak spiritual truth.

The Holy Spirit communicates the heart of God. He can be trusted to communicate to you wisdom, guidance, correction, and encouragement. This is without error or confusion. He's faithful to reveal the truth if you seek to know it. He's God's voice. As part of the Trinity, He fully understands God's word, so His communication will be exactly as God intends—no variation or altered meaning.

How does all this work? Once a believer in Jesus, God's Spirit resides in you. He communicates with your spirit. You'll learn to recognize His "voice." You'll develop an intimacy with God through the Holy Spirit. Access to Him, however, is dependent on your accepting Jesus as your Savior. The Trinity—God, Jesus, and the Holy Spirit—works as a whole.

Are you becoming frustrated with studying Scripture? Are you trying to hear from God, but there seems to be disconnect? The problem may be related to Jesus. If you have never accepted Jesus as your Savior, believing He took on human form, died for your sins, and resurrected, then the Holy Spirit isn't in you. Your translator and interpreter is missing. This becomes your first step: get to know Jesus.

Are you experiencing the same frustrations yet a believer? I think every Christian at some point experiences what they consider as silence from God. Stay in prayer and Scripture. Repent of intentional and unintentional sin. Keep seeking, and you'll begin to hear again clearly from God. He still speaks your language.

August 2 Grey or Gray?

Acts 4:12

"And there is salvation in no one else; for there is no other name under heaven that has been given among men, by which we must be saved."

The words used to convey a thought or describe a thing, in most cases, has various options. There's usually more than one word to get the point across. In some cases, there's even an acceptable difference in how a word is spelled. *Grey* is just as right as *gray*. It's amazing how diverse language is. It continues to grow as new words are adopted as their cultural use determines. But when it comes to salvation, there's only one way: belief in Jesus.

All other worries and stressors of this life aside. All wrong decisions regretted. In the end, your salvation is the most important matter you need to settle. It trumps everything. A relationship with Jesus is the only way to heaven. He's the answer to all this life's disappointments, pains, unfairness, prison, and anything else you'll encounter between your sunrises until your body dies physically.

The verse today is Peter's statement to the elders, rulers, and scribes after his and John's arrest for preaching and healing in the name of Jesus. Jesus had already been crucified, resurrected, and returned to heaven. Peter and

John were testifying to this truth and that Jesus was the only way for sins to be forgiven and salvation received.

God made no other provision. There's no grey area. There are false religions that do not teach about the same Jesus as Peter is preaching about. Belief in the true God will be the God who sent Jesus to be born of a virgin and die on a cross for all mankind's sin.

There's also not an indefinite period of time to decide about Jesus. If you sense the Holy Spirit dealing with your heart, do not ignore the promptings. Every day is a gift and once death comes, there's no other opportunity to make a choice. Some religions may teach there's still hope for salvation after death, but that isn't what Scripture teaches.

Do not linger in the gray. God loves you and desires to spend eternity with you. He laid out the perfect redemption for you. It's through Jesus. There's nothing you have to do, but believe.

August 3 Trapped

Philippians 4:13

I can do all things through Him who strengthens me.

It's a horrible feeling to be trapped by your circumstances. It's a feeling that your circumstances control your schedule—and your life. A sense of helplessness accompanies such a season. You want to get off the speeding train you sit in, but there seems to be no way to slow it down, let alone exit. You boarded from a consequence of your own poor decisions or that of someone else—possibly your husband. But now, what's the answer to bring back some sanity to your world and the everyday demands that keep you exhausted?

You must surrender your circumstances to God for whatever purpose or step toward the exit that He has planned. This is the only way to reach a level of peace while you wait for freedom. There must be a laying down of your ability to perform, accomplish, and likely mentally survive by your own power. This may be a moment to moment realignment of your thoughts to bring your heart back to that place where you can say, "Today is okay," despite today looking just like the one prior.

Pray in those moments when strength is what you need to go one more moment forward. You can be candid with God. He already knows your heart. Ask for His help to endure.

Sometimes the most challenging thing to ask of God is to change your heart about your circumstance. It's a deeper level of surrender in a way, because you give up your right to be in a poor, frustrated mood. Instead, you ask God to help you come to enjoy or find favor within the circumstance. This is particularly hard because it will feel like you're giving God the okay to keep you where you are longer. Release that fear. He may just be waiting for exactly that type of prayer before opening the way of escape.

I had a job once that was, by default, the only thing I could get given my life circumstance at the time. I was miserable. It was a horrible job and experience. I cried many days when waking to my trapped reality. I was forever searching for a way out. In my exhaustion and the barriers surrounding me, my surrender came one day in the bathroom stall at that job: "Lord, if this is where I'm to be right now, please help me learn to find contentment in this place."

There was no great change in my circumstances. The job remained horrible, but God showed up in the trying moments to answer another version of that bathroom-stall prayer. There came a reminder that everything in that moment was designed by God for my good. Peace came with that. I knew that I was headed to something better. I could trust God to take me on the "perfect" path, even the one that I was eager to exit.

You can trust Him with your entrapment too. He will strengthen you to endure and ease the burden by being your contentment. Being obedient to His path is your way out.

August 4 — Individuals within 4k

Mark 8:3

"And if I send them away hungry to their home, they will faint on the way; and some of them have come from a distance."

Technology has provided TV fans a resolution option of 4K. Televisions have come a long way from the external antennae and limited channel options. This high definition option equates to nearly 4,000 horizontal pixels. The details are so vivid on the screen to almost look 3D. The greater the resolution, the more lifelike.

Jesus is into details as well. Within the crowd of four thousand, He knew the individuals. He knew some came from a long way. He was concerned for them individually. Those there received both fish and bread. Each was equally served.

The disciples saw the crowd as a crowd. They questioned how such a number could be fed. Their compassion was possibly more immune to being stirred because of the number of people they saw scattered across the landscape. But Jesus saw the individual need. He had compassion singularly.

Our God is so awesome that way! There's no limit to the details He's able to see in our lives. It's an astounding aspect of His omniscience. I take comfort in knowing that He sees my every need and that of my husband.

Billions on the earth, over a thousand men on the prison compound, my husband in his cell, and me sitting alone in my house. God sent Jesus to meet every one of us individually. He came to meet our spiritual needs, but He knows all our other needs intimately too.

Your life is seen by God in limitless pixels. He watches over every second of your life and that of your husband's. You can rest in this truth. Keep following God like the people did in this passage of Mark. He knows how far you have been and what you're facing now. He knows you're "hungry" and tired. Out of His compassion He will satisfy your need with an overflowing menu of good things.

August 5 — Reason or Faith?

Judges 6:39

Then Gideon said to God, "Do not let Thine anger burn against me that I may speak once more; please let me make a test once more with the fleece, let it now be dry only on the fleece, and let there be dew on all the ground."

It may not always be easy to move forward in life or even stay put if there remains indecisiveness between reason and faith. Stepping out in faith may not seem reasonable when the circumstance is considered. But some faith steps defy conventional wisdom. God is wise. He's reasonable. So how do you balance the two?

You may be at a crossroad trying to decide which way to turn. One way seems to be God's call, but it's not reasonable. But choosing reason may result in missing God's best. Like Gideon, you may need to throw out some fleece.

God had called Gideon to deliver Israel from her enemies. He assured Gideon that he would be successful. Yet, Gideon couldn't help but consider the reasonableness of what God asked of him. The enemy was camped and ready to attack. In response, Gideon asked God for signs of reassurance in the plan.

Gideon recognized his own weakness and dependence on God. God responded to this humility and encouraged him. A piece of fleece became either saturated or completely dry to confirm the successful task that lay before him. With this encouragement, Gideon's faith bolstered to move forward. It carried him through the even tougher and more unreasonable request to intentionally reduce the size of his army.

You may be faced with unreasonable expectations. Maybe others are advising you based on a human perspective. And it likely makes sense when you consider it. But do you also hear the voice of God prompting a different course of action? If so, always go with God. Maybe neither voice is clear enough to determine the best way. If so, in humility, ask God to clarify and confirm in a way that you'll recognize as His voice. It will be your version of that piece of fleece. You'll then have the benefit of not only knowing the way, but also growing a closer walk with God as you continue on your life's path.

August 6 Hang in There

John 6:68-69

Simon Peter answered Him, "Lord, to whom shall we go? You have words of eternal life. And we have believed and have come to know that You are the Holy One of God."

Sometimes you might want to bail on this whole life of prison. Maybe even life itself seems too hard. The difficulty and continued energy it takes to manage your days wears you down. You see not only your own difficulties, but also the continued decline of the world each news broadcast. Mass shootings, terrorism, depraved actions of people, loss of things beautiful and innocent, from forest fires to animal cruelty. You may be angry with or questioning God from a heart that's quite frankly tired of it all.

But if you bail, where will you go to find peace? Countless people pursue peace and contentment through dead-end avenues all the time. Lasting peace is never found in worldly things. Troubles remain or just come dressed up another way. Hopscotching out of your difficulties to what seems like greener pastures will not resolve the longing in your heart.

God is the only answer to this life's problems—including prison. He provides life. He brings joy and contentment. And best of all, He brings hope. This life isn't all there will be. All these burdens will go away when Jesus returns. And until such time, He actively loves and helps in the present.

Peter recognized that Jesus was the way to everything his heart desired. Many had abandoned Jesus at the point in the verse today. Peter and others knew running away from Jesus wouldn't satisfy their needs. They didn't have an easy life, yet a life without Jesus would have been more unbearable. And as Peter said of Jesus, "You have words of eternal life." In other words, You're our hope for something better than what this life has to offer.

It must be mentioned, however, that if your trying emotions are interfering with your ability to function or you feel as though you're losing all hope, you may be experiencing true clinical depression. A Christian can be clinically depressed despite the deepest faith in God. Consider professional support if this sounds like you. God remains just as powerful, but He may choose to heal your mood through a medical professional.

If you, otherwise, know it's merely weariness and a longing for a life without pain and sadness, Jesus still remains the answer. Get some rest, stick close to Him, and always be assured that you have the answer with you already.

August 7 Faith Filled

John 6:8-9

One of His disciples, Andrew, Simon Peter's brother, said to Him, "There is a lad here who has five barley loaves and two fish, but what are these for so many people?"

Andrew was from Bethsaida. He was a fisherman along with his brother Peter. Jesus chose him as one of His disciples. Early in his calling, his faith was energized by what he knew of Jesus from John the Baptist and the hope that Jesus was the Messiah promised in Scripture.

There isn't a lot written of Andrew by name in Scripture, but what we do know presents a life of eager faith, yet with the common reservations in its expression. He seemed to battle human reason as he spent time with Jesus and beheld His deity. The Scripture today is an example.

Jesus had already presented the question to His other disciple Philip about how the five thousand people could be fed. Philip answered from human reason: it was simply not possible. They were in the middle of nowhere and had no resources to purchase that much food. Andrew, on the other hand, saw the same barriers, but we see a glimmer of his faith by his actions. It's like he wanted to believe, but was not quite sure.

Andrew doesn't confidently bring the boy's bread and fish to Jesus with the expression, "I know you can take care of this Jesus. Here you go, do your thing." His actions reflect faith, but his words reflect a man with one foot still rustling around in human reason not sure of which place to plant both feet.

The fact that he brought the meager helpings to Jesus in the first place shows faith in the possibility. He wanted to believe! Yet, he provided an out for his faith in case Jesus didn't follow through: "But what are these for so many people?" As a disciple, he had personally witnessed Jesus do amazing things; however, he couldn't release his foot to cross over to unwavering faith.

Jesus didn't respond harshly to him, or the other disciples. He simply instructed them in how to participate in what He was going to do. He took care of the need; everyone received more than enough to eat. In fact, there was a surplus.

Jesus is so gentle in how He deals with our unbelief. He wants us to see the impossible as possible when He's orchestrating the events. His desire is for us to have confident faith. But when it's shaky, He continues to seek us. He continues to teach us. He doesn't give up in exasperation and say, "Forget it! You just won't ever get it!"

If God is asking you to believe in meeting a need that only a miracle can provide, go to Him with whatever faith you can muster. Bring your fish and loaves and possibly wavering faith. He will take what you have and multiple it—including your faith.

August 8 Cultivating Respect

Ephesians 5:22-23

Wives, be subject to your own husbands, as to the Lord. For the husband is the head of the wife, as Christ also is the head of the church, He Himself being the Savior of the body.

Being in prison is a very vulnerable position for any man. Having your lady free and away from your oversight, protection, and love is difficult for him. Feelings of inadequacy can quickly build along with jealousy, anger, and depression, any of which can destroy your relationship.

So I would encourage you to continuously build your man up. Encourage his leadership in your household. Seek his input as you would if he were there with you and nurture abiding respect as you choose to follow him. I have not always agreed with my husband's desires for me or us, but if the decision didn't involve anything sinful or otherwise in opposition to God, out of love and a desire to bring our relationship into a godly design, I would accept his decision. It's an expression of love that he greatly needs — respect.

I see an example of this every day when I look upon the long hair and panting tongue lying near me. Did I want the dog I have now? No. I knew the added responsibilities, the time, the nuisance, and everything she and her hair would bring to my life to further complicate it. The greater issue, however, was that my having a dog was very important to my husband. My living alone has always held concern for him. He knows what evil looks like because he lives amongst it daily. He knows the potential bad that can happen when expected or worse, not expected.

So I now have a dog. And when not yet housebroken and on one of our many 2:00 a.m. trips outside, in the seemingly always rainy mornings, I would simply sigh to God, "The things we do for love," and consider how He did tremendously more than be inconvenienced when He gave up Jesus to die on the cross. I would shake my head with a sense of resolution and take a deep breath to keep bitterness from entering my system and remind myself that I'm called to love my husband as Christ loves me. Sacrificial love means being inconvenienced sometimes.

Seek ways you can now follow your husband and honor his requests of you. The benefit to your relationship will outweigh most any difficulties arising from the choice, and I know God will honor your efforts. **

✝

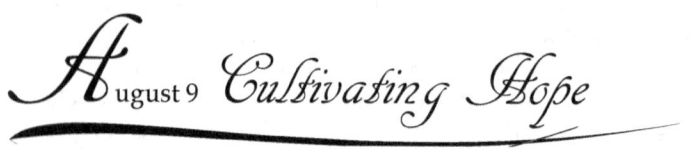
August 9 — Cultivating Hope

II Corinthians 1:9-10

Indeed, we had the sentence of death within ourselves in order that we should not trust in ourselves, but in God who raises the dead; who delivered us from so great a peril of death, and will deliver us, He on whom we have set our hope. And He will yet deliver us.

Paul was recounting to the church in Corinth that his life-threatening events demanded an answer for what he truly believed about Jesus. Did he really believe there's life through Jesus after death? Paul faced many threats on his life and he could honestly say that those experiences could be faced with hope, because his faith was the most real when faced with the reality of death.

There are some who experience startling or ominous moments when death is close. There's time for the mind to contemplate whether in seconds or days the sobering reality that this life is about to end. Paul shares the encouragement that even under such duress, hope remains for the Christian.

Paul possessed extraordinary faith, but at times his life was threatened, his trust in Jesus only deepened. He believed God could deliver him, whether in this life or after death. He had hope regardless of which outcome God allowed.

These are the invaluable lessons, the rich deepening of our faith, that no one usually volunteers for. Paul says in verse nine that God allowed him to go through what he had so he wouldn't trust in himself.

Paul was a dynamic preacher. He was fiery and persevered through great sufferings. What better person to tell us — with all certainty — that hope can be maintained in the face of death? We get the encouraging fruit from his hardships.

Each of our experiences on our spiritual journey should cultivate our hope. In spite of hardships and dry seasons of life, hope is something that can grow. It's the irony of God's garden work. Even if death encroaches, deliverance is promised for those who believe in Jesus.

I do not know any greater hope for any of us, especially the prisoner. Especially the lifer. Especially the person on death row. The Gospel is hope. Better things are to come regardless of where you are now.

August 10 Healing History

Isaiah 61:1

The Spirit of the Lord God is upon me, because the Lord has anointed me to bring good news to the afflicted; He has sent me to bind up the brokenhearted, to proclaim liberty to captives, and freedom to prisoners.

Always on the lookout for a bargain, I stopped by a yard sale brimming with possibilities. I find it fun even looking through stuff I'm not looking to purchase. On that afternoon, however, a peculiar pattern emerged during my browsing: I was finding things like I once owned. The difference was that mine had acquired damage which destined them for the dumpster, not resale.

There laid a rug, same color, style, and size of the one I had many years before. Mine was marred by stains during the housebreaking days of my dog. It also bared the growing years of the same dog through unraveled places she used as a toy. On a table was a small vanity mirror with an attached jewelry holder. Mine was discarded years before after the mirror broke.

I understood the message God was speaking to me. It was a metaphor for how God takes our damaged pasts and heals us. Through Jesus, we lose our stained, frayed and damaged parts and are restored to God. Our past doesn't determine our value for the future.

Isaiah was one of God's greatest prophets. In the verse today, he's indicating the coming of Jesus and His role to bind up and heal us, to free us from sin. This is exactly what He wants to do for every person, including every criminal. God sent Jesus to every person to receive forgiveness for sin. It doesn't matter what a person's past looks like.

Jesus heals history. But the beautiful thing is that He does it individually. Your husband's past is intimately known by God. Just like He knew each little item I previously owned and orchestrated my seeing them again at that little yard sale years later, God is personal. There's nothing that He doesn't know about your husband's past, present, or future. He wants to heal his history which led to his incarceration and repurpose his life for good.

August 11 Sin Spreads Harm

Joshua 7:1

But the sons of Israel acted unfaithfully in regard to the things under the ban, for Achan, the son of Carmi, the son of Zabdi, the son of Zerah, from the tribe of Judah, took some of the things under the ban, therefore the anger of the Lord burned against the sons of Israel.

Joshua had just led the Israelites to victory over Jericho in an amazing show of God's power. As part of this victory and giving glory to God, all the booty from the attack was to be dedicated to the Lord; none was to be kept by individuals. The gold, silver, bronze, and iron items were to be brought into the tabernacle. Achan, however, couldn't resist the wealth before him, and he secretly kept back a beautiful robe, gold, and silver. He hid them in his tent.

In the next battle for Israel, an easy victory should have been accomplished. The enemy was severely outnumbered. Joshua was certain of victory, but this didn't happen. Israel was defeated by a weaker and less numerous enemy. Sin in the camp removed God's protection and blessing. Achan's sin brought disaster on the entire community.

This was discovered and Achan and his family were destroyed. Once cleansed of the sin, Israel went up against the same enemy again and was successful. God's blessing returned.

Sin isn't without damage. Secret sins harm just as known ones do. Sin harms the sinner and others. Achan's sin influenced his family, bringing their death as well. Achan's sin influenced his community with many dying in battle who likely wouldn't have otherwise. Achan's sin was known to God, and his sin was ultimately against God.

There's no sin which is insignificant. God hates all sin. Sin interferes with our relationship with God. It places us outside of His protection and blessing. He never stops loving us because of our sin, but He does allow consequences from it. These consequences impact others as well; often those we love.

As you walk through this prison journey with your husband, you'll be faced with secret temptations or be the victim of those of your husband's. Sin must be dealt with. Seek restoration with God by removing the sin you can control, because not doing so risks tremendous harm in ways that you'll most likely regret. And never cease praying for your husband in the areas where you know he struggles, because ultimately you experience the fallout of even what he attempts to hide.

August 12 Which Is It for You?

Luke 7:7

For this reason I did not even consider myself worthy to come to You, but just say the word, and my servant will be healed.

Humility or poor self-esteem? The centurion soldier in this story had sent some of the elders to Jesus, asking him to come to Capernaum. The centurion's servant was seriously ill, and he knew Jesus could make him better. The elders bragged to Jesus about the centurion and how "worthy" he was to receive a miracle.

Jesus agreed to come with them, but before they make it to the house, the centurion sent some friends to stop them, because he didn't see himself worthy of Jesus's presence in his home. This was also his reason for not going to meet Jesus in the first place, as the verse above states. The centurion instead asked Jesus to simply speak the words; there was no need to physically see his servant. His faith was heralded by Jesus, and his servant was healed.

The centurion was humble. Despite his worthy accomplishments, there's no evidence of pride in his actions. In fact, others praise and provide evidence to his character. He was a loyal, competent, and well-liked man. His feeling of unworthiness was from the right motive: an understanding of who Jesus is.

Sometimes we struggle with self-esteem issues. Having our husbands incarcerated can impact our perception of ourselves. We may not feel worthy. But these feelings are sometimes from the wrong perspective. Often we absorb what we hear from others about us or our husbands — whether true or not.

Resist the temptation to diminish your value because of your husband's situation. If you know you're exactly where you're to be, be confident in this. You're highly valued by God. He's faithful to build this confidence in you as you seek Him. And as you get to know God more fully, your worthiness will diminish in the right way. You'll be humble before God, focusing on His worthiness, not the lack of your own.

August 13 Sparkle

Colossians 3:23

Whatever you do, do your work heartily, as for the Lord rather than for men.

    I often think upon a 56-year-old man whose life was briefly profiled on the news. Unlike most news, it was a feel-good story. He had a troubled past, but was given an opportunity for employment at a car wash Mr. Sparkle. His first assignment was the usually avoided street performer.

    This man was seen each of his work days, walking a small area by the road, wearing a sign which advertised the car wash. He smiled and engaged drivers through his upbeat and energetic behavior. The key to his impact was that he truly seemed to love what he was doing.

    When his past was summarized, he presented a life changed and complete gratefulness to God for the blessings he had received. He explains that he sees himself working for God, and with this perspective, his desire is to be pleasing to the Lord. This man's routine of starting his day reading Scripture was included in the story—the book of Proverbs, specifically.

    How many of us would settle for a job such as that, especially at his age of 56. He endured heat, standing on his feet for hours, and likely for a small wage. But he did the job faithfully. I was also struck by the images of his workplace. He didn't station himself on the sidewalk alone. There was a worn area of grass where he worked, placing himself as close to the road as possible. It was another example of his going above and beyond in his assignment.

    And it made an impact. So much so that the media featured him. What a testimony for God's ability to transform and impact a life! God had not given up on that man.

    Take encouragement from his story. Your husband's past can be redeemed as well. Second chances are God's specialty, and His heart seeks those with troubled pasts. God works heartily for them. Pray for your husband's surrender to the Lord. With surrender, he will sparkle with new life and renewed energy to be pleasing to God.

☦

August 14 — The Savior's Touch

Matthew 8:3

And He stretched out His hand and touched him, saying, "I am willing; be cleansed." And immediately his leprosy was cleansed.

    Jesus healed most often through touch. It wasn't that He needed to physically touch any person to heal, because He can just speak a word and do anything. But we read throughout the New Testament of His touching a blind person's eyes, laying His hand upon the sick and the dead to bring healing and life. It seems it was another way of His expressing compassion and relating to us in our humanness. He was approachable to us, not a stand offish deity that barked commands from a distance. That type of interaction He reserved for demons. We never read where He cast out demons by touch. Touch was a special connection He would do out of love.

    The verse for today is just one example of the Savior's touch to bring healing. The man knew Jesus could heal him. He was like the crowd flocking to Jesus for help and to hear more of His teachings. Having leprosy, this man may have been lingering on the outskirts waiting for an opportunity to make his plea to Jesus. Lepers were outcasts, physically and socially.

    But even if this man physically joined the crowd of "typical" people to seek Jesus's help, his very disease would have likely been the key to his gaining access despite the crowd. Others would have scattered, not wanting to make that unavoidable, yet dreadful contact when pushed along in a crowd next to someone disfigured and "unclean."

    This man knew Jesus wouldn't be afraid to touch him; Jesus wouldn't cringe away as a person in a crowd might. This man sought the acceptance and compassion of Christ. His faith was rewarded and he was cleansed immediately at Jesus's touch.

    In a way, incarceration is the leprosy of our day. Hundreds of thousands are removed from society and labelled "unclean." That label keeps everyone at a distance. No one wants to mix company, knowingly, with a felon who could possibly be a risk to their own well-being. Even after release, employers scatter and some linger at a distance wondering if it's safe.

    Thankfully, Jesus isn't part of that crowd. In fact, He seeks each of us in our leprous spiritual state. And like the man in today's Scripture, we have full access to Him. It matters not how sick we are spiritually. As He says in

Matthew 9:12: "It is not those who are healthy who need a physician, but those who are sick."

Jesus is willing to heal your husband too. No crime can make Jesus turn away. He just has to come to Jesus in faith, asking for His healing touch. Jesus can reach through the barriers of prison and cleanse any man's physical body and more importantly—his heart.

August 15 Individual Love

John 6:40

"For this is the will of My Father, that everyone who beholds the Son and believes in Him, may have eternal life; and I Myself will raise him up on the last day."

This is one of the greatest things I love about God: He's personal. He isn't a far-away god busy taking care of bigger and better things. He manages all the big things, but He loves me so personally that I feel as though I'm walking through a supernatural world consisting of just Him and me. How grand is that!

I gain peace in knowing He's with me constantly. He talks with me, makes me laugh, shares my tears, understands my desires, corrects me when needed, encourages me, and teaches me. He intimately knows me, because He created me.

John records Jesus's words in the verse today. Jesus is speaking of His promise to anyone who puts their faith in Him for salvation. He will personally resurrect him or her at His second coming. He says, "I myself will raise him up on the last day." Wow! How grand is that!

There will be a lot of activity going on at Jesus's return. Magnificent things will be seen and heard by all. Yet with all the grandeur of the King of Kings descent from heaven, He will individually see to it that every believer be resurrected. All that are His, He will not lose.

I used to consider the possibility of becoming "lost" at death. What if my spirit is just floating around in another realm and I do not know how to get to heaven or how to direct my spirit. What if all the angels are busy? What if I'm overlooked for whatever reason? Silly thoughts I suppose. But, I actually have the promise of God that Jesus will personally see to it that I'm not forgotten at death or at the second coming.

This personal love is available to you too. God wants you to experience His personal love. He wants a relationship with you. He wants to be personal to you in a supernatural way.

Being a prison wife can be lonely. People may be around, but few may understand your journey. God has been with you since your creation. He knew this journey would be part of your life. He hasn't deserted you or your husband now that prison has arrived. He remains on the throne.

And despite all the big issues of the world that you might think probably occupies His time, God equally is aware and involved in your days. He shares all your moments with you. Take comfort in this. You cannot do any better than to have God on your side.

If you aren't experiencing the supernatural. If you do not think you have ever heard from God. Seek Him. Get into Scripture and pray. He will personally show up. You're that special to Him. And so is your husband.

August 16 — Refiner's Rescue

Psalm 66:12

Thou didst make men ride over our heads; we went through fire and through water; yet Thou didst bring us out into a place of abundance.

God's refining fire can be ignited by our own sin, another's sin, or simply God's allowance of a circumstance not attached to the fault of anyone. If we cooperate with the refining, a place of abundance remains on the other side of the difficulty. God is faithful to do this for His children. He did it for the Israelites as the psalmist refers to in this verse, and believers in this age are afforded the same.

There are many analogies in Scripture comparing cleansing impurities from metal by fire to growing us up spiritually. The fire allows a blacksmith to mold metal. When heated, it can be hammered and reshaped for a specific purpose. God uses our trials to reshape us. He doesn't leave us in the fire. He desires to rescue us and use the "better" of what results for our purpose and His glory.

We may choose to stay in the fire sometimes, because we hold tight to sin. But He's patient. Just takes some of us longer in the heat. You may have witnessed the life of someone and wonder, "What is it going to take?" Most likely, we were that person at one point in life, gaining a similar remark to our life's path.

If we are in the firepot for no fault of our own, we ask, "Why, God?" I'm the worst for analyzing every angle of a situation, trying to figure out where I went wrong. I feel defeated and grumble. Then I get upset that I'm grumbling, then I descend into apathy. What a mess! Yet God still faithfully rescues me and teaches me.

Precious things come by heat and fire. But only if we seek and trust God's hand to pull us out of it.

August 17 Broken for Broken

Isaiah 53:5

But He was pierced through for our transgressions, He was crushed for our iniquities; the chastening for our well-being fell upon Him, and by His scourging we are healed.

There's a toil on the spirit when faced with repeated rejection. I never had much experience with this until I sought employment after I was placed on probation one time. I had always been able to find work rather easily given years of experience and two degrees. However, one wrong decision wiped it all away and I was unable to work in positions I could before. I was forced to seek entry-level positions making barely above minimum wage in most cases.

Sadly, my credentials which got me a job in the past became the very things adding to the pile of rejected applications. My application screamed with red flags. Why is this girl applying here when she has a master's degree? Interviews were rare and when offered, explanation as to why I was "ineligible" to work in my profession led to the same outcome — rejection.

I wanted to scream, "I'm not a bad person!" But I couldn't blame an employer for the hiring decision made when not afforded the opportunity to know me personally. Every interview was ended with building tears and crushed confidence as I walked to the parking lot. But worse yet, the shame of my sin which led to the tainted background check was the heaviest to bear.

This was something I battled frequently. It's hard to hold your head high when shame is choking you in its filthy smog. It was hard to make eye contact with most anyone when needing to explain my probation status. I felt dirty and worthy of rejection. I knew I wasn't a bad person, but I responded as if my permanent value as a person was determined by my past.

Amazingly, this isn't the truth. Jesus was tortured and shamed for the sin which placed me on probation. He ultimately took the punishment so I could be eternally with Him after I die. Everything shameful and sinful from my life was healed at the cross. He was crushed so I could be whole. He was scarred so I could be without blemish.

Having your spouse incarcerated may be the foundation which spotlights possible shame on your life. You may be rejected because of your own sin or that of your husband's. Cling to the truth that God hasn't rejected you if you're His daughter. God will never say, "You should be ashamed of yourself!" He will lovingly convict when necessary, but will also love the broken pieces of your life back together again.

August 18 *When Everyone Leaves*

Matthew 26:56

"But all this has taken place that the Scriptures of the prophets may be fulfilled." Then all the disciples left Him and fled.

I was involved in a robbery when I worked at a liquor store. It was one of the most frightening experiences of my life. Being held at gunpoint, trying to comply with the commands of the one waving it next to my head, had me speedily contemplating that my life was going to end that night. When the man got all the money and thankfully left, breathing was only allowed a brief rest. When other employees who had ventured to the parking lot to see which direction he may have fled, they ran back in yelling, "He's coming back! Lock the doors!" At that terrified moment, the manager pitched me the keys and he, along with everyone else, fled to the back of the store.

I was the only woman working that night. Big, "tough" men were my coworkers. People that I thought I could depend on—particularly a supervisor—left me alone at a time of extreme need. It was life or death by my perception at that time. I was abandoned to the outcome that everyone else ran away from. Thankfully, the robber didn't come through those doors. Thankfully, none of us were physically harmed that evening.

Jesus experienced abandonment by His closest friends. All the disciples fled at a time of Jesus's greatest need: His arrest and coming death sentence.

They had already spent their time sleeping after Jesus had asked them to keep watch with Him and pray. He asked them repeatedly to wake up and help Him keep watch, yet they proved to be unreliable. Jesus was loyal to them, but they failed to stick with Him when things got hard.

You may be experiencing disappointment in someone close to you that has left the scene because of your husband's crime. Your support may have fled with his arrest or incarceration. I can assure you, however, that Jesus hasn't left you. At the time of Jesus's arrest, everyone left Him. He knows how it feels. Others may be unreliable, but He's faithful to stick by your side to be your helper and support. He doesn't run away when times are hard; in fact, He only draws closer.

August 19 When God Says No

II Corinthians 12:8-9

Concerning this I entreated the Lord three times that it might depart from me. And He has said to me, "My grace is sufficient for you, for power is perfected in weakness." Most gladly, therefore, I will rather boast about my weaknesses, that the power of Christ may dwell in me.

Paul called out to God three times to remove the "thorn" which tormented him. Scripture doesn't say what the thorn represented. It was obviously causing Paul great pain—spiritually, emotionally, or physically. Maybe all three. Paul endured much in preaching the Gospel. Even Jesus said in regards to Paul's conversion: "For I will show him how much he must suffer for My name's sake" (Acts 9:16). The suffering from the thorn was specifically designed to keep Paul dependent on God.

God promised His grace to help Paul bear the burden of his thorn. Paul accepted this answer. He precisely asked three times. There's no indication that he asked anymore. Did he still grumble at times about the thorn? I doubt very much, if at all. He goes further in Scripture to describe the contentment he learned to possess not only with whatever plagued him, but the hardships of persecution, distresses, and insults—for Christ's sake.

Paul's thorn was there to humble him. Many men in prison try to beat prison by becoming stronger than it is. They rely on themselves, not God. They do not boast in Christ; they boast about their evil past to show themselves strong. If not a believer, this fits. If a believer, they may be facing their greatest test in obedience—for Christ's sake. You may also be too.

Jesus asked God three times to remove the cross, but God said no. Paul asked three times for God to remove the messenger of Satan, his thorn in the flesh. God said no. They both surrendered to God's will.

You may be asking God to remove a difficulty and yet the difficulty remains. Maybe He has actually told you no. God has promised you His grace. He wants to show Himself strong in your life. He sees your ability to overcome and wants to help you see the victory despite your weaknesses. Open yourself up to His grace. You'll likely be astounded to see just how strong you are and what He can accomplish through what buffets you right now.

August 20 Worthy in God's Way

James 2:5

Listen, my beloved brethren: did not God choose the poor of this world to be rich in faith and heirs of the kingdom which He promised to those who love Him?

One of my pet peeves is seeing someone donate stained, torn, and cleaning-rag-ready clothing to charity or thrift stores. The greater frustration is then seeing those items on the rack for someone to purchase. People with minimal funds are catered leftovers that should have been taken directly to the dumpster. Without saying it, a judgment has been made of the patrons of those businesses: they aren't worthy of anything better.

James instructed the early church to not show partiality in their congregations. He provides the example of showing special attention to a well-dressed, wealthy man who enters the sanctuary and disregarding the poor man who enters. James challenges them to consider that the poor man is just as much an heir in the kingdom as the wealthy one. And when you consider wealth, what greater riches are there except those awaiting us in heaven? What greater surname could one have than that of being God's son or daughter?

This holds true for prisoners as well. The man on death row who has his salvation is just as privileged as the mega-church preacher. He's a child of the King with all the rights and privileges. He's part of the greatest royal family. How awesome is that!

I applaud churches that have an active prison ministry. And hopefully that ministry exists because they see the men and women incarcerated as worthy, as fellow heirs in the family of God—or wanting to bring them into it. The persons they serve should be treated with the same respect as they would show that fine-suited gentleman who gets to freely enter the sanctuary on Sunday. Some of the most faith-filled people live behind bars. Some of the most faith-filled women have a husband in prison. You're likely one of them!

God's economy is upside down compared to this world's. The least are in a position to experience God's best, because they aren't distracted by the riches of the world. The rich are at greater risk to overlook God, because man shows so much favor and special attention that they forget they need God.

God shows no partiality when it comes to His love. The prisoner—your husband—is a worthy person. So much so, Jesus allowed Himself to be executed so your husband would have a place in heaven with Him.

August 21 Days of the Water

Proverbs 5:15

Drink water from your own cistern, and fresh water from your own well.

This chapter of Proverbs is a warning against adultery from the perspective of a man. He describes the grave consequences for falling for the temptations presented by another woman. He encourages the young man to seek his sexual pleasures through his own wife. Verse fifteen describes it as drinking from his own cistern and well. He describes the waters at home as "fresh."

Fresh waters are active. They are flowing. They are drinkable and desirable. This tells me that the wife at home isn't inactive in her sexual interest for her husband. She isn't stagnant or stale in this area. She's a refreshing source of pleasure to him.

For our husbands, this can be the hardest part of a prison marriage: lack of physical intimacy. It's the hardest thing for us to foster within the limited avenues of contact that we have. No privacy and no conjugal visits for most of us. To keep things fresh is no easy task for something that we know should ideally "flow." The writer of this Proverb says the husband should remain "exhilarated" by the love of his wife. So what can we do to keep love fresh?

We can use our femininity to allure our husbands and be sexually appealing. Femininity becomes part of meeting our husbands' needs for intimacy without the need for physical touch, which is removed with prison. Femininity becomes powerful and can reinforce the marriage bond.

So consider what feminine aspects of yourself that your husband enjoys and try to do those things. Dresses? Manicured nails? Hairstyle? What womanly feature about you does your husband enjoy?

Romance letters, sexy pictures, flirtatious phone calls, perfumed letters. These are other ways to show your husband that you're interested in his sexual needs.

I'm challenged in keeping the waters fresh at home. I'm busy, I'm not very creative in that way, and I'm financially limited to invest in beauty for myself. But the biggest barrier usually is simply the discipline to invest the time. It's so easy to become stagnant.

The irony is my husband is more likely to consider godly things, consent to righteousness through my influence if our "physical" relationship is attractive to him. I know the waters at home hold tremendous power that isn't limited to physical pleasure. I just need to be intentional to stir the waters.

Stir up your waters. Dive in. Add some flavor. Make time to improve the quality of the water your husband drinks. The benefits will flow beyond the physical.

August 22 Futures Rewritten

Daniel 1:3-4

Then the king ordered Ashpenaz, the chief of his officials, to bring in some of the sons of Israel, including some of the royal family and of the nobles, youths in whom was no defect, who were good-looking, showing intelligence in every branch of wisdom, endowed with understanding, and discerning knowledge, and who had ability for serving in the king's court; and he ordered him to teach them the literature and language of the Chaldeans.

Daniel held much promise. He was a handsome young man, intelligent, and mature. He would be a fine husband for any young bride, likely the desire of most. But these qualities led not to a future bride, but captivity in Babylon. He was one of the youths handpicked by Nebuchadnezzar's officials to return to Babylon to serve in the king's court. He was schooled for three years, then assigned his work. He remained a servant his whole life, with no indication in Scripture that he was allowed to marry or have a family. There's speculation that Daniel was castrated as was the custom for many who worked closely to the royal family.

Regardless of whether he was a eunuch or not, Daniel's bright future was suddenly removed and replaced with a different life. He was uprooted from his family and home, taken to a foreign land, and forced to serve a pagan king. If he were then castrated, this would have been physical trauma added to what he had already experienced emotionally.

Daniel, however, was a man characterized by great faith. God was an active part of his life. His walk with God didn't start in Babylon; it was a daily habit well before Nebuchadnezzar captured Jerusalem. This faith enabled him to overcome the losses, and actually gain favor with the king. God's favor never left him.

Prison alters a person's future, whether guilty or innocent when sentenced. For men serving a long-term or life sentence, the bright possibilities of having a wife or family may have been removed. Wives in this situation likely grieve the absence of dreams taken away with their husbands.

I gain encouragement from Daniel. He had everything taken away, yet he trusted and remained faithful to God. He directed his focus to serving within his captivity with no less quality than if he were in his hometown doing life freely. He processed the certain grief and praised God for His goodness.

You and I may never have the future we desire with our husbands. Grief rightly comes with this, but our lives can bear spiritual fruit even if not the children or the home life we desire. Spiritual fruit in many ways is the best of all, because it has eternal impact. Our lives can matter for eternity if we choose to overcome the losses and embrace our new life to God's glory. God will direct your purpose within this new life, and you'll be amazed at how many blessings can come out of captivity.

August 23 God's Varied Workforce

Amos 7:14-15

Then Amos answered and said to Amaziah, "I am not a prophet, nor am I the son of a prophet; for I am a herdsman and a grower of sycamore figs. But the Lord took me from following the flock and the Lord said to me, 'Go prophesy to My people Israel.'"

God's call isn't limited to specific vocations. As a Christian, your career is merely the place God uses you. There may be many special assignments while at one place of employment. Maybe there are persons He wants to reach through you, maybe it becomes a stepping stone to greater responsibility. Opportunities for advancement—or possibly even loss of a job—remain part of God's planned career path, because He's always your ultimate boss.

Amos worked with sheep and trees. In those days, he would be considered a lowly farm worker with less value than other modes of life. But he obviously loved the Lord and the Lord entrusted him with a great message. Much as David was called from the field to lead Israel, Amos was called from the field with his own special assignment. It was not a life-long career as David experienced, but his short-term call to prophesy was just as significant. There's no calling greater than the next; it's about being faithful where God has you and being available for the next assignment.

Prison can complicate your employment. Maybe you're working two jobs, because your husband's income is no longer part of the budget. Maybe you relocated to be closer to your husband, leaving a job that you enjoyed. Maybe your job opportunities have been impacted due to unspoken discrimination related to your husband's incarceration. Maybe you rarely get to visit because of your work schedule.

God is in all your jobs: the good, bad, and horrible ones. Even the ones you took outside of His will. He may have you somewhere for a season. He may ask you to stay at that horrible job, because He's fixing your mess or planning something better. Regardless, He desires to use you where you are now. Your job is special, because God has allowed or willed it for you at this time. Prison may have brought you to it in some direct or indirect way, but only through God's application process.

You're a valuable employee to God, regardless of what you do. Some jobs have greater responsibility, but that doesn't take away from the importance of the one you may fill now. Amos likely returned to the fields after he delivered God's message. God didn't see His shepherd-farmer as the world did. Amos didn't see his work as separate from working for God. It was his life's work regardless of how he made a living.

✝

August 24 — Health Matters

III John 1:2

Beloved, I pray that in all respects you may prosper and be in good health, just as your soul prospers.

Health is important. God sees our bodies as His temple, thus we are to treat it well. Good health extends beyond the obvious. It allows God's work to continue through us without the barriers often arising when health issues enter. Praying for healing and good health is scriptural. In the verse for today, John is greeting his friend Gaius with a general hope that he's well in all ways: physically as well as spiritually.

My husband's health is an area of dealing with prison that has always covered me with a hovering concern. His immediate safety of course, but also the long-term effects of a poor diet, living on concrete, environmental stress, and lack of decent hygiene items such as a good toothbrush. And if he ever has a problem, getting a timely response to his expressed illness adds to the worry for his health.

I pray daily that his health be protected. I pray for whatever damage that has been caused be halted and healed. When he's in need of something or a regular exam, I pray for competent and timely care.

I wish I could remove the stress he lives under. That in itself is the biggest threat to his health. Unrelenting stress damages a person. So as part of praying for his protection, I pray for his peace. I want him to rest securely, whether asleep or not.

I always joke with him that if he ever gets out, I plan to have him get every test and exam available, from head to toe. His eyes, teeth, ears, skin, blood, everything! And of course, if he remains in prison for life as sentenced, I'll continue to prayerfully intercede that all will remain well.

This is another aspect of this journey that I have to regularly give to God. That hovering concern for my husband's health can be smothering, especially if I know he's sick or physically injured. It's a helpless feeling. I wish I could trust DOC in this area, but I cannot. And that being from experience. But I do trust God.

Your husband's spiritual health will always be more important to God, but He cares about his body too. It was His greatest creation! He created him in His own image, so of course He wants the best for your husband physically. Pray that his health prospers, just as his soul does.

August 25 *Time Is of the Essence*

Genesis 1:14

Then God said, "Let there be lights in the expanse of the heavens to separate the day from the night, and let them be for signs, and for seasons, and for days and years."

I do not really understand why God designated days and years at the time of creation when the design was to be eternal. But with perfect minds, I suppose Adam and Eve would have done fine keeping track of it. The use of our time was certainly damaged with the fall; life became fragile. Death now happens. People are part of our lives for only determined amounts of time — including our husbands. Our use of our time should reflect this understanding.

The relationship I want with God and my husband are time dependent. Living out my purpose is time dependent. It only takes one tragedy in the headlines to stir me out of complacency to invest in what really matters. I can review the previous week and regret that I missed opportunities, because I chose to watch one more episode of a TV series from 1990 that I have seen countless times! Why?

I really do not know. We cannot live hypervigilant about death or tragedy, but there's a need to be intentional with how we spend our time. Prison robs us of so many opportunities already. It would be regretful to leave the visitation park after wasted silence in anger at our husbands or seated in front of a computer for hours doing nothing of value when that dreaded call comes that rocks our world.

So wake with a sense of direction. Spend time with the Lord first and foremost. He will refine your goals and mold your priorities. He has to be first to get anything else to line up correctly. He's your best defense against regrets. He has a plan for each day. His life of significance for you consists of purposeful days, and only He knows the best way to accomplish your best life.

After that, try to invest in what matters before you sit down at the computer or TV. I try to write to my husband before I do anything else. A quick check of email often branches into reading articles, looking at websites, or lengthy detours I never planned — but always seem to happen. Before I know it, I have only a few minutes to jot a few lines to my husband before the next thing on my list demands attention.

Try to set aside a block of time once a week when you can focus on your husband. Whether it be a special love letter, doing things of interest for him, getting creative with personalized cards, or doing anything that will build connection. Consider it like your date night.

Make the most of your visits. I know they can become routine, but if you find yourself watching the clock out of boredom or restlessness, something needs to change. Try never to leave in anger. It's a terribly hard place to resolve conflict, but it's even harder once you walk out that gate. He may not get to call you that night or the next or ever.

God created time and controls it's ending, but we are given the privilege of managing it. Prison forces its management into our lives, but with intentional decisions and God's help, we can feel good about how we did the time with our husbands — and hopefully without regrets.

August 26 Unleavened Is Best

Galatians 5:9

A little leaven leavens the whole lump of dough.

Any baker knows that it doesn't take much yeast to impact a bowl of dough. Those little packets are potent. It's an active ingredient. Given time, it expands the dough beyond its original size and texture. Paul in the verse above is comparing false teaching to leaven. The Galatian Christians were being led astray by unsound doctrine. He urged them to have nothing to do with it and to stand firm in the truth of Jesus's teaching.

Sin cannot be compartmentalized. Just like leaven, it permeates the entire loaf. Paul knew that sin is subtle and slow "leavening" away from the truth of God's word can have severe consequences. It will impact the believer's entire life. Satan uses the gradual accommodations for sin to destroy the person or at the least, a person's testimony.

Prison might as well be presented to you in those little envelopes like yeast. It's full of bad influences and sin that actively expand into your life and your husband's. Once introduced, accommodations begin to slowly replace what you know to be right in God's eyes.

Your husband might already be well entrenched in the prison culture. His acceptance of sinful behavior will impact you. It will cause conflicts if you stand firm like Paul encourages of the Galatians. Loving a man who is incarcerated will often bring you to a test of who do you love more: God or your husband?

As hard as it can be, choosing God is always the best. You'll not escape the negative consequences of your husband's willful sin, especially if you begin participating in it with him. It may seem like no big deal at first, but that's exactly how the subtle accommodations permeate to pull you away from God's will, protection, and blessings. And that's a scary place to be, especially when dealing with prison. Your best support of your husband is sometimes telling him no.

August 27 — All Who Sin

Romans 5:8

But God demonstrates His own love toward us, in that while we were yet sinners, Christ died for us.

Stigma often comes while walking through days of prison with your husband. I understand the basis for the struggling thoughts of others when considering a commitment to a man who has committed a crime, particularly a violent one. My stomach sickens with grief when I hear a news anchor recounting the details of evil released upon another person. With most difficulty, I look at the crime scene photos and the body of my husband's victim on a slab of metal. Knowing my husband was responsible cuts to that deep part of my heart. The raw sense of knowing God is needed in this world glares at me.

You may be married to a violent offender. It's a difficult role to fulfill as a wife. This is especially true when you're coming to grips with his actions that reflect the opposite of love. How can hands that lovingly hold you have caused such harm? You may have been shocked with your husband's arrest, not fathoming how he could have done such a thing.

But it doesn't always have to be a violent past to create the condemning reaction of others. Thievery, drug offense, tax fraud—incarceration from all depths comes with judgment that often extends beyond the man to the family still trying to love him when he's at his most difficult to love.

The problem is others also try to keep you in whatever past took your husband to prison. They doubt good can come from him or such a depth of wrong. Your husband's depth may be murder. He may sit on death row. It may be from habitual depths according to the law, which now demand a harsher penalty. My reminder to you is that there's no depth beyond God's reach. There's no man considered valueless to God and no man whom He didn't send Jesus to die for. Jesus loves the murderer equally as much as that finest minister. Jesus died for all, equally. Thus He desires to redeem all.

Others who criticize, shame, or judge you because of your husband's crime or sentencing, thankfully, do not determine your or your husband's value. They sin as your husband sins. They need Jesus just as much as your husband does. No one is good enough to enter heaven on their own actions, regardless how law abiding a person may be. Christ died so all could come to salvation and live eternally in heaven. Let this truth encourage you when others behave toward you in ways that causes you to feel otherwise.

August 28 Even the Smallest

Revelation 22:18-19

I testify to everyone who hears the words of the prophecy of this book: if anyone adds to them, God shall add to him the plagues which are written in this book; and if anyone takes away from the words of the book of this prophecy, God shall take away his part from the tree of life and from the holy city, which are written in this book.

Adding a letter to a word can have dramatic impact on its meaning. "S" added to "laughter" becomes "slaughter." Quite a difference. Some may humorously understand why adding an "s" to "mother" becomes "smother." Just one letter added or taken away can communicate something totally different. It's just as critical that God's word not be altered, even slightly, because what may seem like a minor adjustment can communicate significant error. God desires everyone to hear the truth, not a close or different version of it.

John wrote the verses above as a warning to support how serious God's word is. He's referring to the book of Revelation which he was authoring, but throughout Scripture, God stressed the importance of obeying His commandments and following His teachings. Everything written in the Bible is without error, and God expects it to remain unchanged.

Sadly, not all prison chaplains teach the truth of Scripture. They can be from different doctrinal backgrounds. Just because they serve in the spiritual role doesn't equate their beliefs to true Christianity.

Another thing to consider: chaplains are available to all inmates, regardless of faith. This expectation can result in subtle accommodations or keeping quiet about the truth in serving men of religious diversity. It would be a very hard role to fulfill in such situations. But to add or take away from Scripture would hold a serious consequence to both the chaplain and the man he was attempting to minister to.

Callousness can also come from working in prison. I have experienced chaplains who were downright ugly in their speech and attitude. If someone were to observe them from afar, they would never guess they were spiritual leaders. Those were disappointing days for me.

These type things can be unfortunate, because as prison wives, we want to see the chaplain as a spiritual resource. Of course, there are some very good chaplains in the system. We just need to be alert that the title alone doesn't equate to a teacher who supports what the Bible teaches. It's okay to ask them what they believe! And of course if they show a pattern of harshness in their mannerisms, then I would suggest caution in your interactions with them. They may be more dedicated to pleasing the DOC than God.

You can also pray for the chaplain. He has an awesome responsibility if he takes the word of God seriously. Any spiritual counselor does. He has the opportunity to impact many lives. He also has the challenge of accomplishing this within numerous restrictions. It's a valuable role in the prison and one that must be handled delicately to make sure even the smallest of errors aren't intentionally fostered simply because his flock never leave the fence.

August 29 — Apple of His Eye

Zechariah 2:8

For thus says the Lord of hosts, "After glory He has sent me against the nations which plunder you, for he who touches you, touches the apple of His eye."

Have you ever considered that you're the apple of God's eye? All believers are. Or at least we should want to be. Being the apple of someone's eye confers admiration and zealous interest. The apple is equivalent to the pupil of the eye. It's the pupil which rests in the center of the eye and allows the light into the eye so the other parts of the eye can operate to reflect the light and produce an image. Wherever the eye looks, the pupil is there, front and center.

Being the apple of God's eye means He's always focused on you. Wherever He looks, He sees you. You're the center of protection and love. God stays focused on you for your good. This is the benefit of being His daughter.

In the verse for today, Zechariah is referring to the opposition Israel faced after returning to Jerusalem at the end of the Babylonian rule. They were still in bondage, but under the Persian government. The Israelites had lost energy for rebuilding the temple which was destroyed when the Babylonians took the city. The opposition seemed just too much. But God imparted to them that despite His discipline of them, He remained jealous for them. Anyone who messed with them, messed with Him. Zechariah was sent to encourage them to push through their fears and the enemy's attacks and complete their place of worship.

Similarly, when David's life was being threatened, he pleaded with God to "keep me as the apple of the eye" (Psalm 17:8). David didn't want God to turn His eyes away from him, meaning His protection. He wanted God to see and understand all that he was going through.

That's the joy of walking with God. You know that He always sees you, and you're always under His watchful eye. You do not have to explain or catch Him up on what's been happening in your life since your last conversation. His eyes never left you. That's such a tremendous comfort.

Whatever you're going through, God is attentive. You're in the center of His vision. He hasn't turned His head the other direction in disinterest. It may seem as though He's busy looking elsewhere, but He isn't. However He's dealing with you today, even if seeming in the far sights of His vision, you have not dropped out of His sights.

August 30 *Reluctant Servants*

I Samuel 16:2

But Samuel said, "How can I go? When Saul hears of it, he will kill me." And the Lord said, "Take a heifer with you, and say, 'I have come to sacrifice to the Lord.'"

Sometimes God asks us to do things that causes us pause. He may prompt us toward a decision that stirs up anxiety. We usually "educate" Him on the risks, the what-ifs, and maybe even our ineptness as if to say, "You've got the wrong person." There are plenty of persons in Scripture, thankfully, who shared such experiences from whom we can draw encouragement. In the end, God knew what He was doing. His call and instructions can always be followed confidently.

I do not readily think of Samuel as having cold feet about anything. He was a strong mouthpiece for God, but even he had his anxious moments and times of questioning. In the verse today, Samuel was responding to God regarding the assignment to go to Bethlehem to anoint the new king. Saul had been ousted and the boy David was off in his father's field tending sheep unaware that his life was about to change dramatically. Samuel was the one who had to tell Saul that he had essentially been fired, and now he was to go appoint his replacement. He feared Saul's response.

Seems a natural reluctance under the circumstances. Of course, Samuel obeyed the Lord despite his reservations. Others in Scripture have done similar: Moses was reluctant on several occasions, Gideon was fearful and requested signs of assurance, and Ananias made sure he let God know of Paul's persecution of believers. But all followed obediently. They trusted God with the outcome.

I have been in the camp of wondering if God knew what He was doing. He has asked me to resign from jobs that I loved, asked me to move to places I wasn't sure I wanted to go, and asked me to speak up in times I wanted to be invisible. All His requests were part of the path He was taking me or the development of my character. Some of the hardest requests involved being God's mouthpiece in challenging my husband's actions. I would sigh in reluctance wondering if God knew — as I did — how my husband was going to respond. The conversation would always end, "I know. I'll do it."

God may have many assignments that will tap your courage. They may involve being a godly example when it's unpopular. They may involve your husband's choices in prison. They may involve your calling. Being reluctant is human. Great men of Scripture struggled with the same. But there's tremendous satisfaction when you step forward in obedience and do what God asks. His pleasure will sing over you and your spirit will breathe a peaceful "Well done."

August 31 Wonder Why?

John 11:33-34

When Jesus therefore saw her weeping, and the Jews who came with her, also weeping, He was deeply moved in spirit, and was troubled, and said, "Where have you laid him?" They said to Him, "Lord, come and see."

I'm fascinated by Scripture that gives us the stories of Jesus interacting with people. He asks in verse 34 where they had buried Lazarus. Did He really not know? He could have walked to the burial site without directions, but He engaged those in the moment with a question. They were eager for His intervention, and they led the way as if He were dependent on it.

It's interesting to consider why Jesus asked and did the things He did. He knew Lazarus had fallen ill. He knew exactly when he died despite not being there. He intentionally waited four days to perform the miracle of raising Lazarus from the dead. I can understand some of the witnesses' statements about why Jesus exerted His power in some situations and not in others. Specifically, John records for us in verse 37: "Could not this man, who opened the eyes of him who was blind, have kept this man also from dying?" Sure He could have! But He chose not to in order to bring greater glory to God and build the faith of the witnesses.

There are verses in the Bible that refer to Jesus knowing the hearts of people, or better stated, what they were thinking. He knew Peter would deny Him three times. Yet other times, He asked questions. Before feeding the five thousand, He asked the disciples how many loaves of bread were available. Before driving out the demon from the child with seizures, He asked the father how long the boy had been afflicted.

Jesus was fully God and fully man. How He blended the two is beyond our grasp. He brilliantly carried out His ministry and compassionately fulfilled His mission. He beautifully engaged people in a perfect way, whether the goal was for their encouragement, repentance, admonishment, or teaching.

Get fascinated by Jesus and Scripture. The Bible is about Him, from the creation account to His Revelation. There's so much richness in God's word. It's your life's guide, from decisions to your purpose. It's about God's love and desire to be in relationship with you, now and eternally. That's why Jesus came. His life is a fascinating read! Read it with renewed enthusiasm.

September 1 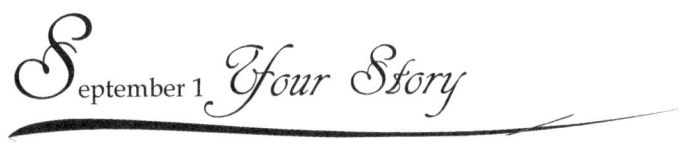 Your Story

Daniel 4:2

"It has seemed good to me to declare the signs and wonders which the Most High God has done for me."

Everyone has a testimony. It's usually a bad-to-good story of how God sustained and changed a life. In order to share, however, the joy and gratefulness has to exceed the shame or stigma. No one likes to broadcast their dirt! But everyone has it. Some pasts are just muddier than others. In most cases, the darker the past, the greater the testimony to God's ability to change a person. Satan, however, will use shame to keep a person silent.

King Nebuchadnezzar makes the statement above after he had lost his kingdom and was driven out to live as a wild man seven years in the fields. He was forced to eat grass and live like an animal. He began to look the part even. But he finally surrendered his heart to the Lord and his kingdom was restored.

He had plenty to be embarrassed about: the way he looked, the pitiful state his life had become after so much prestige and power. Yet when he proclaimed his testimony, he didn't hold back. He addressed his words to "all the peoples, nations, and men of every language that live in all the earth" (verse 1).

Nebuchadnezzar was arrogant throughout his ruling years. He was very cruel. He was responsible for throwing Shadrach, Meshach, and Abed-nego into the blazing furnace, so hot it killed the soldiers standing next to it. And after witnessing their deliverance, issued a decree that if anyone spoke against God, that person would be dismembered and their homes destroyed. Needless to say, he caused a lot of harm as ruler. Yet, even with such a past, God extended mercy when Nebuchadnezzar—at his lowest--surrendered.

We can learn from his life and how he shared his dirt. He thought it was important to let others know what God had done for him. He didn't shrink away in shame when his former officials approached him about returning home. He allowed himself to enjoy his redemption!

For many of us, there's time between the transformation and the boldness to share our testimony. That's fine if God is using that time to heal what has been broken. But if the silence is from shame, God isn't behind that feeling. His forgiveness brings peace, not humiliation. His acceptance, regardless of past sin, ignites the words of a testimony, not a mute disgrace.

Maybe God is stirring in you or your husband the words He wants you to share. Remember everyone has dirt, so do not think you're the only person who has messed up. Most of all, remember that God's work in a life is good and glorious, not shameful. It's not about the bad, but what God has done with it.

September 2 — Isolating Consequences

Judges 18:27-28

Then they took what Micah had made and the priest who had belonged to him, and came to Laish, to a people quiet and secure, and struck them with the edge of the sword; and they burned the city with fire. And there was no one to deliver them, because it was far from Sidon and they had no dealings with anyone, and it was in the valley which is near Beth-rehob. And they rebuilt the city and lived in it.

The town of Laish is described almost as a sanctuary. It was in the valley, tucked away from the world, and the people enjoyed a peaceful way of life. The land was rich and plentiful, providing everything they needed. They settled into this haven and lived isolated from others, enjoying their privacy and comforts.

Well, the very things that hallmarked it as desirable and promoted self-sufficiency are what led to its annihilation. Men of the tribe of Dan spied out Laish and attacked. It was an easy target. Scripture says that there was no one to deliver Laish, because they had isolated themselves from other people and support.

For some prisoners, isolation in a one-man cell is actually very attractive. It can be difficult to go to sleep not knowing if the stranger sharing a cell plots harm. So a one-man cell brings a sense of security due to restricted access from the general population and no roommate. But as a prisoner's wife, remaining isolated from others can leave you vulnerable to attacks, emotionally and spiritually.

No Christian is meant to do life alone. We need other Christians. If you have a great church family, keep it going. I know that it can be difficult connecting in a church, particularly if you weren't a member prior to your husband's incarceration. But what happens if you aren't connected?

You lose other Christians' input and perspectives of anything you're dealing with. You lose the encouragement of other believers (who would likely pray for you as well). You lose the opportunity to worship and hear from God through the pastor. And you lose opportunities to serve.

Satan would love to keep you from church. He knows in doing so the church is weaker, and so are you. He will use the difficulty of prison to keep you discouraged with the goal being to have you lose hope. Really hope in anything: your life, your husband's changes, and God's goodness. You'll also be at home, not using your spiritual gift so the church will not benefit as God designed. All the consequences are cumulative, and your life loses power and effectiveness.

I have to fight to stay connected in community. It doesn't come natural or easy for me. I dread the "shake hands and greet your neighbor" that's heralded at most any church I have ever attended. But I understand community is important. It's rather a discipline for introverts like me. It might need to be for you too.

What I do find, however, is that God rewards my commitment. He will show up to speak to me on a Sunday morning when I would have not heard otherwise if I had been absent. I get a fresh encounter with Him either through the worship music or message. I get reminded that my life isn't all about me. And through this commitment, when trouble comes, unlike Laish, there's help available.

September 3 O My Soul

Psalm 42:11

Why are you in despair, O my soul? And why have you become disturbed within me? Hope in God, for I shall yet praise Him, the help of my countenance, and my God.

On my bad days, my personality can be my worst enemy in the legalistic, graceless expectations I make of myself. I'm always seeking to do the right thing and bothered when mistakes are made. This expectation resides on me spiritually. I desire to be pleasing to God in word and deed, and any emotional breakdown that prompts an ungodly reaction toward my husband or a situation frustrates me, as failure tends to do. I condemn myself spiritually when the person I desire to please—God—hasn't. It's a skewed perspective that prompts thoughts that Satan knew would follow if he could get me to that point: "I can't do anything right. What a terrible person I am." I can tell myself that I have nothing to contribute to anyone or anything.

It doesn't take long in such a conversation with myself to rob my day of needed joy. Sadness often comes, and my energy for prison and life again runs low. Weariness reflects through my regular letters to my husband and the less frequent romantic ones if the sadness lingers. Satan tempts me with depressing thoughts, and if I take the bait, he wins the battle. The more ground I give him, the more he takes.

Fortunately, God knows my personality and my struggles. He created me! He faithfully provides me a timely hug to refuel my perspective with truth and encouragement. The Holy Spirit throws me a lifeline through Scripture or something in my world to be that cheerleader I need. I often empathize with God in how much time He spends reassuring and loving me to get me through some days. I'm dependent on Him daily and am frequently reminded that He desires my dependence. Although He desires me to learn from the experiences so that I can live in victory over my thoughts—and those Satan adds to them—He's amazingly gracious when my thoughts turn to tears, a rant through the house, or an extended lull in bed.

Prison might trigger days when you only want to remain in bed and somehow escape through sleep all that you woke to. The barriers of prison may begin their looming with the rise of the sun, collecting more darkness as your mind begins to consider the closest one to you. It's one barrier, and then on to the next, then another connected to it, and then once sufficiently smothered in your thoughts, you must sigh through the cloud formed to even make it out of bed.

But stay in the battle! You're loved and treasured by God. Get up—spiritually and physically. You may stumble, and even when you do not grab the lifeline the Holy Spirit throws you, God will faithfully lower you to the floor to cushion the fall and remains ready to pick you up again. Each fall adds to your experience, and if you allow God to use it, the next battle goes better.

✝

September 4 — He Wants You

Acts 8:26

But an angel of the Lord spoke to Philip saying, "Arise and go south to the road that descends from Jerusalem to Gaza." (This is a desert road.) And he arose and went; and behold, there was an Ethiopian eunuch, a court official of Candace, queen of the Ethiopians, who was in charge of all her treasure; and he had come to Jerusalem to worship.

Uncle Sam's image and, most popularly, his finger portrayed the Army's call to individuals: "I want you!" It displayed the singleness of contribution one person could make to America through serving in the military. The message hoped to connect with the audience on a personal level.

God has His finger pointing at all of us. And He sends individuals to share His message: "I want you!"

Philip was sent to explain the Scriptures and the Gospel to a single Ethiopian who was returning home from Jerusalem. God sent an angel, who sent Philip, who then sent the Ethiopian back home so he could share with persons in his circle of influence. It was part of God's design to evangelize the nation of Ethiopia. That one eunuch, in a position of influence, could impact many for the Gospel he came to believe in. He likely made a tremendous contribution once home.

God is personally interested in your husband. In his salvation and sending him to an audience as a witness. His audience may be to many or just one other prisoner, one at a time, much as Philip was called to minister to the Ethiopian. You may need to pray for a Philip to be sent to your husband. You may be his Philip.

God is interested in you too. He operates by personal invitation only. "You" isn't plural. That's how awesome His love is; it's all about His loving each person.

Is there anyone in your circle of influence that needs to hear your story? Has someone entered your life whom God is using to grow you in your faith? Your contribution can be as unique as you are. The eunuch had a position that not just anybody got to do; he managed the royal finances. There's only one you, and that's so special to God that He's seeking you out for His personal service.

September 5 Knowing God

John 1:14

And the Word became flesh, and dwelt among us, and we beheld His glory, glory as of the only begotten from the Father, full of grace and truth.

    To walk with God and experience His comforting presence, you have to come to know Jesus, desiring Him to be your Savior from sin and Lord of your life. God then sends His Holy Spirit to live within you. This triune relationship will provide everything you need to make it through these days, whether they be sad, frightening, lonely, or amazingly stressful. There's no substitute for God's guidance, presence, or love. And all of this begins with Jesus.

    For some of you, Jesus may not be a part of your life. You may not know much about Him, God, or the Holy Spirit. If you're unfamiliar with what Scripture says about Jesus, start in one of the first four books of the New Testament. These books provide the story of Jesus's life. Bible teachers often recommend the book of John as a great introduction to Jesus. John was Jesus's closest disciple. Use a Christian translation most appropriate for you. Also, ask God to lead you to a local Christian church where the Bible is taught and Jesus is glorified in all His deity.

    Once you believe in who Jesus is and as your relationship with God grows closer, you'll experience the greater presence of the Holy Spirit in your life through the Scripture you read. He will communicate with you through the Bible, others, your world, and situation. You'll begin to recognize His voice, and once experienced, I pray you also will long for more of His presence.

    You do not have to feel alone in your everyday world of prison. God desires to walk this path with you. He wants to be your cheerleader, comforter, and guide. He has been with you every moment of every day before prison became a reality in your life. And today, there are no tears missed by Him in your emotional breakdowns whether they land you in the floor or your face in a pillow. In that silent cry no one else perceives, He sees. He knows you intimately and invites you to know Him.

September 6 — Heart of the Matter

Proverbs 4:23

Watch over your heart with all diligence, for from it flow the springs of life.

    You can find endless situations of prison to feel victimized. Delays in a visitation line, high-priced phone calls, rude officers, or commonplace corruption that's present in every correctional system—it all comes with prison. You may also find yourself in more situations where you feel compelled to defend your husband or your marriage. But always remember that your marriage is about your relationship with your husband, not the system or defending against the criticism of others. Even in the smaller situations that create that upsurge of anger or defensiveness, do not let it detract from enjoying moments with your husband or erode a peaceful heart.

    The goal is to graciously release persons who criticize to their own perspective and rest in knowing God is on your side. It doesn't mean that you'll not be hurt, but you can accept the hurt once you understand you're fully accepted by God. And in releasing a person to their perspective, try to do it without an embittered attitude. "I don't care what they think anyway!" isn't doing it with grace. Grace comes from the heart, and it gets released from the heart. There's peace with it. A gracious response doesn't retaliate in words or thoughts.

    When feeling victimized, it's also good to do a pride check. Are you defending your husband or yourself? Are you upset because someone doesn't have the image of you that they had before knowing your husband is incarcerated? Pride has a competitive nature and doesn't like taking that lower, perceived defeated position. Your embittered emotions can be connected to pride, because it's all about self. I have been done wrong in some sense, I have been misunderstood, I have been hurt, or I have been whatever.

    To accept being misunderstood or wrongly criticized is showing humility, being meek. Jesus did it all the time. If you're in a conversation where you find yourself getting upset over the other person's words, drop the rope. Why try to convince them? You do not have to compete for your marriage's acceptance. The only person who matters accepts you already — God.

It may just be you and God who believe in your husband or marriage. But let me assure you that's plenty! You haven't given up on your husband, nor has God, even if the rest of society has. Just take caution over your own heart's reaction to those who think differently.

September 7 — What Part Are You?

Romans 12:4-5

For just as we have many members in one body and all the members do not have the same function, so we, who are many, are one body in Christ, and individually members one of another.

Paul is explaining that believers who make up the church have been gifted in different ways to fulfill different service needs within the church. It's how the body of Christ is to operate. When everyone serves within their giftedness, the body thrives. He also stresses a quality to the service. Service should be done with the right heart. This attitude most likely flows when you find how you "fit" within the body. You're not an eye trying to be a foot, or an ear trying to be arm; all of which would just be frustrating.

Being devoted wives and supporting our husbands will always be our primary calling. But God also desires to use us individually to serve other believers. We wouldn't have been gifted individually or saved individually if God didn't desire to use us individually. He desires to use you and me beyond the role of wife to serve within the church.

There was a time when I saw my role as simply living life with my husband, being there as his supporter in all ways, being a teacher in spiritual matters when possible, and remaining always in prayer. I was loving God and my husband, but only haphazardly serving in the church.

I never considered myself "religious" enough to be involved in what I considered *real* ministry. I had volunteered, but those events never kindled a sense of fit. I did it, because I felt it was the right thing to do and knew it was important. But without a deeper connection to the where, whom, and how I served, I concluded there must have been something wrong with me since excitement seemed to flow through everyone except me. I saw others as better Christians because of this. How could I genuinely consider my service efforts as ministry, since my heart lagged in its passion? Without a passionate heart accompanying me, I struggled to believe the service could be completely pleasing to God.

Please, do not misunderstand me. I'm definitely not saying that we never help within or outside the church beyond how we are gifted. But in regards to my primary service to God—beyond serving my husband—I hadn't even considered if God had any other plans for me. I thought I was to be the unsung prison wife doing what that role needed while also helping at church in unintentional ways.

But I wasn't meant to do just random, good activities within the church when the opportunity arises. Neither are you. God has a special way for you to serve.

In my case, God has given me a heart for communicating Scripture. I love learning about Scripture and how God actively uses it. I get a righteous stirring in my spirit when I hear errors made in it. I have also always gravitated toward words and writing. My personality also prefers the sidelines. Combine these things with my life experiences of prison and you're reading the product of one of my gifts.

Serving in intentional ways, based on your spiritual gift(s), can be an exciting aspect of your life despite the reality of prison difficulties that you face daily. It will be part of what builds contentment into your life. Venture to discover your fit. If not familiar with the gifts, I would encourage you to do a Bible study on the spiritual gifts. Then it becomes a matter of stepping out and getting involved. Everything will sync when you find the part you play within the body.

September 8 *Types of Time*

Ecclesiastes 3:1

There is an appointed time for everything. And there is a time for every event under heaven.

When your relationship has the barrier of prison, steps toward anything seem to move like molasses. Nothing moves fast enough when it's entangled in a system where security is paramount, and the way it seems to accomplish this is have everything move painstakingly slow. Ironically, time moves too fast when there's finally an opportunity to be with your husband either through a visit or phone call. These are always such bittersweet logistics of having your husband incarcerated. Once resolved to the surrender of another visit or call ending, you then hurriedly look to the calendar either on your wall or in your mind to see when the next opportunity can be had. Then comes the wait—yet again.

The writer of Ecclesiastes discusses "set" time and "seasons" of time. The word time in the verse today are two different Hebrew words: z^emân and 'êth. There's a set time for everything which would be a scheduled visit for example. There's a season of time which would be your husband's time of incarceration. The season of time carries with it a sense of rightness in that God still manages the seasons of our lives just as He does the exact time of our birth or death. The writer sees God as the scheduler of both time and seasons.

It's the season of incarceration that's the harder to walk through. It taxes our endurance and patience. We more easily become weary than the impact a one-time good or bad experience might have on us. But if we consider that God has divinely allowed the season, we can trust that God is still managing all the time (z^emân) within it. He doesn't relegate us to a season, then go about His business as if to say, "I'll be back on your husband's release date." He goes with us through all the events, within every day of the season. The season is His appropriate time to do a good work within us.

In your best effort, try not to get bogged down with the weight of the season. It's God's desire to carry the weight for you. Hand it to Him. He can carry it with perfect ease. Continue to enjoy the visits and the phone calls, and relax within the wait of everything else, knowing God is in control.

September 9 *Mightier Help*

Zechariah 4:6

Then he answered and said to me, "This is the word of the Lord to Zerubbabel saying, 'Not by might nor by power, but by My Spirit,' says the Lord of hosts."

My past is full of failed efforts at love and each provides an example of where God was not the source or center of my efforts. It reflects my history of doing love the world's way. To go in my own strength would find my emotions always too fragile, my ability to control my reactions lacking, and my tendency to want to control and change what I didn't like by means of guilt, manipulation, or a critical attitude. The self-help prescription would soon fail and so would the relationship.

This may be where you are today. You may not see any solution in sight as the same battles ensue. Your battles are also waged in the midst of a correctional facility, likely leaving you with a greater sense of vainness and exhaustion in your efforts. You may be thinking: "I want my marriage to survive, I want my relationship to be different this time, but I don't know how!" Take encouragement! God's words remain, "Not by might nor by power, but by My Spirit."

The prophet Zechariah was to speak these words of encouragement to Zerubbabel, Governor of Judah, at a time when God's people, the Israelites, had been allowed to return to their land following seventy years of Babylonian captivity. The motivator behind this release came from the divinely inspired heart of King Cyrus, who desired the rebuilding of the temple in Jerusalem to be initiated and by way of his royal decree this pursuit became a reality. The temple area had laid desolate since Solomon's magnificent structure rested there.

So for the postexilic Israelites, a dream was granted by a merciful and loving God. It was much as a restored love relationship between two persons estranged and reunited enjoying all the newness as when the relationship first blossomed. But in a pattern so familiar to the Israelites, they lost their motivation with only their fervor lasting for as long as it took the foundation of the once longed-for temple to be completed. The emotional, self-help prescription failed them.

Zechariah was to stir the Israelites on in their efforts, break them from their lethargy, distractions, and selfish pursuits to resume the love relationship represented by the construction and completion of the temple. With his words came the promise of God that God's Spirit would enable them to be successful.

This can be your motivation as you persevere alongside your husband. Cling to God on the path He has placed before you lest you become complacent and loose the passion to continue the work. A prison marriage is work, but it isn't without hope. God's Spirit is available to help.

September 10 *Missing Him*

Song of Solomon 5:6

"I opened to my beloved, but my beloved had turned away and had gone! My heart went out to him as he spoke. I searched for him, but I did not find him; I called him, but he did not answer me."

There's definitely a different way of moving through life when your husband is incarcerated. You do life as best as you can with the understanding that your husband, in prison for possibly even life, is unable to enjoy days with you beyond what he can experience through words or pictures on a page, pricey phone calls, or regimented visits. There's a singleness you maintain despite your hearts being inseparable.

In the Song of Solomon, the bride's longing for her mate is expressed in today's verse. She wants nothings else but to be in his physical presence, to be held and loved by him. It's the focus of her thoughts. She's awaiting their union when all these desires are received. He desires her equally so. It's such a beautiful representation of marriage as God designed.

If your heart is longing for your husband, consider the good of your love that it represents. Your situation should stir feelings of loss. If the Shulamite bride in the Song of Solomon was indifferent about being away from her mate, what affection would she hold for her marriage vows? It's when the singleness you experience takes your heart away too that danger lurks.

God understands the longings that you have. He understands that empty ache that comes with missing someone terribly. He knows how hard it is for you to see other couples doing the simple things that they sadly take for granted. He understands when no one else does. His Spirit will comfort you through the lonely days, especially the simple moments they contain that you usually miss the most.

September 11 Tragedy Remembered

Proverbs 6:16-19

There are six things which the Lord hates, yes, seven which are an abomination to Him: haughty eyes, a lying tongue, and hands that shed innocent blood, a heart that devises wicked plans, feet that run rapidly to evil, a false witness who utters lies, and one who spreads strife among brothers.

Bad news travels fast. Horrible events travel even faster. A national tragedy leaves a wake of numbing silence when word reaches the ears. It burns into memory the location, time, and emotions when it hits. Unbelief works to get absorbed into reality. It's part of the human experience when faced with an unexpected and unconscionable event that was carried out by another human being. It makes one question how dead a conscious must be to do such a thing?

But it's good to remember. Sensitivity to human experience and the gift of life are necessary for compassion and appreciation of both. Today brings solemn peacefulness. A moment of silence for some who do not believe in God. Prayers made to God for those who do believe. Understanding likely grappled with by both.

For those personally impacted by a tragedy, acceptance and understanding are likely ill-grasped regardless of the time that passes. But hopefully, assurance comes — in time — that God hates evil too.

For you, there may by another day of the year marking the anniversary of a tragedy. Your husband's crime, the death of someone innocent, or some other permanent scar that's a reminder daily of the loss you have experienced. Please know that God is close and longs to bring comfort to your heartbreak. He can fill the hollow place and bring you through these difficult days and the anniversaries of the future that are solemn.

Loss can make you dread the future, because it seems nothing but more days of feeling sad and empty, a weary journey that seems impossible to make. God is in the future, and just as importantly, He's in your today. He's available and ready to smother you with help and loving assurance. Take His hand. Fall into His presence. He can be trusted when everything around you cannot be. He's on your side and desires to walk with you through the memories or your current reality.

September 12 — Resurfaced Way

Genesis 19:15-16

And when morning dawned, the angels urged Lot, saying, "Up, take your wife and your two daughters, who are here, lest you be swept away in the punishment of the city." But he hesitated. So the men seized his hand and the hand of his wife and the hands of his two daughters, for the compassion of the Lord was upon him; and they brought him out, and put him outside the city.

You may have been one to see the darkness of prison looming in the distance as you anxiously walked each step with your husband prior to his incarceration. Or you may have been one to watch him run full-speed ahead ignoring your cries of warning that the darkness is getting closer and seems only a short distance from him. I can still see the dread of that darkness when I watch my husband walk unwavering toward it through decisions that he makes since incarcerated. As a result we both deal with any negative consequences for our marriage. As wives, we too are now on this same path that brought our husbands into the darkness, but the key is to now accept God's resurfaced way out. Even if your husband will not walk the resurfaced way with you, go anyway!

My husband historically lingers behind me on the path much like Lot in the angels' escort of him and his family from the certain devastation of Sodom. He wants to hold onto the sin or somehow feels that he cannot survive otherwise despite God clearly showing him the way of escape and to a better life.

God sent angels ahead to warn Lot, but he amazingly didn't respond in urgency to the stated consequences: destruction of the city. Lot hesitated. He even disputed the angels' instruction for him to escape to the mountains. He requested an alternate safe haven.

God was compassionate and the angels spared Lot's desired city of refuge in the destruction of the land surrounding Sodom and Gomorrah. Unfortunately, God was providing the way of escape, but Lot seemed to go kicking and screaming the whole way. Whatever attachments he had made with the city of Sodom, they were strong.

Your husband may behave in like manner. God may have to figuratively grab him and tear him away from the sin that binds him. But while He's doing that, you keep running for the mountains! God will honor your steps, and you'll impact your husband in the right direction. Your faith will become augmented with each forward movement, building your confidence and desire to remain on God's resurfaced path as you experience the joy and fulfillment that comes into your life. And through God's compassion for you and mercy on your husband, you'll see your husband behind you. And in that commodity of time, hopefully, he will begin leading.

September 13  The Sin in Us

I John 1:8

If we say that we have no sin, we are deceiving ourselves, and the truth is not in us.

Early in our relationship, I could always sense when my husband had other things occupying his time besides me. He seemed very distracted, with his letters being less affectionate and shorter. It created insecurity and indirect hurt, because as a lady, I want to be my man's world. I would think to myself: "What else does he have to do that he can't find time to write!" My imagination could create endless situations for what or who was occupying his time. The hypothetical could make me crazy, but in my husband's case, he unfortunately usually did worse than the imagined, so we had a tremendous issue of trust early on.

In those days, I would try to impact his heart through similar correspondence. I would be aloof and intentionally not share. I would have loved to have heard some upset in his letters in response to the same distance, some suspicion for how I was spending my time, but typically I got little to no reaction, just his frustratingly unaffected words.

Relationships can be played with all familiarity despite prison being involved. That's because we are the same whether our man is incarcerated or at home. The issues we bring to the relationship remain and will remain unless we work at doing things differently. There's responsibility on both sides for problems that exist. Prison is a problem, but not the only problem, and as wives on the outside, we need to recognize that all of the relationship problems do not rest on our men alone simply because they are the ones imprisoned. This cannot be our winning claim for each fight.

John is reminding us that everyone sins. Personal sin was taught by Jesus, and regardless of salvation, the sin nature remains in a person. Salvation and freedom from sin are separate. Salvation removes the eternal penalty of sin, but the believer still has the capacity to sin. There were people in John's day that believed the mind and the body were separate in terms of sin's consequence. You could do immoral things with your body, and not sin in doing so. This of course was a false teaching that John was refuting.

John further explains that a Christian will commit sin, but to intentionally practice a known sin in one's life brings into question one's relationship to God. A Christian may stumble over the same sin, but there's conviction and repentance. Someone who feels no conviction doesn't repent, thus remains in their sin. To which John asserts is incompatible with knowing God.

In our marriages, we can often be blind to our own sin or we minimize our negative qualities, usually making excuses for our actions. It's easy to condemn our husbands' faults while justifying our own. Such pride is further proof of our sin nature.

If your tendency is to place blame mostly on your husband for problems, John would encourage you to get to know God better. As you do, your awareness of sin increases. With awareness comes the desire to work on your own issues, not self-righteously point out your husband's.

September 14 — Finishing Faithfully

II Timothy 4:7

I have fought the good fight, I have finished the course, I have kept the faith.

The hardest part of any project is usually finishing it. Excitement can fuel progress initially, but with time — and usually unexpected problems — enthusiasm starts to wane. It turns into real work. I have had this happen many times during home improvement projects, yardwork, and organizational ideas at work. Drudgery fuels more so my desire to quit, and the words "What was I thinking?" soon follow.

In some cases, however, we are at the mercy of the assignment — like prison. We didn't choose to start it, and we definitely do not get to decide when it ends. It can be drudgery out of the gate, so sustaining enthusiasm to finish well is very hard to generate.

Paul invested a lot into Timothy and continued to do so up until his death. The verse today was written by Paul in anticipation of his execution. Paul was in prison when he wrote this letter to Timothy. He was in a sense reflecting on his life of service and was confident that he did all he could to serve and preach the Gospel faithfully.

Paul started strong and finished strong. After the first beating, shipwreck, or imprisonment, most of us would have been questioning if it were time to quit. His ability to sustain the good fight and finish the course was directly related to his reliance on the Lord. He did everything through the strength God provided, not his own.

This is the key to finishing the prison course. God's strength is needed. Opposition and adversaries are on the sidelines, not cheering fans, because the track is the narrow road to God. The jeers are to discourage and trip you along the course and especially as you approach the finish line. Temptations are thrown at you all along the course.

You may be losing heart for the race. You may not care any longer if you make it to the finish line along with your husband. You just want relief. In these cases, be brave enough to ask God to refresh your spirit for the work of prison. I say brave, because in your heart, you may be afraid that God may just answer that prayer and you would rather be done with it all.

The beauty of God's help, however, is once supernaturally inspired to keep the faith, you'll be so grateful that you didn't quit. He can bring excitement to the path as you grow close to Him in your dependency. You can watch amazing things happen in your husband and marriage through your reliance on God. And as Paul encouraged Timothy, having fought the good fight and finished the course, you can be that encouragement to others new on the path or those growing weary you pass along the way.

September 15 — Tithing in Trust

Malachi 3:8

"Will a man rob God? Yet you are robbing me! But you say, 'How have we robbed Thee?' In tithes and offerings."

I have not been a perfect tither. I have been legalistic about the amount to the point of rationalizing for putting nothing in the plate if it wasn't the full 10 percent. I have put my tithe toward non-profits other than the church. I have used my tithe to help out of friend. I have used my tithe for my own personal "ministry." Consistent tithing has been a hard discipline for me. The variations of what I find to do with my tithe (or not do) is directly related to my income. And this really just becomes a trust issue. Do I trust God to provide for me?

I have to admit that I get uneasy when money is running low or my income becomes interrupted. I begin looking for all ways to cut expenses. Sadly, my tithe becomes part of my financial consideration. I begin rationalizing what would God have me do in such situations as if He has plan B or C or D. I would look for any plan that would allow me to hang onto some of the money or accommodate better the financial changes.

I have "robbed" God according to Malachi. But I have also robbed myself of a tremendous blessing. Altering my tithe amount or frequency as my financial situation changes prevents God from showing Himself faithful to me. I start to think practically from a worldly perspective instead of faithfully from a godly one.

Beyond the tithe, Malachi speaks to the Israelites about not providing their offerings as well. This was above and beyond the tithe. God purposes us to be generous. Giving the tithe is the minimum. We are also expected to give offerings above it. Like my tithe, I do this inconsistently. It's again dependent on my finances at the time.

God has shown me my sin in this area times before, and I repent. I do well for a while, then I find myself again in the same faith decision. Will I trust God with my finances? I hope to permanently make a faith decision and tithe in trust—regardless of circumstances. From there, hopefully, I'll be an above-and-beyond giver—consistently.

Prison impacts finances. Less money or more things to pay for. We all know how costly visits can be! I would challenge you to consider giving back to God, regardless of circumstances. Not from legalism, but from a heart that wants to seek and do God's will.

September 16 *Coveting Normal*

Exodus 20:17

"You shall not covet your neighbor's house; you shall not covet your neighbor's wife or his male servant or his female servant or his ox or his donkey or anything that belongs to your neighbor."

I was in a season where I was not hearing from God as I always had. I knew and felt His presence, but our interactions had changed. He wasn't "talking" to me as I was used to. So I began to consider what sin was in my life that would be interfering. There were two specific areas that I knew were problems. But I had been regularly confessing and dealing with those. But during a study of the Ten Commandments, it struck me like a brick that I was guilty of covetousness. Seeds of envy were growing in my heart in my desire for a normal life.

I was under house arrest at the time, unable to find a job to cover my expenses, unable to see my husband, living in a glorified shack as I came to refer to the structure which was called my residence, and wondering how on earth God was going to redeem the mess I had made of my life.

It was a very discouraging period. I would see people in different situations during the day and think to myself, "Look at all those normal people, doing normal things." This was opposed to my being stalked by law enforcement, restricted to where I could go and when. I would see someone on a job and think, "Look at her with her normal job," as opposed to my being branded and rejected from employers because of one mistake on my record. I would drive by homes and say, "Look at all the normal homes where normal people live."

I felt far removed from a normal life, or at least what I was used to. Although I recognized how my poor choice resulted in my circumstance, I couldn't let go of the thought that the degree of my outcome was unfair. I should be able to get a normal job, do normal things, and live in a normal house. There was bitterness in my attitude and almost resentment seeping into my thoughts about people who had what I was lacking.

I had to repent of my heart's sin and invest in thanking God for what I had and the potential consequences from which He spared me. There was also a surprising deeper lesson in contentment I learned in my reflections.

I have always hallmarked my ability to be content, but I considered how this was always still within my ability to choose excess if I wanted. Nothing extravagant, but if I wanted to order a pizza, I could. If I wanted to buy gourmet coffee, I could. My new circumstances didn't allow for such luxuries. Yet when I considered this, I knew that I still had much in the big picture. And I again repented.

Your circumstance might have you saying a similar thing, if not about material things, your marriage: "Look at all those normal women with normal marriages." You long for a typical marriage with your husband. You long to experience even his annoying habits in real time. You long to snuggle with him while watching TV. You long for his companionship in the everyday matters.

The longing isn't sinful. It's when the deeper seed of envy and bitterness sprout that you need to stop and get your heart right before God. Consider the volume of your thoughts. If it's weighted toward the negative, try to outweigh this with praise and gratitude to God for what you have. You're a blessed lady, loved by the Lord.

September 17 *Positively Minded*

Philippians 4:8

Finally, brethren, whatever is true, whatever is honorable, whatever is right, whatever is pure, whatever is lovely, whatever is of good repute, if there is any excellence and if anything worthy of praise, let your mind dwell on these things.

I have a terrible habit of meditating on an issue until I get myself emotionally charged through the replays in my mind. My quiet nature plays out in my negative ponderings, similar to the peaceful and reflective ones. The negative, however, transforms into brooding or worrying if I'm not careful.

This weakness in me demands alertness, because it will seep into my thinking quickly, undetected. I'll find myself stewing over a situation or conversation, responding in that talk I have with myself—and the dog if she's around—with my blood pressure rising with my words. It just takes one little annoyance at that point to release a buildup of past injustices or hurts, successfully ending the fragile discipline I had over my emotions. Such a state of mind does nothing to help my marriage and help me make it through this prison journey with joy.

In my battle, if the thought about another person, my husband, a situation, or myself doesn't fall under one of the descriptors in the verse above, I have to say, "No! That's not true! I'm not going there!" If my thoughts aren't true, right, noble, pure, lovely, admirable, excellent, or praiseworthy, I say, "No!" I must say whatever interrupts the spiral or contemplation. I know if I do not, the progression of negativity rolls downhill quick. It's almost as if Satan pulls it down to his level to stoke any wounds I have. In my best strength, I get mad at Satan for trying to rob me of my mood, my day, and ultimately my marriage. It remains a daily battle.

Aligning your thoughts with this verse will help you build successful days of prison. It directs your focus to God, and this reminds you of that bigger perspective. It will help you think more positively about your husband, which will strengthen your marriage. It will stop a bad day from feeling worse, which goes a long way when you're trying to stay content within the wait of prison.

If you have concerns, hurts, or fears, talk to God, but do not waste mental energy wallowing in the negativity. It produces nothing but more of the same. And thinking as Paul teaches isn't about ignoring your reality. It's rather trusting that God has you covered, and His covering will always take care of you even when the negative clouds linger.

September 18 — Hope in the Morning

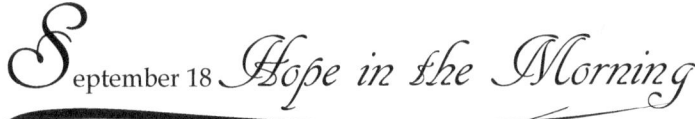

Lamentations 3:22-23

The Lord's lovingkindnesses indeed never cease, for His compassions never fail. They are new every morning; great is Thy faithfulness.

Jeremiah lived when Jerusalem was destroyed by the Babylonians. He prophesied it. It was his heartbreaking warning to his people. But they ignored it. What a dread to overcome him when the future he warned about approached the gates. The book of Lamentations is extreme grief and mourning put to words. Jeremiah was there when rulers were displaced and captivity became a reality for the Jews. He could write with a passionate sense of loss, because it had been his life.

Jeremiah suffered much with his calling. He persevered through imprisonment and abuse when crying out his warning, and he grieved with others when exiled and the city burned and plundered. But his devotion to and walk with God made his heart hopeful. He knew God could be trusted. Thus Lamentations is sorrowful, yet not without hope as the verse for today captures.

Mornings hold the potential for a better day. When going through sorrow, we often pray and hope for sleep to give our hearts respite. When we rise, any glimmer of God's faithfulness is enough to sustain us. And He's faithful to provide it. Jeremiah knew this. He writes of great sorrow, but as an eyewitness to God's goodness too.

You may have great sorrow today. You may just be feeling numb — and possibly considering it a blessing in some sense. You may just be burdened and stressed from various situations. Prison is likely contributing to one or all of these.

The same God of whom Jeremiah speaks is your God as well. Refresh your heart in the mornings knowing God is kind. He will not allow the hurt today without a better day planned. Keep getting up with the assurance that God never sleeps or tires, and He's never running low on love or compassion. He has been watching over you all night, waiting for you to wake. Let the new day be His greeting, "Good morning, My daughter." Let a fresh perspective come with the morning. Let hopefulness arrive. Let things that seemed impossible somehow now seem doable.

September 19 *Humor Helps*

Proverbs 17:22

A joyful heart is good medicine, but a broken spirit dries up the bones.

    God built laughter into our personalities. I know that He has a sense of humor. I have experienced it in my daily walk with Him. He surprises me. He makes me laugh.

    Scripture confirms the benefit of humor. It's good for the body. There's something therapeutic about laughter. It's a great stress reliever and a lot more fun than aerobics. I'm not a TV person, but sometimes I just need a lift through laughter, so I'll stream a comedy for a 30-minute reprieve. And usually it helps.

    Dry bones in Scripture represents death, spiritual or physical. Job describes a physically healthy person as the marrow in his bones being moist (Job 21:24). Ezekiel saw the vision of the valley of dry bones which represented Israel's spiritual apostasy. Prison can break your spirit and dry up your bones.

    There was a time when laughter was absent from my days. I hadn't realized how long I had been walking on dry bones. My spirit was depleted, but I had grown accustomed to it. I was actually taken aback one day when I heard myself laugh. It was one of those deep, genuine laughs, not a surface smile and chuckle. I stood there, frozen, in almost disbelief. I couldn't recall the last time I had laughed like that. It was a sad realization of how dry I really had been.

    Thankfully my husband has a great sense of humor. He makes me laugh. His wit never ceases to leave me shaking my head in amazement. It's quick and clever, and truly funny. There are times when we do not always agree on what's funny, but it's good to laugh together.

    A laughter break is good for you. Your husband, like mine, may be already providing you some. There are some great Christian comedians. You may have a favorite movie that lifts your spirits. Do not get to the point as I did and hear the strange sound of your own voice laughing. Let it be a familiar sound to your ears. Your body and spirit will benefit.

September 20 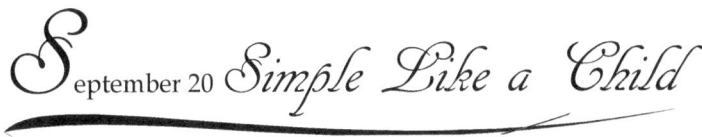 Simple Like a Child

Psalm 116:6

The Lord preserves the simple; I was brought low, and He saved me.

I wonder if others, like me, long for the simplicity viewed when watching programs like *Little House on the Prairie*. It's a combination of nostalgia of my youth and the burdens of adulthood. I was a simple youth watching simplicity, but not even realizing it. Choices were fewer for those on the screen. Contentment was a closer necessity, and life was slower. The hard work of the Ingalls isn't fully grasped by anyone of this generation, but it seems working hard to better one's life from the past, as we pursue today, destroys us in the process.

My husband often comments to the same. He has watched prison transform into a more violent, sin-saturated warehouse. He gets tired dealing with the daily filth. The energy to maintain constant bravado to support not being a victim takes its own toll. The stress and vigilance damages him in their goal to protect. He just wants simple.

The simple we are both describing is really, at the heart, a desire for care-free assurance that removes that smothering negative culture we lived within. And that assurance comes only through faith in God to save us eternally and then protect us in the everyday lives we wake to.

Scripture associates simple with childlike. There's an innocent dependence when you're a child. That's how God desires us to rely on Him. Jesus applauds childlike faith. Salvation requires childlike faith. Our faith going forward from there should remain as so. Life isn't childlike, issues are complex and the world is harsh in its negative maturity, but faith in God to preserve us through this life is simple: just believe.

Humble dependence is difficult for prisoners. The bravado my husband mentions interferes with allowing God to protect. It's hard to live in peaceful assurance regardless of what's going on around you. I appreciate greatly the level of trust a prisoner must have compared to what I have muster in my days. To live as God requires in prison takes tremendous faith in God's promises. So much so, it may even seem naïve to do so. It's the epitome of childlike faith.

There are true threats within the walls. I understand why prisoners make weapons from the resources they have. It's wrong, but I understand. Those of us on the outside lock our doors, install security systems, and carry concealed weapons. Our husbands live among the people we guard against and they are expected to be defenseless.

In being so, however, they have the marvelous opportunity to get to know God in a way most will never receive. God is close to the simplehearted. There's an amazing walk with God for those of such faith. They will experience intimacy that will encourage them to continue in the faith.

Your husband may need simple faith for salvation. He may be saved and need faith to live righteously where he wakes, in childlike dependence. I cannot imagine being in that environment and needing either. In a way, as wives, we must release their protection to God in childlike assurance that He's all they need to be kept safe.

September 21 — *Prey Away*

Genesis 15:11

And the birds of prey came down upon the carcasses, and Abram drove them away.

This must have been no easy task. Vultures that I have come upon do not frighten easily. They are ravenous and relentless in dealing with their deceased find. Approach them on a highway and you're a nuisance they reluctantly scamper away from to immediately return to the carcass. Some stay stationed on the pavement unmoved by a passing car. So I would think Abraham's task would be met with equal perseverance.

We do not know exactly how long Abraham waited on God. He brought the offerings God requested and laid them in halves, and then waited. God had already communicated to Abraham about his inheritance of land and the great offspring who were to come through him. But God waited until it was dark before He responded to the offering. It was during the wait that the birds of prey came.

And that's how it can seem when we are waiting on God for the next step. Attacks come to steal away and interrupt the purposes of God. The enemy can be relentless, and like the vultures, there's usually not just one. They lurk and wait, hover near until the optimal time to descend upon their target. Trying to stay the course God has ordained can seem as a battle.

But like Abraham, do not leave your post, your calling, your path, or whatever version of offering God has entrusted you with. Abraham likely worked tirelessly to keep the birds away, but we do not read of his resting until God caused him to fall into a deep sleep.

Figuratively, treat God's plan that He has revealed to you the same way. Guard it continuously. The enemy will wait until you're weak or distracted and try to snatch away the good God is doing. Be alert to it.

Prison attracts vultures of all varieties. They would love to devour your faith and interrupt your walk with God. They would love to see you give up your husband to them, to stop praying for him, to give up on your marriage, and ultimately, allow them to drag it all away.

Abraham was given the good and the bad news about Israel. But their destiny would be reached, despite the bad, and it would start with him. So keep up your fight as well. What you're protecting is linked to your destiny — your husband's included.

September 22 *Sad, but Still Saved*

Judges 16:30

And Samson said, "Let me die with the Philistines!" And he bent with all his might so that the house fell on the lords and all the people who were in it. So the dead whom he killed at his death were more than those whom he killed in his life.

There are some who consider Samson's death a suicide. There are some who believe suicide sends a person to hell. Scripture doesn't support this. There are sadly many prisoners who choose to take their own life, possibly out of despair, and most likely because hope has left their life, but this action doesn't condemn them to hell. Rejecting Jesus is the only choice that results in hell — none other.

Samson had been captured by the Philistines after Delilah gave him up for money. His eyes were gouged out, and he was imprisoned. When they brought him to the arena to mock him, he asked God to allow him to avenge them for what they did to his eyes. Standing between the pillars, he pushed them, collapsing the structure, killing himself and over three thousand Philistines.

True, he knew his actions would cause his own death, but was it motivated by anger, depression, or repentance? Was he also wanting to be used by God to avenge them as an enemy of the Lord's? Did his anger come from the depression of all he had lost: his eyesight, his position as judge, his freedom? We do not know these details, but we do read in Hebrews where Samson was hallmarked for his faith (Hebrews 11:32). This doesn't seem to be a person who will reside in hell.

And if you consider Samson, he was God's anointed judge. God's favor was on him before he was even born. Samson had supernatural strength given to him by God. And in the end, God answered Samson's prayer and provided that same strength again to accomplish the task which would take his life. I do not think God condones suicide, because life is precious to Him. Samson's death likely had a different motivation.

So I tend to lean away from the perspective that Samson committed suicide, and I definitely believe he will be in heaven. He offered to die to avenge an enemy of God's children—himself included. That makes it more like a soldier going into a battle, despite knowing the grim odds.

If you're touched by suicide, remember that the saved go to heaven, regardless of how they die. If a person has a relationship with Jesus, this secures their eternity in heaven. There's nothing they can do to lose their salvation, since they didn't do anything to earn it in the first place. It's through God's grace only.

There's thousands of prisoners who need prayer that they will rediscover hope for their lives through Christ. And with that, they will avoid being added to the sad statistic of prison suicides.

September 23 *Loving a Black Sheep*

Mark 10:27

Looking upon them, Jesus said, "With men it is impossible, but not with God; for all things are possible with God."

Sheep are designed to be prey. They have no claws or fangs to attack, capture, or effectively tear through flesh. Blood neither pours when they feed, nor stains their mouths in the satisfaction of their appetites. They are meant for the relaxing consumption of the pasture, not the carnivorous demands of the predator.

Sheep do not kill. They are the social and passive of the pasture. Their eyes, displaying large, scenery-absorbing pupils, are set more to the sides of their heads for the field of vision innate for defense, not the stalking of a weaker foe through a piercing vision channeled forward.

Such is also their flock mentality. Always connected through vision, the flock remains linked and alert to signal danger to the herd if one of the stalking comes into view. They are in many ways defenseless and easily marked for slaughter by a predator that runs faster and maintains its own innate weapons to capture and kill them.

Maintaining wool of varying colors, the sheep seems to have been created to meet the needs of others, not themselves. Food, milk, or clothing--giving of itself for the foundational needs of others, in its design, sheep live a sacrificial life.

But what of the "black sheep"? He's in opposition to the good, the innocent, and the passive. The black sheep desires more to be a predator, to use others for benefit, and to attack in the face of danger, not run. Not interested in the preservation of the flock in the mutual defense of others, the black sheep isn't a protector of others, but of self. In its deviant nature, is it possible for the black sheep to live among the white of the flock? Can the innocent lamb, frolicking gently in the fold, live safely with the black sheep who stalks within the same field?

You may feel you have a dichotomous marriage: the innocent lamb and the black sheep. But God is interested in all sheep. He loves your black sheep more than you do. And the great thing about being a part of God's pasture…all sheep start out black. Your black sheep isn't without hope. With God all things are possible.

September 24 *Strength to Forgive*

I Peter 4:8

Above all, keep fervent in your love for one another, because love covers a multitude of sins.

Day and night, praying without ceasing, on my knees, during the routine of my day and in that evening weariness, I prayed. I prayed with tears, crying out to God to rescue my husband from harm. He believed his life to be in danger. That belief spawned a level of prayer in me only originating often from such a time of crisis.

And God seemed to answer. The crisis safely passed. But on my first opportunity to see my husband, a visit that was much anticipated quickly proceeded into hurtful territory. The urgent situation I pled before God had been a lie.

The truth was revealed as I sat across the table from husband. I was numb with a righteous anger that wanted to start flipping tables in the visitation park as Jesus did in the outer court of the temple. He sat there feeling justified in what he had done. I sat there in that exploding hurt that has nowhere to settle, because the moment, the surroundings, and the emotions imploded on me at the same time.

I wanted to run. Away from my husband, away from the cold and public room that never allowed me the freedom to share even the good times with him in privacy, and certainly never accommodated the moments of serious hurt as I faced then. I despised him in that moment. He lied to me, but worse yet, he knowingly allowed my distress and urgent prayers with the believed truth that his life was in danger. Sitting before him, listening to his justifying words, I felt my blood turn hot.

God's Holy Spirit had to restrain me through those incredibly hard moments when fleeing was my temptation. Somehow, God cemented my butt to that plastic chair! He communicated to my spirit that leaving wasn't the answer. Restraining my flesh and my words were needed. God knew both our personalities, and He knew leaving wouldn't help my marriage. My anger was okay; it was righteous in the face of my husband's lie. My reverence for God and prayer were all disrespected by his actions. But loving my husband, meant communicating in that moment, not fleeing.

And he listened. God seemed to have cemented my husband's mouth shut! He listened to what that lie burdened me with. He saw his usual fragile wife tearless and angry. His callousness softened, and he apologized. The visit moved forward, and God's Spirit enabled forgiveness to have victory.

What could have been an abbreviated time ending with two emotionally charged persons at odds, exiting without resolution, our visit was restored. We enjoyed each other, shared, laughed, and parted with our usual all-consuming kiss and warm hug. Love showed up in the form of God. I couldn't have done it any other way.

I share this story to encourage you in whatever battles you're facing with your husband. It's immensely hard to resolve conflict with prison being a constant antagonist. Sometimes there's no opportunity to resolve issues to the extent they deserve because of the restrictions on your time and simply the public nature of all your contact. I had to choose on that visit to accept my husband's apology and allow the visit to move forward in a positive direction. Sometimes, you have to drop the rope and let things go. And the

Holy Spirit is the best person to tell you when and how that's best accomplished. And He can give you the strength in those moments to do it.

September 25 *The Discipline to Pray*

Psalm 6:9

The Lord has heard my supplication, the Lord receives my prayer.

One morning at 2:00, the Lord called me to pray for a co-worker whom I later discovered was going into labor and required an emergency C-section. Another morning, I was prompted to pray for my neighbors. And within the hour, the ambulance arrived at their home. I have been prompted to stop at a convenience store out of my routine to witness an angry-hearted person speak and behave in ways that added to the heaviness I felt when the cheap bell signaled my entrance. I prayed for the child I saw who was listening to the same words that made me shudder.

God calls us to pray, but I never heard Him ask me to pray as in the examples above until I got serious about prayer at other times. The routine, daily time I spent talking with God opened up the opportunity to be used in more intimate ways. And I have been eternally grateful when I consider the times my husband has been on the receiving end of those promptings.

Time alone with God and the prayers that go up from our knees hold the power for where our ultimate victory in life—and prison—begins. It's how God can use us in miraculous ways in people's lives—including our husbands'. Life-changing prayer is intentional prayer. And this remains the challenge.

I easily keep in conversation with God throughout the day, but to take time away, in silence, and on my knees to commune with God is a discipline that can easily get bypassed. I often feel rushed by everything awaiting me for the day. I may rationalize, "I'll pray on the way to work in the car," and skip my time on my knees, exchanging it to my hands behind the wheel. It isn't that this type of prayer doesn't have its place. It certainly does! It's for me, however, more reflective of my ongoing conversation I have with God anyway. So regardless of its value, there's a different level of intimacy I achieve with God when everything else in the world is shut out, and God is allowed my focus.

Quiet prayer time with God also slows me down. Sometimes I do not realize the pace I have been keeping until I'm on my knees and fighting sleep! Even in the eagerness to do for God and the pace and sacrifice it demands at times, God never expects me to do so much that I sacrifice time with Him. I can really share my heart with God when alone. I can cry into my mattress if I need to. I can be still before the Lord, and He can speak to my heart in ways I would never hear in the busyness of the day.

Wherever you're in your walk with God, begin to pray intentionally. Set aside time daily. And as you experience your closeness to God growing, you'll begin to see the power of prayer in your life. And do not ignore the promptings of the Holy Spirit. You never know what's happening in the moment for why it's been communicated to you. Even if you're not sure of what you're sensing, there's only good that results from talking with God.

September 26 *Never Alone*

II Timothy 4:16

At my first defense no one supported me, but all deserted me; may it not be counted against them.

Paul was imprisoned and expecting his execution. It seems at his first court appearance no one was there to support him. He gives an account to Timothy of those who deserted him. But he also mentions his hope that it may not be counted against them.

He shared with Timothy that he faithfully accomplished the mission God gave him: sharing the Gospel with the Gentiles. He hoped to see Timothy before winter. There's nothing further in Scripture as to whether he was able to or not.

Paul desired earthly support, but he learned about the faithfulness of God when earthly relationships were absent or unreliable. He doesn't share the details of the circumstances for the lack of support at that first hearing. Possibly even well-intentioned persons disappointed him. But God didn't leave his side.

At times we feel abandoned in our lives. People will disappoint us. Family, friends, co-workers, neighbors, and yes, fellow church members. People may be well-intentioned, but life is busy. They cannot be there for us all the time even when they desire to be. Some may purposefully disappear and that hurts. But this is when we actually get to experience the faithfulness of God. Until such a time, we have the truth of Scripture in our heads, but it's made real in our hearts in our time of need.

You might have felt as Paul did: abandoned when you needed people the most. You might still be experiencing this. It's a horrible feeling when you're left to face a challenge alone. But what Paul says in the next verse is true for you: "But the Lord stood with me."

September 27 — Negative Nellies

Deuteronomy 20:8

"Then the officers shall speak further to the people, and they shall say, 'Who is the man that is afraid and fainthearted? Let him depart and return to his house, so that he might not make his brothers' hearts melt like his heart.'"

In the verse for today, Moses is reminding the leaders of how to select men for battle. Positive-minded men who believe in God's ability to bring them success were to be chosen, not the fainthearted and timid. Negative faith can be a fatalistic attitude. Persons with such an attitude rarely keep it to themselves. Moses knew negative faith defeats the heart, and victory doesn't come from men with hearts influenced toward loss before the battle even begins.

Negative attitudes are draining. They can be contagious. Chronic complainers are hard to be around, especially if you aren't cut from the same cloth. It's amazing the impact one Negative Nellie can make on a team, in a business, or in relationships. Scripture speaks to the principle of guarding against their impact by limiting their contact and participation.

It's very hard to stay positive when your life involves prison. The struggles of your marriage may invoke chronic sympathizers. Although these attitudes are meant to express positive regard for your circumstance, they simultaneously deflate your own motivation. You say a hope-filled comment, and they respond with a statement of pity "for all you're going through."

Expressions of concern are appreciated, but there must be a balance with positive, uplifting encouragement. Sometimes I wish instead of a comment that smothers my outlook (said in concern), I would receive a statement about my strength or endurance for my encouragement, not a sigh reminding me of all the barriers before me.

You can manage the impact of Negative Nellies. You may need to limit contact to manageable levels for your own well-being. If you always tend to feel worse after talking to a person, that's a good sign that some limits need to happen.

Managing the content of the conversations can help. Simply do not volunteer or encourage a conversation that's likely to give the person the opportunity to "share in your troubles." An aloof "I'm fine" may be the best response, then move on to something not related to your personal situation like the sale of grapes you got at the store or how pleased you are with something. Keep it positive.

There are times when you might actually need to confront someone on how their negative focus makes your walk on this journey even harder. I have had to do this. Sometimes the person isn't aware of the pattern of their interactions with you, so a conversation about this can help.

Your battle is to overcome prison with your marriage intact. Believing in God's ability to do this is your focus. People who spend more time reminding you of the power of the enemy and not the power of God discourage your heart. You do not want Negative Nellies battling with you. Their efforts are really just friendly fire that damages in its own way.

September 28 One Day at a Time

Matthew 6:34

"Therefore do not be anxious for tomorrow; for tomorrow will care for itself. Each day has enough trouble of its own."

Life comes in days, but our minds use the capacity of abstract thinking to consider most time beyond the current day and the hypothetical outcomes we will experience. Scripture encourages us to live within each day. Not that we do not plan and consider the future, but these are to be done in positive ways, not with reluctant anxiety.

Jesus spoke of not worrying about tomorrow. We keep the Lord first in our lives, then He takes care of our needs. Jesus relates this to all aspects of our lives. He wants us to ultimately rely on Him, not our bank accounts, personal connections, talents, or strengths. And in doing so, He will provide.

I saw His provision in action when I relocated for a job. I didn't have enough time (or money) to secure a place to live before I left. Crazy to consider loading a moving van and heading out three states away with no place to go. But I already experienced God lining the job up for me in a miraculous way, so all I knew was to go and trust He was going to work it out.

I arrived on a Thursday. I found the most perfect house to rent on Friday. I moved in Saturday, and started my new job on Monday. Whew! It was an amazing display of God's orchestration.

Not that I didn't get concerned at points. I viewed one tiny apartment, smaller than a hotel room, consisting of rotting cabinets and disgusting furniture left behind by a previous tenant. According to the landlord, it was move-in ready. When pulling out of the parking lot, I nervously expressed to God, "Okay, Lord, this isn't looking good."

But God had indeed planned the place for me and He led me to it. It was spacious, sitting on a lake, and less money than the cramped squalors closer to the city. It even had a fenced backyard for my dog. That was icing on the cake that God baked for me.

Seek to live a righteous life. Study and apply God's word to your life. You'll not be perfect, but God's grace and provisions will be there for you. When you get anxious about the days beyond the one you're in, be reminded of God's promise to take care of each day as it arrives.

September 29 *Mad at God*

II Samuel 6:8

And David became angry because of the Lord's outburst against Uzzah, and that place is called Perez-uzzah to this day.

Ever been angry at God? Ever had an outburst of anger in your soul against Him, then tremendous fear because of your irreverence, believing you're surely going to be struck by sudden death? Have your words been hateful to Him?

I have one vivid moment in my life when I accused God of not keeping His promise to me. My heart cursed Him. I have never been so bold to make such an outcry to Him again. I was angry and disappointed at that time. I felt that He had misled me, and I believed that I was suffering undue consequences for it.

When the words of my heart were coming forth, I knew I was overstepping. Way overstepping! I had an immediate sense of regret and fear. The Lord I loved and who was my life, I treated harshly. The awesome

God who is ruler over everything, I disrespected. I waited for discipline. But it didn't arrive. Only my tears of repentance.

When I read of David's moment of anger toward God, I sympathize with him. They were bringing the ark back to Jerusalem, and when it seemed at risk of toppling over, Uzzah extended his hand to steady it. God killed Uzzah for his actions.

It had been a joyous day. They had been dancing and playing music to the Lord in celebration of the ark's return. The journey turned tragic for what I'm sure David saw as a man's good intentions: Uzzah didn't want the ark to fall off the cart on which it was being carried. I'm sure David was thinking, "Cut us some slack here! We're trying to do a good thing!"

But the ark was a holy vessel. There were many instructions for its transport and access. The Israelites knew it was not to be transported on a cart. The Philistines had initially captured the ark and transported it on a cart, but they were a pagan people, not accountable to God for such things. When David saw Uzzah killed, dread fell upon him and reverence for God and the ark.

So our anger gets rightly corrected from our reverence for God. Ideally, reverence should trump our anger before our emotions lash out. But I'm grateful the Bible includes accounts of great men of God who struggled at times in their lives as we do. I'm grateful God is slow to anger and patient—when we aren't.

Your angry moments with God are hopefully only moments. It's possibly from prison or another circumstance that seems unjust. A persistent anger, however, will be detrimental to your relationship with Him. He will not turn His back on you, but yours turned against Him removes you from your source of life. Hopefully, you feel Him wooing you to return to Him fully.

September 30 *A Prodigal's Mom*

I Samuel 8:3

His sons, however, did not walk in his ways, but turned aside after dishonest gain and took bribes and perverted justice.

Samuel was a great prophet and you would think his children would be godly. You would think his influence in the home would be astounding since he was God's anointed to the people. Yet we read in the verse for today that his sons didn't walk in his footsteps. They were dishonest and greedy. The people even taunted Samuel that the behavior of his sons was one of the reasons Israel needed a human king like all the other nations: the prophet's sons were not qualified spiritually.

It makes you wonder what led to Samuel's sons being disobedient to not only him, but also more importantly, to God. Was he gone a lot? Was he inconsistent in his discipline? Did his wife play some background role in their choices? Regardless, the sons chose to sin individually despite knowing differently.

This should bring encouragement to your mother-n-law if she did everything "right," yet your husband still was rebellious in the face of knowing right from wrong. She may be carrying a lot of guilt regarding his current incarceration.

Parents of prodigals experience a complex set of emotions. It's very difficult for them to separate the burden of responsibility from themselves — especially mothers. Hindsight becomes a constant weight of regret even if parenting was done "perfectly."

You can be an encourager to your mother-n-law if she's laden with guilt regarding your husband's imprisonment. Remind her that at some point he became responsible for his own actions, despite the negative influences growing up. Hopefully, the court gave mitigating value to those experiences beyond his control. Tell her the story of Samuel to lift her off the floor from that weight of guilt, sharing how even a great man of God had wayward sons. Bring this fresh perspective that will lighten her steps through forgiveness she may need to extend to herself.

October 1 — Godly Appeal

I Timothy 2:9-10

Likewise, I want women to adorn themselves with proper clothing, modestly and discreetly, not with braided hair and gold or pearls or costly garments; but rather by means of good works, as befits women making a claim to godliness.

The most common reason a woman is turned away at the gate on visitation day is her wardrobe. Too revealing, too tight, too short, no undergarments in some cases. And I would boldly add: ungodly. By far, when I have seen a woman turned away, I would honestly have to agree with the officer's decision. You might throw this book away at this point, because this can be a very controversial issue. It can be a convicting issue. I know, because I have been through the Lord's convicting displeasure of my wardrobe.

If we honestly consider Scripture and God's word on sexuality, dressing provocatively is a sin. It does nothing to keep a man's thoughts pure and undefiled. A woman doesn't want her husband looking lustfully upon another woman, and most times spiteful thoughts erupt for that woman causing her man's eyes to wander. Yet the same woman can dress in the same manner being that spiteful target of another wife. Visitation day can highlight this.

Immodest dress is so commonplace that the consequence is silence due to immune consent. I have seen women on the stage in a church service wearing what you would see in a dance club—cleavage and all. It has become acceptable. So you have men in the congregation on Sunday mornings battling lustful thoughts, and his wife sitting there in many ways, disrespected by another Christian woman.

A good question to ask when getting dressed: "Am I dressing attractively or dressing to attract?" And this really becomes a heart question: "Do I want to please God?"

Scripture tells us to avoid even a hint of sexual immorality. This includes our wardrobe. Paul cautions us "to make no provision for the flesh in regard to its lusts" (Romans 13:14). God knows that sexual sin destroys relationships, and He puts safeguards in place to protect marriage not to be legalistic and unfashionable.

Men in prison are sexually deprived in many ways. It's a struggle for them to keep their thoughts and behavior pure. So sitting in the visitation room with competing images to his wife serve only as a stumbling block. As women, we must be aware of how our dress affects men. It's the man's responsibility to deal with how the temptation affects him, but according to Jesus, it's also our responsibility not to contribute to his stumble. It's a mutual desire to put God's interests before our own.

You'll find that the closer you walk with God, the closer His standards fill your closet. And that's a good thing.

✝

October 2 — God-Given Authority

Romans 13:1

Let every person be in subjection to the government authorities. For there is no authority except from God, and those which exist are established by God.

This is probably my husband's least favorite verse in the Bible. It challenges him daily. It doesn't say only the good authority. The corruption and bad officers within a prison promote defiance. Most men are in prison because they couldn't abide by the law. And that was when they were living free in society. To move into a facility with even more restrictions, supervised by often antagonistic personalities, with the same expectation of compliance as when he was free is almost comical if it weren't the truth.

Congregate rehabilitation doesn't happen. Prison rules and authority cannot change a heart. They might deal out consequences, but lasting change only happens when the subjection is in the heart. Only God can change a heart to submit to the rules in place.

And this type of change doesn't happen all at once generally. It mirrors a person's spiritual growth. Scripture calls this process sanctification. It's becoming more like Christ. As your husband is able to conform to the likeness of Christ, the more he's able to submit to authority. It's about submitting to God first.

As a wife, remember what your husband is up against. His own personal tendencies, sandwiched between bad officers and bad inmates. Most all are trying to exert their own authority with no one really respecting anyone else's. Change has to battle against all of them.

But God has the power to change both: your husband's heart and his circumstances. God's grace will follow your husband as his heart surrenders. And this will impact those day-to-day things that make doing time difficult. God can make changes in which officers get assigned to your husband's dorm, who the warden is, and which roommates come and go.

Your main job as his wife is to pray. You may have to make calls and advocate for your husband on some occasions, but your primary power rests in the Lord's response to your prayers. God has given you the authority to ask in Jesus's name according to His will. And a heart change toward Himself is always in His will.

October 3 — Today Is a Gift

Hebrews 3:12-13

Take care, brethren, lest there should be in any one of you an evil, unbelieving heart, in falling away from the living God. But encourage one another day after day, as long as it is still called "Today," lest any one of you be hardened by the deceitfulness of sin.

    I had to visit a client in jail one afternoon. The room available to me as a professional visit, to my surprise, was actually within the pod. I was escorted and locked in a male pod with inmates walking laps around me as I waited for my client to get out of the shower. I felt horribly awkward. When I left after seeing my client, I was escorted and locked into a sally port connected to the pod. My escort was to be there shortly.

    I waited—and waited—for the opposing door to roll, but it never did. To my surprise the door to the pod opened and an inmate entered. The door rolled, and we were locked in there together. That awkward feeling only grew. Finally, a passing officer glanced through that narrow, fortified glass and did an immediate double take with a panicked face. I was immediately escorted out.

    The jail was having a hard time finding someone available to escort me. It was not a priority. It instantly became a priority when potential harm was observed. That officer was going about his daily job when he dropped everything to take care of the situation.

    We can approach life in the same way. We run on cruise control until a close call happens. It's rather a sobering encouragement to consider every day a gift. The reality is people die every day without knowing Jesus. There's an urgent need for them to be escorted into the loving arms of the Lord and away from harm.

    The writer of Hebrews is stressing the urgency in getting right with God before it's too late. He's saying people can be deceived into thinking they are okay spiritually, when in fact they are backsliding. They are missing opportunities that may not be available tomorrow. Every day truly is a gift of which they may have lost sight of, because sin has blinded them. They are no longer devoted followers of Christ.

    A risky lifestyle leads to a greater risk for death to come prematurely. Prison is a dangerous environment. Harm is housed, requiring sally ports and guards. There are unbelieving men there, living solely under the mercies of God each day. It may be your husband.

God doesn't want anyone to perish. He uses believers to snatch unbelievers from harm before it's too late. Do not let it be a close call to realign your priorities. Do not miss opportunities to be a spiritual blessing to someone else today. God can help you set and keep your priorities. He can stir your devotion to the things that matter. You can start today!

October 4 A Prophet's Camera

Ezekiel 1:1

Now it came about in the thirtieth year, on the fifth day of the fourth month, while I was by the river Chebar among the exiles, the heavens were opened and I saw visions of God.

The days of the Polaroid camera to memorialize a visit seems to have passed. It's been a good thing. They require more care than digital prints to extend their life over the years. Framing them becomes an irregular project. Officers often tear them up looking for contraband since the thickness already lends itself to suspicion. I'm not sad to see them go. No more wasted fortunes on mistimed blinks and quirky expressions.

God's prophets captured their messages by writing them down on some form of paper. God would give them a vision and they would describe it as if looking at a photo or scene playing before them. He would speak to them and they would write. Ezekiel was one of the writing prophets.

I wonder if God had to repeat Himself so the prophets would take it all down accurately, or replay the vision like a transcriber might. Consider the volumes of statutes that Moses wrote down. Did he do that all from memory or did God take him through it line by line, waiting on Moses to complete a sentence before moving on. It's fascinating to consider.

Whatever process God used, there were no "Polaroid" limitations. The prophet said exactly what he meant. He didn't appear to be "blinking" or "not ready." As with all Scripture, the books of the prophets are without error.

Prophecy can be a challenge to read and will take intentional study to best grasp, but as a student of the Bible do not shy away from these works. You can find application to your life in all the Bible, even what might seem dry and irrelevant to your life now. Even if you do not understand it fully, you'll still find blessing in the reading. It speaks to your desire to get to know God. He wouldn't have included them if He thought they were optional reading. He can use any part of the Bible, any verse, to speak personally to you.

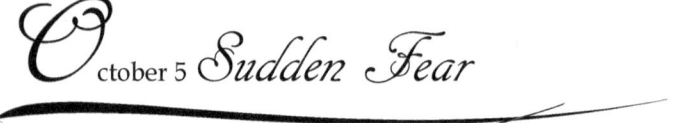

October 5 Sudden Fear

Proverbs 3:25

Do not be afraid of sudden fear, nor of the onslaught of the wicked when it comes.

Do you ever worry that you're not going to make it? Typical marriages struggle and do not make it, so how on earth do you expect yours to survive? I have waves of fear about the long-term ability to keep my marriage together. I envision all the temptations that could drag my husband away from which we might never recover. I see the barriers and wonder if we are up for the journey. I anticipate loads of pain and consider, "Do I really want to go through that?"

But what I have come to realize is that God doesn't speak to me in panicked bursts. And if I consider the rush of fear, I have balanced my marriage purely from the efforts of me and my husband, not on God's ability to sustain us. I'm also aware that evil lurks in the air about me, speaking defeating thoughts.

We can be the victims of spiritual terrorism at such times. We consider that what happens to other couples could likely happen to us, especially given that prison makes everything worse. It's similar to never going to a parade or stadium due to prior terroristic attacks in such venues.

Fear is the goal of the terrorist. In the spiritual sense, Satan promotes fear to render us powerless in our marriages. He loves to paralyze us from moving forward in the purpose and place God has for us, and he would love it if we would bow out altogether.

I had one such attack when I was actually listening to a Christian radio program. The guest was a former pastor. He and his wife were sharing the struggles they experienced in their marriage; he had been unfaithful to her. In that moment, I heard the thoughts, "He was a pastor and look what happened in his marriage. Why do you think it won't happen to yours?" But the words were not inquisitive; they were taunting.

From there my thoughts fearfully traveled to consider if I should even be writing a devotional book. What a hypocrite I would be. If I cannot be assured my own marriage will survive, who am I to encourage others? I was soon deflated in my outlook for my marriage and my purpose. Thankfully, I recognized the need to rein my thoughts and to remind myself of what I knew to be true both with God and Satan.

God doesn't taunt me. He doesn't invoke shock and fear when He needs to tell me something. But Satan will use such tactics. I know that God values my marriage. It's His will for marriages to thrive and reflect His love. I know that every marriage can be a powerful testimony to the power and love of God—mine included. Most importantly, I know that God can be trusted. I can trust Him with my life, my purpose, and my marriage.

Do not listen to the defeating thoughts that suddenly form in your mind. They cannot be trusted, whether they are your own or from Satan. Spiritual attacks are real. Satan terrorizes believers who are making a difference and fighting for their marriages. Do not succumb to the lies. Settle your fearful thoughts on the solid truth of God's character, His word, and His love for you and your husband. So live fully into your marriage without the reservations of what might happen in the future.

October 6 Do Not Have a Prayer

Numbers 13:31

But the men who had gone up with him said, "We are not able to go up against the people, for they are too strong for us."

When the men came back from surveying the land, they basically told Moses and the people, "We don't have a prayer against the people living there." God had moved the Israelites into position to move forward in possessing the land of promise. The team gathered information on the geography, who lived where, and also returned with produce from the land, confirming it was rich in resources. The land flowing with milk and honey awaited. Yet fear circulated amongst the tribes due to the ominous report by the survey team. Only Caleb and Joshua voted to move forward in faith and claim what God had promised.

Unfortunately, Caleb and Joshua were outnumbered. God determined at that point He would keep the Israelites in the desert until that unbelieving generation died off. Any person twenty years old or older wouldn't enter the Promised Land, except Caleb and Joshua. So Moses continued in the frustrating task of leading the Israelites in their 40-year wanderings until all persons of that generation died.

The aspects of the task which frightened the men were the fortified cities and the size of the people. They didn't see how they could win against such odds. They didn't seem to consider the miracles of their exodus. God also had previously given them victory over the Amalekites when they sought out the Israelites for war after they came through the Red Sea. This same group of people were part of those now feared by the men.

We should all strive to be a Caleb or Joshua when faced with scary odds. A prison chaplain once told me that my marriage has a 1 percent chance of surviving because my husband is serving life. Those are horrible odds! Yet I know when that 1 percent has God supporting it, odds can be overcome.

If you're in the minority statistics, you do have a prayer if God is leading you. He has the resources and plan for your success. Do not let prison be your fortified city that shrinks your faith to the point of defeat. Do not let the system be the towering people of the land that makes you feel like there's no hope. God doesn't want you floundering in the desert of your prison journey or giving up the fight. He wants you to boldly move forward in the power that He supplies.

October 7 *Above Jewels*

Proverbs 31:10

An excellent wife, who can find? For her worth is far above jewels.

The culture speaks to us about what's perceived to be beautiful and worthy. Women should be perfectly formed, flawless in complexion, independent, sexually provocative, and carefree. Her status is further heightened if she has a successful husband attached to her.

Scripture counters all these things and says a godly woman is more valuable than all the jewels in the world. She's more valuable than any earthly wealth. Her concerns are the well-being of her husband and children. She sacrifices for their good. She's thoughtful and generous. She's wise.

Scripture says beauty is vain. To put one's hope in external beauty is a dead end. We all know this, but it's hard not to compare ourselves with others based on how we look. It takes an intentional, inward recalibration to be confident in the beauty God values.

A godly woman supports her husband. She treats him good. He's proud to be her husband. She contributes financially if needed. She works hard at the office and at home, doing what it takes for her family's best.

And most of all, she fears the Lord. This is the heart of how a godly wife remains more worthy than jewels. The Lord is the standard by which she approaches her life.

Your husband is blessed beyond measure if you're striving to be a Proverbs 31 wife. He may not appreciate your godliness at all times, because prison clashes with most things godly. However, fearing the Lord will keep your path straight. A devoted, godly wife finds strength in the Lord to remain beside her incarcerated husband. God fully understands your value. He has given your husband a priceless gift. This true assessment of what's beautiful and worthy can carry you through until your husband finds what's right before him.

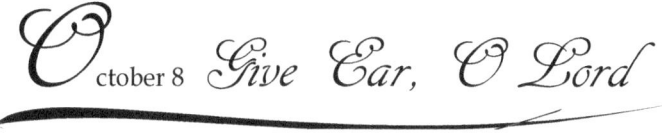

October 8 Give Ear, O Lord

Psalm 140

If you ever need a prayer to cry before God when scared for your husband's safety, Psalm 140 is it. David wrote the psalm. Wherever he used "me" put your husband's name. It's a powerful psalm and mirrors threatening situations your husband may face.

David just spells it out in verse 1: "Rescue me, O Lord, from evil men; preserve me from violent men." His need was urgent, and he saw God as the only source of help.

A person's mouth usually starts the problems in prison. The tongue is a harsh weapon used in prison, and it wreaks horrible consequences. It stirs up wars as David describes it in verse 3: "the poison of a viper is under their lips." He was being threatened and slandered. Their words were wicked toward him.

David's enemies were physically plotting his harm. He was a target. Prison is popular for premediated attacks on an identified foe. And sadly, the reason can be very insignificant. Yet in that environment, the small infractions and offenses become escalated to justifying violence no matter how slight the original upset.

David needed God to show up and save his life from all these things. He closes the psalm by reminding God of His character: "I know that the Lord will maintain the cause of the afflicted" (verse 12).

Hopefully, your husband will escape being in a place where such a prayerful psalm is needed. But there remains a chance he will be if incarcerated long enough. It's the nature of the landscape. Even now, he may be facing such a situation that has your heart weak.

Your husband may have earned retribution from someone else, or he may be simply a target based on erroneous information from a source that cannot be trusted. Regardless of where you are today, your best line of defense is to lay out your petition before God as David did. Share this psalm with your husband. If he can come clean before God, asking for forgiveness for whatever part he may have played in the situation — if any — God will hear such a cry for help from a humbled heart.

October 9 — Joy of the Lord

Zephaniah 3:17

"The Lord your God is in your midst, a victorious warrior. He will exult over you with joy, He will be quiet in His love, He will rejoice over you with shouts of joy."

God sent prophets repeatedly to Israel, urging them to return to Him with full devotion. He longed to bless them. Yet as Zephaniah warned of the coming punishment, the word of God through His prophet was again ignored. Yet God repeatedly extended His mighty arm through the words of future restoration. Today's verse is part of that prophecy. Israel would once again be the object of the Lord's joy. As grafted vines into His family, all Christians can share in this aspect of God's design for His children.

Imagine, God receiving joy from us. I wonder if I make God laugh — in that good way. I hope He finds my personality enjoyable. I hope I make Him proud. To consider bringing Him joy makes me smile.

To be restored to God, the intimate blessings of His presence surrounds you. His love gently guides you; His walk with you isn't pressured, but pleasurable. I have heard it described as a dance. You walk in sync with Him through your obedience and He reveals more about Himself to you. You hear His singing over you.

The Lord is all-powerful, yet all-loving. Life and prison can go together. You can have joy in the Lord; He can find joy in you. He can powerfully lead you through this season, and do it so gently, like a whisper of love.

The Lord will correct a wayward heart, like the Israelites, but He also offers a renewed relationship full of joy that can only be found when walking with Him.

October 10 — Until I See You Again

Deuteronomy 28:32

"Your sons and your daughters shall be given to another people, while your eyes shall look on and yearn for them continually; but there shall be nothing you can do."

This verse reminds me so much of my perspective when leaving my husband after visitation. If I do not look over in the direction at the officer bidding my exit, he will not see me and somehow allow me more time with my love. Maybe the clock is wrong and I really have ample more minutes. But of course that never happens, and I solemnly submit to the alert that it's time for me to leave. There's nothing I can do about it.

It's in the leaving, keeping my husband in view to the last most possible second, that increases my yearning. He's being taken away from me by strangers. And there's nothing I can do about it. It's the bittersweet reality of visits. The walk in is light and anticipated; the walk out is heavy and dreaded.

Today's verse is part of the consequences that God outlined for the Israelites if they broke their covenant with the Lord. Captivity would be one of the outcomes. But by the time it happens, nothing they can do will change it. It was determined by God beforehand for their disobedience.

The dreadful separation at visit's end is part of the consequences of prison. We each have to exit into our different worlds: my husband to the drab and darkness of cement; me to the sunlight and comforts of home. He remains in the hands of strangers, but I take a deep breath when I step beyond the gate, knowing that God has us both in His hands.

Then I begin the new feelings of anticipation when I can see my husband again. I pray to God on that drive home. I thank Him for our visit. I take in the scenery of His creation. I pray He keep my husband safe. And the routine continues — visit to visit.

God shares in your yearning when you have to leave. Some family members choose not to visit, because it's just too hard to see their loved one on the inside. The pain is too great. But God also instills hope for the future, and this hope can be the strength to make the visits in between sweet.

October 11 A God Ending

Philemon 1:15

For perhaps he was for this reason parted from you for a while, that you should have him back forever.

I find much encouragement from Philemon. It's a short book, but full of encouragement for any prison wife. The useless turned useful — this was Paul's description of Onesimus, who was Philemon's slave. Onesimus ran away and came to know Paul who was in imprisoned in Rome. He came to know Jesus through Paul's teaching. And with this, Paul saw the new man with Onesimus's salvation and he advocated for Onesimus's freedom. Paul sent him back to Philemon with a wonderful character letter and offer of paying restitution of whatever Onesimus owed. The beautiful perspective captured in the verse above was part of the message to Philemon.

Paul was acknowledging the providence of God within the situation. Onesimus wronged Philemon according to the law at the time. He deserted his master, but God providentially used the time to connect him with the apostle Paul. And he ultimately met Jesus through Paul which changed him forever. He was transformed into a godly man.

Paul was confident that Philemon would do what he asked, and it's a wonderful story of Onesimus getting a new life. He was freed both spiritually and legally. Meeting Jesus was the key to his new beginning.

I cannot help but smile when I read this story. I have read it many times over and I still smile with each one. There's a deep joy for a man I have never known, and I envision how incredibly nice it would be for my husband to receive such mercy. I also respect Paul for taking a chance on Onesimus, seeing his potential, and making the effort to give him that second chance.

God's providence still operates today. He works in the lives of all, behind the scenes, orchestrating circumstances to bring about His will. God values criminals, just as He did Onesimus. He desires to change the man, then the life. He may just have allowed your husband's current incarceration to return him a new and better man. There may be a "Paul" in prison that your husband needs to meet. And if he meets Jesus in prison, you'll have him truly back forever.

October 12 *Willingly for You*

Mark 14:36

And He was saying, "Abba! Father! All things are possible for Thee; remove this cup from Me; yet not what I will, but what Thou wilt."

When I first moved to Florida, I was new to just how hot the sand can become when baking in a scorching afternoon. Believe it or not, I have never been to the ocean and only have mere winks of memory for being on any type of sandy shore. And it was not a Florida shore.

My introduction to sandy temperatures came when I mindlessly walked my dog along the unpaved lane where I lived at the time. My poor dog repeatedly stopped, sat down, and refused to move. In my frustration I insisted she move forward, and in my opinion, "Quit acting silly!" Sadly, it took her defiance—along with repeated lifts of her paws, one then the other, dancing to limit contact with the sand—before I actually took notice.

I touched the ground with my hand and yanked it back. My heart broke into miserable pieces looking upon my dog, trying so hard to be obedient, yet unable to endure what I asked of her. The broken pieces further melted, knowing I was the one responsible for her pain. I gathered her in my arms and carried her back home.

When I reflect on this memory, it reminds me of what Jesus did out of obedience to God and love for me. It reminds me of His crucifixion and resurrection. And it can bring me to tears, just as watching my faithful dog experience physical pain because of my actions.

Jesus asked God to remove the cross. But He followed the request with a statement of obedience to God's will. Jesus surrendered to the will of God. It was my sin which caused that outcome of such pain for Him. Yet I can envision Him looking down at me from the cross, much as my beloved collie looked up at me—in pain—with loving and innocent eyes that say, "I'm here because of you."

And much as I picked up and carried my dog home, in no more pain, Jesus resurrected from the grave and went back home to heaven. With my salvation, I'm assured of being carried into His heavenly home one day as well.

The pain of prison will end one day. Either in this life or with the life event that carries you or your husband to your eternal home. I pray Jesus gets to carry you there. If you aren't sure of your salvation, please do not delay getting sure.

October 13 — Penny-Wise

II John 1:10

If anyone comes to you and does not bring this teaching, do not receive him into your house, and do not give him a greeting.

I have always thought it would be a nice ministry to own a bed and breakfast or possibly a small apartment building in which the wives of inmates could stay at a reasonable price while visiting their husbands. The costs associated with visits prevents many women from seeing their husbands regularly. It's not reasonable for us to move every time they are moved, so we surrender to long drives, hotel stays and the accompanying expense. Sadly, when the cost of canteen for the actual visit is added to the weekend, it's not cheap to simply want to spend time with our husbands.

Unfortunately, I have neither the experience nor finances to consider such a business undertaking. Furthermore, if I were running a bed and breakfast on weekends, when would I get to see my own husband, I comically conclude any time this comes to mind. But it would be nice to provide such a convenience and blessing to traveling wives.

Conversely, in the verse for today, John is cautioning "the chosen lady and her children"(verse 1:1) not to provide hospitality to traveling evangelist who were not teaching the true Gospel. It was commonplace to host such men, providing support for their ministry. John was concerned that in doing so, it would communicate to others that she endorsed their message or indirectly enabled false teaching to spread.

There were false teachers during that time who didn't believe God took human form in the person of Jesus. They also separated the spiritual from the physical, believing that a person could sin with their body and still be okay spiritually.

I enjoy supporting ministries that impact prisoners when able. This may be where your heart settles as well. Yet we need to be wise. It does matter what ministries you choose to support. We do not want to inadvertently support wrong and harmful beliefs. Just because a ministry is charitable doesn't mean it's Christian. Even if Christian, it may be a false religion.

Pray about your giving. Take time to investigate the organization. Read about their beliefs. What's their mission statement? Look for established financial endorsements or comparable information that helps you decide that your donation will be used wisely.

You work hard for your income. You sacrifice financially because of your husband's incarceration. God is all about helping others and ministries, but only if they do not oppose what He teaches.

October 14 Take the Next Step

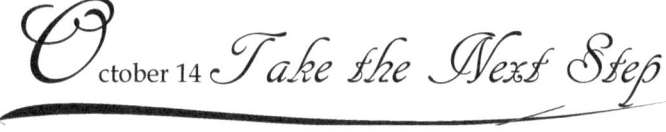

I Samuel 15:22

And Samuel said, "Has the Lord as much delight in burnt offerings and sacrifices as in obeying the voice of the Lord? Behold, to obey is better than sacrifice, and to heed than the fat of rams."

I walked into the house with my dog when she planted herself at the threshold, refusing to enter. I was shocked, because she had never done that before. She expressed her dislike for coming in from her outdoor fun by halting at the door. Soon after that peculiar event, I was listening to a Christian radio program and the pastor made reference to disobedience to God being like standing at the threshold and not stepping forward. My spirit had that recognizable feeling: God was speaking to me.

And I knew what He was talking about. I was putting off a decision that He had made for me. My procrastination circled around wanting to be certain I heard correctly, dislike of the decision, and worry for the outcome. In my delay, I was praying for clarification. Well, God made it clear that day. By not following through, I was being disobedient to His will.

Walking with God will present such moments as these. You'll be at the threshold, paralyzed from forward movement, wanting really to retreat to where it's easier and seemingly more enjoyable. You consider every angle to how you can delay stepping forward, maybe even from reasonable concerns. Other times, it's simply because it's an unpleasant option.

I have found that if it's something I want to do, I leap over that threshold without regard, with my banner flying: Prompt Obedience! I'm carefree in faith and looking forward to all God has planned with the next step. It's the exciting part of walking with God.

But obedience to God's will include both types of decisions if you're serious about walking close to Him. He uses the challenging steps to test and build your faith, teach you more about Himself, and ultimately prepare you for the steps beyond that one.

Once I surrendered to God's will in my threshold moment, peace flooded over me in a warm spiritual embrace. There was no longer that disconnected anxiety that came with my idle considerations of what to do. Moving forward settled my heart and brought peace. The decision was no less difficult, but I could confidently accept that it was the right one.

When you find yourself at the doorway, unsure if you should enter, consider these things: Has God revealed the answer to you in Scripture? Are you truly uncertain about what God has asked or just scared to do it? It's okay to ask for clarification. But once certain of God's answer, delaying is still disobedience. A delay may result in your losing a blessing God has planned.

God's peace and blessings come with walking obediently to His will. You can trust Him with what lies beyond the threshold. He wouldn't say, "Go," unless He had everything waiting exactly as it's supposed to be. The only thing missing is you.

October 15 — When I'm Not Enough

Romans 5:5

And hope does not disappoint, because the love of God has been poured out within our hearts through the Holy Spirit who was given to us.

What I have learned during these years of prison is that I'm not enough to carry my husband through what he faces on the inside. He might even say, "You're all I need," but I know this isn't true. If it were, the temptations in there wouldn't overpower him, my being in his life would keep him content, and his desire would be to please me above everything else.

I'm not enough to keep him joyful and hopeful when he listens to a man commit suicide in the next cell. I'm not enough when he sees stabbings and violence, when he's threatened, when he sits in an unconditioned cell drenched in sweat or when he freezes in a lower-level cell surrounded by cold cement. I'm not enough when he wakes in the knowledge that he's "home" for his natural life.

As his wife, I do a lot for his well-being, but I cannot share in the life that he sees from his bunk or experience the moments which settle sadly into his heart. That connection is reserved for God. It's through the Holy Spirit that comfort comes in those moments. It's the Holy Spirit who can give my husband pause before a decision, encourage his heart when he wants to give up, or when there seems no good happens in a day.

Paul describes in chapter five of Romans, the power available through the Holy Spirit to face adversity and overcome it, because there's a greater hope found in our salvation. Adversity comes, but believers have the hope of eternity with God. This inspires perseverance. As we persevere, our character gets developed, and with this, our hope is renewed. Our understanding of this hope is communicated to us through the Holy Spirit.

God loves us like no other person can—even a spouse. His love fills that void in the heart where true peace and contentment reside, no matter the difficulty. This cannot be generated from the presence of, marriage to, or support from any other person. It's a special bond only held with God. He knows our thoughts and hearts intimately. He knows the unique impact every adversity has on us. That's why He's the perfect Comforter, Heart Changer, Encourager, and Counselor.

So acknowledge that your love isn't enough for your husband to be victorious over prison. You get the awesome privilege of loving your husband, but the hope he needs to persevere through the world he wakes to daily requires the love of God actively working inside of him through the Holy Spirit. This hope doesn't disappoint.

October 16 *Family of One*

Proverbs 14:10

The heart knows its own bitterness, and a stranger does not share its joy.

Many churches produce a directory. The compilation portraits of the leadership and members usually come about every few years. It's the family units of the greater family of God. It's also another experience on this path of prison which can remind me of how raw my hurt can be. It spawns from the repeated offer to pose for a portrait without my husband as if I'm single. I can be easily offended, because my heart is more fragile at those times.

Often there's no comment even made about my being married. My husband is invisible to them in many ways. I'm approached as any other single person. My hurt response wants to rudely ask, "Now, why would I want to take a family portrait without my husband?"

But I know I cannot blame them, because people do not mean to be insensitive. And my quiet nature contributes to the invisibility of my husband, because I simply do not talk much about my personal life. And, yes I know, people pose by themselves, but they are whom I consider the truly single.

Some people continue in their pressure even after I explain why I choose to decline to sit for the photo. Their reasons are never convincing and further proof they do not understand why I feel as I do.

And there's really no way for me to further explain how my husband would feel. He already misses being home for special occasions (which I do send pictures of to help him feel a part). But if I were to sit for a family portrait, it would only highlight our separation in an intentional way. So I choose not to participate. This may not be an issue at all for you and your husband. I share it by way of example for the verse today.

The proverb beautifully captures my heart when something like this comes up. Only my heart truly knows the bitterness I fight against from the everyday losses, but the deep joy of my marriage is the positive of this path that no one else can truly know either. That makes my marriage uniquely awesome and more fulfilling than a million portraits of us.

You have the positive to hold onto in your marriage that's yours alone to experience. No one can take that from you. Your faithfulness to your marriage is building into your life a joy that no one can share in. Take pleasure in the good your marriage offers. It's uniquely yours.

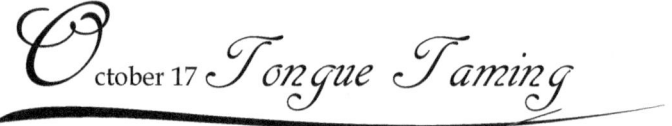

October 17 Tongue Taming

James 3:6

And the tongue is a fire, the very world of iniquity; the tongue is set among our members as that which defiles the entire body, and sets on fire the course of our life, and is set on fire by hell.

Words are the greatest instigator of evil in prison. Vulgar cursing, degrading comments, coarse jokes, angry threats—it is a restless evil (verse 8). So much harm is caused by the tongue in prison. James wrote about the power of the tongue. If a man can control his tongue, he can effectively manage any other area in his life.

Think about it. If the same discipline it takes to control your words was used in other areas of your life, how successful would you be? You would probably exercise more regularly, procrastinate less, complete projects, and stick to a budget.

The Lord created us with the ability to learn language and communicate. We were made to worship Him. James challenges us to consider how we can praise God with the same mouth that curses.

For many, it's habit. I used to curse out of habit. I think back on the words that rolled off my tongue and it makes me wince. Sadly, I recall even boasting about the curse-word combination that was my favorite to use. I thank God my language got cleaned up when my heart did, but it took intentional choices, especially at times of upset. I still slip a word now and again when my emotions are in upheaval. Thankfully, God and the dog have been the only witnesses. And thankfully, both are forgiving.

It's really a heart issue. A heart bent toward loving and pleasing God will consciously try to speak words that are pleasing and appropriate. Habits can be broken, but the heart must be motivated to make the effort. Just as ugly and mean-spirited words can be stopped, encouraging and positive words can be added.

Let your husband experience what godliness sounds like. I'm quite certain he hears obscenities and ugly tones every day, throughout the day. Let your words to him be uplifting and positive. Give compliments to him. Try not to curse in anger or habit. You can be a witness to a disciplined tongue from which sweet blessings flow, not bitter poison.

October 18 — Rewritten from Love

Jeremiah 36:23

And it came about, when Jehudi had read three or four columns, the king cut it with a scribe's knife and threw it into the fire that was in the brazier, until all the scroll was consumed in the fire that was in the brazier.

Over the years, communication with my husband has been primarily through letters. Our letters have become representative of our growing love as the endearing greetings and things shared blend to form a story of memories and experiences. A typical couple have pictures to capture the memories of times shared. For us, it's in a string of continuous letters recorded across several years in handwritten form. Letters hold the laughable moments, the fights, the sadness, the excitement of love, the typical and uneventful days. But with prison, they also hold the moments of anxiety, fear, separation, and frustration.

The receipt and screening by prison staff on his end has been a progressively accepted intrusion, because this is the reality of prison mail—it's neither private, nor confidential. With the hardness of the environment and indifference that's shown for many aspects of an inmate's life, I sometimes relax in the assumption that this is carried through to the person who handles the mail, making it seem less a violation. Fights, love letters, family happenings, and the day-to-day events are open to the eyes of whoever is working the mailroom that day. But the indifference becomes a frustration when mail is lost or damaged.

Jeremiah's "mail" in the form of a scroll was ripped piece by piece and burned by King Jehoiakim. God directed Jeremiah to essentially write down everything He had spoken to Jeremiah since his initial calling to be a prophet. It was another attempt to get the people to turn from evil and back to the Lord. Once delivered to the king, however, he only listened to a portion of it. His distaste for what it said and continued rebellion resulted in his disregard, yet again, to God's word. He destroyed it.

Every time I read this passage about the scroll being burned, my heart breaks for Jeremiah. I have one letter damaged by prison staff or "lost," and I experience a level of grief that my words didn't reach my husband or arrived in pieces. That scroll contained the account of 22 years of God's word. Jeremiah dictated every word to his faithful scribe Baruch. The exhaustive effort that went into composing that scroll is nothing short of amazing. No computer, no audio recordings, every word was written by hand.

Even more astounding is that he was obedient to God's instruction to simply rewrite it. Can you imagine? I lose a couple of paragraphs to a power outage and want to cry at the thought of rewriting something. A compilation of over twenty years of information would be devastating. Yet, Jeremiah faithfully completed it again, "and many similar words were added to them" (verse 32).

Being a prophet was no easy assignment. But I'm so grateful there were men like Jeremiah willing to accept the call. Men of such tenacity for God's word and willingness to accept mistreatment in all forms out of their love for Him. Thankfully, we have their writings and experiences preserved in the compilation called the Bible.

When prison beats on you when you're already down, or rips and burns the good you try to provide to your husband, you might become sorrowful. But do not let their actions rob you of your tenacity to stick to your calling, your marriage, or anything else God has instructed you to do. Rewrites become no problem when God has assigned it.

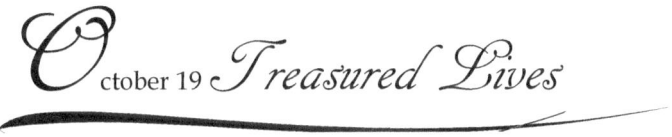

October 19 — Treasured Lives

Isaiah 57:18

"I have seen his ways, but I will heal him; I will lead him and restore comfort to him and to his mourners."

I have a heart for the less valued and easily see the possibilities for restoration. I love to see older homes restored. I see scuffed and flawed furniture at a thrift store and see a beautiful eclectic piece given a little work. My eyes see treasure in a dilapidated house and the future beauty in things someone has discarded as junk. My husband's heart, his life, and all the potential for a great future have always received this same hope.

God sees him that way too. He has great plans for him — despite prison. My husband's life has been repurposed through God's mercy. He sees him as strong and courageous. God sees him as a powerful witness to His glory brought about through amazing changes accomplished in a place of evil and from a history marked by violence, drugs, immoral, and illegal behavior.

I consider myself truly blessed to have been given the same vision and entrusted with loving my husband, a person who most would look over as not worth the time, effort, and certainly not the love. Thanks truly to God that His vision isn't so shortsighted. Thanks truly to God that I get the humbling privilege of loving and being loved by a man chosen by God for an awesome purpose.

God has the restorative plans for your husband's life too. Everything is designed, and He's willing to make a beautiful life from whatever damaged it in the first place. There are endless possibilities with God.

Chances are you see that treasured life as well or else you wouldn't be at his side now. Prison wives have a deep heart for hope. We are labeled desperate, pitiful, naïve, and maybe even crazy for remaining in our marriages. But what we have is a God-sized hope that in the hands of God any life can be restored. We see the value in a life, because we know God values that same life.

So go ahead and envision your husband and your life with him through the eyes of hope and God's power to create a beautiful future.

October 20 *Bless the Children*

Mark 10:16

And He took them in His arms and began blessing them, laying His hands upon them.

I wonder what became of the children that Jesus blessed that day. Did they become young disciples? Did they have a memory of that day Jesus touched them? I'm sure their parents told the story to them. You would have to think that Jesus praying and blessing your child would have great rewards. But is there a guarantee?

Scripture teaches that each is responsible for their own belief in Jesus, so a parent cannot obtain salvation for a child in that sense. A child isn't saved just because a parent participates in a baby dedication ceremony. However, Scripture is clear that a parent can impact a child's spiritual development if the child is raised in a home where God is center and taught godly principles. The role model of the parent is important. Children may be wayward at points, but there's an investment prior to that season which encourages their return to godly living.

Are you concerned that you missed opportunities with your children to rescue them from a negative future? Does your husband make it more difficult, because he doesn't provide a role model for what a godly father looks like? Is a child showing that rebellious spirit that you fear will lead to legal involvement if not reined in?

Jesus has a special place in His heart for children. He says to not hinder the children from coming to Him. He says that childlike belief is what salvation faith is like. There are warnings to persons who lead a child into sin.

Do everything you can to teach your children about God and Jesus. They are more open to the Gospel when young. Take opportunities to involve them in church activities. Consider if there's a godly man who could mentor your son. Guard who and what comes into your home that doesn't support your beliefs. And take your child to Jesus through prayer, much like the parents did in the verse today, asking for God's blessing and protection.

October 21 Making Honey

Judges 14:14

So he said to them, "Out of the eater came something to eat, and out of the strong came something sweet." But they could not tell the riddle in three days.

As a wife, you hold attributes of your husband dear. You know the deeper things about him that others do not always appreciate. This is how it should be. But often others weigh any positive attributes with less significance as those that led to his incarceration. Many believe that just because he can be good, his bad outweighs any positive contribution that he ever makes to your love. This easily boils down to the question: "Why do you stay with him?"

The verse above is the riddle told by Samson to the wedding party gathered for his marriage. He offered a prize of clothing to anyone who could solve the riddle. Samson was anointed by God with incredible strength, and this was proven on a path where he killed an attacking lion with his bare hands. Later, on his walk to his wedding ceremony, the carcass of the lion lay full of bees and honey. The Lord has used this verse to remind me of the continued work He's doing in my husband.

My husband has incredible strength. Serving two life sentences, ex-death row, and over twenty years already served in a harsh environment has demanded strength. I admire him greatly in this. My husband also has incredible sweetness, and he shows me love in adoring fashions. There's much good. I see him as the whole person, and the whole person is whom I love, unconditionally. Others see mostly the strength that becomes violent, has an ugly mouth, or causes problems within the system he survives in. I see this as well. And it's hard to go through the days when this type of strength creates consequences that make doing a prison marriage difficult. But I also know that God desires to use this strength for His kingdom work.

Fortunately, God also sees the whole person of my husband: the potential, the sweetness, the good forced to live in a brutal landscape where attacks from lions can come out of nowhere. The sweetness is worth holding onto, because it's a reminder that out of the harshness, God can bring the sweet.

Hold onto the sweetness and positive in your husband. Others may not give it credence, but God sees. He has plans for the good you see. He will also use the things, which others see through an inadequate perception, to bring about incredible changes in the lion that may best represent your husband now. Continue to be your husband's number-one fan. Admire his strengths, appreciate the good, and never lose faith that God continues to make honey within a powerful person. You're blessed to be chosen by God to love your husband as only you're qualified to do. So do not be discouraged if you feel as though you're the only person who seems to know this—God knows. **

October 22 *Alas!*

Daniel 9:4

And I prayed to the Lord my God and confessed and said, "Alas, O Lord, the great and awesome God, who keeps His covenant and lovingkindness for those who love Him and keep His commandments, we have sinned, committed iniquity, acted wickedly, and rebelled, even turning aside from Thy commandments and ordinances."

"Alas" is used to exclaim great grief or distress. Many of the prophets used this word in their supplications before God. They absorbed the gravity of a situation and verbally tried to express their heart's anguish in this often introductory word in their appeal to God.

You do not hear this word used much in modern conversations. Definitely not in text or blog posts. It likely comes out as "OMG!" An abbreviated expression, but conversely not always associated with distress and rarely truly directed to God.

There's something special about praying Scripture back to God, using words of Scripture in your heart's cry. It's His word, thus never trite or diminished in power. The true heart of the writer is expressed, and this can help you capture the same depth of appeal to God when you pray. "Alas" can reflect a pure emotion, not a surface response like "OMG."

Many of the psalms are great for this. Many of the prayers recorded in Scripture, like of Daniel, Jeremiah, and of course, Jesus, are powerful expressions. You can personalize it to your situation, because it's the heart and emotion of the prayer and reverence to God you're capturing.

Prison deals you grief and distress at some point, and generally, there's an unrelenting somberness that tracks you on this journey. Evil accompanies every step it seems. "OMG!" doesn't seem to account for your need, but "Alas, Lord!" communicates your desperate need for God's help. It says, "Please, hear my cry, Lord!"

Reverence God's power through speaking His divine word. You'll connect with Him in a special way. It will deepen your prayer life, and in doing so, you'll tap into power not available previously.

October 23 Weeds Now

Matthew 13:30

"Allow both to grow together until the harvest; and in the time of the harvest I will say to the reapers, 'First gather up the tares and bind them in bundles to burn them up; but gather the wheat into my barn.'"

The city had placed a walking path between two main roads. Very parklike. Nature grew on both sides, and trash cans and benches rested at varying points for use by the patrons who often use this path as a cut through now available on foot or bike.

During the final phase, sod was placed along the sides of the concrete path and watered regularly. Clean, crisp, and healthy grass lined the path. At least initially. When later walking through that area, I noticed that the picturesque grass was marred by plenty of weeds.

The city didn't plant weeds. But they encroached and weaved themselves into the soil. To pull up the weeds would result in uprooting the true grass as well. I was reminded of Jesus's words in Matthew about heaven and its application to the evil allowed to grow with the good.

Prison is a very hard place to live righteously. Prison surrounds those men trying to remain clean and healthy and righteous. The evil seems relentless, circumventing the good, weaving the impact of its deeds to all around. Regardless of effort, it seems the good is being choked out by the bad.

But this apparent discouragement doesn't reflect the reality of God's sovereignty. God hasn't forsaken those who are His living amongst the weeds of prison. In fact, He's acutely aware and intentional within the circumstances. God is fully in control. His power isn't weakened by evil. In fact, His allowing the weeds to remain is proof of the power over evil He possesses.

Your husband is in good hands if he's a child of God! No amount of evil will change God's favor on him. It may be difficult to see the blessings on some days, but God hasn't forsaken him. He remains destined for heaven—the ultimate blessing. While on this earth—and in prison—he will face evil, but his faith in Jesus has already determined the victory.

The challenge for him is to remain aware of how evil operates. In verse 25, we read: "But while men were sleeping, his enemy came and sowed tares also among the wheat, and went away." In your prayers for your husband, consider praying not only for his encouragement, but also for his wisdom to recognize when the weeds are creeping in. Evil may seem blatant in prison, but Satan deals with individuals very cunningly.

But take heart! God's harvest in the end has already been determined. Your husband is part of God's kingdom! He's safe in the most perfect way.

October 24 Seeking Silence

Psalm 63:1

O God, Thou art my God; I shall seek Thee earnestly; my soul thirsts for Thee, my flesh yearns for Thee, in a dry and weary land where there is no water.

I struggle to understand people who constantly need some type of noise surrounding them. A TV always on, the radio in the background, someone always around to talk with, no alone, no quiet—and this is what's pursued to my bewilderment. But I have to consider, this preference is comparable to their possibly not understanding someone like myself who pursues the opposite. Despite how we are wired, however, being still and quiet is a valuable way to grow spiritually and hear from God in ways not available when all around us is noise.

This is an aspect of my husband's prison time that I grieve—his inability to get away from the noise of his surroundings. Regardless of hour, there's always noise. Voices, echoing metal, clanging doors, a roommate's presence—never an opportunity to be truly alone, to sit in silence and meditate on God, or listen acutely for His voice.

Although I know Scripture speaks to the value of this discipline, I also know that God isn't limited by our environments. I think those of us who have the opportunity to nurture our relationship with God through quiet moments with Him do miss out on a huge blessing by not taking the opportunities that we have. For a prisoner, whose opportunities have been taken away through circumstances, I think God especially blesses the effort made to connect quietly despite the unending noise.

This can be another area where you can pray for your husband. If he's wired to desire constant activity around him, a prayer might be for him to cultivate an appreciation for silence. If he's the opposite, he's likely more emotionally drained by his surroundings and needs special prayer to mentally cope with his reality.

A quiet heart can be pursued even if the ears are forced to keep listening to the background noise. And this is ultimately the purpose of being silent before God. It's to quiet our hearts, meditate, and be attentive to His presence and His voice.

October 25 — Out of My Desire

Philippians 4:4

Rejoice in the Lord always; again I will say, rejoice!

I just ended a miserable weekend of feeling sick with sinus trouble. To the doctor on Friday, vomiting, a headache that I was sure to crack my skull if I were to move too quickly—rejoicing I was not. It seems when I'm nauseated nothing else matters in the world. But there I stood in the sanctuary on Sunday morning with a sick feeling that wouldn't leave. Rejoicing worshippers surrounded me.

My attitude crash-landed that morning. I was definitely better than Friday, but the lingering sickness had me not rejoicing, but whining. It was all about me, as it had been the entire weekend. The Lord knew how I felt physically—and I was grateful for that—but He also knew where my heart was in the slow process of recuperation. I prayed for health, but despite feeling better, my spiritual energy continued in its seemingly helpless state. Could I not even sing one line of a praise song to God who blesses me beyond anything I deserve! I wonder what would have happened if through the discomfort, I had put just as much focus on thanking God that I did on complaining to Him.

God has always been more interested in loyalty of the heart than sacrifice of the body. It's the heart behind the sacrifice. I had made it to church that morning almost out of guilt for skipping when I was still able to function in some capacity. But my worship was empty.

There are plenty of days on this path of prison when whining could be a common expression, if not from my mouth, from my heart. Every day brings with it a bucket of complaints if I care to start dipping. Most days I do okay, but there are times when my resolve falters, and dipping begins. This is when that plane of emotions starts plummeting and everything looks more miserable as I get lower.

Whether sickness, a car repair, or prison, I can always find something imperfect in my life. But there are amazingly more blessings—many I take for granted as I dwell on the things lacking. Instead, I must look for the blessings within the days and see God's hand in all that touches my life.

Paul doesn't say only rejoice when we feel good. He says, "Always!" Even if not in the physical energy of a healthy body, our hearts can always rejoice in sincerity. And with that comes a connection with God not otherwise accessible. I long for my sacrifices to be acceptable in His sight, because He's worthy. I'm also grateful for His mercy when they fall short. What a beautiful God we serve! **

October 26 — *You Can Overcome*

Jeremiah 1:19

"And they will fight against you, but they will not overcome you, for I am with you to deliver you," declares the Lord.

I gain great encouragement when I consider how much my husband has overcome in his own life. His past was perpetrated on him by men who were to be that loving father. If you ask him today about the stepfather who openly rejected him and treated him cruelly, he will share with you a heart that harbors no resentment. He appreciates the part of that father who taught him to fish and to ride a bike. His birth father exposed him to crime and drugs early in life, physically abused him, and did little to provide a stable and secure home. But my husband overcame this too.

Several years ago, my husband desired to reconnect with his birth father, a man he hadn't seen since he was thirteen. We could never locate him through our own efforts, but amazingly, my husband received a letter from him sent through a social worker. His father was within hours of the prison, residing in a nursing home due to a stroke. Amazing how God operates!

His father was dependent for the basic needs of life, and his mind didn't escape without injury. We soon discovered that much of his personality remained, but with a childlike manner at times. My husband received closure in many ways after his father's death within that same year. Thanks to God's grace in allowing that last earthly reunion to end in a much different way than those of the past. God's grace allowed my husband to overcome the many wrongs done to him. Wrongs that on some level contributed to his life's path to prison. My husband made criminal choices, but he was unable to choose his childhood life.

Ironically, I get angrier about people in my husband's past than he does! I get resentful toward those people who should have treated him better, protected him, and taught him respect for authority — especially respect for God. I have to practice releasing his past influences and experiences with the truth that God has won. My husband's past has and continues to be redeemed for the good. I do not know if my reaction comes from the losses for him or myself. It's probably a twisted version of selfishness. Regardless, I'm challenged when I regularly see forgiveness he extends to people who do not deserve it, and how he moves forward without a root of bitterness anchored to his relationships.

Oftentimes, I think this path of prison is more about what God wants to do in me than my husband. My husband may be the one in prison, but often he's the better person. I'm humbled and challenged by this.

Give praise to God for the mercies and strength given to your husband to overcome some great opponents from the past. But also recognize the current growth He's doing in you to deliver you to a deeper character by overcoming the situations fighting against you now.

October 27 *Battle Buddy*

Exodus 14:13-14

But Moses said to the people, "Do not fear! Stand by and see the salvation of the Lord which He will accomplish for you today; for the Egyptians whom you have seen today, you will never see them again forever. The Lord will fight for you while you keep silent."

When I went through ROTC Camp Challenge, my bunkmate was also called my "battle buddy." We were to look out for each other and form a comradery. By way of simply being around each other, this was encouraged. She was automatically my partner for many of the trainings. I recall vividly when we were paired for bayonet training. We squared off and learned the skills necessary for hand-to-hand combat. Neither of us, however, enjoyed the prospect of ever using them, and we both used a diminished and unmotivated call of "kill, kill, kill," during our mock sessions.

Spiritually, God is even more than our battle buddy. He conquers the enemies we face and thankfully, doesn't need to train! He steps in and defeats perfectly. And it's within a sobering reality He works, not a make-believe world of good and evil.

In the verses today, Moses and the Israelites were faced off with the Egyptians at the Red Sea. They had powerfully left the slavery of Egypt by the mighty hand of God and were headed to the Promised Land. The Egyptians pursued them. And what seemed like a defeat coming toward them, God stepped in between the conflict and defended on their behalf. He provided the miraculous escape through the Red Sea. Moses was the cheerleader, calling out, "Do not fear!"

The Israelites saw no solution to their situation. They had nowhere to go. They were trapped, squaring off with their enemy. Through human eyes, there was no hope. What they learned that day was that nothing is impossible with God.

He can do anything in your situation too; there's nothing too hard for Him. Where the legal system fails, He can win. Where evil battles, He's victorious. He's all-powerful. He created everything and everything remains in His control. Still do all that you can do in your situation, pray, and be faithful. And when the Red Sea arrives, stand by and see the salvation of the Lord on your behalf.

October 28 Stick to Your Purpose

I Corinthians 3:15

If any man's work is burned up, he shall suffer loss; but he himself shall be saved, yet so as through fire.

When I finally retired my antiquated flip phone, I faced the daunting task of purchasing a smartphone. I had grown tired of fighting a losing battle of doing life with a simple phone that couldn't adapt to the demands of technology. It seems progress forces itself on us, ensuring we either get on board or be denied the ability to participate. So my all-reliable, simple phone had to be replaced.

My purpose in having a cell phone is primarily to make or receive phone calls. What a concept! However, when researching smartphones, very few reviews even addressed the issue of call quality. The original purpose of the phone was ignored. All the bells and whistles took the spotlight of the reviews. It was evidence to the reality that the cell phone's purpose for most people had changed.

This change in purpose may hold very little danger when cell phones are considered. But for our lives, replacing God's purpose or being distracted by the bells and whistles of life can have regretful consequences for us. We will miss God's best and deny ourselves of the awesome peace that comes with being in the center of His will.

Anxious longings, unsettled feelings, wrong-turn consequences, missed opportunities—all these things can result from drifting away from what God has planned for your life. And most importantly, you'll miss that deeper relationship with God that's only available when doing life fully with Him.

Prison doesn't change your purpose. The unique and awesome ways of God allow your divine purpose to be weaved within the off-path, wrong choices of yourself or those which others make that impact your life. God redeems the bad—perfectly.

It doesn't mean all consequences are removed. But your life can be saved eternally and your purpose redefined to fit God's will. The things which have no eternal value will be lost (the bells and whistles of this life). But those things you do within God's purpose will bring you eternal reward.

Seek God, ask Him to guide you into your purpose, and stick to it. If you do not have a relationship with Jesus, your first step becomes getting to know and accepting Him as your Savior. Having your salvation and living your life in God's will—these are the ways to redeem the losses that come with prison.

 October 29 Above the Mire

II Peter 2:22

It has happened to them according to the true proverb, "A dog returns to its own vomit," and, "A sow, after washing, returns to wallowing in the mire."

There were sloughs in areas where I grew up. They were low-lying, usually muddy, and marshy. A "mire" is a similar word to describe the same type of landscape. In Scripture, the mud of a mire is often used to represent sin or a low, troubled place in life. In the above verse, Peter is referring to the false prophets who after hearing the truth still chose to return to a sinful lifestyle—the mire.

A man has a strong challenge in shedding his old lifestyle when he enters prison. He's surrounded by those still participating in the filth. Some give up and find themselves returning to what previously entangled them. This happens more times than not. When leaving prison, just the same, most find themselves diving back into drugs, violence, or whatever led to their incarceration.

What would Peter say to these men to resist this sad outcome? He would tell them to diligently practice a list of qualities: faith, moral excellence, knowledge, self-control, perseverance, godliness, brotherly kindness, and love (1:5-7).

He would also remind them of the eternal outcome for their encouragement. The new heaven and earth will come. Evil has been defeated despite what they see. God doesn't want anyone to perish, thus He delays in bringing judgement (3:9). He allows the mire of this world (and prison) to remain, because He loves those still choosing to stay in their sin. Your husband may be ready for eternity, but others aren't. God requires His believers to be patient while He extends patience for the benefit of those still wallowing in a dead-end lifestyle.

God is able and willing to provide your husband the power to remain godly, but a surrendered heart will be needed. This will be a daily challenge; he will not be perfect. But practicing the qualities Peter mentions will release God's favor on him. Peter knew that practicing these qualities will produce the accumulated effect of a transformed life, bent toward God, not the wayward path back to the mud.

You can be your husband's cheerleader, his support, and his prayer warrior. Pray for God to flood him with the strength to resist the temptations he faces daily that wants to lure him back into bad choices. And if he does slip, love him through the time to get back on solid ground. God will give you the strength to do this as well. It's all about loving God and others while waiting on the best outcome for all.

October 30 Grace to Forgive, Again

Luke 17:4-5

"And if he sins against you seven times a day, and returns to you seven times, saying, 'I repent,' forgive him." And the apostles said to the Lord, "Increase our faith!"

What the apostles seemed to be saying is "This is too hard, Lord. You must help us in this!" Saying I have to keep forgiving someone who continually wrongs me is a hard thing. Life requires that you forgive often. But the wrong is especially hard to release if the person doing the hurting is your husband. We have so much emotionally invested in our spouses that we can sometimes get exhausted when the same hurts find their way to our hearts through their words, actions—or in some cases, inaction. We forgive, but nothing changes. So the Lord's standard is high. The apostles realized this and knew for them to be able to do it, they needed help. In our flesh, we are prone to harbor resentment for promises not kept, harsh words that pierce deeply, or love that isn't appreciated.

Prison presents many hurts that need to be forgiven, sometimes every day, sometimes several times a day, because as the wives on the outside, we often carry the hurts along with us. Our newly defined world of prison is a constant reminder of hurts that we are experiencing.

When you're once again taking care of the yard work alone, you may need to practice forgiveness. When the kids are going crazy and you have no one to help, you may need to practice forgiveness. When the bills are piling up and there continues to be only one income, you may need to practice forgiveness. Hurts will boil to the surface depending on the day, your mood, and once there, your response will help build either a bridge of forgiveness or a wall of resentment. You and your husband are physically separated, but a wall of resentment will be even more detrimental to your marriage than any prison wall.

You may be saying, "I want to forgive, but I don't know how. Nothing ever changes anyway!" I have been there raging in my body. In those moments, I want to rage on my husband, but as usual, he isn't here! I'm aching and angry, and he isn't even aware. He's miles away in a cell, probably listening to a ballgame or talking trash on the vent, oblivious to my pain. What do we do at those times?

Be like the apostles. Say, "Lord, increase my faith!" Cry to God in your anger, cry to Him your bitter tears, but do so with a heart desiring to receive help to forgive, not escape. In your own strength, you may be unable to forgive. For those deep hurts, you really have to immerse yourself in faith and trust that God continues to work in your husband. Give God your pain, and in the process, you'll find strength to forgive while He holds you. **

October 31 *Darkness Changed*

Genesis 1:5

And God called the light day, and the darkness He called night. And there was evening and there was morning, one day.

Horror stories, crime, nightmares—darkness is often associated with evil or the potential bad that lurks in the bushes. But this isn't how God purposed the darkness to be used. We read in Genesis that God created the cycle of night and day, the moon and sun, and the stars. Darkness was good. It represented God's creation for beauty not for evil. But when sin entered the world, it changed the darkness.

Darkness is now used to hide sinful behavior. The beauty now harbors the creative minds of men to do evil. The criminal chooses darkness as his accomplice. Sexual sin is more appealing in darkness. The nightlife doesn't bring righteousness to mind, but carousing, drunkenness, and adrenaline for wrongdoing.

As the years move forward, sin needs less darkness to operate. The world is becoming more sinful and accepting of things that violate God's original design. The criminal boldly operates in the daylight, adultery is promoted through around-the-clock websites, and homosexuality is applauded and celebrated in public.

But in the end, darkness doesn't win. Evil will not be glamorized. Bragging for wrongs done will be brought down to knees before a righteous God.

It's a dangerous time in which we live, but even more so for those who choose to revel in the darkness. In their believed power, they are in danger of eternal damnation. And what they believe to be appealing will turn out to be their worst nightmare. They will suffer the consequences of rejecting the good and being deceived that the darkness will protect them. Sadly, they will discover they have been deceived by Satan and will become victim of the serious evil they once pursued.

And they will have no power to change the darkness of hell once there. It's only during this life that hope remains. That hope is in Jesus. He's the only escape. Be assured, God will reclaim the darkness, and when He does, screams heard will not be from crime, spooky scenes created in Hollywood, or cheers of unrighteousness. They will be in futile repentance of those who rejected Him.

Prison exists because of sin. Your husband is there because of sin. Darkness lives in the hearts of men, which causes actions which are illegal. Reclaim the darkness while there's still time.

November 1 — Comfort in Suffering

II Corinthians 1:3

Blessed be the God and Father of our Lord Jesus Christ, the Father of mercies and God of all comfort.

Suffering takes on a whole new personality when you have a close relationship with the Lord. It doesn't mean the pain is any less, but there's spiritual and emotional comfort, continued guidance when walking through the pain. The truth that God never leaves you is made real when in the valley.

But God's ability to comfort us depends on our closeness to Him. I can look back on my life when heartache and difficulty entered and see how God's comfort wasn't as "real" to me as it is now. His presence was no less, but He used the pain to cultivate my young faith, to seed the foundation. There was no grand revelation or spiritual event. The pain in many ways was my focus. But God met me where I was, and I matured from there.

I wouldn't trade what I learned through those early trials, nor give up my accumulated faith that's now the result. There's a sweet reward in the comfort I experience now when trials come. The trial may be fierce, but the personal hand of God communicates with me in ways never experienced before. God knows just how to "hug" me. He speaks to me through Scripture. He puts patterns in my day to whisper His presence to me. We communicate, and He's active in my suffering.

He's the God of all comfort. All levels of comfort for all different places in our spiritual walk. God will use suffering in a specific way depending on what He knows we need to learn at the time. We can always be assured that if we are His child, our suffering will not be wasted.

Prison may be a foundational place where you're seeking God. You may only see mostly pain right not. Maybe God doesn't seem real to you either. You know He's there, but He seems distant.

Please do not give up on God. Continue in the truth that you know. Get in the Bible and read. Anywhere! Pray. If you do these things, and continue to seek God, He will draw close to you. And with this, His ability to comfort you on this journey will leave you in awe of His goodness, and you'll have confident hope that everything truly is and will be okay.

November 2 Stumbling to Our Knees

Ezekiel 14:1-3

Then some elders of Israel came to me and sat down before me. And the word of the Lord came to me saying, "Son of man, these men have set up their idols in their hearts, and have put right before their faces the stumbling block of their iniquity. Should I be consulted by them at all?"

Many times, we want God's blessing without considering what our level of obedience has been. We cry out in crisis wanting God to rescue and fix our problems. But how much have we sought His will prior to the crisis? We do our own thing until we hit a stumbling block, then we seek God for help. Can we expect Him to fully bless us in the midst of our rebellion? In the words of a pastor, "God can't bless a mess!"

Israel was coming to the Lord's prophet to hear from the Lord regarding their captivity, as they were under the dominion of Babylon at the time. Ezekiel and other prophets had been telling the Israelites what God required of them, but they continued to rebel. They stepped out of God's will and disregarded the warnings, thus their exile and captivity commenced. Even within their captivity, they continued in their disobedience, worshipping idols.

God was gracious to the Israelites, repeatedly. But they consistently strayed from His love. They let other things and interests interfere with their relationship with God. They let fleshly temptations allure them, and ultimately, they became self-seeking instead of God-seeking. That's until trouble hit.

Prison presents many crises. At least, it has for me. There have been many situations when I feared for my husband's life, when I urgently wanted God's protection, and when I wanted His favor. These were situations when I was on my knees, crying out to God for mercy and deliverance.

God desires for us to seek Him in times of trouble. But He just as much wants us to seek Him in the less eventful times of life, when all seems to be going fine. God's will is found in the everyday, not so much the times of chaos. He wants to guide us and protect us, but if we stray, our disobedience is often what makes us stumble. The prayers of a righteous man are powerful and effective (James 5:16), and righteousness happens as we walk daily with God.

When you're in a crisis, your prayers are going to be far more powerful if you were there on your knees the day before when all was well. Do not wait for the eventual crisis to occur before you seek a closer relationship with God. Prison will deliver a crisis. As my husband says, "Things go from zero to sixty in here." Be walking with God before you have to run to Him. **

November 3 Glimpses

II Kings 6:16-17

So he answered, "Do not fear, for those who are with us are more than those who are with them." Then Elisha prayed and said, "O Lord, I pray, open his eyes that he may see." And the Lord opened the servant's eyes, and he saw; and behold, the mountain was full of horses and chariots of fire all around Elisha.

How much more our faith would embolden if we could see the work on our behalf in the spiritual realm. The Lord allowed Elisha's servant a glimpse into the realm of angels.

The king of Aram had sent warriors to capture Elisha, because he was repeatedly informing the king of Israel of the Arameans' military plans, thus thwarting them. It was not that Elisha was the secret service of the king, gathering information as any spy would. He was rather a prophet of God who supernaturally received the military information. Elisha was foremost a servant of God, not the king.

Soldiers thus arrived to the city where Elisha was staying and began circling it. It seemed all was lost because of the surrounding foe. Dread fell upon Elisha's servant. But Elisha knew a greater power stood with them — God's army.

And because of his anointing, faith, and obedience, Elisha's prayers to God were powerful. He requested his servant's eyes be opened to the spiritual realm, and God granted this request. The servant saw the supernatural forces protecting them.

His servant needed encouragement and a boost in faith. He needed tangible proof to "not fear" as Elisha encouraged of him.

I have heard tell of missionaries who were protected by angelic forces brought to light by the orchestration of God to be seen by an approaching enemy. I have experienced the also reality of evil in overt ways which was a sobering reminder of the realm that's active beyond my vision.

Prison can seem like a surrounding enemy posing certain harm to your husband or to yourself through the fencing which extends indirectly to your life. Be reminded that God is all-powerful and is constantly going to battle for you. Even though the battle is held in places you have no access to, your faith allows you to believe that victory always remains in the mightier army of God.

November 4 *Brother Daniel*

Isaiah 6:8

Then I heard the voice of the Lord, saying, "Whom shall I send, and who will go for Us?" Then I said, "Here am I. Send me!"

Long before missionaries have a testimony of God's amazing work seen within the lives they devote their lives to reach, they have a story. They have a testimony of their own salvation which placed them on the path to reach others with the love of Jesus. Some are the children of missionaries. Some were late in life coming to know the Lord. Missionaries are diverse in their personal testimonies. Brother Daniel is one of those dear missionaries.

His story is about a man who had everything by the world's standards. He was a career success. He had wealth and status. He followed the value of the world to make as much money as possible. One morning, loaded with cash and a pistol, he headed out for the office Christmas Eve party. His life changed in a matter of hours.

The party which started out with morning drinks traveled to his home that afternoon for continued fun. Drunk, arrogant, and out of control, he got into a fight with another man. This man fled. Daniel grabbed his pistol and pursued him with all plans to kill him. The car chase transformed into seven squad cars pursuing him. That chase ended with a four-hour standoff with a host of police and media in a cold, drizzling rain with evening upon them—and the temperature dropping. Daniel, sobered somewhat, decided he didn't want to die, so he surrendered. During that first night in jail, the voice of the Lord said to him, "Daniel, I've been waiting for you."

That event took away everything, but it set Daniel on the Lord's path. He has been serving the Lord ever since. He has been part of evangelism to China, Mexico, India, Alaska, Vietnam, and Bangladesh. He has been soul winning for Jesus for over thirty years now.

Brother Daniel is another example of what God can do with a life surrendered to Him. God pursues us and orchestrates even the negative events to halt a negative path. Your husband's incarceration could be the most loving thing God could have done for him, short of sending Jesus to die for him.

Brother Daniel surrendered when he heard the voice of the Lord in that cell that night. Just because your husband possibly hasn't surrendered yet, doesn't mean God is still not pursuing him. Do not give up on the testimony your husband will have when his night comes.

November 5 No Comparison

Isaiah 40:25

"To whom then will you liken Me that I should be his equal?" says the Holy One.

Sometimes we get immune to concepts that we hear repeatedly or observe played out before us. We can stop thinking critically simply from familiarity. This has been especially true when we consider good versus evil. Hollywood, books, television, and most media tend to see the sides of good and evil as opposing equals. God versus the Devil. How grossly inaccurate this is!

Satan is a fallen angel. He voluntarily gave up his position of serving God. He has never been God's equal. God created him. Although powerful, Satan will never reach equality with God—although he continues to try. God allows free will even of the angels. And Satan took his free will to abandon heaven and war against God.

Have you ever stopped to consider why Satan does not just take God on one-on-one in heaven? Why does he bother with spreading evil here on earth, seeking mankind to destroy? It's because he isn't powerful enough! His only way to get back at God is to attack God's other creation—man. Satan attacks in pursuit of keeping man's soul from saving faith in Jesus. He knows he's defeated, so his obsession is to take as many souls to hell with himself as possible. Satan hates us, because God loves us. He doesn't care for man. People who worship Satan, somehow believing Satan will reward their service are seriously and gravely deceived.

Satan will be unable to save those in hell, because he will be there as well. Nor will he care that anyone is there anyway, beyond the satisfaction that he kept them from heaven. So it won't be about their service or loyalty to him, it will always be about his pride and obsession to get back at God.

Satan will never rule over God. He will never reign as a conquering foe. Good has already won. God tarries in eliminating evil once and for all, because He wants every person to accept Jesus as their Savior and to be with Him eternally.

There are many religions circulating within prison. If not teaching the Bible and Jesus as our Redeemer, then it's a false religion, orchestrated by Satan to deceive. Satan has found a playground in prison. He's delighted that evil deeds sends the persons God loves to prison. Because once there, it's very hard to see the good.

But, again, Satan isn't God's equal in this war. Take encouragement in this when it seems evil is always winning. Do not be deceived that all is lost. All power is held by God. Pray for prisoners' eyes to be opened to God's saving grace. Pray they be no longer deceived by Satan's tactics to keep their soul from the nurturing, loving, and saving love of God through Jesus.

☩

November 6 — The Good Influence

Proverbs 21:9

It is better to live in a corner of a roof, than in a house shared with a contentious woman.

    I came across a book at a thrift store that struck a familiar chord. I puzzled, "Where do I know this book from?" I then recalled having checked it out at the local library several years before. The version I held in my hand at the thrift store donned "Bestseller" and came "Recommended" from a famous celebrity. Strangely, I couldn't recall much about the story. I wonder if my impression of the book would have been different if I knew it was a bestseller before I began reading. Maybe the anticipation of quality would have impacted how I experienced the book. Maybe I would have paid more attention to the details or allowed myself quality time in which to enjoy the book better. Quite possibly.

    This effect can be a good way to approach our marriages. If we believe that the good in our husbands is there, we will be more apt to find it. Maybe we will focus more on the details of his life or spend more quality time with him if we see the value in investing the time.

    There's good or you wouldn't have married him. There was something that attracted you to him. It's still there, but you may be "reading" him as if he's an unadorned, back shelf find at a thrift store. You may be finding all that's wrong and your relationship becomes likely a series of arguments based on these points.

    Proverbs teaches us that to constantly find fault and ignite arguments is unwise. In doing so, a husband finds basically anywhere else better than living under such constant disagreement. He seeks escape. Although in prison, his escape will result in a further emotional distance.

    We all risk falling into this pattern of correcting and harping on issues. They are in prison so there are certainly issues! But to focus on the things lacking in our spouses or the wrongs done by them (from our perception) does nothing but create further separation that we already fight against because of prison.

    When was the last time you could easily list things that you love about your husband? Consider specific things he has done recently to show you love. Make a point to communicate these things to him. Try to avoid always finding fault, while also looking for the good. Show him that he's valued. He needs to know that you still think of him as a bestseller. If you do this, you'll likely find the story reads like it is.

November 7 Concrete Images

Isaiah 28:16

Therefore thus says the Lord God, "Behold, I am laying in Zion a stone, a tested stone, a costly cornerstone for the foundation, firmly placed. He who believes in it will not be disturbed."

The backdrop for most every prison photo I've seen is cement. Sure there's a painted landscape or something to lessen the sterile setting, but it's still cement. When my uncle was in prison many years ago, you could stand in front of a poster taped to the cement of a swimsuit model in a tropical scene. I'm sure there weren't many wives thrilled with a permanent image of that either.

Isaiah was giving us a picture of Jesus in the verse today. Jesus even referred to Himself as the stone rejected by the builders. He describes Himself as the cornerstone. A cornerstone in the foundation determines the sound placement of all the other blocks. The quality begins with the cornerstone.

Jesus used Isaiah's prophecy and that of the psalmist (Psalm 118:22) when sharing a parable about a landowner who goes away and leaves tenants in charge of his crop and property (Matthew 21:33-46). When ready for harvest, he sends servants to redeem some of the produce, but the tenants assault or kill each servant that he sends. So the owner decides to send his son, thinking they will surely respect him. Yet, just as with the others, they kill his son. Jesus then presents the question: What will the owner do with the tenants when he comes. The people respond that the owner will destroy the tenants and obtain new tenants.

This parable was directed to the religious leaders at the time due to their severe rejection of Jesus and ultimate plot to have Him killed. The servants in the parable represent the prophets who were sent ahead of His coming, but who were persecuted and killed for their message. Because the Jews rejected Jesus, the Gospel was taken to the Gentiles (the new tenants). The Apostle Paul primarily preached to the Gentiles, and he referenced the Old Testament verses when speaking in Acts 4:11: "He is the stone which was rejected by you, the builders, but which became the very corner stone."

Paul went on to say in verse 12: "And there is salvation in no one else; for there is no other name under heaven that has been given among men, by which we must be saved."

So the next time you stand before that decorated cement with your husband, consider Jesus is the costly cornerstone and thank Him for your salvation. This remains your hope regardless of how many such images you have taken over the years or the number to come.

November 8 Safe in Jesus

Philippians 3:1

Finally, my brethren, rejoice in the Lord. To write the same things again is no trouble to me, and it is a safeguard for you.

Passwords are a necessity of doing life online. They have become increasingly more needed to safeguard your personal information and against misuse of your accounts. The risks demand more complex combination of characters than ever before. Similarly, you cannot trust all the emails you receive even if the sender appears to be a friend. There are persons out there whose primary goal is to infiltrate the safeguards in place for harmful purposes. The best you can do is do all you can to keep the safeguards secure.

In chapter three of Philippians, Paul reiterates a warning to the Christians in Philippi to beware of the false religions and people who were opposing the Gospel. He comments that it's no trouble for him to repeat himself, because the issue was of upmost importance and safeguards were needed.

There were people of his time whose goal was to nullify Paul's preaching and spread harmful beliefs. They were aggressive in their tactics, trying to slander his testimony and the Gospel. They were the legalistic who attached themselves to tradition and the religious laws made by man. Paul distinguishes true belief from their false. Yet he's also quick to note that he claims no confidence in his flesh, only in what he has through Jesus. Jesus was his ultimate safeguard against the threats and his assurance of salvation.

Paul encouraged the Christians to stand firm in what they knew to be the truth. Not to be deceived by or overcome by the evil working against them. Paul wanted them to stay alert to the threats, but also be joyful. To him, there was no level of persecution that could remove joyfulness, because of the hope if one knows Jesus.

This world is threatening. There are no safe zones, even in the privacy of one's home. Worst yet, evil doers have an open door through the internet if a weakness is found. Yet, we cannot live in persistent anxiety of harm. God wants us to be joyful and trust Him with things that are beyond our control. Many things of prison are beyond our control, but we can respond to reasonable concerns, like we do with our personal information, and commit the rest to the Lord for safekeeping.

November 9 *Hard Work*

I Thessalonians 2:9

For you recall, brethren, our labor and hardship, how working night and day so as not to be a burden to any of you, we proclaimed to you the gospel of God.

Paul made tents as a way to earn income while he evangelized. He likely did other types of manual labor too, depending on the circumstances and needs at the time. He wasn't above working hard. Scripture is clear that we are to work. Laziness is rebuked, just like get-rich-quick efforts. Honest work for honest pay should be our goal. God designed and purposed us to be productive.

Your husband may have been the only wage earner at the time of his incarceration. While there are likely complicating variables to replacing that income, getting a job should be part of the consideration. And likely you do work. But in case you do not, consider this an opportunity to explore options or set new goals.

Prayerfully consider how God has gifted and designed you. Maybe this is your opportunity to pursue that life-long dream, but you never had the motivation. It's said: "Necessity is the mother of invention," but so it can be with a job path. Realize that God knows your needs. Pray that He would open the door to that job that's out there.

Maybe getting a new skill or trade would be of interest. Furthering your education possibly. There's an abundance of options online these days. Get excited about learning something new which could also help add some cash to your budget. Local career centers can also help with assessing your skills, writing resumes, and interviewing. A center can often connect you with employers in your area.

And if working outside the home is simply not an option, that's okay. Just be honest in your motivations for that choice. If it's more of a desire than a need, then you could possibly be missing a great opportunity God has planned in the redemption of your circumstance. If income isn't a concern then you're blessed, and you have wonderful opportunities to serve others without the burden of financial stressors. Go for it!

Be productive with the time while your husband is away — out of necessity or desire. Work hard in or outside the home. Many of you likely do both. You're to be commended on your strength and work ethic. God will continue to direct your days and provide in response to your faithfulness to what He has entrusted you with. Your skills and opportunities are under His sovereign care.

November 10 *The Drifter*

Joshua 2:18

"Unless, when we come into the land, you tie this cord of scarlet thread in the window through which you let us down, and gather to yourself into the house your father and your mother and your brothers and all your father's household."

I was living in a rural area, unemployed, broke, and facing a circumstantial "eviction" because my house was no longer going to be offered as a rental. I also faced giving up my pets in the fallout. I had no contact with my husband through it all, because he was in confinement — as usual. I sat dismayed and wondered why God had allowed it all to happen. I was highly discouraged and quite frankly having a bountiful pity party. I only invited God so I could pour out my woes to Him.

Nothing was right in my life that day. I even whined about the way I looked, from my homely sweatpants and ratty shirt to the multiple blemishes beaming from my face. I felt horribly unattractive and my mood matched. Then came the knock at the door.

Oh, perfect! A visitor was the last thing I wanted. I was embarrassed for anyone to see me, nor was I emotionally up for company. But the knock was unavoidable. I called through the door, "Who is it?" The return voice was unfamiliar. "I'm looking for a friend," I heard her say.

I guess it would seem foolish, but I opened the door and saw before me a raggedly dressed woman. She was unkempt to say the least. Her face was blemished by a large sore on her cheekbone. Yet despite her appearance, she was wearing a smile. The old woman repeated that she was looking for a friend by the name of "Angela …" The last name I couldn't make out. All I knew was that I was not the Angela she was looking for.

She proceeded to explain that she was walking along the road and saw my car and thought possibly it looked like the one her friend drove. I assured her I didn't know of the person she sought. She thanked me and walked away. I closed the door.

I was overcome with the oddness of the whole encounter. And it struck me: in every way that I felt ugly in my appearance, she looked worse. Down to the same place on her face where I had my worst blemish. And who walks along a country road looking for a friend who happens to have the same name as me?

I immediately went outside in further curiosity and looked to see if she was truly walking. But the lady was nowhere to be seen. Maybe she had already traveled to the next house and someone was answering her same questions as I had. Maybe she actually had driven, despite my not hearing the vehicle. But the next day upon coming home there lay upon the doorstep a scarlet-colored ribbon. Where did that come from? And then it struck me.

I had just read in my Bible study about the scarlet thread Rahab tied to her window to distinguish her home from the others which would spare her family in the attack detailed in Joshua. Within the footnote for that verse, the commentator had written that the scarlet thread was often seen as a symbol of salvation to both Christ's messengers and those whom they visit.

My heart skipped a beat. I knew God had sent me a messenger. An angel? There are no female angels mentioned in Scripture. So I do not believe so. I only know that God showed up in a very real way to assure me of His presence, His personal interest in all my concerns that day—and my not-right life as I saw it to be. I think He was also reminding me of the simple truth that He's my friend.

I came away feeling wowed by the intimacy of God and comforted. God used a cheerful drifter, who looked worse in dress and complexion, to give me a fresh perspective of my troubles and to simply say, "I love you, Angela. I got you."

If you ever need a "hug" on this journey of prison, there's no greater hugger than God. In all of life's trials, He can comfort like no other. He will even send a stranger to your door if need be.

☩

November 11 The Mind's War

II Corinthians 11:23

Are they servants of Christ? (I speak as if insane) I more so; in far more labors, in far more imprisonments, beaten times without number, often in danger of death.

My uncle was a veteran. He was also a death row inmate. He had full-blown PTSD from his military service which included two tours in Vietnam. He was executed in 1993 despite being psychologically damaged at the time of the murder which placed him on death row. My husband, on the other hand, has been psychologically damaged from his cumulative years incarcerated. He refers to it as Present Traumatic Stress Disorder.

Over twenty years in prison has resulted in countless negative experiences which have impacted him on all levels: emotionally, spiritually, and physically. His eyes have witnessed trauma. He has been a victim; he has been a perpetrator of harm like a soldier from the need to survive in a hostile environment. If soldiers can be diagnosed with PTSD from time-limited service in a threatening environment, surely men incarcerated with no end to the tour of duty can experience the same.

But in the name of security and justice, men are expected to rehabilitate despite psychological damage being done to them at the same time. Sadly, many who achieve release are in worse shape than before they arrived. They return home with all the scars from a battle.

I consider all that Paul experienced in his service to God: persecution, beatings, imprisonment, and trauma at sea. He lived under constant threats. He writes that he went hungry, naked, and despaired even unto death at some points. But at the end of his life, again a prisoner, he presents himself through his writings as being psychologically strong and at peace.

Paul countered all the negative experiences through the power of the Holy Spirit. God was in active service through every moment of Paul's service. This is clear through his testimony. He attributes no strength to himself.

I do not think Paul was immune from damage, but the events of his life more so shaped and emboldened his faith. They didn't bury him in psychological wounds.

Few have the faith of Paul. But men in prison can learn from him the preservation skills to limit the damage prison inherently projects on a person. God is the best treatment for the present stressors your husband lives within. He's the best ally in the battle. He's the best prescription for any "post" symptoms which make coming home more complicated. Professional support has its place, but without Christ, it will always be missing what only God can accomplish in the heart and mind of the one wounded.

November 12 New Heart Desire

Ezekiel 36:26

"Moreover, I will give you a new heart and put a new spirit within you; and I will remove the heart of stone from your flesh and give you a heart of flesh."

I surprise myself in how hard an exterior I can put around my heart. It can be there from bitterness, resentment, distrust, or frustrated exhaustion. My aloofness in emotions is sadly satisfying at times. In essence, I shut down and shut people out. To withhold conversation, emotion, or interest accomplishes what my heart desires and what I know would be improper to speak. It's comfortable being distant. But I also recognize that such a heart doesn't please God.

A cold heart hinders the work God wants to do through me. It has the potential to harm my witness. Both rob God of the opportunities He purposes to produce fruit in my life or that in someone else. And despite knowing when the "temperature" of my interactions with someone is dropping quickly, my cold heart can still be stubbornly defiant. I can confidently allow the interaction to run its course with the cool air escaping with my limited words.

Ezekiel's words to Israel teach me who is needed to replace my cold heart with a godlier one: the Holy Spirit. He will always be the key to a heart change. It's by the Holy Spirit that I'm able to overcome the negative ways I may treat others when I disengage emotionally. Warning bells sound at the same time I begin to savor the sin which is at the heart of my ungodly heart moments. This is the Holy Spirit alerting me to the wrong reaction I'm feeding.

Ironically, I more often allow the Holy Spirit to curb my reactions toward my husband, while everyone else gets the mute feature of my personality. I think it's because I enjoy my husband. I value our relationship more. It's easier for me to forgive and to extend grace to him than others. It's a lot harder to voluntarily participate in a positive heart change when the person on the other end is someone I would rather avoid altogether. I run from such "growth" opportunities. It's more satisfying to be bitter or angry at someone.

Maybe you can relate to this struggle. Prison marriages are hard, but other relationships can be too when God's standard is applied to them. This consideration keeps me humble to my husband's struggle in reacting with the right heart to the relationships he faces each day. His are, quite frankly, more challenging than any I typically face. I understand when he fails in this area. Would I fare any different? Success for any of us only comes by surrendering to the help of the Holy Spirit.

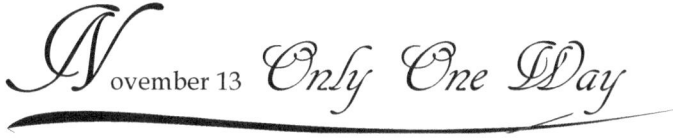

November 13 *Only One Day*

II Corinthians 6:14

Do not be bound together with unbelievers; for what partnership have righteousness and lawlessness, or what fellowship has light with darkness?

Being unequally yoked is a familiar concept in Christian circles. Most times we think of it in terms of marriage. A Christian shouldn't marry outside the faith. There are sound reasons for this. God purposed marriage as a team for His glory and purposes. This cannot be accomplished if the spouses have different spiritual beliefs. There are also the conflicts which will arise about how the children will be raised. So, most agree like-minded faith is best.

But I've also found that being at different points spiritually causes its own type of conflicts that make a Christian marriage hard. The prison culture even further complicates it, and puts me and my husband at odds. I go one direction while he pulls another. He attempts to pull me to follow his prison-accepted path, while I'm using all my energy to keep from being dragged that way.

We are locked together by the same yoke willingly, because we love each other and chose to be married. Both Christians, but at different points in our relationship with God. There can be tension when the path comes to a crossroad of decision. A yoked pair can only go one direction. We can see the path differently, experience different levels of conviction, and battle for our positions.

As wives, we must not give up the battle. We need to be that light and accountable voice for God's path. It will take a lot more energy to resist than giving into the pull your husband may be placing on you. You may not always win. But keep walking within the yoke of your marriage toward God. Pray for your husband's surrender to the right path.

By God's grace, harmony will increase in the travels with your husband. Tension will subside, and the energy required to walk toward God will lessen. Hopefully, your husband will actually begin to pull you that way in his desire to be on the right path, leading the way.

Trust that God is on your side. His will is for both of you to draw near to Him. Your husband may see the yoke as a ball and chain some days in the conflict it can create, but in the end, he will be so thankful that you never let him off easy to go the way of the prison.

November 14 Happy Birthday

Jeremiah 1:5

"Before I formed you in the womb, I knew you, and before you were born I consecrated you; I have appointed you a prophet to the nations."

Today is my brother's birthday. Growing up, birthdays weren't really celebrated with huge significance. They were recognized and some atypical food or occasional "party" orchestrated, but mostly they were low-keyed.

God, on the other hand, never saw our births as just another day. Happy Birthday! truly was an excited exclaim on the day you were not only conceived, but born. It was divinely timed from an extraordinary perspective. Your life was planned with astounding forethought. The purpose linked to the time of your birth should excite you too.

It also may bring a solemn reflection if, like me, much of your life has been off the mark despite being relatively "good" from society's perspective. You may consider the years possibly wasted by not being close to God as you are now.

But it's never too late to redeem your birthday. God is still eager to grow you up into the purpose that He designed before you were even born. As Jeremiah says, God knew you before you were born. His life plan for you was determined before you were conceived. Jeremiah was to be a prophet. You're gifted for a calling as well. Your entrance into this world had God's blessing on it.

This is true for your husband too. But it may be even more difficult for him to see his birth as that astounding and important. He may not see any good that came from his birth or childhood. Sin may have robbed him of it. However, God can and desires to redeem the awesome birthday plan for your husband too. Others may share his same birthday, but he was uniquely made and delivered on that day for reasons only he can fulfill. God knows why and longs to bring it to fruition.

Celebrate birthdays with a new perspective. See the awesome connection to a timeline of events that your life impacted at your first breath, and that of your husband's.

November 15 *Accidental Message*

Matthew 26:27-28

And when He had taken a cup and given thanks, He gave it to them, saying, "Drink from it, all of you; for this is My blood of the covenant, which is poured out for many for forgiveness of sins."

I accepted the communion tray and grasped the tiny plastic container filled with grape juice. Problem was it wouldn't release from the tray. Wedged in or stuck by residual juice I didn't know, but I fought against the little shell thinking it should surely pull free. Well, it did. But not without some spillage. I whispered to the usher, "I'm sorry." He responded in an equally hushed tone, "That's alright."

The interaction swept over and through me in a way only recognized as the Holy Spirit. That accidental interaction was a picture of why I was taking communion in the first place: Jesus spilt His blood for my sin. My acceptance of this through "I'm sorry," is met with His "That's alright."

I'm forever alright because of what Jesus did for me. No matter what comes to me He's with me forever, and He has reserved my place with Him in heaven. Nothing in this world can change that.

I needed that message that Sunday morning. I awoke to a solemn and troubled heart for so many things. That morning, tears came easily while I sat with coffee, simply sitting before the Lord in my morning routine. I just wanted to remain there forever. But life awaited. As it has every morning — whether I want it to or not.

That Sunday I knew all that communion represented. I understood my salvation and Jesus's sacrifice. But thankfully God knew that I needed a closer, more intimate reminder of His presence and provision. His message stirred in the same heart that had trouble facing the day.

God is intimate with your days too. Your fragility is known to Him. He's compassionate and understands why your heart might be struggling even today. He wants you to remember His presence and provision. Jesus paid with His own life to give you both. He willingly did it, because He loves you that much.

 November 16 *Small Reminders*

Matthew 10:31

"Therefore do not fear; you are of more value than many sparrows."

A walk through a busy parking lot often sends birds fluttering away from their survey of the area for crumbs and edible remnants of the customers' walks to or from their vehicles. It seems their daily hangout to scavenge a meal. I hadn't really noticed any birds on such a mission where I was working, which made my notice of such more pronounced when I walked to my car that afternoon. Sparrows perfectly spaced around my car, as if they were set to lift it and carry it away as pall bearers would a coffin. They were not hopping around; they were just sitting calmly, each in its place.

It wasn't a foreboding feeling in my spirit at the sight of those tiny birds. It was an immediate sense of peace and protection. God spoke to my heart that I was in His care. He reminded me that I was so incredibly valuable to Him. It was the message of the verse above. I'm more valuable to sparrows in God's eyes.

Scripture speaks of God's knowledge and interest in every living thing: plants, wildlife, people, birds, including the tiniest activity of a sparrow such as one in a busy parking lot. Nothing escapes His knowledge. He knows the very number of hairs on my head to every thought. With this, He also knows my every worry.

He knows your every worry. And whatever it's today, He's got you surrounded in love. His love for you is greater than many sparrows which in Jesus's time were valued at mere pennies. If He watches over one valueless sparrow in the expanse of this great world, you can be assured He's watching over your life.

Do not forget how big God is. The power He possesses sustains all creation. Yet His power gently abides in your life through His willingness and desire to share your day and help you through whatever you face.

November 17 — Out of Harm's Reach

Psalm 27:5-6

For in the day of trouble He will conceal me in His tabernacle; in the secret place of His tent He will hide me; He will lift me up on a rock. And now my head will be lifted up above my enemies around me; and I will offer in His tent sacrifices with shouts of joy; I will sing, yes, I will sing praises to the Lord.

When my dog was a puppy, she was thoroughly attached to my presence. She followed me room to room — constantly. If I ever slipped out of her vision, I could hear her scurrying throughout the house looking for me. When she met my mother-n-law's dogs for the first time, their surrounding interest was too much for her. She extended herself upwards, resting her front paws on my legs, with a pleading facial expression to rescue her from the foe she believed the other dogs to be. And once lifted into my arms, high above the pack, her anxiety lessened, and she was quite content to remain there. I was her security in all circumstances.

This is how God wants us to feel about Him. He wants us to seek His presence in all situations. And when we are fearful, He wants us to know we are confidently held in His arms and protected.

He's faithful as David wrote in the psalms. David rejoiced in God's protection and love. He was rescued repeatedly from harm's reach and he recognized God as his ultimate defense. When others abandoned him and he felt alone in his hurt and hardship, David knew God had not forsaken him.

Prison seems always like that circling foe, whether for true harm or the residual weight of all it brings into your life. It's hard to relax when harm seems it could reach out and touch your life at any moment — or that of your husband's. You need the circling security of God's presence and protection to settle into while on this journey. It will bring peace and joy and a solid height from which you view your circumstances.

And you'll never outgrow your need for God. A puppy usually gains independence, much like a child, and distance becomes more comfortable. This is fine if you're a dog. But God's children learn it's best to remain close, because the days of trouble will come. When close, you need only look up to be assured you're safe. The enemy may keep an eye of interest on you, but you're safe in God's arms, high above the harm.

November 18 — True & Faithful God

Judges 3:26

Now Ehud escaped while they were delaying, and he passed by the idols and escaped to Seirah.

Ehud was a judge appointed by God to deliver Israel from an oppressive enemy. This time it was Moab. The Israelites were enslaved to Moab for eighteen years, because they once again "did evil in the sight of the Lord" (verse 12). God extended compassion when they cried out to Him. With Ehud's anointing, he plotted and killed the king of Moab. Chapter 3 includes the description of how he gained access to the king and subsequently stabbed him to death. As Ehud fled the scene, Scripture includes the detail that he "passed by the idols." It's a stunning detail that speaks volumes.

Moab was an idolatrous nation. The people worshipped mere images such as statues and small carvings. They were fashioned by man with no real spiritual power. They were dependent on man to be made and to be moved from one spot to another. They were simply objects. Their true lack of power is magnified by the detail that Ehud ran passed the idols during his escape.

The idols didn't respond or come to the king's rescue. They didn't warn the king of the threat approaching. The idols didn't prevent Ehud from leaving. They were no threat to him, because they possessed no power. They simply stood in place and remained lifeless—as they had always been.

The people of Moab put their faith in false gods. God became angry with the Israelites when they worshipped the same. In the end, the false gods couldn't rescue. They couldn't help the king; they couldn't rescue the Israelites.

There's only one, true God in this world. Today's idols of money, status, position, and material possessions can never touch the awesome power of God. There's no authority higher than God. Putting anything on a pedestal above God is the heart's equivalent to the physical idols Ehud passed.

Many things fight for our attention and admiration. We easily misplace secure feelings. We attach them to earthly things or even people. We easily make idols of hobbies, celebrities, and technology. We may place more faith in a well-known attorney than God. We may depend on connections to better our husbands' or our own standard of living. We remove God from

His rightful place and cease to depend on and to worship Him as He commands, deserves, and desires.

Ehud walked into the king's chamber—and out—under the sovereign power of God. As judge over Israel, he kept God at the center of the Israelite community. You need God's true power to successfully walk in and out of this season of prison. You can rely on Him to respond to your cries and your needs. He sees and works for your best interest. He also desires to stay at the center of your life, even long after your rescue.

 November 19 *Embrace the Wait*

Psalm 37:3

Trust in the Lord, and do good; dwell in the land and cultivate faithfulness.

Prison provides an ironic opportunity in its extended wait to enrich our faith. It's not a one-time difficulty that we push through and get over. There are multiple difficulties over an expanse of time that seem to crawl along at a snail's pace. It's within those daily, exceedingly slow moments that we have to choose God over the idle frustrations within the wait.

In the verse above, David writes to "dwell in the land." Chapter thirty-seven focuses on God's faithfulness despite the apparent success of the wicked. God hasn't forsaken those who trust in Him. The land may be filled with evil and those who delight in doing wrong, but he tells us to basically hunker down and trust God. Do not run from the bad. Do not abandon your faith. Instead, turn your energy toward Almighty God and invest your time in the things of God.

Enrich your faith during this time of prison by reading Scripture more fervently. Seek God's heart for how He wants you to spend this time. When the day brings a greater bad than the usual, trust in the mightier power of God to handle the situation on your behalf and within His perfect will. Dig deep into the truth of what you know about God; do not try to escape by the path not in His will.

The more you remain steadfast in your faith within the land of prison, the greater your faith will grow. Make your life all about God, not prison. Make your faith a priority, and you'll see God do wonderful things within this wait.

Your life or marriage may not have turned out as you planned, but God can take the bad of your life and use it for good. He can make your husband useful from whatever circumstance that may seem hopeless to you right now. He's the perfect travel guide in this life, even if life's path now takes you routinely through prison gates. You can walk confidently — with peace — through those gates and in your exit to your everyday life.

Embrace the waiting by cultivating your faith. You cannot remove prison at this season, so allow God to use the season for an astounding work in your life and that of your husband's. Remove the victory of the wicked by surrendering the battle to God. It isn't a weaker position, but a faithful one which will only become stronger as you stand firm.

November 20 *When Words Fail*

Psalm 34:18

The Lord is near to the brokenhearted, and saves those who are crushed in spirit.

Some days you may not be in any mood to read these devotionals. You may be actually catching up on a few because you just couldn't bear to read a genre of uplifting words this week. Maybe you began reading, but quickly slammed it shut, saying to yourself, "Blah, blah, blah!"

This describes me on some days. The deep unrest in my spirit or mood doesn't absorb cheerful or hopeful moments spread across a page. Even my favorite devotionals leave me unsatisfied. I know the devotionals reflect truth, but I'm in no place in my heart to hear it. I have a deeper need that it cannot reach.

When I'm depressed, angry, and heavily frustrated, moving toward an outcome of feeling encouraged and cheerful is unappealing. It's those shameful moments when I'd rather remain in my low mood, because doing otherwise frankly takes too much energy. So devotionals remain unread until God nurses me back from my spiritual stupor. And He faithfully does this through His word and presence.

God gets the worst of me at those times, but He lovingly listens to my complaints. He knows how to encourage me when a devotional cannot. He's intimate with the core of why I feel as I do in the first place. This special place is for Him alone to heal — in the perfect way He knows I need.

And that's why I say these devotionals aren't to be a replacement for your time in Scripture. They supplement it, but are never meant to be the means to satisfy all your spiritual needs. They can never replace God's presence and meditating within it. They can never replace your prayers.

God does use devotionals. I love how He orchestrates their reading at sometimes the most brilliant moments. They can spark deeper study of His word. They can refresh your perspective. I wouldn't write a devotional book if I didn't believe in how God uses them. But I also recognize its limits.

When you're hurting the deepest and struggling the most to stay positive, keep seeking God when the words of these pages are inadequate. He remains active in your life through prayer, Scripture, and His presence. Other sources may seem dull when at your lowest, but God is never dull. He can breathe life back into your mood and days when no one else can.

So welcome back! Or I'll see you in a few days.

November 21 Revive Us

Habakkuk 3:2

Lord, I have heard the report about Thee and I fear. O Lord, revive Thy work in the midst of the years, in the midst of the years make it known; in wrath remember mercy.

It's difficult to see a future blessed with goodness when facing years of incarceration. Just getting to the future seems a mountain blocking even the sun of what may lie on the other side of it. Days seem dampened by the dreary rain from clouds that never move along. But I believe most of us do not want to arrive to the other side the same as how we arrived. Neither for us or our husbands. We want a new and good start. We want to see the sun, but without the same mountain of reasons why prison arrived in the first place.

Habakkuk expressed his heart for God's mercy in the midst of Israel's punishment. He desired redemption from the bad. They had been enslaved by Babylon through God's allowance due to their rebellion against Him. Their captivity would last many years. But Habakkuk clung to God's faithfulness and His word that they would be revived.

Within the years of hardship, Habakkuk knew Israel couldn't remain as they were. Their heart needed revival to leave their captivity a different people. And in that process, he prayed for God's mercy, knowing it would only be through God's mercy, because Israel—quite frankly—didn't deserve it. Surrendering to God was the way to reach the other side a better people.

Prison holds the same opportunity. The pressures and hardships can shape our heart for the better if surrendered to God. It would be a shame to leave the same way we arrived. I want to overcome the mountain and see the sun, not the same clouds.

And I know I will, because God is faithful. He revives my heart daily, within each day of this journey, to bring me closer to the good. He's merciful in the process, forgiving my stumbles up the mountain through my wrong choices and sin. I must endure the years along with my husband, but within them a new and fresh start is being prepared. You can count on God's faithfulness as well.

November 22 The Trap of Bitterness

Ephesians 4:31

Let all bitterness and wrath and anger and clamor and slander be put away from you, along with all malice.

You have probably encountered a bitter person during your unending wait at the gate. You might see yourself in this description. She's the person complaining at length about the wait, criticizing the officers and the system, huffing and puffing at any interruption that further delays being processed into the prison. She makes negative jokes about the incompetence of the officers working. She conveys they are the single cause for the delay. Furthermore, they are intentionally doing it to make her suffer. This wasn't such a person's first visit to a prison.

Who knows where the bitterness was a seed in her life, but prison came along and embittered her further. There was one injustice that she couldn't get over. It went unchecked, and because of our sinful nature, the seed began to sprout. With time, a root emerged and eventually the person standing before you in line was created.

This is the danger in allowing a negative and resentful thought to sit in your mind; it doesn't just lay idle and lifeless. It feeds on itself until another cause of injustice is placed on top of it. This gives it more to feed on. The soil then gets well tilled for the next injustice, another similar conversation, or extensive wait.

I hate the waits too; however, complaining isn't going to move things along quicker. I do not perfectly manage my frustrations either, but when I start to get increasingly frustrated, I may sigh, but I know I'm responsible for my reaction to the situation. So I intentionally defer my focus.

I often use the time for prayer. I pray for my husband, I pray for the officers I see working, and I pray for the embittered person in front of me complaining. I may start a conversation with someone who seems to be timid with the surroundings to try to put them at ease. One time, I softly sang hymns to God, praising Him, to endure the biting wind gusts that were accompanying the forty-degree dreariness of rain. I find anything to keep bitterness from finding a place to settle. I have a lifetime of such waits before me. The waits cannot become more important than the reason I'm there.

Paul teaches in Ephesians that bitterness grieves the Holy Spirit. It hurts God's heart. It hurts you too. Bitterness is related to an unforgiving attitude. It stresses you physically and emotionally. It makes you a miserable person and a miserable person to be around. It will make this prison journey seem eternal.

Bitterness is the challenge for our hearts when faced with prison. There are plenty of injustices. But try standing in line with a different perspective. It will free you from a prison of another sort, and you'll find more peace in this journey.

November 23 — Desert Supplies

Deuteronomy 2:7

"For the Lord your God has blessed you in all that you have done; He has known your wanderings through this great wilderness. These forty years the Lord your God has been with you; you have not lacked a thing."

The desert is often described in Scripture as a "wilderness." We think of a desert as an unwelcoming place. Nothing thrives in the desert. A desert has few, if any, natural provisions. To survive, provisions have to be brought into it or received from beyond that landscape. In the verse for today, Moses was recounting how God provided for the Israelites during their desert wanderings. It conveys that life and provisions were out of reach, except through God's divine orchestration.

The Israelites brought provisions when they initially fled Egypt, but these wouldn't sustain them through the years they faced. Eventually, their resources were depleted, and they seemed nowhere near arriving at the Promised Land. They hated the circumstances, but were really at the mercy of their situation. Sadly, only a few of their number recognized God's role in coming through victoriously.

Prison can definitely be a vast desert. The years ahead will require God's provisions. You may enter this journey full of hope and confidence and your own "provisions," but prison has a way of wearing you down. Like the scorching, dry heat in the desert, it's the daily reality. Once you're out of hope and confidence, the landscape provides nothing to replenish you. It will let you perish in the statistics of broken marriages.

God, however, will watch over you with blessings if you let Him. He will be your source for life. He can infuse your journey with the nutrients you need to sustain your marriage and your hope. Your struggles aren't hidden from Him. He sees your good and bad days. He knows how you have been treated at all points along the way. He knows how thirsty you are for refreshment. You'll find that He's all you need when you have nothing else. You can keep walking through the wilderness, and survive, with God walking with you. He carries a full supply of anything you might need along the way.

November 24 *Loads of Thanks*

Luke 7:47

"For this reason I say to you, her sins, which are many, have been forgiven, for she loved much; but he who is forgiven little, loves little."

I still find myself thanking God for my washer and dryer. As I toss in a load even these many years since their purchase, I say a word of thanks to God that I have them. After thirteen years of hauling loads to the local Laundromat in every type of weather, I appreciate immensely the luxury of the convenience I now have. No more purchasing rolls of quarters knowing the change machine would be most likely out of order, no more strategies to snag the best dryer, no more hours spent on a plastic seat supervising a load's completion while watching unsupervised kids run amuck around the place.

Gratitude is often equal to how great a need has been met. Going without a washer and dryer all those years made me all the more grateful for the set I finally was able to purchase.

The verse above follows a parable Jesus told Simon, a Pharisee who was hosting a meal for Jesus in his home. During the meal, a woman entered and began wetting Jesus's feet with her tears. She then wiped them with her hair, kissed them, and poured perfume on them. Scripture seems to indicate this woman was a prostitute, although it doesn't say explicitly. Simon was indignant toward Jesus thinking it was not proper to allow such a "sinner" to touch Him. She was a lowlife in Simon's eyes.

Jesus told Simon a parable about two debtors. One owed a lot of money; the other little. Both were unable to pay back the money, so the moneylender graciously forgave all their debt. Jesus's question to Simon: Which of them therefore will love the moneylender more? Simon answered, "The one whom he forgave more."

Jesus did know all about the woman's sin. And she apparently did too! Because of the greatness of her sin, she sought forgiveness, and Jesus's forgiveness was graciously given. The love she expressed to Jesus matched her need.

Being a Pharisee, Simon was bent toward pointing out someone else's sin, ignorant to his own. Simon didn't see his true level of need for Jesus, thus he didn't express love or thankfulness to Him to the extent the woman did.

Once we recognize where we have been and what the Lord has done for us, gratitude follows. The greater the sin, often the greater the gratitude. The longer the wait, the more appreciative of the arrival.

You may have loads of sin that you have been carrying for years. Jesus wants to remove the burden, cost, and wasted time. He wants to forgive your sin. And in doing so, your thanksgiving going forward will be found in the realization of the eternal life you possess.

November 25 *Purposeful Pain*

II Timothy 4:5

But you, be sober in all things, endure hardship, do the work of an evangelist, fulfill your ministry.

I do not do pain very well. Prolonged physical discomfort exhausts my mood, and I persistently complain within the persistent aches. I believe that it takes a great character to overcome physical distress that never leaves. I think of those with chronic disabilities and pain, or prisoners of war who experienced traumatic abuse over extended periods of time. My pitiful efforts to endure pale in comparison to the sometime lifetime discomforts of such persons. I seem to endure emotional distress far better than physical ones. And maybe that's the outcome of how God blends our personality and our experiences. He orchestrates both ultimately for His glory. Once we recognize that, the pain of whatever our circumstances can be endured with greater success.

I used to plead with God to change my heart to one less emotional or fragile to tears. I used to admire the emotional "cinder blocks" of those unmoved by the emotional. But God never answered that prayer the way I wanted at the time. And I'm okay with that—now. I see the good He can do with a fragile heart. A cinder block heart would have never stayed with my husband all these years. A cinder block heart wouldn't hold compassion for the prisoner or those impacted by his incarceration. I accept the emotional hardships of this journey, because God has proven Himself faithful to use and redeem and bless through the difficulties. I trust that's how those with physical struggles overcome theirs.

I cannot live someone else's journey. Nor was I meant to. I can be inspired by another's success over challenges and apply as best I can their recommendations for victory, but I'm responsible for what God has called me to overcome. Maybe one day it will be physical discomfort. For now, I fail repeatedly at that type of endurance. I succeed better through this emotional journey of prison, because it's the cards I've been dealt. It's what God has purposed to be a ministry to others.

Whatever the "pain" your life provides, God has fitted it to your purpose and personality. It's hard to embrace what you only want to disappear, but there remains tremendous blessing for you and others because of your journey. Prison likely holds a piece to your purpose. You might not do some types of pain very well, but I bet the pain of prison has success written all over it. If not, God wouldn't have brought you to it.

November 26 Justice for All

Micah 6:8

He has told you, O man, what is good; and what does the Lord require of you but to do justice, to love kindness, and to walk humbly with your God?

As the years progress, I've become more alerted to the inconsistencies and unreasonable sentencing of the system. Some have no record, yet make one mistake and are punished severely with prison. Others have multiple charges, yet are given yet another community opportunity to do right. Even with great evidence that harm was not intended, "justice" demands the unintended harm be paid for by someone. Families and communities cry for justice without interest in the devastating impact an unreasonable sentence has on a life—and those connected to it. The good isn't allowed a voice or to weigh the justice scales fairly.

God hates injustice. The book of Micah recounts God's indictment of the people through His prophet Micah about their ethical decline and moral corruption. God states His case against Israel who were oppressing the poor, cheating in business, and lying, while the leaders did nothing to intervene. So God did.

God punished the wicked in Micah's time. He will right every wrong committed in our day as well. Everyone will answer to God for this one life lived on earth. The righteous are rewarded; the wicked condemned. He allows injustice, but everything gets redeemed in the end. And that's good news!

God hasn't forgotten those in prison. He encourages us not to forget, especially those wrongly imprisoned and those persecuted for preaching about Jesus. Each life in prison matters to God, regardless of how they arrived. It matters to Him how a prison is operated and how those in charge choose to treat the persons living there. He gives hope to the wrongly accused. He restores the over-punitive sentences. He gives a voice to the victims of the system.

November 27 Is This Love?

Romans 8:35

Who shall separate us from the love of Christ? Shall tribulation, or distress, or persecution, or famine, or nakedness, or peril, or sword?

Some would argue a contradiction in this verse. If Christ loves us, why should we be experiencing tribulation, distress, and all the other horrible experiences of life in the first place? Paul wrote about Christ's love and firmly believed it was genuine, despite all the bad things that happened to him. It's a common struggle for our thinking, because we all know that love should be kind, merciful, selfless, right, lovely, and all the other positive descriptions that we also read in Scripture. If someone puts us through hardships, persecutes us unjustly, and treats us badly, we wouldn't describe them as loving. And that's just it. The sin within people causes those things to come, not Christ. God allows experiences, but He doesn't take pleasure in our pain.

This is key to remember when walking your journey of prison. A lot of bad exists any given day. But God's love is unchanging. This is the stable and secure foundation that holds your world together when everything crashes against it. If you're new on this journey, you're probably still reeling trying to get your body steady so you can even begin walking. What God is doing within your journey may not always be clear. Any Christian worth his or her salt would never tell you that it will be all the time. And why this peril of prison has entered your life now may seem total blackness in clarity.

But trust God's love. It hasn't left you. It remains as pure as always, undefiled by the world of problems around you. Take His hand in your swirling, and the steady, loving grip of Jesus will faithfully be there. Your pain isn't pleasing to Him; He hates the sin which has brought it into your life. He wants to bring you out of the mess and in the process, you'll have a deeper understanding of just how much He loves you.

So there's no contradiction when a loving God allows bad things like crime, prison sentences, and wives left alone on the outside. Like Paul, we can be assured that nothing prison can do to us will ever separate us from Christ's love. Prison takes a lot away, but Jesus has never left. Your faith is something no one can remove from you, and just as your faith is, there is your hope.

November 28 *Mental Mess*

Isaiah 42:11

Let the wilderness and its cities lift up their voices, the settlements where Kedar inhabits. Let the inhabitants of Sela sing aloud, let them shout for joy from the tops of the mountains.

Do you ever feel like you're a mental mess? I sure have. Usually one of my "fits" ends in tears to God, telling Him what a mess I am. My mental mess is really my mental stress being exacerbated by various things in the moment. Everything-going-wrong kind of moment. I also recognize (in hindsight) that Satan capitalizes on those moments to instill fear, doubt, and ultimately despair.

Sadly, he gets me to that point on some days. After I've allowed God to nurse me back to faith, I regret so much for not putting out Satan's fiery darts after the first one pierced me. But the reality is I'm often my worst enemy, not Satan. I just welcome him into my fit.

The snowball of thoughts descend with my mind jumping to the worst scenario. It's at these times that I'm almost glad that I live alone, and that my husband isn't a witness to such a decline in my mood. If I have to find a silver lining, that would be it. I get the opportunity to "work" on my attitude and heart, alone. Just God and me. I can fuss to God or to Him about myself without the restraining presence of another person.

But I also recognize the limitations on my spiritual growth when I surrender to a poor mood without even a personal filter to hinder the impact on no one else except really myself. Sometimes I excuse my words and actions with the stance that I have the right to throw a fit—look at everything that's going wrong!

But the reality is I'm hurting myself with my bleak outlook, even if I know deep down everything is okay. It's like any bad habit; I know it's bad, but I choose to do it anyway. Satan might sprinkle more kindling on the fire, but I usually start it—out of habit.

Changing a bad habit requires reminders and motivators. I had a friend who wore a rubber band on her wrist to remind her to refrain from making negative statements. Some people write notes and leave in pertinent places. Do whatever helps you, because we have to stay above our circumstances, not deep in our mental stupor under all the things wrong in our lives.

If you live alone, there's spiritual privacy. These can be precious opportunities for you to work on your mental messes as they accumulate in your head. If you can do it when no one is around, you're doing better than most of us! Rant praises, not complaints. Speak aloud of God's goodness, not fitful words of malice for another. As Isaiah says in the verse for today, "shout for joy!" You can be assured that less mess in your head helps clean up your outlook.

November 29 Consider Your Days

Haggai 1:5

Now therefore, thus says the Lord of hosts, "Consider your ways!"

It's ironic that the word "ways" in Hebrew is translated as "Derek," which is my husband's name. So every time I read it, I cannot help but replace his name with it. It's always amazing how God orchestrates my reading such verses as He also imparts thoughts to my heart. For today's verse, I was convicted with the reality that I had grown less focused on my husband's situation, God's purposes for him, and my role in both.

In some ways, you could equate it to taking a vacation. I was preoccupied with my own life, my own comforts. I had recently relocated, started a new job, and was in many ways, beginning to feel like I had a normal life. Prison was far from my reality, because I was physically away from it all, enjoying the positive changes I had been blessed with. But I soon heard the voice of God simply saying that my "normal" life isn't where He planned for me to be. "Consider your Derek!"

And I knew He was right. But it was just so much easier acting like prison was gone. But it was a false reality. And as God stirred my thoughts, He also orchestrated many other encounters which reminded me of what was important. Every day I was faced with the topic of prison, inmates, and prison ministry. In my heart, I said, "I know, Lord. I've been lazy about my purpose."

There's such a temptation to bow out of this whole prison thing. The accumulated stress and work it demands can get you feeling like, "I need a vacation!" But to enjoy its absence from the wrong motivation is dangerous. Thankfully, God doesn't allow us off the hook of purpose so easily.

And with this surrender comes peace that actually lasts and is deeper than the passing ease of days trying to escape God's call. Consider your husband and God's will for how He wants to use prison in your life for His glory. It's there; it just might seem further away with other things shielding its view. Do not be afraid to surrender to the life prison brings to you. As Haggai teaches us: building a life without a focus on God brings dissatisfaction. Our vacation efforts leave us ultimately wanting more of what can only be found back in the place where God is — and that place may be prison.

November 30 — Nothing Greater

Hebrews 13:6

So that we confidently say, "The Lord is my helper, I will not be afraid. What shall man do to me?"

Fear of rejection. It's with us it seems from an early age. It's what drives most teenagers toward certain people, choices, and behaviors. Adults struggle with it in their careers and relationships. Older folks are stigmatized and brushed aside. It's important to even loners to be accepted at least by someone. Behind everyone's personae, regardless of how confident, is a vulnerable place which can be wounded. Being married to a prisoner certainly presents uneasy interactions and uncertain outcomes on the acceptance meter.

Why does it matter? I suppose it shouldn't, but that's not where most of us live. We have to live at workplaces, neighborhoods, churches, and family gatherings. We have to be faced with our reality anytime we walk out the door with our wedding band on. Will we be truly accepted or awkwardly acknowledged?

The writer of Hebrews encourages us to take confidence in the Lord. By meditating on this larger picture of God's sovereignty over our lives and His goodness, there really is nothing in the world we should fear from other people. In the end, God's got our backs. We may be rejected from some here on this earth, but ultimately, what does it truly matter? God's eternal goodness rests upon us—and that brings a confidence that can come from no other place than the supernatural presence of the Holy Spirit.

Share your concerns with God. It's not pleasant to be unfairly rejected purely based on your husband's residence. I can understand where people's perspective may originate, but it doesn't make the rejection any easier. What does make a world of difference is remembering that God is your Helper. His mighty power and love rests upon you. There truly is nothing anyone can do to you that's greater.

If you need further encouragement about this truth, read Psalm 118. The verse for today was taken from that psalm. It's definitely worth reading. It's full of so many encouraging truths about God's character and love. You can just feel the psalmist's joy. The words are for your encouragement and confidence too.

✝

December 1 — What's in a Name

Genesis 35:9-10

Then God appeared to Jacob again when he came from Paddan-aram, and He blessed him. And God said to him, "Your name is Jacob; you shall no longer be called Jacob, but Israel shall be your name." Thus He called him Israel.

Many prisoners have aliases — AKAs — that follow them wherever their criminal record leads. They receive nicknames in response to some aspect of their personalities, interests, or experiences. In biblical times, however, names were often given *in anticipation* of something.

God changed Jacob's name to reflect the future of the nation of Israel that he would father. Israel means "to struggle with God." Israel did this throughout their history. Similarly, Jesus called Simon by Peter, meaning "Rock" to reflect his future contribution to the foundational growth of the church.

My husband shares the same name as his father. But his mother, in an effort to shield him from the negative attributes of his father, began calling him by a nickname from a very young age. In many ways, this reflected her hope that he would grow into a person of a different character than the man who fathered him — a man who contributed mostly biology, abuse, and whatever financial support that could be acquired from shooting pool. Many would say that my husband turned out worse than his father.

In Jacob and Peter's case, the power was not in the name, but in the person behind the name change — God. By giving a nickname or changing a name, none of us can impart a change or future we desire for a person. Only God can change a person's heart, and that's often what a prisoner's nickname reflects. It may reflect a past of violence, drugs, women, or gang affiliation.

Fortunately, God sees your husband's potential. He has an amazing future planned for him, and He wants nothing more than to lead him to that chosen purpose. Pray that God grow your husband into the name of his calling. God has the power to change what society has labeled or a past of wrongs branded into your husband's life. God created him, and He did it with amazing forethought and an exciting assignment for him to fulfill. It's never too late for change to begin! **

December 2 — Giggles with a Ladybug

Philippians 3:20

For our citizenship is in heaven, from which also we eagerly wait for a Savior, the Lord Jesus Christ.

    I have a small plaque hanging above my desk with a painted bunny reclined on flowers, obviously laughing profusely with a little ladybug who is sitting atop one of the flowers. The caption reads: A giggle a day keeps the glums away. I gaze at the image when I'm feeling low and chuckle at the simplicity. I wonder what's so funny between the two and consider how obviously their world doesn't involve real life.

    But it's also a reminder to me to not lose sight of the life I desire within each day. Each day looks more promising if done within the moments, not the overshadowing collection of days not yet experienced. The weight of the worries for the future keeps the glums close. It seems a forever challenge for me to hold my worries loosely, knowing that God is in control and has me covered by His grace and love.

    I also wonder if heaven will be full of moments like between the bunny and the ladybug. I hope so. And I believe it's safe to say there will be no worries and burdens like we carry here on this earth. We can experience a sustained calm and contentment that, for now, gets quickly interrupted by life here. Or for me, just a glimpse away from my plaque. Both send my mind back to something foreseeably gloomy and the conscious effort to keep the glums away.

    Paul reminds us in this verse in Philippians of the hope of heaven, when all things will be made right. He stresses through his book that nothing compares to the future we have in Christ. It was his constant encouragement. He meditated on this truth and couldn't help but share the joy which filled him. Despite how hard his circumstances were here on earth, the reality of heaven and being with Christ, spurred him on in his attitude and purpose.

    With Christmas approaching, the glums may seem closer or more frequent. Christmas in a visitation park is less than ideal, and for some of us, it will be shared only through a phone call or letter. But the reason for the season is always perfect—Jesus. Yes, it's a cliché, but it's an earthly saying that's remarkably true.

Jesus is the reason for the season. He's also the reason we can consider bunnies and ladybugs, giggling in a patch of fresh flowers, knowing all will be perfect in our world one day too. Heaven came down through Jesus so we can one day be there with the glums nowhere to be found.

December 3 *Healed & Free*

Luke 13:11-12

And behold, there was a woman who for eighteen years had had a sickness caused by a spirit; and she was bent double, and could not straighten up at all. And when Jesus saw her, He called her over and said to her, "Woman, you are freed from your sickness."

The woman desired to be healed, but she didn't have the power within herself to do it. The demon kept her bound for eighteen years. What agony! I wonder if she knew the demon was the source of her physical affliction. I wonder if her crippled back came on suddenly without explanation. Maybe like many of the day, she thought a specific sin kept her in that condition.

She came to the synagogue to hear Jesus speak. I'm sure she likely heard of His healing and miracles as well, but Scripture says that Jesus noticed her and called her forward; she didn't initiate the request to be healed. Was she more infatuated by His words or merely polite and respectful of His authority, not wanting to approach Him without permission. I'm sure she considered the opportunity to be healed before going to the synagogue that Sunday. She likely wanted to be healed physically, but her real problem was the spiritual part of her. Jesus healed both.

I then wonder why the demon allowed her to go to Jesus, knowing he was no match for Jesus's power. This demon had invested eighteen years in this woman's misery, so why give up the fight then? Was he not able to restrain her movements beyond those crippling her back? It's interesting to consider. But this woman went faithfully to the synagogue on that Sunday, possibly as she had the eighteen years up to that point.

The synagogue official scolded the people there in response to the healing, telling them to come on any other day to be healed. Don't you think in those eighteen years she had done that? Yet there was no power in the officials to heal her. Maybe this official's pride was damaged, having seen this woman seek healing before without success. I admire her tenacity. She had lived with a debilitating condition for years, but she persevered through the days.

Just as so, I struggle on some days to consider my husband's daily existence in prison. He wakes daily with no relief from what surrounds him. I admire his tenacity too. He has persevered through the years—one day at a time. He will tell you that the years have been long. He gets weary like I'm sure the crippled woman did. My husband will also tell you that he isn't without hope. Jesus sought him out, and it made all the difference in the world, despite his world still being prison.

There are so many persons incarcerated who are possessed by evil influences. They are bound by sin and the demonic. I believe in present-day demon possession. It's not just a biblical story of the past. Whether possessed or bound in their own sin, their spiritual condition is the heart of their problems. In either case, the answer remains Jesus.

December 4 *Hetairos*

Matthew 26:50

And Jesus said to him, "Friend, do what you have come for." Then they came and laid hands on Jesus and seized Him.

Jesus addresses Judas as "friend," but the Greek translation "hetairos" which is used three times in the New Testament generally describes a person who isn't a true friend. This person seeks his own well-being through the connection with the person or falsely portrays being a comrade. Most of us would agree that Judas was not a true friend to Jesus.

False friends abound in prison. Every man mostly looks out for himself and considers how a connection can benefit himself. Lose the benefit, lose the friend. Friendships develop for reasons not related to the relationship. Some men desire protection and multiple companions provide this when things turn ugly. Some men desire a contact for their addiction. These façades provides a sense of loyalty and social acceptance, but there's no depth or genuine concern for each other. I consider them as "frequent acquaintances."

You may be the only true friend on this earth your husband has in his life. It's hard to be a friend when it calls for accountability or tough love. Confronting your husband about sin is true friend behavior, but likely one that isn't accepted easily. A true friend loves at all times. You love your husband when he's unlovable. The surface friendships in prison do not do this.

Your husband may not always want to hear what a true friend has to say. He may prefer to coast along in sin or rationalize his choices without rebuke from you. Prayerfully consider how to handle such moments. Silence and prayer may be the timely option for the moment. It may also be time to lovingly confront. Just the consideration of the choice is more evidence that you're the steadfast friend he needs.

The false friends will come and go from his life. Prison transfers also make it difficult to develop lasting and potentially godly friendships. It's a world where the superficial connections dissolve quickly when faced with change or a misunderstanding. Hopefully, his contacts aren't premeditating evil against him. Jesus knew Judas's heart and intentions and anticipated his actions. Hopefully, your husband's friends are merely the run-of-the-mill superficial type, not a true threat to his well-being.

It's another burden of prison that we as wives can take to God in our prayers. You may not be recognized immediately for the investment emotionally, yet be assured that God applauds your efforts. God is smiling on the way you love your husband by being his true friend.

December 5 *Where's the Joy?*

II Corinthians 1:22

Who also sealed us and gave us the Spirit in our hearts as a pledge.

Joy requires too much energy. This is my perspective in the low of difficulty. How do others do it? This is my question when I repeatedly fail to be joyful when I know I should be. The futility of failing in my efforts and the anxious anticipation of failing again only makes me want to cry, not rejoice. So how is anything overcome, like prison, like life, when my heart cannot keep pace with the expectation of what I see in others? I should be joyful, yet I'm not—at least outwardly.

Logically, I know I have a diagnosis of depression. I'm reminded every morning when I take a pill. So sometimes I feel that this is simply the lot for my life. God has wired me toward vulnerability that gets played out in solemn words, because my emotions cannot tolerate other forms of expression. I have these seasons of struggle. You may return here at points in your prison journey whether you have a diagnosis or not.

I come and go from this place. So much so, I cannot imagine why I get bewildered when it arrives—yet again. I even get anxious when I consider the end of my life arriving without having figured out the correction to this flux.

Yet within this place, I'm reminded of the deeper joy that blends with the reality of altered chemicals in my brain and symptoms which label me with a diagnosis. Joy is still there, because that deeper sense of contentment and hope remain greater.

And this is where the genuine me lives. Because God allowed me to be emotionally impaired, I can better appreciate the awesome beauty of true joy. The two can live together, but my expectation of what it looks like has to change. Joyful living isn't always smiles and praise songs as I may see in others. Its true evidence is a quiet song of the heart, despite a heartache. It's a knowing smile expressing a confidence that all is okay, when everything in the world isn't. Tears of this reality can blend with sadness to create beautiful moments with the Lord which remain out of reach to anyone else. This type of joy is an intimate, spiritual experience, not always that outward expression I mistakenly believe must be there.

And this is where joy is found—in the soul sealed by the Holy Spirit. Other sad emotions might come and go; and He allows that. But the presence of the Holy Spirit never leaves. He permeates any other emotion in my heart at the moment. I continue to battle my perspective that a chemical imbalance tries to smother, and I recognize my role in the spiritual disciplines that aid that little pill every morning. And hopefully, I'll have more success in the overall war. However, I never lose my confidence in the love and peace that God supplies to fill me with holy joy.

Prison complicates my heart's struggle. As it may yours. So I seem to write more frequently of this battle. I believe I'm not the only person wired by God with joy "issues." I also believe His word and why He tells us to comfort others as we have been comforted (2 Corinthians 1:4). These words I believe will help another lady needing a reminder that joy for the Christian doesn't always look like a happy place from the outside. It's about God living in that inner space with you.

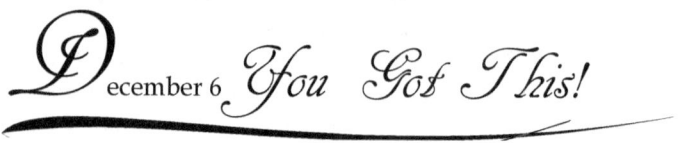

December 6 — You Got This!

Psalm 31:24

Be strong, and let your heart take courage, all you who hope in the Lord.

"You got this!" speaks not about me, but God! I do not feel as though I have anything. Life's challenges are way beyond my ability to manage. I have days of varying confidence levels, but I'm quickly reminded of my inadequacies when a stronger force comes against me. I cower behind my Helper and cry, "Help!" But the quote, reproduced in mass upon various gift items, tunes my mood up a bit.

Inspirational quotes have endured and inspired for generations. They seem to have cemented appeal to us. Coffee mugs, trinkets, plaques: the local gift shop displays our weakness for quick infusion to our perspective. There are plenty of inspirational quotes which can actually speak truth if we know who is behind the outcome. "You got this!" is thus a reminder from God to me, not actually the person who delivered it printed on a coaster.

We obviously need little injections into our day or the retail market wouldn't overflow with such things. Christian outlets included. Those little sayings and verses can benefit us, even if we still sigh when we read it. God can orchestrate and use the little in mighty ways. Less can be more, because it inches our hope forward.

Pretty things which boast a few encouraging words bring an appreciation that hasn't been extinguished in why the words were needed in the first place. Hope isn't lost—essentially. The lighter side to life can break through the yuck.

Do not forget to surround yourself with small things you enjoy, even if it's a simple saying. You may peruse those words at just the right moment. They are part of the good things to put into your mind. You already have enough difficulty and concerns sharing the space. Also remember that God is the ultimate inspiration that you got this!

December 7 *Love & Limits*

Proverbs 19:14

House and wealth are an inheritance from fathers, but a prudent wife is from the Lord.

    I usually work two jobs. Sometimes, I feel as though my husband's requests are my third one. One time I got a letter with his expectation that I write the local radio station and complain about the song list and rotation. He included his list of all the bands and songs that he advocated be played. He's locked in a cell with his radio being his primary occupation. My first thought: "You're kidding me!" I took it almost as a disrespect of my time. Of all the things that I was certain that he knew I was dealing with, why on earth would he "burden" me with such an unimportant thing. But it's his world and what's important to him. Did I write the letter? No. I sent him the address so he could write the station himself.

    I love him, but my life (out here) has to be manageable. I have to work. I have to put limits and find ways to meet my husband's needs while also looking out for my own. Scripture speaks to considering others before yourself, sacrificing, and persevering in doing good. But it's reasonable to balance the demands when you find a way. So opportunities like the one above I take.

    I struggle with guilt for not always doing for my husband. I sometimes feel guilty when I'm sitting on my day off and watching a movie, especially when there are still things I could be doing for my husband. Yet, I remind myself that rest is needed and that he and I have different life responsibilities. He's serving life. I'm doing life out here. Sometimes he needs to be reminded too.

    I stay organized and do what I can to accomplish all this life demands. I take care of my husband within the same days. The limits are loving. For myself and him.

December 8 — Butterfly Living

II Corinthians 4:6-7

For God, who said, "Light shall shine out of darkness," is the One who has shone in our hearts to give the light of the knowledge of the glory of God in the face of Christ. But we have this treasure in earthen vessels, that the surpassing greatness of the power may be of God and not from ourselves.

    God's creative nature in nature fascinates me. The life cycle of a butterfly is one such fascination. Although it also challenges my understanding of why the cycle is designed as it is. The butterfly spends most of its life cycle becoming an actual butterfly. As a caterpillar, it molts several times until ready to settle in and start its real transformation in the pupa state. Everything about the caterpillar changes in this state. From the inside out, a totally new creature emerges. Once free from its grounded state, many unfortunately only live mere weeks, if that.

    This is what I struggle to understand. All that effort to attain to the beautiful outcome to only live a week. What a shame I say to myself when I ponder its life. I consider how it can represent a Christian's life if not careful.

    God's saving grace transforms us into new creatures, sets us free to be beautiful creatures. Yet, so many of us waste our transformation. There may be a butterfly on the inside that never really takes flight. No one gets to experience or be touched by our beauty as He designed.

    I for one do not want to be a Christian "butterfly." The beauty — yes, but for a brief matter of time — no. I want to stay motivated for what eternally matters. And that requires intentional decisions. It requires me to stay focused and allow God to direct my days for the eternal best. I shy away from butterfly living on some days — and seasons sadly. But He remains faithful to capture me in His "net" for the good reminder that I need, just when I need it.

    It's the best way of doing life regardless of how prison impacts my life. God provides the lift off the ground following a battle during a bad day. He ushers His gentle wind of encouragement that powerfully renews my wings for traveling another day. The beauty He created in my heart and the continuing reminders of His love are worth sharing with others who may still be grounded or yet to be transformed by His offer of salvation.

December 9 — Replay

Ecclesiastes 7:9

Do not be eager in your heart to be angry, for anger resides in the bosom of fools.

Do you rehearse the hurt? Do you anticipate the story you'll tell with eagerness to recount the anger, savoring the support or empathy you expect to receive from your audience? Such exchanges in most cases do not calm your heart, but rather stir it up. We wrongly believe satisfaction will come with the telling, but it only feeds the anger, raising our blood pressure, tainting our perspective, and delivering unworthy words to another. Ecclesiastes teaches us that looking forward to such exchanges is foolish.

God knows our thoughts. So why does it seem more satisfying to share the bad with others—repeatedly? Sharing troubles with a friend for genuine, beneficial input is different than venting for the sake of being affirmed in your attitude. And once you have involved someone in your plight, they typically ask for updates in future conversations. You have set the stage for another replay of what you have already stewed over.

Conversations are tempting arenas to replay the negative. It's a form of gossip that seems to harm your own spirit more than the reputation of the person who has upset you. Speaking worthy words usually takes intentional steps for us. It's about denying the flesh. A big step is reminding ourselves that God is fully aware and fully involved. The emotions attached to the replay are bitter and resentful usually. These emotions grieve the Holy Spirit. This reminder can also help dull the enticement of replays.

If you can resist the temptation and let a conversation go without hitting the replay button, you'll have achieved a tremendous victory. It feels good to be victorious! That feeling is charged with the energy that your actions have been pleasing to God. That feels so much better than any negative applause you may get from someone listening to a story you have told not only in your own mind repeatedly, but to a list of others who are no better for the information.

Scripture says that it's foolish to seek out conversations that only serve to fuel your anger. Pause before you become lured into this. Gain control of your emotions by allowing the Holy Spirit to redirect that energy toward godly words and thoughts.

December 10 Life Remotely

Psalm 48:14

For such is God, Our God forever and ever; He will guide us until death.

    I wish life were like a remote. Pull up the guide, peruse the possibilities, and make a selection. All possibilities for future times could be considered. One channel may seem good initially, but maybe that program is about over and a dreadful show will air after it. Such options could be ignored in scanning page after page of programming. Those bringing enjoyment for the better part of the day could be indexed and watched whenever. Even if a show is unfamiliar, we can gain more information before committing to a decision. Wouldn't that be nice in life!

    Yet that isn't within our ability to do with life. Most of us would have avoided many poor decisions and "selections" if that were the case. We can view a menu of life choices and feel overwhelmed and indecisive, because we do not have enough information or fear paralyzes us from taking the next step. Our battery life for decision making runs low, so procrastination settles into the screen and it's easier to stare at the uninteresting than explore options that may end up wasting our time.

    But God doesn't want us seeking our own way through the choices in life. He knows that we do not have all the information. We cannot see the future "programming." He does. So His remote is crucial to successfully enjoying the days before us, remaining productive, and overcoming the "bad shows" which can be a part of any season of life. His remote is charged with His word and His Spirit.

    Prison can confuse the choices. It alters the programming and from a distance seems nothing is interesting or worth the time. It demands you sit through the drudgery without the option to skip ahead to the end. You long for the commercial breaks to lighten and brighten the screen before you. You may be resisting settling into the time of prison. But I would encourage you to release what's ahead to God.

    Let God choose what you watch and how you spend your time through the choices He has for your days now that prison is a part of the scene. It will bring richness and excitement from where you never thought possible. He has the perfect choices already decided and "programmed" for you. You can walk through the days ahead with confidence when you know God selected the events within the hours and even the commercial breaks. He doesn't always remove the negative consequences when you take back the remote, but He continues to work all things for your ultimate good.

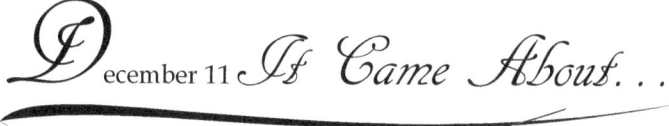

December 11 — It Came About...

II Kings 8:5

And it came about, as he was relating to the king how he had restored to life the one who was dead, that behold, the woman whose son he had restored to life, appealed to the king for her house and for her field. And Gehazi said, "My lord, O king, this is the woman and this is her son, whom Elisha restored to life."

    We never know fully what God is doing behind the scenes of our lives. It's the place where faith is grown once the past events are considered. God's orchestration becomes a witness to His sovereignty when all events converge into the present reality. The blessing becomes sweeter when His loving care is seen long before we were aware of what He was doing. This can be seen across days, months, years, and a lifetime of experiences to bring about blessings.

    In today's Scripture, the woman returned home following the famine and planned to resume her life with her son on their property. The laws at that time allowed people to reclaim property that was originally theirs despite even possibly someone else taking over its use. She went to the king to present her case for this to be granted. Her son had been earlier raised from the dead by the prophet Elisha and this was one of the events the king's servant Gehazi was sharing with the king just as the woman arrived to appeal to the king for her land.

    What were the chances? The timing was perfect! But the woman had no idea before she headed out that day that she would be the topic of conversation between those men. She likely had anxiety and worried on the way, wondering how to make her appeal. Maybe she even practiced out loud her speech. But all the while, God had already prepared her victory. He supernaturally orchestrated the events to bring her success. On her walk out, I'm sure she wondered why she wasted such energy on being worried beforehand. God cleared the barriers on her behalf.

    There's much going on behind the scenes of your life as well. God is up to bringing about the good through ways and encounters unknown to you now. He desires to "wow!" you when the encounters and circumstances come together at that most divine moment. You can walk through these days of prison, trusting that God has been preparing the details within the days for your good long before you arrived. This can bring you peace and a testimony that will begin "And it came about…"

December 12 *Dirty Pride*

II Kings 5:1

Now Naaman, captain of the army of the king of Aram, was a great man with his master, and highly respected, because by him the Lord had given victory to Aram. The man was also a valiant warrior, but he was a leper.

Naaman is an interesting fellow in Scripture. He was a great military man. He was highly regarded by the king. The verse today describes him as a valiant warrior. But he was also a leper.

He's interesting because despite his leprosy, he was respected. He had a comfortable life with servants to assist and a wife to love. One doesn't think of such descriptions when a person has such a disease; they were usually outcasts. It seems he was even liked enough that his wife's servant desired his healing. And with her mention of Elisha the prophet as a source for this, the king amply supplied Naaman on his journey to seek the prophet's help.

Elisha instructed him to wash himself in the Jordan River seven times to remove his leprosy. The Jordan is a dirty river in Israel. Naaman was frankly insulted that Elisha asked such a thing. Despite his own disease, he thought he was too good for the Jordan. His servants had to encourage him to reconsider his actions given what was at stake. Naaman had hope to be healed, but even with the severity of his physical condition, his pride almost prevented its occurrence.

People can think of prisoners as the "Jordan." Dirty and undesirable. There's an unspoken sense that everyone else is better, because their wrongs have never been publically or legally judged. It's easy to diminish our own faults when someone else's seem dirtier. This is because our thoughts of what defines a person as "good" is mostly a comparison of what we consider "bad."

Naaman almost considered his leprosy as better than lowering himself into the waters of the Jordan. People usually compare themselves to someone lower, because they do not have to acknowledge their own faults. But God considers goodness only in comparison to Himself. The world's goodness is a source of pride. When compared to God, we are all so far from goodness that this truth brings humility.

Do not let others' thoughts and blind pride make you feel you or your husband are any less valuable. You have been blessed with the knowledge of why you need a Savior. Those who do not aren't even aware they are still lepers.

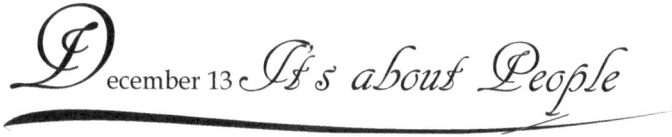

December 13 — It's about People

Ruth 1:21

"I went out full, but the Lord has brought me back empty. Why do you call me Naomi, since the Lord has witnessed against me and the Almighty has afflicted me?"

Today's verse is Naomi's statement to the women of Bethlehem after she returned from Moab. She originally left with her husband and sons, because of the famine in Bethlehem. They remained in Moab several years. But once she lost her husband and both sons, she made plans to return given the news that the famine was over and the harvest time was underway.

So why does Naomi state that she left full and returned empty? She left during the famine which wouldn't indicate a time of fullness or plenty. She returned during the harvest which would indicate abundance, not emptiness. Her description was related to the relationships in her life. The people who were important to her made her life full or empty, not the amount of food she had.

She was in Moab many years, but she only chose to leave once her relationships vanished. The food wasn't enough to have her stay. This is the realization we would be wise to consider as the world works so effectively to distance us from relationships in our lives, sometimes in the same neighborhood.

Your husband has been removed, and life makes it complicated to keep that relationship connected. But there are likely other family or friends who remain accessible to you and may just want to be your "Ruth." People who want to support you and are interested in your well-being. But you have to invite them into your life.

Naomi tried to push Ruth away and urged her to turn back from following her. But Ruth persisted and Naomi gave in. You may assure others that you're fine and decline support or minimize your needs. You may be battling the shame of your husband's circumstance just as Naomi may have felt ashamed that she bailed on Bethlehem and her relationships there when things got hard.

But God wired us for relationships and dependent on others to fulfill our needs which are usually beyond food. Family and friends can be a resource for the necessities, but like Naomi, she knew the emotional connection to others brought value to her life regardless of how much material things she possessed. Make a point to be involved in the lives of those near you. Chances are you both will find a blessing.

December 14 Press On

Haggai 2:4

'But now take courage, Zerubbabel,' declares the Lord, 'take courage also, Joshua son of Jehozadak, the high priest, and all you people of the land take courage,' declares the Lord, 'and work; for I am with you,' says the Lord of hosts.

Haggai was the prophet whose message was one of encouragement. Many others in Scripture provided warning to Israel and outlined the consequences for not obeying God. Haggai shared the good available for hearing his message and following through. He was part of the rebuilding project of the temple in Jerusalem after it was destroyed by Nebuchadnezzar. He reminded the people why they were punished, but he was mostly interested in conveying to them that God was restoring their place of worship and to press on with the project.

There had been opposition to the rebuilding and the people faded from the scene, turning to their own interests, figuring there was no way to complete the temple in the face of the oppression. Haggai was sent to remind them that God wanted the temple rebuilt and that He would help them accomplish it. But they still needed to do their part.

There was wood to be gathered and rock to be quarried. There was a lot of labor to be done. Everyone needed to pitch in to prepare the material and fashion it together. God promised to orchestrate its completion, but He required their devotion through the discipline of good old-fashioned work. The goal couldn't be accomplished otherwise.

God values hard work. There are Scripture stating the downside of being slothful. If God has called you to do something, do whatever's in your power to do; He's responsible for everything else. I have found God to provide the encouragement I need when I get weary or unmotivated. One simple word from Him is all it takes to fill me up with the emotional energy that I'm lacking to move forward. Taking tangible actions flow from there.

Regardless of what you face in your goals, He will help you successfully complete it if He has instructed you to do it. Do not let things like prison stand in your way of doing the work required to meet the goals God has given you. Prison may be part of the opposition, but rise up and do the work despite its presence. God is leading the way and has everything planned for your success.

December 15 God's Heart for All

Ezekiel 33:11

"Say to them, 'As I live!' declares the Lord God, 'I take no pleasure in the death of the wicked, but rather that the wicked turn from his way and live. Turn back, turn back from your evil ways! Why then will you die, O house of Israel?'"

I get disturbed in my heart when I hear or read of the pleasure someone takes in another's death. This is often seen when the legal system carries out the death sentence and the victim's family expresses a twisted joy in watching or knowing the perpetrator has been killed. I recall a bystander being interviewed after teenagers stole a car for a joyride and ended up crashing the car, dying. He commented to the media, "They got what they deserved."

Really? A stupid teenage decision deserved death? I would think a somber acceptance of the outcome would be more fitting—in all cases. Occasionally, the victim's family will extend compassion and forgiveness for the person who wronged their loved one. I always think that's an awesome reflection of a heart impacted by Jesus.

You may encounter some very callous people during this season of prison. They may not present an ounce of empathy for your situation. "Three hots and a cot" are more than prisoners deserve from some people's perspective. The fact that death row inmates have a TV infuriates some. Some believe the death penalty coddles inmates; they should experience physical pain during the execution, because that's only fair considering what they did to their victim. The emotion behind the outcome in such cases is pleasure. If the TVs were removed, if the mattresses were removed, if pain were inflicted, a heart is satisfied.

But God doesn't take pleasure in the death of the wicked. He takes no pleasure in seeing people endure consequences of wrong decisions. Scripture is clear in this. He's just and holds people accountable for their sin, but His heart desires their repentance. He desires them to seek Him and learn to love righteousness, not sin.

Find reassurance in knowing that God's heart isn't like the people who find gratification in the punitive circumstances of others. He's a loving Father who disciplines and allows consequences from a just character, not happy revenge.

December 16 Go

Revelation 3:2

'Wake up, and strengthen the things that remain, which were about to die; for I have not found your deeds completed in the sight of My God.'

If I'm not late, I'm not on time. I say this jokingly to myself as I once again look at the clock, which has moved forward within my procrastination to what I need to be doing. I'm not opposed to my schedule for the day, just preoccupied with other things in the moments leading up to it. I find this more often when I do not have a deadline for the day. I relax in the freedom of time to the point I casually move toward the responsibilities, losing time in the process. Not an earth-shattering situation, but this approach to God's call on our lives risks missing the best within the call.

Prison's impact on our days shouldn't create lengthy moments of ponder when our minds idle in the thoughts of uncertainty — or at least there should be a disciplined limit to say, "Enough! It's time to move forward." God hasn't removed our purpose with the arrival of prison. He uniquely blends it into what we now face. The uncertainty can be transformed into excitement when you alter your perspective to one of hope. And hope is what keeps you moving forward, ironically, while you wait on prison to leave.

One thing you can do is set small goals within the days. This is especially true if you do not have a deadline of accountability from an external source. For example, when writing, I set a number of hours each day I'm going to write, usually a block of time. Other things creep in and attempt to distract me, usually my own mind's wandering or the phone, but I have to intentionally stop the temptations and stick to my goal. Otherwise, a day will end and I'll feel discouraged that I let yet another opportunity leisurely pass into unproductive time.

You have to determine your own deadline and steps within the days to accomplish what God has called you to. Write it down. Remove distractions. And start. Listless longings for a better day within prison will not move you forward into your purpose. Action steps will. Daydreaming is okay, but it can slothfully turn into procrastination. By taking the reins on your purpose, you can disallow prison the opportunity to waste time in your life despite it coming along for the ride.

December 17 *Godly Conflict*

Matthew 9:17

"Nor do men put new wine into old wineskins; otherwise the wineskins burst, and the wine pours out, and the wineskins are ruined; but they put new wine into fresh wineskins, and both are preserved."

Conflict comes into most all long-term relationships. Family, spouses, coworkers, friends: we aren't clones of one another in our personalities and experiences, thus our perspectives and opinions do not always align. We stumble through most occasions of disagreement and hopefully resolve to disagree if nothing else. If a Christian, we should approach conflict with a new heart and a new perspective. The goal isn't so much to "win" the argument, but rather maintain the relationship by keeping godly thoughts and actions despite the outcome not being exactly what we feel is right.

Jesus taught this example through the verse for today. A believer in Him will behave differently than before salvation—or at least should recognize the need and work toward it. To approach conflict as you did in the past may result in ungodly responses and little focus on maintaining the relationship. Old wine (actions and thoughts that are ungodly) do not fit who we are in Christ (new wineskins).

Old habits are hard to break, however. We easily slip into prior patterns especially when it comes to dealing with conflict and other people. Marriages tend to develop a pattern of interaction based on the experiences we bring into it. Prison marriages are no exception, because it's still about two people trying to live life together despite differences. Prison just complicates resolving the differences.

The key difference in the old and new wineskins is the presence of the Holy Spirit. We have God's Spirit to strengthen us in our interactions and to give us pause when we want to respond like our old selves. We have His power within us to allow us to be stretched when it seems uncomfortable to respond differently. He can shape us without breaking us. And if we can allow this, our marriages benefit.

Take your new self into your conflicts. Surrender the urge to respond "as usual." Surrender to the Holy Spirit's promptings to do things differently. Do not focus so much on winning, but rather preserving the connection with whom you're at odds.

December 18 *Avowed*

Hebrews 2:11

For both He who sanctifies and those who are sanctified are all from one Father; for which reason He is not ashamed to call them brethren.

Shame is likely one of your greatest nemeses during this prison journey. It's with every new introduction or new conversation that involves your spouse or life situation. You may cower inside when a topic travels into that vulnerable place where you aren't sure if damage will happen to your circumstance or your feelings as a result. You took your vows publically, but now to avow your relationship when he's a prisoner is far more difficult. However, if you can consider what the writer of Hebrews says about Jesus, it can help hold your head a little higher.

Jesus set out to identify with us by becoming like us, to suffer for us. He wanted to experience our sin, though sinless, to communicate to us His love. He freely associated with flaw-filled man without embarrassment. He willingly set aside His heavenly home to live within the sin of this world to redeem us from it. He was not ashamed of us, despite our sin.

Jesus considers us His family. Let that sink in. Consider His deity and the majesty of everything He is. Consider how flawed we are; how much we mess up—repeatedly and severely. Yet, instead of distancing Himself from us, He seeks us out! He wants to be close to us and to have a personal relationship with us. It matters not what we have done. He wants to be the center of our lives, privately and publically.

God isn't ashamed to call your husband a brother. If your husband has repented of his wrongs, God hasn't allowed his crime or current incarceration to remove him from the family. Jesus isn't distant now that prison is present. Your husband is wholly accepted, without hesitation. If the Creator of the universe isn't ashamed of him, you can confidently take steps toward your husband knowing Jesus stands beside him too.

December 19 A True Heart

Psalm 69:33

For the Lord hears the needy, and does not despise His who are prisoners.

God's prophets, Jesus's disciples, and Jesus Himself were harshly treated and imprisoned, many executed. Jesus was publically disgraced, "legally" tortured, and crucified. If God intimately used the legal system and incarceration in the lives of great men and Jesus, why would He not be interested in the circumstances of those imprisoned? How could God not have a heart for the incarcerated?

Society seems only interested in prison for realty TV, the shock value of the sin which sends a person to prison, or the fuel to power the headlines. The prison culture is produced and aired to fascinate and allure. Sin shouldn't be entertaining. The destruction of lives and families shouldn't be broadcast for gossip's satisfaction. God never used prison in such ways.

Prison was, and is, a source of sadness and a consequence of personal and societal sin. Prison was, and is, a place of suffering. Samson's eyes were gouged out by prison officers, Jeremiah was beaten on the way to his prison cell, John the Baptist was pulled from his cell and beheaded out of spite. God doesn't see the impact of prison as light and breezy entertainment. He longs for the prisoner's heart and tells us to pray for those in authority, not glorify the bad of it all.

Prison was the central arena where Jesus fulfilled His mission. But there was no death row for Him. He was immediately ushered to the death watch cell and hastily executed. He died as a criminal, harshly treated by authorities at all points along the way.

God is truly interested in the heart of the person behind bars. He isn't impressed by the sin, only heartbroken. He doesn't enjoy seeing the punishment legally or unethically administered. Society will make sport of prison and the prisoners, but God's heart remains tender for all that you and your husband are living through. It's a serious circumstance that He fully appreciates. Take comfort in knowing this. God doesn't minimize your heartache; He bears you up so you can make it through.

December 20 — Arrested & Saved

Romans 5:20-21

And the Law came in that the transgression might increase; but where sin increased, grace abounded all the more, that, as sin reigned in death, even so grace might reign through righteousness to eternal life through Jesus Christ our Lord.

There are men out there who would say that being sent to prison was the best thing that happened to them. Their arrest and sentencing was their path to salvation. It took prison to turn them toward God and toward a life with meaning. At some point they became aware of their need for a Savior, because they became aware of their sin.

Sure they knew they broke the law. In fact, prisoners usually aren't good at following rules. They often struggle with defiant and deviant behavior. They may justify their actions. But until they grasp the depravity of their life compared to holy God, whether they are truly innocent or guilty in the world's legal system, they are eternally condemned. We all are.

Paul is writing in this section of Romans about justification. No amount of following rules can earn salvation; the religious laws were in place to reveal how bad we are at being perfect. It's only through faith in Jesus; the gift of salvation based on belief, not keeping rules of behavior. And with this truth, the more rules you break, the more you realize God's grace is always greater. Paul is quick to remind that this isn't a license to sin! It's rather the understanding of one's sinfulness that one grasps really how far God's grace reaches.

For the saved prisoner, their understanding is great. They came to understand that there's nothing they could do to earn favor with God. Justification by faith is crucial to one who knows their heart condition and sinful nature. God's acceptance of them as righteous, despite their rap sheet, is further evidence to Paul's preaching: where sin increases, grace abounds.

I do believe in jailhouse conversions. I love to read victory stories of God's amazing grace on behalf of the damaged and hopeless. These are only possible because it's never been dependent on what we do; but rather what

Jesus did on our behalf. He walked this earth and kept the religious laws perfectly on our behalf. He willingly surrendered Himself to death, so we could live eternally with Him. Prison may be a blessing in hindsight to you if your husband doesn't yet have his salvation. Pray for his eyes to be opened to his soul's condition and need for a Savior.

December 21 God in the Flesh

Mark 10:18

And Jesus said to him, "Why do you call me good? No one is good except God alone."

Jesus seems to be asking the rich, young ruler, "Do you believe that I am God?" In his initial question to Jesus, the man addressed Jesus as "Good Teacher." He went further to ask Jesus what he needs to do to inherit eternal life. The young man was focused on works and all the "good" that he had already done in his life, but Jesus was asking him to look deeper into his faith in Him as God in the flesh. Jesus was trying to teach him that eternal life was contingent on his belief in Jesus as God. If he could fully surrender and believe, then he would realize that his works and treasures here on earth couldn't get him into heaven—only his faith.

The rich man quickly withdrew the description of "good" in his next statement to Jesus, addressing Him only as "Teacher." In the end, the rich man walked away disappointed and sad, unwilling to accept Jesus for who He is—fully God, thus fully good.

At Christmas, Christians celebrate Jesus's birth, God coming into the world as a human. He was fully God and fully man. Jesus was a great teacher, but He was undeniably Immanuel, God with us. Mary says in her Magnificat as written in Luke 1:53: "He has filled the hungry with good things; and sent away the rich empty-handed."

Prisoners may be bent toward thinking they could never inherit eternal life, because unlike the rich ruler, they have broken many commandments of God and earthly laws. They have been judged guilty. They may have a flawed concept of the Gospel, like the rich ruler. But it's not about rules and keeping commandments. It's about being in relationship with Jesus, believing He's God. With this acceptance and repentance of the sin in one's life, eternal life is freely given.

December 22 It's There

Psalm 119: 14

I have rejoiced in the way of thy testimonies, as much as in all riches.

    I was on a repeated search for packing tape, and when I finally found it, only a minimal amount remained. So every trip to town and back, there was an afterthought, "I forgot to get packing tape!" There was a specific task I needed it for, so thankfully, the next trip to the store, I purchased it. I completed the task, and all was well. The next week I was sorting through boxes, and when I opened the first box, what did I find? A brand new roll of packing tape. The second box had yet another roll. I had to shake my head when considering all the searching and effort I had made previously when all the while what I needed was right under my nose.

    That's how it can be with the Bible. Everything we need is there, but we have to open it to find it. And like my packing tape, we can usually find a double portion of whatever we need, because God supplies abundantly. Whether it be encouragement, direction, or wisdom.

    In the busyness of our days and distractions, spending time in God's word takes discipline. We may satisfy our conscious on a hurried day by committing to reading it on the next morning. But the next morning may arrive with the repeated commitment getting extended another day. All the while, we struggle within all the reasons why we are so busy in the first place.

    Reflection later often reveals remorse when we quietly sit before the Lord in exhaustion. With the refreshment we obtain comes the wonderment of why we waited so long to pursue the one solution to all our problems. The Bible is amazingly timeless, despite how long we go between days in reading it.

    You may just have discovered the treasure of Scripture. God speaks through it, and that makes it worth reading daily. It will help you immensely on this journey of prison. It's there when no one else may be. It's there when you have only a few minutes or hours. All that God wants to say to you awaits your just opening it. Of all the gifts you may receive this Christmas, you already have the grandest one ever. Do not let it build dust from non-use like possibly other gifts of the season. Let it be a continual source of guidance, encouragement, and godliness.

December 23 *Intimately Known*

Psalm 139:3

Thou dost scrutinize my path and my lying down, and art intimately acquainted with all my ways.

One Christmas, a relative of mine planned her gift giving around a simple list we were to provide of things we would enjoy having, but do not buy for ourselves. I considered it a list of "nice, but not necessary," because that's generally what I tell myself when I place the item back on the shelf. So I provided a list: body wash, new dish rags, house shoes, wall calendar, and other small ideas. And I received much of my list, but it struck me that every item missed the mark slightly in terms of my preference.

She bought me the body wash I wanted, but one with a pump dispenser. I hate pump dispensers! I received the dish rags, but they were white in color. I never buy white. I got the new calendar, but it was a Scripture calendar with landscape scenes. I never buy Scripture calendars! Ironic, yes, but I much prefer animals or something artsy when it comes to calendars. Despite her years of knowing me, she really didn't "know" me in the details. It struck me also that we never have this happen with God. What a pleasure it is to be known fully by God.

David wrote in Psalm 139 about the omnipresence and omniscience of God. He recited God's knowledge of everything about him. He said that God is intimately acquainted with all his ways. God was there when David was being formed in his mother's womb. He was intimately acquainted with David before he was even born. God knew exactly how many days David would live prior to even being conceived.

The same is true for us today, because God is the same. His ability to know us intimately, more than anyone else on the planet, remains constant. He's the Creator and Sustainer of life—with all its details.

I take great comfort in having God know me. Granted, there's no hiding my wrongdoing and sin, whether intentional or unintentional. But this is the beauty of how He's able to support me in my repentance. This is the beauty of how He's able to completely and compassionately support me through the hard times. It's His knowledge of me that resonates a genuine understanding, thus satisfying my soul within any heartache I may encounter.

There's no greater support than someone who knows your every thought and feeling. God gets you. He knows the details of your preferences. He knows the subtle emotions and inner thoughts. He's available to fully absorb your trials and sustain you in precisely the way you need. He knows what prison has done to your life and your heart. And it's through this knowledge that He knows best how to lead you through this season and beyond.

December 24 — Steadfast Saint

Luke 1:13

But the angel said to him, "Do not be afraid, Zacharias, for your petition has been heard, and your wife Elizabeth will bear you a son, and you will give him the name John."

Zacharias doesn't get a lot of attention compared to his son or wife when the stories of Scripture are discussed. His son John the Baptist rightly has his place. His wife Elizabeth gets attached to Mary in the Christmas story, because of their miraculous pregnancies and the sons to be born. And without question, they were significant, prophetic events! Yet I see Zacharias, in the midst of astounding family circumstances, humbly take the shadows as the steadfast priest that seemed to characterize his life. I see God's special heart for him, and it reminds me of the special heart God has for me.

Zacharias was a man of prayer. He had been praying for a son. Elizabeth's barrenness was obviously a burden on his heart. In Scripture, you usually read of the woman's heart-felt prayers when barren. The angel usually appeared to the woman like in the case of Samson's mother and Mary. But Gabriel appears to Zacharias, not Elizabeth, and tells him that his prayers have been heard. He would have a son, whom he would name John.

Zacharias showed devotion to God. After Gabriel appeared to him inside the temple, he was unable to speak due to his questioning. He may get a bad rap for this, but do not overlook what Scripture says in verse 23. He stayed and finished his service despite the amazing experience. Most of us would have probably taken a sick day or at least left early. We would want to run home and share the good news and the opposing wonderment of our muteness. Or we might just be too distracted to be of any use in our service.

Zacharias, however, was faithful to his calling as priest and remained, completing his duties for God.

After John's birth and circumcision, Zacharias's speech returned, and he began praising God. The Lord had kept him mute for nine months, but we read of nothing but praise from him. No complaints, just praise! The Holy Spirit also came upon Zacharias, and he prophesied about Jesus and John's role in preparing the way for Him. At this point in Scripture, the Holy Spirit didn't just come upon anyone. It was reserved for the righteous and for a special message.

So Zacharias was a man I consider the steady faithful that God chose to use in a magnificent way. God entrusted him with parenting the great John the Baptist. He's rather a sideline figure when the Christmas story is discussed, but I do not see any evidence that God considered him that way. He was a crucial part in God's plan.

Do not ever underestimate your value to the purposes of God. You're steadfastly remaining in a wife's role with few praises. You're the behind-the-scenes prayer warrior for your husband's good. You humbly do it daily. It's part of your calling, and why the Lord entrusts you with it. God has a special heart for all you do.

December 25 — A New Gift

Numbers 6:10

'Then on the eighth day he shall bring two turtledoves or two young pigeons to the priest, to the doorway of the tent of meeting.'

The famous song "The Twelve Days of Christmas" lists numerical gifts offered by a "true love," accumulating with each verse the gifts prior. Most are familiar even if unable to recall which offering is provided on which day. This song can provide an analogy of the offerings the Israelites provided the Lord for the purposes of thanksgiving and repentance, leading to the final gift to us in the person of Jesus.

In Old Testament times, the offerings made to God were animal sacrifices. The Israelites were told how many, what kind, and when to offer them. In Numbers, chapter six, offerings of a Nazirite are outlined for the person's service and dedication to God. In the case of a Nazirite coming in contact with a dead person, which would be considered unclean, two turtledoves could be brought to be sacrificed. It was never that God "needed" the sacrifices. It was more about calling the Israelites to obedience. Their obedience in offering the sacrifices showed their devotion to their one True Love—God.

It's very difficult to read of the killing of animals to atone for sin. But ever since God killed His creation to provide clothing for Adam and Eve, His love for mankind has been evident. Thankfully, His love for us moved Him to provide a much greater sacrifice to permanently atone for our sin. Jesus offered His life so that no more animals would be needed. Past offerings for sin have been replaced with a new gift in the person of Jesus.

Christmas hallmarks Jesus's birth. Have you accepted Him as your gift? Unlike the Israelites, your sin can be forgiven by admitting to God that you're a sinner, believing that Jesus died and resurrected on your behalf, and turning from your sin to live righteously. You do not have to offer an animal sacrifice; Jesus became the sacrifice. In accepting this gift, your eternity in heaven is secured. Without accepting Jesus as God's gift, hell is what awaits you.

God takes your obedience seriously. But He wants you to come freely and of your own will. He's your True Love, offering eternal life to you. Please accept this gift this Christmas Day.

December 26 The Crash

Isaiah 9:6

For a child will be born to us, a son will be given to us; and the government will rest on His shoulders; and His name will be called Wonderful Counselor, Mighty God, Eternal Father, Prince of Peace.

So here it is—the day after Christmas. For many, with this day comes more shopping than before the holidays. Excitement flurries even if the sun is shining. After-Christmas sales, returning gifts for the preferred item, so much planned in a new kind of chaos. For others, comes the crash; a solemn emptiness that cannot be identified. It remains out of reach despite a multitude of gifts at arms' length or scattered temporarily about a room. It's that feeling that there must be more. Something is missing from the holiday cheer that failed to deliver anything under the tree.

It's much the same experience I sometimes have on a Monday. Days leading up to the weekend were sprinkled with anticipation of rest and usually more distance from stress. A time to truly enjoy waking up without so many burdens possibly. Yet, at the end of those anticipated days, I awake to that hollow feeling of disappointment on Monday. And what seems an even heavier burden, because I now have regret blended into an already difficult rising.

So what went wrong? Why the crash? My reflection generally leads me to days seeking worldly pleasures before or without seeking God. I anticipate movies I'll watch, meals I'll have, or games I'll play. These are enjoyable and can be temporary stress relievers, but they can never deliver true peace to my soul. And that's the allusive longing that stirs the unrest and becomes the foundation of the Crash.

Peace is ultimately the goal. And that's what Christmas symbolizes — the birth of the Prince of Peace. He must remain the goal of the search and foundation of the longing. Without Him, days will remain short of satisfying. The clock will become your nemesis as it displays the countdown to the inevitable Monday morning or the aftermath of holiday excitement. Prison will only add to this lull.

Usually once the Crash is over and routine of the usual begins, expectations return to the norm. To reflect on the days as "it was just a Monday" resolves your heart to the defeat. Desire to complete a weekend or an anticipated Christmas with genuine satisfaction. Seek Christ this Christmas season and let Him fill up the empty space with peace which faithfully remains after the holiday ends.

December 27 Sobering Encouragement

Hebrews 4:1

Therefore, let us fear lest, while a promise remains of entering His rest, any one of you should seem to have come short of it.

When working at a nursing home, I was trying to secure a "Do not resuscitate" order for a lady who had reached the point in her life where comfort was the goal, not extending her life. Her guardian needed to be in agreement. Amazingly, when I received the approval, the guardian had inadvertently inserted my last name for hers. Seeing my name attached to a DNR approval was a little unnerving. It was a sobering encouragement to consider the brevity of life and how I'm living my own — now.

It was a common response similar to an unexpected death of someone close. It was a sobering opportunity to reflect on the important and unimportant parts of my life where time is spent. And as in times before, I had regrets. If that had in fact been my own DNR approval, could I be at peace with what I had accomplished up to that point? Honestly, no.

Another way I have been sobered is to review the death list of those incarcerated. In an effort to be transparent, some states have opted to make public a monthly list of persons who died while in the care of the prison and the circumstances associated with their death (e.g. suicide, homicide, natural causes). With even more sobriety, I can view their photo.

I can easily picture my husband's face when staring at the image of another. I can easily consider the dead man's family, possible wife. Mostly I consider the condition of his soul at the time he was added to the roster. What if it had been my husband?

Life has sobering moments. It's the outcome of the moments that reflect the quality of the days leading up to it. I thank God for the opportunity to correct my focus before it's my name being considered by another or that of someone close to me. I absorb the encouragement to move into the future with intentional choices to limit regretting them.

Are you ready for your DNR approval? Is your husband? Life is precious. We all agree, but get duped into apathy for things that matter because of "life." Pursue the genuine rest of knowing you haven't lived life short of all God has planned for it.

December 28 — Overcome with God

Nehemiah 2:18-19

And I told them how the hand of my God had been favorable to me, and also about the king's words which he had spoken to me. Then they said, "Let us arise and build." So they put their hands to the good work. But when Sanballat the Horonite, and Tobiah the Ammonite official, and Geshem the Arab heard it, they mocked us and despised us and said, "What is this thing you are doing? Are you rebelling against the king?"

When I began to share more boldly about my life with an incarcerated man and plans to marry him while he remained in prison (for life), opposition came to me through people's words. The motivation for some was a callous "You're crazy" perspective. Others were from a positive concern for my life. Regardless, both encroached on my courage and lured me to question what I knew to be God's will for my life. I had to actively reject in my heart the words I heard, because I knew they weren't from God. I had already heard from God, repeatedly. So I prayed for His strength to stay focused and be reminded of that truth.

In Nehemiah's case, he had been granted favor before the king to return to Jerusalem to lead a rebuilding project. He had sought God's face on the matter many days prior to approaching the king. Nehemiah remained confident of God's provision once he arrived in Jerusalem even when the ridicule and ugly actions of others started.

His project was in the spotlight. Enemies ganged up, taunted, and planned to stop the rebuilding of the wall around Jerusalem, even to Nehemiah's harm. Nehemiah made reasonable accommodations to the threats, but didn't stop what he knew to be God's call on his life.

Moving confidently through your marriage takes courage, especially when ugly words and discouragement try to push you in the other direction or to give up completely. But God is faithful to carry you through with the provisions, grace, and blessings you need to make it.

In Nehemiah's case, the wall was finished. In my case, my husband and I have been together seventeen years as I write this page, all of the years in prison. In your case, I pray the years get sweeter as your love matures against the forces you successfully overcome.

December 29 Steward Your Heart

II Timothy 1:7

For God has not given us a spirit of timidity, but of power and love and discipline.

I saw the little thing as I passed a trailer on a country highway, a lamb tied to a stake in the yard. It had circled the available diameter allowed by the restraint, ending up tethered right next to the pole. My heart sank at the sight and my internal rescue button was pushed. I wanted to stop and retrieve that poor creature and carry it away to somewhere more caring by my perception. I was upset for miles. Of course, I knew I just needed to let the situation go. There was no one beating the young thing. It didn't look malnourished. It was beautiful weather. Maybe the owners weren't the best caretakers by my perception at that momentary passing, but my compassionate heart needed to be restrained in its own way.

Following my heart isn't always a good thing for me. I have acquired strays that later complicated life and finances. Jumping to help someone in need without the prompting of the Holy Spirit has left me in debt long after the needy person moved beyond the crisis and out of my life. I have wallowed in the dumps for things beyond my control. Guilt is affixed to the word "no," leaving me stressed when I agree to do things I really do not have time for. There's a healthy balance. And I have to look for it, because it doesn't always "feel" right.

Scripture would say I need to steward my emotions and be self-controlled. Being hasty can lead to negative outcomes, if not in the moment, eventually. It's hard to recuperate or defend your situation once the fallout arrives. It usually has to ride the course laid from the choices. Dwelling on the wrongs of a fallen world must have limits, for my own emotional well-being. I have to emotionally let go of things I cannot control through self-control.

Being self-controlled is a fruit of the Holy Spirit. He's always available to help me, but I have to seek it. I have to pause and consider; I have to pray. I have to allow the Holy Spirit's voice to win over my feelings. I have to rein in my thoughts and turn away from the emotions that hound me like that image of the little lamb. I may have to remind myself of the hope awaiting this world when Jesus restores and makes right, resolving that I cannot fix everything. This includes prison.

You may need to distance yourself from the unhealthy emotions through surrendering to the Holy Spirit's control. This may mean rethinking your situation, considering your blessings, withdrawing from pressures from sinful origins. It's easier to succumb to your heart, but consider the impact on you. In the case of the little lamb, it wasn't a reasonable upset, which only served to deflate my already struggling heart. What would I have done? Carry a piece of livestock in the backseat of my car until I got home? Then what?

There's plenty of ways we can be used by God while prison remains a part of our lives. We can help and rescue under the Holy Spirit's guidance. We can provide for our husbands within reason and resources. We just need to be cautious if prone to be led by our feelings. God will use your heart in healthy ways; Satan will take advantage of its weaknesses.

December 30 Soul Cry

Psalm 31:7

I will rejoice and be glad in Thy lovingkindness, because Thou hast seen my affliction; Thou hast known the troubles of my soul.

A soul cry is that deep communication of heartache that only God can know. Others may see tears, but the emotions drowning your heart, combined with the enormous complexity of thoughts that accompany those moments are only truly known by God. It's your soul crying. And who better to know the condition of your soul than your Creator.

Your cries may vary in severity, but usually the continual ache remains. I'm not sure if we ever really heal fully from heartbreak. The pain gets blended into who we are until more of the healed parts outnumber the wounds still bleeding. As long as we have memories of the moments, then likely the emotions are part of the whole of who we now are or they are the ones causing the current tears.

The beautiful blending of the rejoicing heart and soul's cry makes us who we are. Prison can travel the length of both. I have seen it on the faces outside the gate on visitation day as one man steps out to his freedom. Those wives watching the reunion smile, but you can see the pain and longing of their soul. The heart of the wife hugging her husband rejoices. We live somewhere between these points most days of this prison journey, but it's likely the aches show up more often.

God hears your soul's cry. He can comfort you like no one else. His Spirit is within you; He communicates with your soul, even when you have no words deep within the pain.

It's hard to explain how you feel to others. Thankfully, God knows it all intimately. Let your soul cry to Him. He can blend today's heartache into the foundation that holds the rejoicing your heart experiences later. Ironically, you become a stronger person with that type of foundation if you allow God to be part of the process. It's really His strength living within you.

December 31 *Trustworthy Statement*

Titus 3:8

This is a trustworthy statement; and concerning these things I want you to speak confidently, so that those who have believed God may be careful to engage in good deeds. These things are good and profitable for men.

Paul's letters to Timothy and Titus are referred to as the Pastoral Letters. He was imparting instructions and guidance to both on leadership for the church. He also encouraged them in their work. He repeated the phrase "trustworthy statement" in his letters to Timothy and it appears again in

Titus. Paul didn't use the introductory clause in any of his other writings. It imparts the meaning that one can fully believe what he says.

It's interesting to consider why he chose to in these cases. It brings attention to what follows or something Paul just wrote about. He used it in regards to his being the worst of sinners, a man's interest in being an overseer, training in godliness, salvation, and the grace of God which saved us.

Paul considered Timothy and Titus his spiritual children. He grew them up in the faith and mentored them. My hope in writing this devotional book has always been to grow your knowledge of Scripture while also encouraging you on your prison journey—and in the challenges of doing everyday life within it. My hope is that you find God all-sufficient for any need or trouble.

We may not share exactly the same path. Our husbands may be polar opposites. Your challenges likely include many things that aren't part of my life. And vice versa. We may be at different spiritual points in our walk with the Lord. I certainly do not claim to be a scholar; I learn every day too.

But we both love and miss our husbands. We both want our marriages to survive prison. We are doing the best we know with the situation that has been dealt to us. We mess up. But we remain hopeful.

As this year closes and you face a new year, rely on God to bring you back to this date in a year with a deeper faith in His goodness. I cannot claim goodness will be in every event, but God remains fully good, all the time. It is a trustworthy statement: God is bigger than prison.